Drug Wars

Drug Wars

The Political Economy of Narcotics

Curtis Marez

University of Minnesota Press

Minneapolis • London

Quotations from "The Smoke of a Thousand Dreams," by Ina Sizer Cassidy, are reproduced by permission of the Bancroft Library, University of California, Berkeley.

Quotations from the interview with Josefina Fierro, conducted by Albert M. Camarillo, Department of History, Stanford University, on 21 March 1995, are reproduced with permission of Albert M. Camarillo and courtesy of the Department of Special Collections, Green Library, Stanford University Libraries. This is one of a series of interviews that will be included in a biography of Josefina Fierro to be published by Albert M. Camarillo.

Portions of chapter 2 were previously published in "The Other Addict: Reflections on Colonialism and Oscar Wilde's Opium Smoke Screen," *English Literary History* 64 (1997): 257–87; reprinted by permission of The Johns Hopkins University Press. Portions of chapter 4 were previously published in "Subaltern Soundtracks: Mexican Immigrants and the Making of Hollywood Cinema," *Aztlán: A Journal of Chicano Studies* 29, no. 1 (spring 2004); reprinted courtesy of the Regents of the University of California. Portions of chapter 6 have been previously published in "The Coquero in Freud: Psychoanalysis, Race, and International Economies of Distinction," *Cultural Critique* 26 (winter 1993–94): 65–93; reprinted with permission.

Published by the University of Minnesota Press
111 Third Avenue South, Suite 290
Minneapolis, MN 55401-2520
http://www.upress.umn.edu

Library of Congress Cataloging-in-Publication Data

Marez, Curtis.
    Drug wars : the political economy of narcotics / Curtis Marez.
        p.   cm.
    Includes bibliographical references and index.
    ISBN 0-8166-4059-9 (cloth : alk. paper) — ISBN 0-8166-4060-2 (pbk. : alk. paper)
        1. Narcotics, Control of—United States.   2. Narcotics, Control of—Developing countries.   3. Political corruption—United States.   4. Political corruption—Developing countries.   5. United States—Foreign relations—20th century.   I. Title.
    HV5825.M2535 2004
    363.45—dc22   2003025125

Printed in the United States of America on acid-free paper

The University of Minnesota is an equal-opportunity educator and employer.

12 11 10 09 08 07 06 05 04   10 9 8 7 6 5 4 3 2 1

For Linda and Paul Marez

Contents

Preface and Acknowledgments

My interest in this project began in the late 1980s, at the tail end of Ronald Reagan's second term as U.S. president. The so-called Reagan Revolution that began with the 1980 presidential election initiated a highly publicized "war on drugs." In U.S. mass culture, however, state drug enforcement looked rather different from mainstream political discourse. Music and films from those years foregrounded the complicity of U.S. military and police forces in international drug traffic; in a number of films and songs, corrupt cops and rogue military personnel actually participate in the drug trade. At the end of Reagan's second term, when it was revealed that his administration had supported cocaine traffic in order to fund counterinsurgency projects in Central America, it appeared as though the former actor was caught up in the plot of a B action movie. At that time I was struck by the conflicting representations of the Reagan-era drug wars, which led me to think more broadly about the role of culture in the history of drug traffic and enforcement.

As my research proceeded, I discovered that the ongoing war on drugs, usually discussed in a relative historical vacuum, was the culmination of a much longer, global history of drug traffic and enforcement. *Drug Wars* thus begins with events of the final decades of the twentieth century, but it ultimately suggests that drug traffic and the movements of people, capital, and ideas that it presupposes have been central to an uneven and hierarchical global modernity. While cultural critics are accustomed to thinking of globalization in terms of capitalism, imperialism, immigration, and the mass media, most have largely neglected the formative effects of modern struggles over drugs. Historically, drug traffic has fueled imperial expansion and global capitalism as well as movements of migrant workers throughout the world. As a privileged target of police power, drug traffic has also helped to support and extend the authority of nation-states around the globe. One of the central arguments of this book is that drug enforcement efforts have supported state disciplinary practices that physically latch onto individuals and groups, particularly workers. Indeed, doctors and policemen have often borrowed terms and scenarios from the field of imperial warfare, thus suggesting the extent to which state-sponsored drug wars have brought the ideological and affective intensities of military power to bear upon the intimate details of everyday life. Drug enforcement has not only propped up state and capitalist power but it has provoked dramatic kinds of resistance to capital and the state. Whether in the form of crime, violent rebellion, labor radicalism, or oppositional cultural production, marginalized groups have directly and indirectly opposed the expansion of state and capitalist power that drug traffic supports.

This book was made possible by financial assistance in a variety of forms. As a graduate student at the University of California, Berkeley, I benefited from an Alcohol Research Center Fellowship, a William Andrews Clark Jr. Memorial Library Fellowship (UCLA), and a UC President's Dissertation Fellowship. Later I received a Ford Foundation Postdoctoral Fellowship for Minority Scholars, and while teaching at UC Santa Cruz I was awarded several grants from the Humanities Division Committee on Research and the Chicano/Latino Research Center.

I am indebted to a host of archives where I researched *Drug Wars,* including the Clark Library, Berkeley's Bancroft Library, the New Mexico State Records Center and Archive (NMSRCA), the Margaret Herrick Library of the Academy of Motion Picture Arts and Sciences, UCLA's Film and Television Archive, and Special Collections in the Green Library at Stanford University. I am thankful for the help of numerous librarians and archivists, particularly Roberto G. Trujillo, head of Special Collections at Stanford; José Villegas, formerly an archivist at NMSRCA; and Suzanne Tatian of the Clark Library.

I received important intellectual guidance and support from the members of my dissertation committee, Norma Alarcón, Catherine Gallagher, and David Lloyd. Other Berkeley professors also shaped my project, and I am particularly grateful to John Bishop, Mitch Breitwieser, and Abdul

JanMohamed for their advice and friendship. Were it not for the encouragement of Janet Adelman while I was working on my master's degree I might never have entered a Ph.D. program. A number of my colleagues in graduate school, including Nina Berman, Bruce Burgett, Cindy Franklin, Matt George, and John Wilkins, provided invaluable friendship and intellectual engagements. I owe a special debt to the members of my dissertation writing group, Kate Brown, Alyson Bardsley, and Irene Tucker.

I am indebted to several colleagues in the Department of English Language and Literature at the University of Chicago who read and commented on my work, including Elizabeth Alexander, Chris Looby, Laura Rigal, Lisa Ruddick, Richard Strier, Bill Veeder, Ken Warren, and Alok Yadov. Special thanks to Lauren Berlant, who provided excellent advice and encouraged me by her example to look for new archives and new forms of knowledge. I thank three remarkable students, Magdalena Barrera, Pat Chu, and Yolanda Padilla. Finally, I am grateful to Barb Crawford, the outstanding staff person who deftly managed the department.

Many friends at UC Santa Cruz provided invaluable support. I would like to thank my former colleagues in American Studies, including Michael Cowan, Dana Frank, and Anne Lane. Special thanks go to Judy Yung, who served as my tireless mentor and whose example of politically engaged scholarship will always inspire me. I am especially grateful to Yvette Huginnie, not only for the great Elvis memorabilia but also for her humor and intelligence in trying times. And there has never been a better colleague and friend than Renya Ramirez—I don't know how I managed before knowing her. Thanks to my fantastic colleagues in the Latin American and Latino Studies department, especially Gabriela Arredondo, Pedro Castillo, Guillermo Delgado, Jonathan Fox, Manuel Pastor, and Norma Klahn. My life and work were made incalculably better by the members of the Transnational Popular Culture Research Cluster, funded by the Chicano/Latino Research Center, including Rosa Linda Fregoso, Sarita Gaytan, Herman Gray, Olga Nájera-Ramírez, Russell Rodriguez, Deb Vargas, Isa Velez, and Pat Zavella. Out of this group I owe special debts to Olga Nájera-Ramírez and Pat Zavella, who, in addition to representing inspiring models of committed scholarship, also helped to make me feel at home in Santa Cruz. Thanks as well to Jim Clifford, Kirsten Silva Gruesz, and Shelley Stamp for their friendship and keen intellectual support. Finally, I thank the phenomenal staff at Oakes College, UCSC, including Kathy Durcan, Veronica Higard, and Deb Reed.

I thank the following colleagues at other institutions for their comments, questions, friendship, and support: Mary Pat Brady, Albert Camarillo, Chris Cunningham, Michael Davidson, Bari Gold, Carl Gutiérrez-Jones, Judith Halberstam, Josh Kun, Enrique Lamadrid, José Limón, Chon Noriega, Beatrice Pita, David Román, Ramón Saldívar, George Sánchez, Kathryn Shevelow, Nayan Shah, Yvonne Yarbro-Bejarano, and Lisa Yoneyama. I am especially indebted to Rosaura Sánchez, who read and commented on large portions of my book and helped me profoundly reshape it at a key moment in its development. Her example constantly reminds me how and why scholarship matters.

Before I went to college, a number of teachers had a formative influence on me, and I would like to thank them: Mildred Dilman, Wayne Hines, and Gloria Souza. Thanks also to Bob Backus and Greg Greenway—two excellent friends.

I appreciate the support of my sister, Melissa Serpa, whose love and friendship have helped keep me going over the years. Special thanks to my amazing parents, Linda and Paul Marez: together they raised me right, teaching me lessons in love, respect, and integrity that I will never forget.

Last, I owe an impossible debt to Shelley Streeby, who has been a better critic and editor of my work than money can buy. For many years during the writing of this book we were separated by time zones and miles of airspace, yet even so Shelley's fierce love held me together whenever my world seemed ready to come undone. To paraphrase one of her favorite poets, all I can give you is love that's beyond the call of love.

Los Angeles, California
September 2003

Drug Wars

As part of her contribution to the "war on drugs," in 1983 first lady Nancy Reagan took the unusual step of appearing as herself on an antidrug episode of the popular ABC situation comedy *Diff'rent Strokes*.[1] Recalling the Reagan administration's drastic cuts in social spending and its promotion of charity and other forms of private initiative instead, the television series featured a family comprised of a wealthy white businessman, his daughter, and two adopted black orphans from the inner city. Mrs. Reagan used the show in part to promote her infamous answer to the drug problem—"Just say no." While serving as good publicity for the president's policies, however, the first lady's injunction did little to limit drug demand in the United States. Indeed, two of the show's child actors, Todd Bridges and Dana Plato, would ultimately develop serious, highly publicized drug problems.

This anecdote could be read as an ironic commentary on the recent history of the U.S. "war on drugs." Although official rhetoric focuses on ending drug abuse, state policies have often had the opposite effect. In the 1970s, for instance, the Nixon administration supported Southeast Asian heroin traffic in order to fund the war in Vietnam.[2] Subsequent administrations in the 1980s and 1990s backed client states in Latin America that were directly involved in the cocaine trade. The Reagan administration supported the "Cocaine Coup," a right-wing military takeover in Bolivia that was funded by drug barons; along with his successor, George Bush, Reagan also sponsored Manuel Noriega's

Panamanian dictatorship, which turned out to be a major launderer of drug money; and perhaps most infamously, the Reagan administration directly or indirectly supported the cocaine trade in the United States in order to fund the contras' attack on the Nicaraguan revolution.[3] Thus, while official sources often represent the drug problem as a menace that the state is dedicated to eradicating, in recent history drug traffic has just as often served to sustain and reproduce state power. The exercise of state power centrally includes forms of drug interdiction, but drug enforcement is part of a larger set of ideologies and practices that might be better described as the management of drug traffic. Nancy Reagan's infamous injunction notwithstanding, the United States, along with other states, has often said "yes" to drug traffic by annexing it to state power.[4]

Corresponding to the expansion and transformation of the state's attempts to manage global drug traffic in the 1980s and 1990s, the contemporary "war on drugs" emerged as a mass-media event, or rather a vast series of events. Capitalizing on an unprecedented boom in cocaine traffic from the South to the North during the 1980s, popular authors produced numerous mass-marketed novels and documentary writings about the drug war. This literature includes the real and fictionalized memoirs of Latin American "drug lords," drug smugglers, and drug dealers, as well as the related stories of policemen, narcotics officers, and agents of the DEA, the FBI, and the CIA.[5] These same characters also appear in paperback spy novels and related forms of military adventure and international intrigue. Perhaps the most famous example is Tom Clancey's best-selling novel *Clear and Present Danger* (1990), in which CIA agent Jack Ryan joins the drug war in Colombia.[6] Similarly, television networks have broadcast diverse images of drug traffic and enforcement. In the mid-1980s these subjects pervaded nightly TV news reports that increasingly covered drug wars at home and abroad. TV news exposés in which handheld cameras followed policemen in their dramatic crack-house raids ultimately inspired a host of documentary "reality" shows such as *The DEA* and *Cops* that focused on drug enforcement.[7] One of the most popular TV shows of the period was *Miami Vice* (1984–89), a crime drama set in south Florida that pitted narcotics officers against cocaine smugglers. And numerous TV movies from the 1980s and 1990s represented the war on drugs, such as *Drug Wars: The Camarena Story* (1990), an NBC TV movie that centered on a Mexican American DEA agent who was murdered by a Mexican drug cartel.

Two forms of music that largely focused on drug traffic and enforcement also emerged at this time. African American and Latino artists from urban centers and drug traffic corridors such as New York, Washington, D.C., Houston, and Los Angeles made rap recordings that reflected upon the conditions and consequences of a new hemispheric crack cocaine economy. And at the same time, many Indians and mestizos in Mexico and the United States produced and consumed *narcocorridos,* ballads about the violent transborder trade in narcotics. Both kinds of music served as the sound tracks to numerous drug-war films of the 1980s and 1990s. Meanwhile, the availability of VCRs spurred the production and distribution of "straight-to-video" films about drug traffic and enforcement. Starting in the 1980s, small Mexican production companies began cranking out cheap, immensely popular narcotraffic films for audiences on both sides of the border. Then, in the 1990s, small U.S. companies catering to black and Latino audiences began to make movies about the inner-city drug trade starring rappers such as Snoop Dogg. Straight-to-video films were matched by numerous big films slotted for wide theatrical release. Beginning in 1983, the year that Brian De Palma's *Scarface* was released, more than thirty drug-war films of this sort were made in the United States.[8]

In these ways, myriad forms of mass and popular culture helped to construct the war on drugs as an object of broad public interest. Mass-media representations of drug traffic and enforcement have helped to generate powerful ideas about state power, foreign policy, and transnational capitalism. And drug-war literature, music, television, and films have become privileged cultural forms for reflecting upon larger political-economic power relations in the Americas. The pervasiveness of the war on drugs across a variety of media has helped make drug enforcement a taken-for-granted part of social reality. The U.S. media is so saturated with such images that even when audiences have no direct acquaintance with drug traffic and enforcement, they may still vividly recall TV, film, or musical scenarios that bring the "drug war" into their imaginative horizons. Commercial entertainments that focus on the war on drugs contain imaginary resources, such as characters, costumes, settings, props, and sounds, that different social forces and groups use to make ideological sense out of geopolitics. The war on drugs, in other words, has an important cultural component. In interpretations and discussions of film and music, diverse groups struggle over the meaning of drug enforcement and related issues of state power and hemispheric political economy. Films and music thereby provide what Fredric Jameson calls "cognitive maps" for imagining local and global power relations in convenient and compelling ways. As a significant part of a widely shared ideological landscape, the mass-mediated "drug war" ultimately impacts intimate details of subjectivity and social relations, serving as a formative, structuring context for ideas and practices concerning race, gender, class, sexuality, and nation.

If as an element of foreign policy the contemporary war on drugs has been directed not only at curtailing the supply of drugs but also at challenging their flows in ways that support perceived U.S. interests, as a set of U.S. domestic and border police practices the drug-war also anchors state power in drug traffic. U.S. drug-war policy for the last few decades has focused on military and police actions at the relative expense of education and treatment. Penalties for drug possession and trafficking in the United States have increased, as have imprisonment rates.[9] This is in part because the police have been granted greater latitude to conduct drug searches and seizures. Recent federal forfeiture laws have further given federal, state, and local law enforcement agencies a financial interest in the drug trade by allowing them to confiscate assets merely suspected of being drug related. As a result, numerous police forces at various levels have reoriented their efforts around drug enforcement as a primary source of funding. The situation has led Eric Blumenson and Eva Nilsen to conclude that "the Drug War has achieved a self-perpetuating life of its own."[10] Antidrug discourse has proven quite successful at gaining support for the state, making it difficult for politicians and others to challenge drug-war doxa. With the support of police and prison guard unions, the war on drugs has helped to give the United States, after Russia, the largest prison population in the world.[11]

The war on drugs has also precipitated a qualitative shift toward the militarization of police power, making it difficult to say where domestic policy ends and foreign policy begins. When President Reagan declared in 1986 that drug traffic constituted a clear and present danger to U.S. national security, he signaled the state's reframing of drugs in terms of the sorts of foreign-policy concerns that have often justified U.S. military campaigns. Through the drug war the United States has partly integrated local, state, and federal police forces into a larger system of military power in the Americas. The Reagan administration practically nullified the Posse Comitatus Act, a law that made it illegal to use the military to conduct civilian police actions. Such legal changes enabled the military to share training, intelligence, and hardware with domestic police powers. The opportunities that drug traffic provides for the expansion of military power in part explain the state's relative disinterest in education and treatment. This is because the demand for drugs is not, strictly speaking, the enemy of state power; rather, drug demand is a sustaining object of power.[12]

Representations of the war on drugs are also complicated by the participation of capitalists, for whom the drug trade has been immensely profitable. The aerospace industry (which supplies drug enforcement planes, helicopters, and other technology), chemical companies (which produce the poisons that are dropped on drug fields), and the prison industry directly benefit from the drug war and hence actively lobby for its continued expansion.[13] Capitalists profit from the drug war in other ways as well. It is estimated that illegal drug traffic generates about $400 billion a year, accounting for roughly 2 percent of the global economy.[14] Transnational corporations headquartered in the United States profit from this economy by serving as formal and informal laundries for drug money. Simply put, as Miguel Ruiz-Cabañas suggests, the process of generating surplus value from the drug trade could be described in this way: poor peasants cultivate drugs in return for very little; highly organized traffickers process and distribute the drugs for sale; the traffickers in turn launder their profits through U.S. banks and through "legitimate" investments in the U.S economy more generally.[15] Every year, the black market in pesos alone funnels roughly $5 billion in drug money through U.S. companies.[16] Whereas merely being suspected of participation, however indirectly, in drug traffic has been enough to justify the seizure of assets from individuals, corporations successfully (if implausibly) plead ignorance concerning their participation in drug-money laundering.[17] And rather than prosecuting corporations that profit from laundering drug money, state drug enforcement efforts instead focus on controlling the poor. By policing the poor but leaving untouched corporate drug profiteering, the state has tended not to interdict drug traffic but rather to manage drug flows in ways that support capitalist interests. By dramatically increasing transborder trade, NAFTA has further encouraged the shift from banks to international trade for laundering drug money. Because of the massive volume and velocity of capital flows, J. Patrick LaRue argues, it has become nearly impossible to stop "the transfer of billions of 'narco-dollars' back and forth across the U.S. and Mexican border." He concludes that Mexican traffickers are riding the wave of state-sponsored globalization and liberalization, "taking advantage of open borders, privatization, free trade zones, weak states, offshore banking centers, electronic financial transfers, smart cards and cyber banking to launder millions of dollars in drug profits each day."[18] In these and other ways, the U.S. war on drugs "regularly serves the interests of private wealth."[19]

Many mainstream depictions of the war on drugs—even reformist and critical ones—center on the most powerful actors and institutions and neglect other social strata. Accustomed to thinking about the war on drugs in terms of drug czars and other figures at the top, we over-look the historical power of the many at the bottom. To describe the mass of such people I use the terms "the poor" and "the subaltern" inter-changeably. In my usage, the terms are broad and internally differenti-ated categories that include laborers—the so-called working poor—and impoverished people who do not work for a wage. Or, as John Beverley defines it, "subaltern" refers to people without a voice that matters to those in power.[20] Although they are generally excluded from forms of power and official documentation, the presence and actions of sub-altern people partly motivate and condition the reactions of more power-ful actors. Through their acts of resistance and rebellion the poor also exercise a certain power over social relations by checking or challenging dominant institutions. In particular, poor people have been an influen-tial force in recent drug-war history. Given austerity measures imposed by international financial institutions such as the International Mone-tary Fund (IMF) and the World Bank, combined with official U.S. pres-sure to accept neoliberal forms of "free trade" that favor U.S. financial interests, local economies in Mexico and South America provide campe-sinos with few opportunities for survival other than drug production. Thus, throughout Latin America, but particularly in Mexico and the Andes, subaltern labor is a primary source of vast sums of contempo-rary narcocapital. One result is that capitalists and states have an inter-est in managing or controlling impoverished populations. In this sense, the war on drugs is reactive, following upon (or attempting to antici-pate) subaltern actions.

Contemporary Colombia is an apt example. Far from stopping the flow of cocaine, U.S. drug-war assistance has supported right-wing para-military groups in Colombia that openly participate in drug traffic. The leader of the largest U.S.-backed paramilitary group, Carlos Castaño, told a Colombian television reporter that 70 percent of the group's budget came from drug traffic.[21] These forces ironically use both drug profits and drug-war aid to attack poor people who chew coca, an indigenous ritual practice so important that among Indians in the Andes it has in part come to define what it means to be a social being.[22] With U.S. support, Colombia goes after small producers as part of an effort to terrorize Indians and mestizo peasants and prevent them from opposing the powerful.[23] As a result, the largest Latin American recipient of U.S. military aid has the worst human rights record.[24] All of which suggests that the threat of subaltern agency partly motivates the contemporary war on drugs in Colombia. Indian and mestizo coca producers in the Andes are often actively opposed to drug eradication projects that threaten their survival, and the possible consequences of their opposition serve as a partial check on drug enforcement, for while the United States has "the physical capability to destroy coca fields in short order, the tactic could only be used if the United States also wanted mass uprisings against it."[25]

A related situation exists in Mexico, where the state has used U.S. drug-war weaponry and equipment to attack the Zapatista rebels, even though the group has no connections to the drug trade. As the spokesperson for the Zapatistas in the United States, Cecelia Rodríguez, explains: "The Mexican armed forces have been accused by human rights monitors of murders, disappearances, kidnapping and rape. Nonetheless their requests for military equipment and expertise have been granted time and time again. Under the guise of fighting drug traffickers, the U.S. government has bolstered an anti-democratic and corrupt Mexican government with a laundry list of high-tech military equipment that has been used to violate the basic human rights of the people of Mexico."[26] Yet subaltern people in Mexico also limit the state's ability to prosecute the war on drugs. According to J. Patrick LaRue, the North American Free Trade Agreement that required Mexico to end crop subsidies has encouraged many growers and peasants to take up marijuana and opium cultivation. Faced with the alternative of maquiladora work for subliving wages, La Rue concludes, many poor Mexicans instead choose to work as mules to transport drugs for the traffickers.[27] As in the case of Colombia, where the possible mass opposition of small producers prevents the government from completely obliterating the coca fields, here we might imagine that the possibility of similar resistance has checked Mexico's drug enforcement efforts.

Within the United States, the drug war has also targeted the poor. At the beginning of the 1980s there were a few thousand people in local, state, and federal jails; today there are almost 2 million. People of color convicted of nonviolent drug crimes account for the majority of the increase. Although African Americans reportedly represent 13 percent of all monthly drug users, for example, they make up 74 percent of those imprisoned on drug charges.[28] While critical commentary has focused on the alarming number of black men in jail, the war on drugs has also greatly increased the number of black women in U.S. prisons. One reason for this is that especially during the 1980s, women who smoked crack were criminalized for giving birth to so-called crack babies, infants born with low birth weights and smaller than normal heads. Medical research has indicated that such symptoms are the result not of cocaine use but of poverty.[29] Nonetheless, thousands of black and Latino women were arrested and in some cases convicted of abusing their unborn children by smoking crack while pregnant.[30] Because someone convicted of a felony can no longer vote, the drug war has disenfranchised large numbers of African Americans. Nationally, about 13 percent of all black men are so disenfranchised, whereas in some Southern states the rate is 30 percent.[31] Ira Glasser, former executive director of the American Civil Liberties Union (ACLU), therefore concludes that drug enforcement has become a "replacement system" for segregation and racial subjugation.[32] The war on drugs thus taxes our representational powers because, unlike conventional wars that are imagined as a domestic "us" against a foreign "them," here the "enemy" is subaltern people both inside and outside the United States.

Finally, the war on drugs is inseparable from its mass mediation. Different media do not simply mimic official accounts, or report on a preconstituted thing called "the war on drugs"; rather, the media helps to construct the war on drugs by representing it. The media is thus a semiautonomous agent or set of agents in the war on drugs, and for this reason state officials strive to control representations of drug enforcement. From Nancy Reagan's "Just Say No" campaigns to her husband's criticisms of Hollywood films "that glorify drug use," to the entire "culture wars" of the 1980s, politicians have sought to shape the media and use it to promote the war on drugs.

And yet the process of representing the war on drugs remains an actively interpretive one that leaves room for critical revision and dissent. As we shall see, in the 1980s and 1990s numerous films and popular songs contradicted dominant accounts. What is more, different audiences, notably subaltern ones, have critically appropriated and reinter-

Drug war O.G. ("Original Gangsta"): Al Pacino as Cuban drug lord Tony Montana in *Scarface* (1983).

preted even the most dominant media forms. In what follows, I suggest that drug-war music and films provide competing representations of state power, transnational capitalism, the mass of the world's poor, and the role of the mass media itself in the war on drugs. Drug-war culture, in other words, is an important source of dominant and insurgent ideas about the role of the United States in the global political economy.[33]

Perhaps the most influential recent example of drug-war culture is the film *Scarface* (1983), written by Oliver Stone and directed by Brian De Palma. Loosely based on Howard Hawks's *Scarface* (1932), the 1983 version updates the story by focusing on the violent rise and fall of a Cuban immigrant and cocaine kingpin named Tony Montana (Al Pacino). It begins in 1980 with the Mariel boat lift, in which Fidel Castro allowed thousands of Cuban citizens, including large numbers of prisoners, to sail to Florida. Montana, a small-time Cuban criminal, is one such émigré who, along with others, is held in a makeshift Immigration and Naturalization Service (INS) detention center. After his release, Montana quickly (and violently) works his way up to the top of the local cocaine trade, marrying his former boss's mistress (Michelle Pfeiffer) and entering into a partnership with a Bolivian drug lord named Manuel Sosa. When Montana refuses to murder an investigative journalist and his family, however, Sosa sends a well-armed troop of mercenaries to murder him. In the film's final shootout, Montana wields an automatic machine gun and even a rocket launcher against his assailants before ultimately dying in a rain of bullets. An important precursor to a wide range of subsequent films and popular rap songs,[34] *Scarface* will serve as a template for my analysis of 1980s and 1990s drug-war culture.

"Say hello to my little friend": Representing State Power in the War on Drugs

When *Scarface* was first released, critics were struck by the film's violence, particularly its elaborate and graphic gunplay.[35] Tony is involved in a fatal shootout with a Colombian cocaine trafficker in broad daylight in the streets of Miami, as well as a showdown with two Uzi-wielding Colombian assassins; and in the film's final scenes he faces off against Bolivian mercenaries armed with assault weapons. Although earlier movies arguably contained similar amounts of violence and gunfire, *Scarface* was unique in that its props were drawn from the war on drugs. The film prominently features assault weapons like the kinds used by U.S. drug enforcement officers and supplied by the United States to Latin American clients for use in the war on drugs. In one gruesome scene, Tony watches as Sosa, who has ties to the military, executes one of his associates by hanging him from a helicopter. This use of the helicopter as a weapon recalls the deployment of a variety of helicopters in drug wars throughout the hemisphere, from U.S. urban centers and the U.S.–Mexican border to Mexico and Colombia.[36] And finally, Tony fires on the Bolivian mercenaries with a rocket launcher while demanding, "Say hello to my little friend."

Scarface established a pattern that was emulated in a host of subsequent drug-war films, including the immensely popular *Clear and Present Danger* (1990). In that film, the president and members of the CIA conspire to mount an illegal drug war, secretly dispatching a special forces unit to Colombia where they blow up a drug plane, destroy an underground cocaine processing plant, and drop a "smart bomb" on a meeting of cartel leaders. One cartel member responds in kind by organizing a paramilitary attack on CIA agent Jack Ryan (Harrison Ford) and his colleagues. Colombian narcoterrorists masquerading as motorcycle cops fire on Ryan's caravan, even using rocket launchers that kill one of the agents. Although, as Richard Slotkin has demonstrated, U.S.

filmmakers and audiences have long been fascinated with gunfights, in the last three decades the focus has shifted from Old West shootouts and cops-and-robbers handgun battles to spectacles involving military hardware.[37] More precisely, military hardware has migrated from battle-field scenes and genres to "civilian" settings and genres.[38]

In addition to film, rap music also registers the militarization of the drug war in the inner city. The narrator in Ice-T's "High Rollers" raps about players with Uzis and twelve-gauge shotguns. Three years later, Ice-T costarred in and recorded the theme song for *New Jack City* (1991), directed by Mario Van Peebles. There Ice-T raps a first-person narrative from the perspective of a black, urban drug dealer who singles out his Uzi for praise. In the title song to *Deep Cover,* a drug-war film with plenty of gunplay, Dr. Dre and Snoop Dogg narrate elaborate automatic-weapon exchanges with the police. Similarly, on their 1993 release *Black Sunday,* the members of Cypress Hill include three songs about guns, "Cock the Hammer," "Hand on the Glock," and "A to the K." Rappers also "sample" the sound of automatic weapons, incorporating recorded gunshot loops to produce musical rhythms. The Geto Boys' "Trigga Happy Nigga," for instance, includes the sound of repeated gunfire and recorded dialogue from *Scarface.*[39] Rappers further refer to the surveillance helicopters used by the LAPD, as on the cover of Kid Frost's 1992 CD *East Side Story,* which depicts the performer in his car being pursued by two black helicopters with spotlights.[40] These and other rappers more or less came of age in Los Angeles during a high point in the militarization of drug enforcement, when the LAPD began using military hardware such as helicopters, small tanks, and high-tech surveillance systems as part of antigang programs such as "Operation Hammer."[41]

The assault weapon as hip-hop prop further suggests the extent to which local conflicts are embedded in the hemispheric geopolitics of the war on drugs. Recalling the contra cocaine scandal, in which it was revealed that the CIA was complicit in contra drug traffic in the United States, Representative Maxine Waters explains the appearance of assault weapons in this way:

> In South Central Los Angeles we wondered where these guns were coming from.... They were not simply handguns, they were Uzis and AK-47s, sophisticated weapons brought in by the same CIA operatives who were selling cocaine because they had to enforce bringing the profits back in. It was at about this time when you saw all these guns

coming into the community, that you saw more and more killing, more and more violence. Now we know what was going on. The drugs were put in our communities on consignment, out to the gangs and others. If they did not bring the profits back, the guns were brought in so they could enforce their control.[42]

If Uzis and AK-47s have been appropriated for U.S. film and rap narratives, then, it is in part because the militarization of the drug-war has made such weapons available for cultural work. As a result, props from the drug-war arsenal have come to saturate the imaginary "object-world" of performers and audiences.

Similar claims could be made concerning weapons in *narcocorridos* and Mexican *narcotraficante* films. *Narcocorrido* performers sing about AK-47s, incorporate the sound of machine-gun fire into their songs, and wield weapons on their album covers.[43] Further recalling both *Scarface* and gangsta rap, many *narcocorridos* include references to the surveillance helicopters commonly used in U.S.-sponsored drug enforcement.[44] *Narcocorridos* often underline the distinctly military character of the war on drugs, as in Pepe Cabrera's "La Mafia Muere" (The Mafia is dying), a song that commemorates "Operation Condor" (1977–78), a massive military operation in which ten thousand Mexican soldiers and members of the Drug Enforcement Administration (DEA) burned marijuana and opium fields, used planes to spray herbicides, and conducted commando raids on various ranches in Culiacán.[45] As "La Mafia Muere" suggests, the emergence of *narcocorridos* in the northern states of Mexico, particularly Sinaloa, coincided with the militarization of borderland drug enforcement, a historical context with analogues in the United States, as the preceding discussion of gangsta rap suggests. Indeed, in the late 1980s gangsta rap and *narcocorridos* emerged side by side in Los Angeles, as Mexican campesinos moved into historically black neighborhoods such as Compton and Inglewood.[46] Similarly, the 1980s marked the emergence of *narcotraficante* films, low-budget, Spanish-language movies set in the northern Mexican borderlands and loosely based on *narcocorrido* narratives. Initiating the film cycle, *Lola la Trailera* was hugely popular on both sides of the border. The film is about Lola, a female truck driver, and her undercover cop boyfriend, who struggle to destroy a gang of drug traffickers. Like a host of subsequent imitators, many of them made for the straight-to-video markets in Mexico and the United States, *Lola la Trailera* features military hardware, including grenades and helicopter gunships.[47] Taken together, such films and music register a qualitative shift in the representation of violence toward high-tech military conflicts associated with the war on drugs and other forms of state-sponsored counterinsurgency.

Some cultural producers have reinterpreted the war on drugs as the basis for a new, automatic-weapon aesthetic. This automatic-weapon aesthetic presupposes an abstract visual logic that organizes the dance-like movements of armed bodies into compositions of color and light. The production design of *Scarface*, for instance, is dominated by a high-tech visual palette whose hallmarks are the rich reds, pinks, purples, and blues of automatic-weapon fire.[48] The Colombians armed with Uzis attack Tony at the Babylon Club, a circular, mirror-filled nightclub. A clown is performing on the club's stage as the Colombians open fire on Tony, who fires back and flees around the room past a rain of bullets and shattering glass. In this way the film represents the gunplay as a sort of graceful acrobatics that complements the imaginary circus. The explosive battle that ends with Tony's death is even more spectacular. Set inside his south Florida mansion, the climactic sequence involves shots of Tony, from a second-floor landing, exchanging automatic gunfire with a ragged army of Bolivian mercenaries as they cross the vast entryway and scramble up the grand staircase. As Tony fires at them the camera cuts to reaction shots of impacted bodies flying backward in space and down the stairs. By subsuming combatants within formal aesthetic patterns, these carefully composed, highly choreographed gunfights obliquely depict the epistemological contours of the drug war, in which bodies and populations are subordinated within larger military structures. Drug-war films such as *Scarface, Deep Cover,* and *El Mariachi* use guns and gunplay in order to represent the structures of military power that, by definition, are irreducible to the anthropomorphizing and individualizing conventions of Hollywood filmmaking.

Many filmmakers and musicians have attempted to reassert creative agency in the face of shrinking social agency by modeling their representational work on forms of military power. As the war on drugs emerged over the course of the 1980s and 1990s, cameras were reimagined as automatic weapons. A good example is the use of new technology called a gun synchronizer to capture the colorful flash of an automatic weapon. As the cinematographer for *Scarface*, John Alonzo, explains, "It has always been a problem when you're shooting 24 frames and someone is shooting a gun. You may or may not catch the flash. . . . The synchronizer [solves this problem because it] prevents the gun from firing unless the camera shutter is open."[49] This new "hardware" in effect makes the automatic weapon an extension of the camera. In response to a drug-war world in which larger state military structures subsumed individual autonomy, filmmakers like De Palma attempted to reassert directorial agency by linking the camera to military firepower. This is particularly apparent in his penchant for swooping crane shots in which the camera, looking down on a mass of extras, slowly glides down and into the crowd until it zooms in on a particular pair of characters. Such scenes seem to mimic the bird's-eye view of drug-war surveillance hardware, including not only helicopters, but also military jets and automated aerial "drones" equipped with cameras. De Palma's use of crane shots to reproduce aerial views, particularly in the context of a film about cocaine traffic, reminds us that a good deal of the new drug-war hardware includes visual surveillance technology such as infrared electronic sensors to detect motion, imaging-enhancement systems to sharpen sensor images, night-vision goggles and infrared weapon sights, and closed-circuit television surveillance systems.[50] Indeed, the makers of *Scarface* practically aligned themselves with official perspectives on drug traffic, even using police videotapes as sources of inspiration.[51] As the producer, Martin Bergman, noted, drug enforcement agencies "were very anxious to have this film made. It was an anti-drug film, very much so. They wanted this film made and I think we pleased them."[52] This alliance between filmmaking and military power is even more pronounced in the case of *Clear and Present Danger,* a film so closely identified with U.S. military power that its makers thank the army, the navy, the marines, and the Department of Defense. Moreover, the action sequence previously described, in which a caravan of CIA agents is attacked by narcoterrorists, has been incorporated into U.S. military training videos.[53]

Subsequent drug-war films elaborated an automatic-weapon aesthetic in terms of editing. Over the last several decades, U.S. action filmmakers have cultivated a hyperkinetic style of editing with multiple, quick cuts. While critical commentary has generally associated this editing style with MTV music videos, it partly derives from an interest in automatic weaponry and the war on drugs. One influential example is the climax of Martin Scorsese's *Goodfellas* (1990), which depicts a wired mobster on a paranoid cocaine bender. Composed of multiple quick and jagged cuts, the scene, according to its editor, Thelma Schoonmaker, was designed "for that cocaine rush."[54] This style of editing is more usually compared, however, to automatic-weapon fire. Mainstream film critics, for instance, use phrases like "rapid-fire editing"[55] and "machine-gun editing"[56] to describe the visual style of contemporary action films.

The B-movie master of machine-gun editing is Robert Rodriguez, the director of the drug war film *El Mariachi* (1992). Ironically, Rodriguez participated in a government drug study in order to fund the film, which was made for the remarkably low sum of seven thousand dollars. Columbia Pictures ultimately optioned *El Mariachi* and released it theatrically, but it was initially made for the Spanish-language video market in Mexico and the United States. It is part of larger field of representation that includes *narcotraficante* films and the *narcocorridos* that often inspire them. The film's hero, the unnamed mariachi of the title, is an itinerant singer who arrives in a small northern Mexican town where he is mistaken for an infamous drug trafficker named Azul. The confusion results from the fact that Azul carries an arsenal of weapons in a guitar case. In part to make the film look more expensive than it was, Rodriguez used multiple editing cuts to compose kinetic gun-battle sequences. In order to keep costs low, the director borrowed automatic weapons such as Uzis and a Mac-10 from the local police.[57] But, as Rodriguez explains, the visual effect of machine-gun fire was produced not by the weapons but by the editing. The blanks used in the film jammed the borrowed guns after one shot, preventing them from firing multiple times, and so to generate the illusion of rapid fire, Rodriguez filmed a single shot from three different angles and then artfully edited them together.[58] In this way the editing process mimics the operation of an automatic weapon.

Indeed, Rodriguez suggests that he imagined his camera as a sort of automatic weapon. The photos accompanying his book about the making of *El Mariachi, Rebel without a Crew,* support this claim. On the cover is an image of the director with a "steadicam." The steadicam is a camera mounted on a mechanical arm and then strapped onto the operator's chest in order to produce fluid, mobile camera movement. Invented in the 1970s by a retired U.S. Navy engineer who began tinkering with a "Rommel-era" camera "covered in camouflage paint,"[59] such hardware seems to anticipate the recent tendency to meld drug-war weaponry and communications technology to the human body. Recalling Robocop, the part-human, part-high-tech weapon that battles drug

The automatic-weapon aesthetic: publicity still for *El Mariachi* (1992), in which the title character (Carlos Gallardo) poses with an Uzi in lieu of his guitar.

traffickers in the film of the same name, the U.S. special forces who participate in the drug war are equipped with automatic assault rifles and helmets with built-in night-vision cameras and radio headsets.[60] As if to underline the symbolic homology between film and military technology, the photo of Rodriguez with the steadicam is accompanied by one of him dressed similarly and pointing the automatic weapons he used in the film.[61] In all of these ways Rodriguez imagines his own brand of filmmaking on the model of drug-war military conflict.

Yet, while Rodriguez's mimicry of military technology recalls the visual strategies of *Scarface*—a film he watched on video while participating in the drug study and writing his own movie[62]—*El Mariachi* appropriates the automatic-weapon aesthetic in ways that symbolically counter both dominant media and military conventions. In the first place, it was conceived as a sort of insurgent work, made outside of the Hollywood filmmaking and distribution system for the Spanish-language video market, hence the title of Rodriguez's book, *Rebel without a Crew*. The image of the director as media guerrilla, moreover, condenses multiple, divergent histories of subaltern rebellion against state power that centrally involve participant observation by media makers. Rodriguez appears on the cover of *Rebel without a Crew* wearing a red bandana and a brown, multipocket vest, with a camera strapped across his chest and held like a rifle. Rodriguez here recalls the 1980s "drug war" between the U.S.-backed and cocaine-funded contras and subaltern communities and groups. He resembles the protagonist of Oliver Stone's *Salvador* (1985), a U.S. photojournalist covering the war in El Salvador. This image of Rodriguez also calls to mind the Chicano activists involved in the sanctuary and antiwar movements.[63] The director's photo further draws upon even older representations of Mexican revolutionaries. *Rebel without a Crew* thus imaginatively aligns the director with historical forms of opposition to state military and police power represented in early-twentieth-century Mexican song and story traditions about bootleggers, smugglers, and other rebels who waged pitched battles against state military forces—a topic I return to in Part II of this book. For now, however, I want to emphasize the field of conflicting representations that constitute drug-war culture. *Clear and Present Danger* shares machine-gun props and aesthetics with *El Mariachi,* and the two films similarly subordinate female characters within larger narratives about conflicts between men. Domino, the only significant female character in *El Mariachi,* is ultimately killed in a battle between the villain and the hero, rendering her, as her name suggests, a game piece in a patriarchal game. Although the film reproduces the military and gender scenarios of Hollywood blockbusters, it also addresses subaltern audiences predisposed to sympathize with forces of rebellion. Movies and music are thus contradictory, combining dominant ideologies and diverse critical elements that call into question the legitimacy of the U.S. war on drugs.

"This country was built on washing money": Imagining Narcocapital

In *Scarface* narcocapitalism is personified by a smarmy banker who helps Tony Montana launder millions in cocaine money. As Tony tells his banker, "This country was built on washing money." Tony is also in league with a number of Bolivian capitalists, including Sosa, a large landowner, and Pedro Quinn, the president of the Andes Sugar Corporation. This strategy of individualizing and anthropomorphizing capital is partly countered, however, by representations that instead signify the structural aspects of narcocapital that are irreducible to individuals. Jameson has argued that the "menacing object-world of allegorical conspiracies" in U.S. films from the 1970s and 1980s prominently features representations of communication technology that register anxieties about the erosion of privacy or "the end of civil society itself." Such concerns emerge from changes in the "abstract category of property" that disclose "a fundamental transition from the private to the corporate": "How there could be private things, let alone privacy, in a situation in which almost everything around us is functionally inserted into larger institutional schemes and frameworks of all kinds, which nonetheless belong to *somebody*—this is now the nagging question that haunts the camera dollying around our various life-worlds."[64] In drug-war culture, the saturation of social space by corporate capitalism is represented by new forms of high-tech communications technology that have increasingly been associated not only with the world of "legitimate" corporate finance but also with the drug trade: cellular phones, electronic pagers, and complex surveillance systems. Hence, even in 1983, well before the near ubiquity of the cell phone in North America, the portable phone is an important prop in *Scarface,* and even the drug traffickers in the incredibly low-budget *El Mariachi* own them. And of course such devices have become staples of gangsta rap and *narcocorridos.* A related prop is the large mechanical money counter Tony feeds during two scenes. As figures for global corporate capitalism, counting machines and communications technologies gesture toward the systemic aspects of capitalism that transcend individual human agency.

In addition to the use of props, filmmakers also attempt to represent the supra-individual, systemic facets of capitalism formally, through money montages. A good example is the montage in *Scarface* that depicts Tony's rise to success in the cocaine business: first, a shot of jeweled hands surrounded by stacks of bills which are fed into a mechanical counter; cut to a shot of Tony talking on the phone and then a reverse shot of Sosa on the phone in his garden in Bolivia; then a shot of the Cuban drug lord entering the Tri-American Bank with big bags of money; and finally shots of Tony in front of the Montana Travel Company and the Montana Management Company, the legitimate businesses that serve as fronts for cocaine traffic. A similar montage in *Deep Cover* depicts undercover agent Stevens weighing and packing cocaine, selling it on the street as part of his cover, and collecting and counting money. A musical corollary to the money montage is the use of money collages in CD and cassette art. The CD cover for Grupo Exterminador's *Narco Corridos 2,* for instance, pictures a photo of the band members superimposed over a collage of large-denomination U.S. bills.[65] In these ways drug-war filmmakers and musicians attempt to visually represent capital flows that, because they are dispersed so widely in time and space, are otherwise difficult to depict.

Rap music further references structures of corporate capital in narratives where characters confront the limits of their own knowledge and power in the face of larger forces. A prime example is Ice-T's brilliant theme song for *New Jack City,* "New Jack Hustler," a narrative from the perspective of a crack dealer. The song's object-world is filled with money and expensive commodities. Yet these objects are embedded in a larger capitalist system that reproduces the forms of inequality driving drug traffic: economic inequalities promote the kinds of ruthless profiteering that characterize corporate capitalism, leading the narrator to wonder whether this nightmarish scenario is just another version of the American Dream. The systemic, corporate nature of this system ultimately exceeds the understanding and control of Ice-T's character, and he emphasizes the ways in which it submerges human agency. By focalizing his narrative through the mind of an imaginary crack dealer, moreover, Ice-T uses a state of subjective conflict to reference the conflicted conditions of global capital. In this way the rapper creates a subject that foregrounds the limits of subjectivity itself as a model for mapping the structures of global capital.[66]

Drug-war money shot: Grupo Exterminador's *Narco Corridos 2,* Fonovisa Records.

Similarly, the Geto Boys' haunting "Mind Playing Tricks on Me" points to the systemic violence of corporate capitalism that accompanies the war on drugs. The song consists of a series of paranoid vignettes about imaginary drug dealers living in worlds controlled by vague, malevolent forces that exceed their apprehension and control. One narrator is a virtual prisoner in his own room, where he worries that he is being watched and that his telephone has been tapped, while a second drug dealer confesses that despite his money and power, he constantly thinks that he is being followed and cannot shake his intense feelings of paranoia.[67] "Mind Playing Tricks on Me" refers not only to the kinds of police surveillance that characterize the war on drugs, but also to the world of global corporate capital discussed by Jameson, where privacy is impossible because "almost everything around us is functionally inserted into larger institutional schemes and frameworks of all kinds, which nonetheless belong" to corporations. The acute forms of paranoia described in the song, in other words, speak to the epistemology of contemporary capitalist structures that impinge on subjectivities but resist attempts to represent them in subjective terms.

THE DRUG-WAR POOR

While in portions of this book I focus on drug traffic and immigrant labor, I place workers in relationship to the larger category of the subaltern or the poor in order to address forms of drug-war domination among those who do not regularly work full- or part-time for a wage. In drug-war films, both kinds of poor people are condensed into the figure of the disposable extra. These extras often play the parts of the Latin American peasants who work for cocaine cartels, but their ultimate sacrifice within the film's action sequences suggests the larger disposability of poor people within the global economy. *Scarface's* Tony Montana first encounters such extras when he tours Sosa's Bolivian cocaine plant and sees its workers and armed guards. The film's climax, moreover, includes an army of Latino extras playing the ragged Colombian assassins that ultimately kill the drug lord. Montana, however, dispatches a large number of extras before he is killed. *Clear and Present Danger* includes similar scenes of carnage. There we see U.S. special-forces troops kill numerous extras playing Colombians, including workers in a cocaine-processing factory. The film presupposes a non-subaltern, North American audience and offers the U.S. soldiers as points of identification over and against the Colombians they kill. Unlike the majority of Colombians, the U.S. soldiers have names—John Clark (Willem Dafoe), Captain Ramirez (Benjamin Bratt), and Domingo "Ding" Chavez (Raymond Cruz)—and are given brief, personalizing scenes. As the names of the last two characters suggest, the film recruits U.S. Latinos—themselves potential subalterns—to U.S. nationalism by violently distinguishing them from the anonymous Colombians. As "extras" with respect to an imagined U.S. military multiculturalism, the Colombians are liquidated without narrative remains, representing the "disposable people" disappeared by the war on drugs.

Dominant drug-war representations further suggest how subaltern status is reproduced in terms of gender and sexuality. Beginning in the mid-1980s, TV news reports and other media began to predict that crack consumption by poor women of color would spawn a nightmare generation of irredeemably damaged black and brown children destined to become the criminals and social liabilities of the future. Such representations suggested that women of color were particularly vulnerable to drug addiction and in need of patriarchal protection. In *Deep Cover,* for instance, narcotics agent Stevens befriends Belinda Chacon (Kamala Lopez), a shrill, verbally aggressive Latina who offers to sell her young son to Stevens in order to support her crack habit. Through this mother-and-son pair, the film feminizes and infantilizes the poor in ways that recall discourses concerning crack babies. At the same time, *Deep Cover* makes the war on drugs an imaginary testing ground for patriarchal power. It begins with the patriarch in ruins—when Stevens is a child he sees his own drug-addicted father killed in a botched robbery attempt. As a young undercover agent, his superior officer, Gerald Carver, motivates Stevens by describing crack babies on life-support machines. Soon he meets a model of the drug warrior as father—an older, black narcotics officer who shows the younger man pictures of his children and who dramatically vows to protect them and others from crack. In contrast to the paternal policeman, the film's Colombian drug lords are effeminate and implicitly "queer." Although he is committed to combating the Colombians, Stevens becomes disillusioned when Carver, at the insistence of the State Department, orders him to protect a Colombian drug lord. When confronted with the hypocrisy of official drug policy, Stevens seems to turn away from police work and become a drug trafficker instead, but when his partner in crime shoots the fatherly policeman, Stevens rushes to the wounded man's side and back to the law. The film's final scenes suggest that Stevens's drug-war duty made him a man, meaning a patriarch. Whereas Carver cynically exploits the specter of the crack baby to gain political capital, the film implies, Stevens's paternal concerns are firm and legitimate. Thus, while in many ways the film is highly critical of the drug war, *Deep Cover*'s conclusion redeems drug enforcement by linking it to fantasies of masculine power.[68] As this and a host of other films suggest, the war on drugs of the 1980s and 1990s promoted the expansion of patriarchal power in the name of protecting women and children from drugs.

But whereas some examples of drug-war culture strive to contain subaltern agency, others symbolically promote it. The performers themselves often have subaltern histories. The famous *narcocorrido* star Chalino Sánchez, for example, was a migrant farmworker, a car washer, and a small-time drug dealer before starting to write and sing.[69] And such musicians self-consciously address large audiences of poor people.[70] Indeed, *narcocorridos* are popular not only in the rural villages of northern Mexico but also among young working-class Mexicans in the U.S. Southwest, particularly Los Angeles.[71] Such music serves to narrate the drug war from below. Rap and *narcocorridos* often represent fantasies of a world turned upside down in which poor black and Mexican characters become rich and powerful social actors who battle with and often triumph over the police and other representatives of state power. These two musical forms imaginatively invert dominant state and capitalist relations that subordinate the poor. Which is not to say that *narcocorridos* or rap represent the unmediated voice of the subaltern as such, for both kinds of music are mediated in ways that partly embed them in dominant ideologies and structures. In their fantasies of subaltern power, both forms borrow ideas and images from dominant mass media, including newspapers, TV news, and mainstream action films. And, as their respective critics have pointed out, some examples of drug-war music reproduce dominant forms of patriarchal ideology. Nonetheless, the history of gangsta rap and *narcocorridos* suggests that subaltern audiences take vicarious pleasure in the narcotrafficker's opposition to state power. The tastes of such audiences contradict dominant representations of poor people longing for patriarchal state protections. The U.S. war on drugs thus makes visible historical struggles over the representation of subaltern peoples. In dominant versions, the war on drugs waged in the name of poor women and children serves to diminish the subaltern in the way that the "feminine" is always devalued in patriarchal contexts. As a figure for the poor, the "women and children" trope, moreover, legitimates state action by imaginatively disappearing subaltern agency. From this perspective, state action is justified because the poor are unwilling or unable to act. By contrast, in subaltern representations of the drug war, the poor are powerful social agents who directly confront state representatives. In rap and *narcocorridos,* the police appear as violent and corrupt predators but rarely as protectors of women and children.

Popular female performers, in particular, foreground subaltern women's agency in ways that contradict dominant patriarchal representations of women and the war on drugs. Although men have dominated both musical forms, a number of women have appropriated their conventions to construct female gangsta or *narcotraficante* characters. A case in point is Jenni Rivera, a *narcocorridista* based in Los Angeles whose signature song "La Chacalosa" is about a young, gun-wielding female drug trafficker. As she explains, "the song is about a girl, a daughter of a drug dealer, and how she's on the run. It's a *Thelma and Louise* thing."[72] Although mediated by a Hollywood movie, this song and others have a subaltern address, suggesting the extent to which poor women have become both targets and agents within a male-dominated war on drugs. Moreover, the song represents a world turned upside down, in which a poor woman masters modern communications technology and dominates the drug trade—not to mention the men who work for her. Or, as she summarizes it, "It says that when I was fifteen I didn't get a *quinceañara,* instead they gave me a cell phone and a pager; and a business that would give me lots of money. And then it talks about a lot of different things: that they showed me how to use guns, and I have my plantations in Jalisco and my drug lab in Sonora, and I have people that distribute it for me and I never touch a thing—the men do everything for me. I just make the money."[73] Here Rivera projects a fantasy from below of a dramatic class and gender power reversal that contradicts dominant representations of poor women as passive victims in need of patriarchal protection.

MEDIA WARS

Beginning in the 1980s, the U.S. war on drugs was increasingly waged through the media. The state, for example, directly shaped media representations of the war on drugs in film. As previously noted, local law enforcement agents actively influenced the making of *Scarface,* providing the writer and the director with police files and videos. Later, when it was threatened with receiving an "X" rating, one narcotics agent even testified before the ratings board in favor of an R rating, arguing that *Scarface* was an antidrug film.[74] Similarly, various branches of the U.S. military actively supported the production of *Clear and Present Danger.* In 1990, President George Bush and his conservative allies promoted *Delta Force 2,* a heroic drug-war film featuring martial-arts star Chuck Norris. Bush invited Norris to screen the film at the White House, and the president reportedly "loved the macho story of tough Drug Enforcement Administration guys defeating an evil Latin drug lord."[75] In addition, Republican senators Bob Dole and Pete Wilson sponsored a *Delta Force 2* screening for members of the Senate.[76]

In this film, Norris's character is a special-forces officer, Colonel Scott McCoy, who represents drug-war counterinsurgency in patriotic, paternalistic terms. Throughout the film, starting with the opening scene in which he protects a Vietnamese restaurant owner from a group of skinheads, Colonel McCoy takes violent action on behalf of nonwhite people who are represented as unable to successfully act on their own. As this last example suggests, the Vietnam War is an important subtext in *Delta Force 2*. Shot in the Philippines, the film features scenes of South American peasants harvesting coca who resemble Vietnamese peasants in their rice fields. Fought on behalf of these peasants, Colonel McCoy's one-man drug war symbolically overcomes the "Vietnam syndrome," redeeming U.S. military losses in Southeast Asia.[77] Just as McCoy paternalistically fights on behalf of the third-world peasant, his dramatic mission to capture the evil drug lord Cota is motivated by the murder of two U.S. people of color, McCoy's Latino partner and an African American DEA agent who had infiltrated Cota's operation. In order to avenge his colleagues and free more captive agents, McCoy parachutes into the fictional South American country of San Carlos, where his contact is Quiquina, a local Indian woman. Earlier, the drug lord had murdered her husband and child and then raped her. Norris's character parachutes in as her U.S. savior, but Cota kills her before the colonel gets to him. Because McCoy acts in the name of people of color, their disposability is what ultimately propels the plot of *Delta Force 2*. It thus makes sense that conservative politicians would promote this film, because their own plans for the drug war had the effect of rendering many poor people in the hemisphere similarly expendable.

Other films self-consciously represent the media's participation in the war on drugs through proxy props such as surveillance and communications technology. *Scarface* prominently features shots of Tony Montana's elaborate security system, including scenes built around banks of monitors that alternate between TV broadcasts and security camera feeds. The recorded surveillance images on the monitors mimic the film as a whole, and, by extension, the power of the media in the war on drugs. Similarly, *Clear and Present Danger* represents surveillance technology as one of the CIA's drug enforcement tools. The film first introduces its hero, Jack Ryan, as he meets with the president and his advisers to screen videotape of a crime scene. Furthermore, in order to identify Cortez, the evil drug lord, the CIA feeds a loop of his recorded speech into a voice-recognition database that generates visual patterns on a

Drug-war paternalism: publicity still for *Delta Force 2* (1990), in which "Colonel Scott McCoy (Chuck Norris), deep in the jungle, hides his guide, Quiquina, from armed mercenaries."

bank of computer monitors. If, as Jameson argues, communications equipment has saturated the prop world of recent films, this is in part because such technology has become a weapon in the war on drugs.

As its prominence within drug-war films suggests, television has also been an important drug-war medium. In *Scarface,* Tony simultaneously watches surveillance monitors and the TV news, whereas in *Clear and Present Danger,* scenes of TV news broadcasts serve a narrative function, providing characters (and audiences) with key information. The centrality of TV to Hollywood's war on drugs is matched in the world of official antidrug policy, where first lady Nancy Reagan attempted to influence coverage of the war on drugs by leading a highly publicized antidrug crusade. Acting as what the president called his "cocaptain" in the war on drugs,[78] in the 1980s Mrs. Reagan headed the Just Say No Foundation, an organization whose most significant achievement was to gain favorable television and other media coverage for the administration's efforts. To this end, in addition to her previously mentioned appearance on *Diff'rent Strokes,* the first lady cohosted a two-hour broadcast of the popular ABC morning show *Good Morning America* devoted to drug abuse;[79] hosted a televised drug-abuse prevention forum at the White House; and promoted an antidrug Saturday morning cartoon.[80] In addition to Mrs. Reagan's efforts, starting in the 1980s the state began supporting antidrug public-service announcements on TV, the radio, and in print.[81] And in recent years the government has subsequently provided millions of dollars in subsidies to networks that incorporate antidrug messages into the plots of popular shows.[82]

As part of the war on drugs, the government not only intervenes in the media but also incorporates mass-media marketing techniques in order to disseminate state ideologies. Nancy Reagan's campaign pioneered such work, for the first lady aggressively sought the support of capitalists and their advertising agencies. Companies such as Proctor & Gamble donated large sums of money to her Just Say No Foundation, and in 1988 the company's senior vice president became the foundation's chair.[83] Market researchers simultaneously discovered that the antidrug message has "an almost universal appeal" that "crosses all cultural and economic classes and has few negative connotations."[84] Taking advantage of market research, the state employed advertising firms to create antidrug public-service announcements for TV, radio, and print. More recently, the White House's Office of National Drug Control Policy (ONDCP) launched the "National Youth Anti-Drug Media Campaign." Echoing market researchers, the campaign's goal is to disseminate the state's drug enforcement message "across every economic and cultural boundary."

The ONDCP's media campaign targets subaltern audiences in particular—minority, immigrant, and indigenous peoples living in the United States. According to its official Web site, the campaign's "multicultural outreach" is "one of the largest advertising efforts developed by the Federal Government with messages tailored for ethnic audiences." Around 75 percent of the drug-war ads are addressed to African Americans and "Hispanics." Most of the remainder are reproduced in Cantonese, Korean, Vietnamese, Cambodian, and American Indian languages. Ads also target the U.S. territories of Guam, the U.S. Virgin Islands, American Samoa, and Puerto Rico.[85] The state generates these ads by subcontracting with advertising and public-relations firms that specialize in addressing target audiences. Finally, the campaign distributes drug-war messages through media outlets targeting particular groups, such as syndicated television, magazines, newspapers, radio stations, and Internet providers that address African Americans, Latinos, and

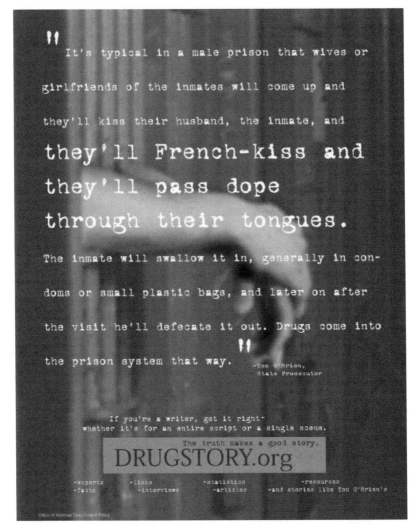

❞ It's typical in a male prison that wives or girlfriends of the inmates will come up and they'll kiss their husband, the inmate, and

they'll French-kiss and they'll pass dope through their tongues.

The inmate will swallow it in, generally in condoms or small plastic bags, and later on after the visit he'll defecate it out. Drugs come into the prison system that way. ❞ —Tom O'Brien, State Prosecutor

If you're a writer, get it right—whether it's for an entire script or a single scene. The truth makes a good story.

DRUGSTORY.org

-experts -links -statistics -resources
-facts -interviews -articles -and stories like Tom O'Brien's

Office of National Drug Control Policy

The drug war goes Hollywood: advertisement for the Office of National Drug Control Policy's Web site for film and television writers, Drugstory.org.

others. In these ways the state disseminates official representations of the war on drugs tailored for largely disenfranchised groups. More broadly, via the war on drugs the state has sought to colonize civil society and annex diverse aspects of mass and popular culture to state power. Or, in the words of the official Web site for the ONDCP's media campaign, the state's strategy is to "leverage pop culture's visibility, credibility, and influence with audiences" in order to generate support for the war on drugs.[86]

The drug war's cultural front extends across a range of media, including film, music, TV, and the Internet. The ONDCP, for example, produces "Drugstory.org," a Web site that serves as an "informational resource for entertainment writers and feature journalists." Advertised in trade journals such as *Variety*, the Web site provides filmmakers with models for their scripts. Drugstory.org features interviews with drug enforcement officials; news stories and government reports on drug smuggling; links to the DEA, CIA, and FBI; and an extensive drug enforcement photo gallery organized by topics such as "Homeland Security," "Special Response Teams," "Concealment Methods," and "Busted." The Web site's stated goal is to provide media makers with accurate and reliable information about the war on drugs. Since most of its information comes from state sources, however, Drugstory.org reifies official representations as the ultimate measure of accuracy and reliability. It thus tends to frame highly politicized constructions of the war on drugs as ideologically neutral. The Web site offers entertainment writers plenty of models for representing U.S. drug interdiction efforts, but no resources regarding two of the central concerns of the present study: the ways in which capitalists and the state have, at the expense of the poor, historically profited from drug traffic; or the ways in which drug-war activities have often focused on the repression of some of the world's weakest and most vulnerable peoples. Such concerns are a constitutive absence in official representations of the drug war.

During the last few decades, then, the state has pursued the war on drugs in partnership with the mainstream media. For this very reason, however, the media has also been a site of conflict, as evidenced by state efforts to manage and control popular music about the drug war. In the United States, the FBI investigated rappers NWA and Ice-T because their songs were critical of the police. Throughout the late 1980s and early 1990s, congressional investigators and parents turned their attention to the media's influence on young people, particularly in the form of popular music referencing drugs. More recently, the Web site for the (second) Bush administration's "National Youth Anti-Drug Media Campaign" distributes academic studies and other information about drugs in music and film. Meanwhile, in Mexico *narcocorridos* are effectively banned from the radio, and in the United States they receive limited airplay.

Rappers and *narcocorrido* performers oppose the mass-mediated war on drugs by foregrounding in their lyrics and imagery the forms of state and capitalist violence that a focus on the dangers of drugs to children displaces. Corrupt state representatives are fixtures of drug-war music. As Robin Kelley and Tricia Rose note, rap music often analyzes racist state institutions, particularly the police and the criminal justice system. In some songs, the police are even represented as complicit in drug traffic. The theme song for *Deep Cover,* for instance, features a narrative by rapper Snoop Dogg in which his character meets with some undercover cops who promise to make him rich if he sells drugs for them. When Snoop's character refuses, a shootout ensues. In the song "A Bird in the Hand" from his album *Death Certificate* (1991), Ice-Cube describes a character who is forced by economic circumstances to sell drugs. The narrator, however, ultimately blames the state—as represented by President George Bush—for producing the economic situation that makes drug dealing an attractive option.[87] As this example suggests, while rappers often focus on the police, they also criticize some of the most powerful state representatives. According to Kelley, "dozens of rap artists... indict 'America' for stealing land, facilitating the drug trade either through inaction or active participation of the CIA and friendly dictators, and waging large-scale 'drive-by shootings' against little countries such as Panama and Iraq." Such music, Kelley concludes, makes the argument that "violence and gangsterism are best exemplified by the state, not young inner-city residents."[88]

Many *narcocorridos* make related claims in their criticisms of the U.S. war on drugs. The song "Los Super Capos," written by Paulino Vargas and recorded by Los Invasores de Nuevo León, concerns the CIA/contra cocaine scandal and the U.S. "capos" or gangsters, such as George Bush, who profit from drug traffic.[89] Furthermore, the song notes that these same figures are responsible for military actions throughout the world, including the blockade of Cuba and attacks on Iraq and the Palestinians. This and other songs call particular attention to the contradictions of drug certification policies, whereby the United States insists that Mexico police drug traffic as a condition for receiving aid but does little itself to decrease domestic demand—or worse yet, actually participates in drug traffic. The song concludes with a direct address to the U.S. state asking it to clean its own fields before insisting on Mexican certification.[90] Similarly, Teodoro Bello has written a popular song called "Por Debajo del Agua," which describes Washington's complicity in drug traffic, and "El General," which asks the question, who certifies the United States?[91]

These musicians participate in circuits of production, distribution, and promotion that bypass dominant routes. New, inexpensive audio technologies such as cassette players made it easier in the last several decades to produce and circulate all sorts of music, particularly songs with challenging views. At the same time, by selling gangsta rap and *narcocorrido* cassettes at gas stations, car washes, bakeries, convenience stores, butcher shops, and especially swap meets, musicians and their small independent labels largely circumvented radio, one of the dominant institutions of music distribution and promotion. Chalino Sánchez, for instance, built his legendary career by driving boxes of his own cassettes to car washes and swap meets in Mexican Los Angeles. He sold thousands and thousands of tapes throughout the U.S. Southwest and the northern states of Mexico without receiving radio play.[92] Small, cheap, and easy to transport or smuggle, the cassette tape is a convenient form of music reproduction for poor people on the go, immigrants who must travel light. Like the audiocassette, the videotape is relatively cheap and easy to transport, and it enables small video distributors to sidestep theatrical release and Hollywood distribution systems. Straight-to-video gangsta rap and *narcocorrido* films are rented at video chains but also at small, independent video stores and other venues. Starting in the 1980s, Mexican immigrants adapted video technology for lives vulnerable to state and capitalist power. Home video enabled poor people to watch films in their living spaces and away from public spheres increasingly subject to various kinds of policing. The emergence of *narcotraficante* videos in the 1980s, for instance, coincided with INS raids on Spanish-language movie theaters.[93] In contexts in which the state and large capitalist interests dominated radio and Mexican movie houses, subaltern audiences countered by turning to music cassettes and home video. Thus, in this case, as well as many others, drug wars are also media wars: in modern history elite and subaltern struggles over the management and control of drug traffic partly take the form of struggles over media representation.

In what follows, I focus on different examples of media struggles between elites and subalterns over drug traffic and enforcement. *Drug Wars* is divided into three parts, each of which focuses on a particular drug traffic from the eighteenth century to the present. Taken together, these three sections—"Opium," "Marijuana," and "Cocaine"—examine the role of state power, narcocapital, subaltern peoples, and media politics in the process of drug traffic and enforcement. Part I suggests that the British opium monopoly was a historical precedent for the contemporary U.S. war on drugs: the state's management of its opium monopoly ultimately served to discipline Chinese immigrant workers on behalf of capitalists. As a result of the first opium war, the British Empire secured a foothold on the Chinese coast not only for opium dealers but also for immigrant labor brokers: opium and Chinese laborers followed each other to China-towns located throughout the British Empire. I conclude that the movements of Chinese immigrant workers decisively shaped the popular British and U.S. representations that were produced to contain them.

In chapter 1, "The Globe in an Opium Bowl: The Opium Wars and British Empire in Asia," I analyze mass-media representations of the British opium monopoly. In order to protect and extend the Chinese market for English opium grown in India, Britain deployed its military in the two so-called Opium Wars. English periodicals circulated a wide range of responses to the opium monopoly and the alliance between capitalists and the state that it represented. Here I consider not only dominant representations of the Opium Wars, including periodical literature about Chinese opium dens throughout British Asia, but also Chinese criticisms of British state power. Chinese observers undercut dominant ideology by foregrounding the aspects of imperial violence that English writers generally suppressed. Taking Chinese rebellions at sea as emblematic, I interpret the figure of the burning ship as the Chinese laborer's critical rejoinder to the imperial "ship of state" and a refusal to be governed by the British Empire.

Building upon this, chapter 2, "Strange Bedfellows: Opium and the Political Economy of Sexuality," suggests that shared debates over the policing of Chinese immigrants in the British white-settler colonies of Australia, New Zealand, and British Columbia, on the one hand, and in the U.S. West, on the other, ultimately supported ideologies of a transnational white male heterosexuality defined in ambivalent opposition to immigrant Chinese workingmen. The figure of the Chinese opium den organized sexualized fears of and desires for Chinese male laborers in England and its colonies. Mass periodicals debated the merits of employing Chinese labor in charged, homoerotic language, with critics alluding to the Chinaman's sexual deviance and proponents praising his unique masculine beauty and powerful body. Similar homoerotic ambivalence reappears in opium den narratives, where male Chinese bodies are alternatively fascinating and dangerous. I conclude that opium den stories reveal the homoerotic investments that subtended British colonial labor relations.

Part II shifts to another precursor to the current war on drugs, marijuana traffic and enforcement in the U.S.–Mexican borderlands during the 1930s. Responding to the migration of Mexicans and Mexican revolutionary politics to the United States, the state employed drug enforcement as part of a larger ensemble of policing practices aimed at managing Mexican workers in general, but especially Mexican radicals. Dominant forms of mass media such as newspapers, radio, film, and commercial art, as well as Southwestern modernist literature and culture developed a symbiotic relationship with that police project. The police used media outlets and techniques to promote their war on drugs while dominant media represented Mexicans in ways that supported law enforcement. By contrast, subaltern Mexican media producers and audiences mobilized modern technologies of reproduction such as photography, radio, film, and live and recorded music in ways that critically addressed the contemporary war on drugs.

Chapter 3, "Anarchy in the USA: The Mexican Revolution, Labor Radicalism, and the Criminalization of Marijuana," concerns the use of drug laws to police Mexican workers and protect mining companies and other capitalist interests in northern New Mexico. Like the commercial art produced to promote travel to the region, the modernist works of the "artist colonies" indirectly supported the surrounding drug war by disappearing it, focusing instead on natural and pastoral landscapes purged of the mines, labor conflict, and the police. By contrast, working-class Mexicans in the region reacted to the same context by appropriating new technologies of mass cultural production such as newspapers, photographs, and musical recordings in ways that opposed dominant drug-war media. Mexicans performed and recorded *corridos* and other songs celebrating bootleggers, smugglers, and marijuana smokers—the various enemies of state and capitalist domination in the borderlands. Such songs were popular because they articulated a collective identity in rebellion against state and capitalist domination of land and resources.

In chapter 4, "LAPD, the Movie: Hollywood, the Police, and the Drug War against Mexican Immigrants," I suggest that modern police power in Los Angeles emerged in response to the radical Mexican presence there. During the 1920s and 1930s, the state used drug and other vice laws to police working-class Mexicans and, in particular, to control the significant number of Mexican women who entered the local labor market in those years. Moreover, dominant media such as newspapers, radio, and film directly and indirectly sustained police efforts. Radio broadcasters and the *Los Angeles Times* complied with police projects by promoting official representations of Mexican criminality. And filmmakers indirectly supported the police by reproducing representations of Mexican sexuality that complemented police profiles. In this way a dialectical relationship emerged whereby Hollywood mimicked police depictions of Mexicans at the same time as the police mimicked Hollywood. I end by analyzing the LAPD portion of this dialectic and the ways in which the police partly modeled the drug war against Mexicans on the themes and representational practices of Hollywood films.

Chapter 5, "La Cucaracha in Babylon: Mexican Music and Hollywood's Sonic War on Drugs," returns to the topic of drug enforcement in Los Angeles, but this time from the perspective of mass-media producers and audiences. On the dominant side of media politics, film studios forged a practical and ideological alliance with the police over the task of controlling Mexicans. The classic Hollywood studios, guarded by their own private police forces, were partly consolidated in practical opposition to the surrounding Mexican populations. Returning to the forms of Mexican music previously analyzed, I argue that with the coming of sound, Hollywood incorporated such songs into films so as to symbolically contain Mexican dissent. In contrast, Mexican immigrants provided Hollywood productions with their own sound tracks, combining film screenings and live musical performances in ways that opposed dominant attempts to police them. Suggesting comparisons with contemporary *narcocorridistas* and rebel filmmakers, the hybrid forms of Mexican spectatorship in 1930s Los Angeles contradicted dominant versions of the war on drugs and the extension of police power over immigrants.

Part III suggests that hemispheric histories of Indian resistance to state power continue to shape ideas about cocaine use and interdiction. Europeans first "discovered" coca when they invaded Peru in the sixteenth century and enslaved Indians to work in the mines and on plantations, including the coca fields. Eventually, the Spanish incorporated the drug into the production process by providing Indian slaves with rations of coca and scheduling regular coca breaks during the workday. Spanish domination in Peru nonetheless remained limited by Indian rebellions, and such rebellions continued after Spanish independence.

Thus, throughout much of the nineteenth century, scientific research and legal discussions of coca were preoccupied with the threat of Indian revolt. A similar structure of feeling continues to inform contemporary U.S. drug-war ideology and practice. Starting in the 1980s, the drug war reanimated historical fantasies of Indian warfare and imperial rivalry in which Anglo America succeeds the Spanish Empire in the West. Indian activists and writers, however, have opposed the U.S. war on drugs by exposing state legal systems as imperial institutions with historical antecedents in the European conquest of the Americas.

Chapter 6, "Cocaine Colonialism: Indian Rebellion in South America and the History of Psychoanalysis," begins by noting that in the final decades of the nineteenth century medical researchers and entrepreneurs, notably Sigmund Freud, revisited the history of the Spanish Conquest in order to promote the benefits of cocaine for Western consumers. In his hurry to advertise the medical and commercial value of cocaine, the future inventor of psychoanalysis imagined himself as a sort of modern conquistador. He thus participated in a larger mass culture of cocaine that was invested in colonial and neocolonial land and resource scrambles that were threatened by the prospect of Indian rebellions. Anticipating the individualizing and anthropomorphizing strategies for representing capitalist relations in recent drug-war films, Freud elaborated a model of subjectivity that imaginatively internalized the international political economy of cocaine traffic in the form of conflicted psychic states. This cocaine prehistory of psychoanalysis suggests that its influential model of modern subjectivity was embedded in and responded to the forms of imperialism that marked the first global cocaine boom.

The final chapter, "Drug Wars Are Indian Wars: Frontier Drug Enforcement and the Ends of U.S. Empire," juxtaposes official U.S. constructions of the 1980s war on drugs to popular writings by Native American authors. Such works highlight the extent to which the drug war targets Indian peoples throughout the Americas. From this perspective, the recent militarization of drug enforcement at the U.S.–Mexico border coincides with longer histories of state attacks on Indian peoples. In the work of Leslie Marmon Silko, in particular, the extension of state legal systems and the criminalization of Indian peoples that characterize the drug war represent settler-colonial warfare by other means— a set of ideologies and practices aimed at subordinating sovereign peoples to U.S. and Mexican state power. In her remarkable novel *Almanac of the Dead,* Silko depicts Yaqui Indian drug and weapons smugglers along the contemporary U.S.–Mexico border. A novel that began as an attempt to write what Silko called a popular "cops-and-robbers novel about cocaine smuggling" ultimately became a complex challenge to U.S. power in the Americas, suggesting that the new demographic realities of the Indian South in the North have provoked a crisis of governmentality for which the drug war is both symptom and response.

Throughout *Drug Wars* I analyze struggles over cultural production that have been integral to the drug wars of different historical moments. Whereas capitalists and the state try to manage contradictions and exclude subalterns from representation, poor people exploit ideological contradictions in order to reinterpret dominant media in other ways, while at the same time striving to capture the means of media production and dissemination. Given historical contexts in which they possess little economic or political capital, subalterns cut alternative channels of media publicity, from the *narcocorridista*'s swap meet, to the American Indian Movement's occupation of Wounded Knee (chapter 7), to the refunctioning of visual and aural technologies by Mexican immigrants (chapter 5). Subaltern interventions in different spheres of cultural production, distribution, and reception often radically challenge dominant ideas and structures governing history, identity, community, class, and citizenship. *Drug Wars* thus examines instances where subaltern people directly and indirectly intervene in mass-media representation. Directly, because they often appropriate records, radio, movies, and other mass media for alternative uses. Indirectly, since subalterns often take dramatic action implicitly or explicitly geared toward gaining attention in a wider public sphere, as when Chinese immigrants burn the ships that carry them into "coolie" slavery (chapter 1), or when Mexican miners forcibly occupy the chambers of state power (chapter 4). To revise Marx's famous phrase, popular or subaltern groups of people make media history, only not under conditions of their own making. I hope that the chapters that follow will contribute to a larger conversation about how drug wars and media wars have shaped global histories of race, rebellion, and modernity.

Part I

Opium

CHAPTER 1

The Globe in an Opium Bowl
The Opium Wars and British Empire in Asia

On the way from Hong Kong to Cuba in 1857, in the middle of the second Opium War, hundreds of Chinese on board the English ship the *Gulnare* rebelled. As we shall see, labor recruitment on the coast of China and transportation to British-dominated ports in Hong Kong and Malaysia relied upon kidnapping and other forms of coercion, so many Chinese were sailing against their will. Moreover, the British ships that transported both opium and Chinese workers were former slave vessels equipped with leg and arm chains, iron gratings, barricades, and armed guards. Under such conditions, the death rate for Chinese immigrants rivaled the deadliness of the African slave trade. And finally, the *Gulnare*'s destination was the notorious labor market of Cuba, where work was impossibly hard and life short. Faced with this dire situation, the Chinese attempted to take control of the ship. When the mutiny failed, they unsuccessfully tried to burn the vessel. Two ship officers were seriously wounded, but as the crew regained control they killed nine Chinese and wounded many more in retaliation. Three Chinese jumped ship, choosing death over recapture.[1]

Such events were relatively common in the second half of the nineteenth century. Between 1850 and 1872, there were at least forty-two cases in which Chinese laborers rebelled against European and U.S. crews whose business it was to transport them into forms of neo-slavery.[2] Indeed, many Chinese took extreme steps such as attacking well-armed guards, burning the ship, or diving into the sea. Although these rebellions would surely make fascinating subjects for fiction and film, both English and U.S. cultural producers have told other stories about the Chinese. In the late nineteenth and early twentieth centuries, an emergent Anglophone mass culture focused not on the ship but on the opium den. Silent films about the Chinese such as D. W. Griffith's *Broken Blossoms* (1919) stage opium den scenes but largely exclude representations of the Chinese "middle passage." While most critics of the film focus on its sensational central portion, involving a cockney boxer, his abused twelve-year-old-daughter Lucy, and a Chinese immigrant to London named Cheng Huan, they generally ignore the remarkable opening frame set in a "Chinese treaty port," "the turn-stile of the East."[3]

In the film's opening frame, Cheng, played by Richard Barthelmess, dreams of emigrating in order to bring the Buddha's message of nonviolence to the Anglo-Saxons. When he attempts to stop a fight between two U.S. sailors on leave in the Chinese port city, however, they push him to the ground and continue to spar. The presence in 1919 of fighting U.S. sailors in a Chinese treaty port suggests a post–World War I preoccupation with the use of U.S. military power across the globe. Given that most of the film is set in London, the sailors signify a historical changing of the guard in which the United States inherited Britain's historical position of imperial power in Asia. But to return to Cheng, his encounter with the sailors only reaffirms his desire to emigrate, and the "Chinese" portion of the film ends with his departure. Conveyed through the streets in a rickshaw, with his luggage following behind, he moves toward the camera before leaving the frame as it fades to black. Next is a dark blue tinted long shot of the immigrant's ship landing in London. An early special effect, the shot was produced by slowly moving a paper cutout of a Chinese junk toward a paper cutout representing the London quays at the mouth of the River Thames.[4] In this opening sequence, Griffith depicts the movement from China to London by editing the two scenes together and thereby eliding the space in between. The Chinese middle passage visually and imaginatively falls through the cracks, as it were, between the scenes that form this part of the story: *Broken Blossoms* focuses instead on the scene of Chinese opium smoking. After arriving in London, Cheng settles in the small Chinese district of Limehouse and becomes a shopkeeper; his "youthful dreams come to wreck against the sordid realities of life." He now frequents a "scarlet house of sin" where he smokes opium into oblivion.

In his survey of early U.S. films featuring China and the Chinese, John Haddad notes that opium dens were highly popular settings in a variety of film shorts, starting in 1898 with Biograph's *A Chinese Opium Joint*.[5] By contrast, he cites only two films that reference, in however truncated a fashion, the process of Chinese immigration: one depicts the arrival in New York of a Chinese ambassador and the other represents Chinese immigrants boarding a ship returning from the United States to China. By generally occluding scenes of immigration in favor of scenes of supine Chinese immobilized by opium, silent filmmakers edited out multiple forms of Chinese rebellion, including not only historical mutinies like the one on board the *Gulnare* but also the more recent Boxer Rebellion (1900) against Western domination in China.[6] The image of the opium den, in other words, represents Chinese immigrants who are incapable of resisting imperialism and coercive labor systems. To be sure, Griffith and others represent the Chinese opium den as a threat to white people, particularly women; and yet in silent films featuring opium dens the focus on Chinese pathology and criminality serves to imaginatively disappear the specter of Chinese opposition to Western domination.

Broken Blossoms is the culmination of a longer history of opium den representations, including not only the film shorts already mentioned, but also the popular practice of photographing opium dens.[7] Visual travelogues of this sort complemented the bustling business of opium den tours in London, New York, and San Francisco.[8] And finally, audiences who could not actually visit the Chinese could nonetheless read about them in the vast and widely circulated popular literature on opium dens. Indeed, *Broken Blossoms* was based on a popular English literary source, a story from Thomas Burke's *Limehouse Nights*. The wide commercial circulation of magazine narratives about opium in London's East End and elsewhere meant that many English readers at the end of the nineteenth century possessed a vivid mental image, however exoticizing and exaggerated, of Chinese opium dens. Several such stories were written by famous authors such as Dickens, Conan Doyle, and Wilde, but many, many more were penned by anonymous or now obscure writers and published in a variety of popular periodicals. Most historians and literary critics who analyze such works, however, diminish their historical reach and geopolitical reach by reading them only as localized responses to Chinese immigrants in London.[9] And yet, the popular excitement mobilized by opium dens was radically out of proportion to the actual Chinese presence there. As Ng Kwee Choo concludes in *The Chinese in London,* "the size of the Chinese population in Great Britain remained negligible" throughout the nineteenth century.[10] Even the most alarmist observers never claimed that there were more than a handful of opium dens in London. The policing of Chinese opium smoking was almost nonexistent and anti-Chinese agitation—violent or otherwise—was sporadic and relatively small in scale when compared with California and Australia.[11] Although opium den texts thus certainly refer to Chinese immigration, local demographics are not, I would argue, their primary interest. Rather than reading mass-circulation opium den literature primarily as a response to the Chinese in England, then, I will instead consider it as a screen for projecting popular knowledge about Britain's Asian empire and the role of Chinese immigrant labor within it.

Opium den narratives emerged in the last third of the nineteenth century as one of the most powerful modes of representing imperial relations in Asia to English readers. These stories—whether forthrightly fictional, professing documentary accuracy, or somewhere in between— played a crucial role in the reproduction of imperial ideologies, for opium den narratives try to enlist ideological support for the British Empire in Asia by disavowing its origins in war and plunder. Opium den writing, in other words, simultaneously acknowledges and denies British attacks on China during the Opium Wars as well as the subsequent unequal political and economic relationships that British military victories enforced. In all of these ways, the setting of the opium den became one of the privileged means, in England and its settler colonies, for reflecting upon imperial political economy in Asia and the origins and consequences of Chinese labor migration throughout the world. In this chapter I analyze representations of opium dens in an emergent English mass media for what they tell us about the global significance of the British opium monopoly and Chinese immigration. Opium den narratives reveal that Chinese migrants were central to Anglophone cultures, impinging in definitive ways upon ideologies of imperial and colonial rule, particularly official and popular historical memories of military conflict and conquest. And the competing representations of Britain's profitable prosecution of two opium wars and its promotion of the opium trade also constitute influential models for understanding subsequent U.S. drug wars, where state and capitalist powers converge in distinct yet related ways, as we shall see in the chapters that follow.

The post–Opium War trade with China supported dense networks of commerce, transportation, communication, imperial administration, and diplomacy that cut across nations and regions. British economic and political stakes in opium extended beyond China, where the drug was marketed, and India, where it was produced, to include large portions of Southeast Asia and the Pacific. The opium trade helped to establish a complicated series of political-economic relationships among Britain and its settlements in Hong Kong and Malaysia; its current and former white settler colonies in Australia, New Zealand, British Columbia, and the United States; and its Caribbean plantations in Trinidad and British Guiana. Stories about opium dens in London represent these tangled global relationships in revised and radically condensed forms. Indeed, for many English readers, opium den discourses helped to make diverse, complexly interarticulated points of imperial interest imaginable as a single entity.

The desire to represent British Asia was partly inspired and enabled by the post–Opium War migration of Chinese workers throughout the world. After about 1850, more than 2 million Chinese traveled to labor recruitment centers in the British settlements of Hong Kong and Malaysia.[12] From there, about a million immigrated to British colonies in Australia, India, Canada, Colombia, New Zealand, and Guiana.[13] During the second half of the century, Britain fostered a symbiotic relationship between the market in opium and the market in Chinese labor. The colonial states in Hong Kong and Malaysia formed alliances with a comprador class of local Chinese capitalists who traded in both labor and the opium that workers consumed. According to Carl A. Trocki, the Chinese immigrant-worker consumers of opium "probably constituted the first mass market in Southeast Asia," and Britain directly benefited from it by taxing opium in its colonies.[14] Chinese immigrants thus contributed to the British Empire materially, through their labor and their consumption, but their very presence in British Asia and sometimes their direct opposition to the British also helped to shape the emergence of English mass culture.

Adapting Toni Morrison's claims about Africans and the African diaspora in U.S. literature and culture, I want to suggest that questions about Chinese emigration were vital to modern British culture. "Explicit or implicit," Morrison writes, "the Africanist presence informs in compelling and inescapable ways the texture of American literature. It is a dark and abiding presence, there for the literary imagination as both a visible and an invisible mediating force." Morrison therefore investigates "the ways in which a nonwhite Africanlike (or Africanist) presence or persona was constructed in the United States, and the imaginative uses this fabricated presence served." She discovers that in response to the Africans in their midst, many white U.S. writers used these fictions to define, by contrast, the meanings and limits of national belonging. Or, as Morrison puts it, "[t]hrough significant and underscored omissions, startling contradictions, heavily nuanced conflicts, through the way writers peopled their work with the signs and bodies of this presence—one can see that a real or fabricated Africanist presence was crucial to their sense of Americanness. And it shows." What this writing shows, according to Morrison, is "the operative mode of a new cultural hegemony"—"the process of organizing American coherence through a distancing Africanism." Morrison concludes that the "well-established study" of racism's "consequences on the victim," should be combined with "another, equally important one: the impact of racism on those who perpetuate it." What effect, she asks, does racial ideology have on "the mind, imagination, and behavior of masters"?[15]

Similarly, I propose to consider not only the profound impact of British imperialism on China and Chinese emigrants, but also the effect of an abiding Chinese presence on the formation of a British imperial imagination. Because of the Chinese presence throughout the British Empire, "the Chinese question" touched almost every aspect of life in Britain. The two Opium Wars were spectacularly destructive events with major ramifications for international political and commercial relations. Throughout the nineteenth century, the Chinese continued to remind English writers and readers of the British opium monopoly and the two wars of conquest that were fought to secure it. The opium wars and trade further helped to initiate the massive global migration of Chinese laborers in the second half of the nineteenth century. Like slavery in the United States and other parts of the world, the international Chinese labor market was a crucial fact of British life that directly or indirectly influenced legal discourse, art, religion, literature, and mass culture. Although I draw upon each of these domains, I concentrate on writing from an emergent British mass culture—including short stories, sketches, travelogues, expository essays, and all sorts of journalistic reportage—that pertains to China and Chinese emigrants. Although canonical works of opium den literature by writers such as Dickens, Conan Doyle, and Wilde are often considered in isolation from their original publication contexts, they were all originally written for popular, middle-class magazines in England and the United States. In conjunction with more specialized publications such as *The Friend of China,* an anti-opium paper founded by English and U.S. reformers, general-interest magazines published Chinese perspectives on the Opium Wars and the British opium monopoly that, however mediated and contained by dominant contexts, nonetheless often contradicted official accounts. The discursively varied context of the general-interest magazine is illuminating because it suggests connections between cultural work and the larger world of political economy represented there, connections that remain invisible when opium den fiction is read in isolation from the magazines in which it was originally published.

In what follows, then, I ask how the mass mobilizations of Chinese immigrant workers in the nineteenth century helped to shape the history of British imperialism. How, for example, did Chinese immigrants help to motivate and condition the dominant discourses that were developed to comprehend their presence in British Asia and the world? How did Chinese immigration produce or provoke hegemonic ideas about nation, race, and empire? Focusing on the opium den, I attempt to reconstruct the traces of Chinese immigrant agency in the expression of imperial contradictions, fears, and denials.

OPIUM WARS

Starting in the late eighteenth century, Britain built an empire in Asia out of opium revenue. The East India Company grew the drug in India, particularly Bengal, and then exported it throughout the world, but especially to the coast of China.[16] Anticipating contemporary contexts, in which the United States used the cocaine trade to fund counterinsurgency efforts in Central America, Britain used funds gained from taxing the immensely profitable opium trade to fund the establishment and extension of British military power throughout the region.[17] Even though China's Ch'ing government (1644–1911) officially banned the drug's importation, the lure of opium revenues proved too strong and so with state support the East India Company used bribery and other kinds of subterfuge to circumvent restrictions.[18] In 1839, however, High Commissioner Lin Tse-hsu attempted to suppress the trade by blockading the residence of foreign merchants and seizing and destroying about twenty thousand chests of opium. With the design of expanding the opium trade, the British responded by attacking the coast of China. The destruction of "English property" would thus become the pretext for what Dilip K. Basu has called "the first major modern colonialist/ imperialist war in Asia."[19]

During the first Opium War (1839–42), numerous cities and villages in southern China were attacked and partially destroyed. Chinese weapons—unreliable small-caliber muskets, spears, halberds, and bows and arrows—were poor matches for English artillery.[20] Britain took advantage of its superior firepower and relentlessly shelled the coast and seized whole cities.[21] Once in control, occupation forces flogged men and cut off their queues, raped women, and looted.[22] Even the dead were not safe, for English patrols opened Chinese graves in search of lucre.[23] Such conduct perhaps explains why Britain's victory inspired little patriotism at home, even in imperialist papers like the *London Times*. At the end of the war the paper noted with relief that its readers would no longer have to encounter stories about British soldiers "sweeping away with cannon or bayonet whole crowds" of Chinese.[24] To end hostilities, the Chinese were forced to sign the unequal Treaty of Nanking. Under its terms China agreed to open four trade ports, cede Hong Kong, and pay a war indemnity of $21 million, about half the total annual revenue of China. Even though the treaty never mentioned opium, however, the war effectively protected drug interests. Anxious to avoid further conflict with Western powers, the Chinese signed similar treaties with France and the United States in 1844. While Britain continued to dominate the opium trade, these agreements guaranteed that several Western nations could trade with a China that, according to Immanuel C. Y. Hsu, had been reduced to "semicolonial status."[25]

The second Opium War (1856–60) was largely waged by Britain to safeguard opium profits and force the Chinese to legalize it.[26] On average, Chinese casualties outnumbered British losses by forty to one, and it was official British policy to plunder villages "as punishment for enemy treachery."[27] The most spectacular looting, however, occurred at the emperor's Summer Palace near Peking. Along with their French allies, British forces methodically stripped the palace of its valuables before burning it to the ground.[28] For many English people, looting was no doubt one of the most notable features of the two wars; the word, in fact, first entered the popular English lexicon during the war years.[29]

The importance of looting as a military imperative in the Opium Wars was publicly acknowledged when, at the end of the second conflict, British officers presented Queen Victoria with a jade and gold scepter and three enameled bowls plundered from the Summer Palace. She was also given one of the Chinese emperor's lapdogs, a "Pekinese" that was renamed "Lootie."[30] Decades after the second war, memories of English plunder remained fresh. In an 1885 essay for *Belgravia,* for example, C. F. Gordon Cummings offhandedly referred to the Chinese vases and ornaments that "became so familiar to us after the looting of the Summer Palace."[31] In this way British acts of looting came to symbolize the history of the opium trade itself for many writers and readers. Meanwhile, in 1858 the East Indian Company was dissolved and after that the task of administering opium production and export fell to the Anglo-Indian government that, for the rest of the century, generally depended for one-seventh of its revenue on the trade.[32] These revenues aside, huge profits were also generated for British opium growers, merchants, and shippers, not to mention the U.S. shipping companies that also transported the drug. By 1870, opium accounted for almost half of China's total imports.[33] Although the trade's volume and value would decrease as the century came to a close, in part because of increased Chinese production, it would remain central to British economic and political interests in Asia until at least 1906, when Parliament finally outlawed it.[34]

In the 1850s, Karl Marx wrote a series of biting editorials for the *New York Daily Tribune* that analyzed the consequences of the trade in opium and the two wars waged in support of it. As Marx makes clear, the Opium Wars helped to turn China into an economic satellite of Britain. Over the course of the nineteenth century, China increasingly exchanged labor-intensive agricultural goods or raw materials for English industrial manufactures and of course opium.[35] China's earlier attempts to tightly control foreign trade could hence be read as unsuccessful efforts to avoid peripheral absorption by the British Empire.[36] Further, Marx frequently foregrounds the brutal forms of force required to integrate China into capitalist world markets.[37] At the time of the Indian mutiny of 1857, for example, Marx argued that "the Sepoy atrocities" were paralleled during the first Opium War, in which English soldiers violated women, murdered children, and burned entire villages.[38] As Marx implies, an obsession with the Indian mutineers' attack on British imperial authority partly served to displace memories of British atrocities in China.

Indeed, imperial violence in China was intimately related to imperial violence in India. In an article on the Indian revolt, Marx argues that "torture formed an organic institution" of England's financial policy in India.[39] This was certainly the case in Bengal, the center of opium production. As Marx also indicates, Indian farmers or "ryots" were often forced to grow opium; those who refused risked beatings, imprisonment, or death. Even the system of cash advances that he refers to was ultimately backed by force. Once accepted, advances initiated spirals of debt that bound ryots to opium production. This combination of economic and extraeconomic coercions was common throughout the nineteenth century, as even the Royal Commission on Opium's report for 1894–95 indicates.[40]

Marx thus indexes a variety of overlapping forms of British imperialism in both India and China when he writes that "the illicit opium trade... yearly feeds the British treasury at the expense of human life and morality."[41] One final implication of the Opium Wars, largely unforeseen by Marx, was British employment of millions of Chinese laborers. Because the wars opened Chinese ports to labor recruiters, they helped to initiate the massive migration of Chinese workers throughout the world. After the abolition of slavery in its colonies in 1833, Britain turned to China for a source of cheap labor. Although the Chinese government officially prohibited its subjects from traveling abroad, the forced opening of treaty ports at the end of the first war in 1842 enabled a number of British firms to establish emigration agencies along the coast to recruit workers for Mauritius, Cuba, and Australia. And finally, at the end of the second war, the Treaty at Peking officially legalized contract labor.[42] Britain directly subsidized recruitment efforts, beginning in 1859 when it appointed an immigration agent for the colony of Hong Kong in order to secure workers for the British West Indies. Seized from China at the end of the first Opium War, Hong Kong became a central embarkation port for workers headed to California, Canada, Hawaii, Australia, and New Zealand. The massive labor recruitment system located on the island colony of Singapore was, however, perhaps even more profitable than the Hong Kong labor market. Between 1829 and 1858, East India Company officials in Bengal largely ruled Singapore. In 1867, it became a British crown colony, and was part of a group of colonies in Malaysia collectively called the Straits Settlements.[43] Like Hong Kong, Malaysia became a major state-subsidized transshipping center for Chinese labor.[44] Although a small number of Chinese capitalists profited from the new "opium regime," the British dominated it,[45] helping to make China a major source of labor for the empire.[46]

Various Anglo governments took a direct interest in the Chinese labor market, for it supplied them with potential consumers of opium. In the United States, the drug was synonymous with revenue, leading Chinese immigrants to call it "the taxed gum." Similarly, import duties on opium were a major source of British revenue in Australia, the West Indies, and especially Hong Kong and Malaysia.[47] As much as 22 percent of all colonial revenue in Hong Kong came from opium duties, while the figure for British Malaysia was between 40 and 60 percent.[48] In those last two colonies, English opium traders sold the drug to local Chinese capitalists who paid duties to the colonial government and then in turn sold it to Chinese workers. Both opium profits and state revenues, in other words, depended on the market in Chinese labor, and vice versa. On the one hand, English proponents of Chinese immigration to Singapore argued that Chinese opium consumption was vital to the colony's economic survival; on the other hand, opponents of laws prohibiting opium claimed that they would impede the importation of Chinese laborers.[49] This symbiosis between the traffics in opium and labor was reinforced by the horizontal integration of the two forms of business. Two of the most prominent emigration agents in South Asia were also major British opium merchants.[50] Similarly, Chinese opium merchants in Hong Kong were also involved in transporting laborers.[51] Opium was sold at exorbitant prices in Chinese-run depots where emigrants were housed just before embarkation, and most English and other ships set aside special compartments for opium smoking.[52] Chinese opium merchants in Malaysia, moreover, also owned tin mines and plantations that employed large numbers of Chinese laborers, and the merchants supplemented their profits by selling the drug to their workers. Plantation owners in other British colonies followed a similar practice, while British firms shipped both opium and Chinese workers to California and Australia.[53] For a number of reasons, opium helped working bodies work longer and harder. In contexts in which little else was available, the drug killed the pain of difficult daily labor, served as a prophylactic against certain diseases, and reduced malarial and other fevers.[54] In addition, colonial employers found it profitable to sell opium as a means of partly recouping their labor costs and binding workers to them in addiction and debt. In this way, capitalists were able to capture and recycle their labor costs and therefore profit from otherwise uncompetitive ventures.[55] For all of these reasons, capitalists and state powers tended to treat opium and the Chinese worker as a single commodity unit with vast profit potential. The opium trade with China thus helped to construct the Asian empire not only through the formation of international commodity chains, as Marx indicates, but also by driving the Chinese labor market that connected multiple spheres of British interest.

In many ways, the opium-driven Chinese labor market resembled the slave system it supposedly replaced but in practice supplemented. When not misled into signing contracts with false promises of good conditions and high pay, Chinese were drugged, pressed into service to pay gambling debts, tortured until they signed contracts, or simply kidnapped. Indeed, tens of thousands of Chinese were kidnapped during the second half of the nineteenth century.[56] The state-controlled labor markets in Hong Kong and Singapore were notorious for their reliance on kidnapping.[57] Similarly, government reports on Singapore in 1876 and 1891 underlined the continuities between the labor market and slavery. And as I noted at the outset of this chapter, many Chinese immigrant ships were former slave vessels. On board, food and water were in short supply and of poor quality. The mortality rate on ships transporting Chinese workers was consequently high, and more than eleven thousand Chinese emigrants died between 1847 and 1866. British vessels were particularly deadly, holding the record for the highest number of deaths per voyage.[58] When they reached their destination, many emigrants were temporarily housed in guarded depots whose conditions rivaled the ships. Once on the job—in mines, as domestic servants, and on plantations—Chinese workers died and committed suicide much more frequently than did Europeans.[59]

The Chinese, however, often resisted the demands of British imperialism and global capitalism. During the second half of the century, Chinese emigrants at times violently opposed their virtual enslavement. British abuse was a constant source of tension in the treaty ports, where Chinese often rioted against British shipping firms. In 1852, Chinese at the port of Amoy rioted against the unscrupulous practices of British companies that were recruiting workers for Cuba and elsewhere.[60] Chinese riots and rebellions also occurred in British territories. On Trinidad plantations in 1866, for instance, the local elite called in police to put down a planned rebellion.[61] Similarly, numerous riots took place in the Straits Settlements during the last decades of the nineteenth century.[62]

We could say, then, that, partly driven by the opium trade, Chinese immigrant laborers actually built British Asia, and not only because they performed much of its labor. Ideologically, "the Chinese question" was one of the few issues connecting places as divergent as the Straits Settlements, Hong Kong, Australia, New Zealand, British Columbia, and even India. As the often-resistant targets of imperial administration and governance in diverse spheres of British influence, the Chinese presence helped to produce an abstract sense of the British government's imperial duty in Asia. A British official in Malaysia named W. A. Pickering argued in 1876 that Chinese labor remained "indispensable to the prosperity of the Straits Settlements" but "require[s] the most careful management and strict supervision." "With a large population of Chinese in the Malay States," he continued, "the peace and safety of our colonies demand that the British Government take an active and chief part in their rule and protection."[63] Here and elsewhere, the agency of a potentially intractable Chinese population generates the perceived need for the mechanisms of "management" and "supervision" that define imperial duties in Asia.

The two Opium Wars, as well as the intertwined opium traffic and immigration patterns that they ushered in, thus had contradictory effects for British imperial power. On the one hand, the opium trade helped give substance to an emerging Asian empire by articulating relationships among British colonial states and British and Chinese capitalists in diverse parts of Asia. In this way, opium traffic served to imaginatively and materially "connect the dots" between different places on the geopolitical map. On the other hand, the opium trade also provoked anti-imperial opposition and undermined the ideological rationalizations for empire. Memories of the British Empire's origins in arbitrary violence, in other words, remained as irritants that threatened to mar heroic representations of British imperialism. In the obvious absence of a liberal "free market" that fairly and impersonally distributed wealth, the opium trade continued to look like what it was—a virtual monopoly secured through conquest. Chinese immigration further provoked new conflicts, new points of resistance to imperial expansion and domination. As we shall see, a host of English writings about China and the

Chinese—but especially opium den narratives—emerged out of these conflicts.

FOREIGN DEVILS: THE CHINESE IN MASS CULTURE

The end of the second Opium War and the consolidation of Britain's opium regime in Asia roughly coincided with the emergence of mass literary culture in England. Before the late 1850s, English entertainment periodicals were divided between working-class publications such as the penny magazines and the more expensive and respectable monthly reviews like *Fraser's* and *Blackwood's*. After that, a variety of magazines hailed a new audience, somewhere in between these extremes, that found the monthlies too expensive (or uninteresting) and the sensational penny magazines too vulgar. The new "miscellanies" or "family magazines" constituted a novel form of mass culture that reached a relatively large, translocal audience that partly cut across class differences, a mix of lower-middle-class and upwardly mobile working-class readers.[64] Combining fiction, current events, historical sketches, and travel literature, miscellanies such as Charles Dickens's *All the Year Round* provided apt material for the "cognitive mapping" of geopolitics.[65] This was in part because such publications juxtaposed writings in diverse registers, from culture to geopolitics. The magazines further encouraged a mode of lateral reading, in which the reader moves from one item to another, and thus potentially from one geopolitical space to another.[66] In practice, this phenomenology of reading implicitly supported the imagination of lateral connections between England and Asia. Thus, while in this section and the next I analyze a variety of different kinds of publications, I focus on new mass magazines because their miscellaneous nature aptly depicts the conflicting accounts of Britain's opium regime.

In the decades that followed the last Opium War, English magazines were obsessed with China and the Chinese. Popular periodicals such as *All the Year Round,* with an average circulation of around seventy thousand, were filled with essays about Chinese culture and society.[67] Topics included Chinese folktales and "superstitions," marriage and mourning rituals, language, gender relations, government, commerce, agriculture, manufactures, and all types of labor.[68] Many publications also presented light, "informative" essays on China, often in the shape of travel narratives with titles such as "A Street Scene in Foochow," "Two Days in Canton," "Shanghai, from a Bedroom Window," or even "A Brush with

Chinese Pirates."[69] They also printed numerous fictionalized accounts of travel in China as well as travelogues and other reportage set in the British colony of Hong Kong.[70] English periodicals of the 1870s, 1880s, and 1890s closely followed the movements of the Chinese and others throughout British Asia. Under titles such as "The Chinese in Australia" or "The Seamy Side of Australia," English readers found accounts of immigration controversies in their white-settler colony.[71] They could also read fiction about Chinese in Australia, such as "Yan," a sensational tale about Chinese servants who attempt to rob their masters in Queensland, or "The Chee Child," about the tragic friendship between two little girls, white and half-Chinese, in Brisbane.[72] Other articles attempted to describe Chinese life in British Malaysia, as in I. L. Bishop's 1883 essay about Singapore, where the Chinese reportedly "monopolize many streets altogether, erect temples, club-houses, opium dens, and gaming-houses."[73] English magazines also depicted the Chinese on the other side of the Pacific, in British Columbia and California. Readers could track the progress of Chinese exclusion legislation in the Canadian parliament and weigh the going rate for Chinese servants in Victoria.[74] Travel narratives and other writings involving San Francisco's Chinatown were particularly popular. Magazine writers composed print tours of Chinatown, editorialized on Chinese-exclusion activities in California, and imagined the adventures of Chinese gold miners.[75] Almost all information regarding the movements and occupations of the Chinese was represented as interesting and relevant to a general or mass English audience.[76]

These publications, moreover, amply demonstrate that the British opium trade was at the heart of British imperial concerns throughout Asia. All aspects of the traffic were covered, from the planting and harvesting of opium poppies to the preparation of the drug for market.[77] One former smuggler, Captain Lindsay Anderson, even published two memoirs of his voyages, *A Cruise in an Opium Clipper* (1891) and *Among Typhoons and Pirate Craft* (1892).[78] Fictionalized versions of such fare were also available, as in Albert Dorrington's story about Chinese and Malay smugglers off the coast of North Queensland, Australia, "The Opium Dealers: Stories of a South Sea Buccaneer."[79] The morality and fiscal expediency of the British opium trade were debated during the 1880s in publications such as the *Nineteenth Century* and the *London Times*, with some writers condemning the traffic as immoral, while others claimed that it was a harmless yet necessary addition to British revenues.[80] Finally, English readers consumed a steady diet of stories concerning opium dens in China, Hong Kong, India, Malaysia, California, British Columbia, and British Guiana.[81]

In the second half of the nineteenth century, an emergent English mass culture became the site of conflict over British opium regimes in Asia. The English mass public sphere contained material that contradicted or compromised official British apologies for opium. One example is the reformist newspaper *The Friend of China*. While the newspaper itself was relatively small and represented a set of minority views, its influence over mainstream discourse is evident in a variety of the larger mass periodicals. *The Friend of China* was the official voice of the Society for the Suppression of the Opium Trade (SSOT), a reform group founded by wealthy Quakers in 1874. The Society shared the Christian outlook, tactics, and membership base of the English abolitionist and temperance movements that it succeeded. Its members included Protestant missionaries who were officially admitted to China under the terms of the treaty that ended the second Opium War. The Society held that opium smoking was deadly and immoral and hence so was the opium trade. The British government, it maintained, had forced opium on China through two unjust wars. The group was concerned that Chinese opium smoking, as well as Chinese resentment of the English for the opium trade, would block the work of Christian conversion. According to Bruce D. Johnson, "propaganda against opium was continuously and repetitively presented to the British public and to other English-speaking countries" by the SSOT. "By 1891, over 100 specifically anti-opium meetings were held annually around Britain, 1,200 attended the annual S.S.O.T. meeting, over 40,000 tracts were issued . . . and some 3,300 petitions with 192,000 signatures were obtained."[82]

For my purposes, the most notable feature of the Society's magazine was its reproduction of a wide range of popular and elite Chinese representations of the opium trade. It reprinted, for example, the pledge of Peking's "Prohibition of Opium Society" as well as a translation of a "stirring appeal" to end the opium trade by a Canton organization.[83] The magazine also published translations of anti-opium tracts and songs that were pasted on walls or handed out on the streets of Canton or Amoy.[84] Related Society publications such as the *China Review* and the *Regions Beyond* printed Cantonese anti-opium pamphlets and speeches, such as the 1883 public London lecture by Mr. Tong King-sing.[85] Indeed, the SSOT regularly sponsored lectures by visiting Chinese dignitaries and merchants. One of its first publications, *British Opium Policy and Its Results to India and China* (1876), by the Society's secretary, Storrs Turner, included lengthy extracts from Chinese anti-opium writings, including Commissioner Lin's letter to Queen Victoria and Minister Tsungli Yamen's letter to Parliament.[86] A series of twelve Chinese anti-opium engravings was also widely distributed in England in the early 1880s. The color engravings, which, according to the *Friend of China,* depict "the opium-smoker's career, from the ruddy youth inhaling his first pipe, to the living skeleton clothed in rags and the ghastly corpse," were originally published in China by the Chinese Anti-Opium Society of Canton. An English missionary sent them to London, where they were sold as a pamphlet in railway book stalls for sixpence. These same images were reproduced by the SSOT as illustrations for use in lectures about the English opium trade. Finally, they were reprinted, complete with translations of the Chinese explanatory notes, in the popular English periodical, the *Graphic.*[87] As this last example suggests, SSOT's public-sphere activities, particularly the *Friend of China,* proved popular enough that mainstream newspapers and general-interest mass magazines followed their lead. Even expensive, conservative monthly reviews such as *Fraser's*—hardly a likely forum for a polemical stand on the opium question—republished anti-opium writing by Chinese authors. Thus, as we shall see, a surprising number and range of English periodicals reproduced Chinese writings critical of the British opium trade.

To be sure, these mass-mediated Chinese texts do not represent the voice of the Chinese subaltern as such. While the anti-opium songs and posters republished in English publications were originally directed at popular Chinese audiences, anti-opium polemics were written by educated and relatively elite Chinese and directed at a literate English audience. Complicating matters more is the fact that while Chinese materials in English periodicals were generally critical of the opium trade, other Chinese actively participated in opium traffic as brokers and in other capacities. Finally, nineteenth-century Chinese subjects, subaltern or otherwise, did not "speak" in direct, unmediated ways; their "voices" were of course mediated by larger forces and contexts, in this case by the reformist mission of the SSOT. Chinese groups such as the Shan-Tung Charitable Society and the Anti-Opium Society of Canton were supposedly inspired by missionaries and partly modeled, as the *Friend of China* claimed, on the SSOT.[88] Nonetheless, the relative visibility of Chinese opinion in the English public sphere attests to the real historical relationships between reformers in England and nationalist or protonationalist reformers on the coast of China.

Located near the cosmopolitan opium and labor trading ports, the anti-opium reformers who published newspapers such as *Shen Pao* represented a small minority of the Chinese population in more or less direct contact with British opium regimes.[89] As the historian Gregory Blue argues, the British opium trade generated two antagonistic forces. On the one hand, the opium trade was "a multinational, collaborative institution that bound Indian peasants, British and Indian governments, a vast mass of Chinese consumers, and an array of Western, Parsee, Sephardic, and most of all Chinese merchants together in an immense revenue-generating system." On the other hand, this system gave rise to "a broad front of international resistance that included otherwise ideologically disparate groups around the shared view that legalization in the service of colonial power was politically, economically, physically, and especially morally unacceptable." By the end of the nineteenth century, this front represented an alliance between emergent nationalist movements in India and China and "religious anti-imperialist and temperance forces" in England and the United States.[90]

Because the circulation of Chinese anti-opium discourse in English periodicals spoke to this international anti-imperial alliance, they played a prominent role in debates over opium. The nature of Chinese opinion was central to pro-opium polemics, with supporters of the trade generally claiming that the Chinese people demanded the drug and that their government profited from its importation. English promoters of the trade further implied that their opponents had fabricated Chinese criticisms of opium.[91] Hence, however much we might qualify or hedge concerning the mediation of the Chinese texts reproduced in English periodicals, they nonetheless threatened the pro-opium forces, which therefore worked hard to discredit them.

Chinese writings and lectures on the opium traffic in the final three decades of the nineteenth century—however translated, edited, mediated, or even contained by English publications—critically unravel influential legitimating narratives of British imperialism in Asia. One often repeated fiction of British commerce with China was that it was part of a civilizing mission. Trade with Britain, it was argued, extended to China the benefits of English commodities and the so-called free market; it even promised to promote Christian conversions. Chinese writers and speakers, however, called attention to the cracks in such rationalizations. Christian missionaries in China and the Pacific often reported that the Chinese responded to their evangelical efforts by pointing out the contradiction between Christian missions and the profitable but poisonous opium trade.[92] In an impassioned letter to the *London Times* in 1875, signed "N. C., a Chinese, resident at present in London," the author mounted a thorough, compelling case for the abolition of the opium traffic. Along the way N. C. countered the common claim that the Anglo-Indian government required the revenue by daring the English government to publicly proclaim its material interest in the opium monopoly and "boldly declare this to the world that all people may know how a Christian nation is treating China."[93] Similarly, the *Leisure Hour* reproduced in 1881 a critical analysis of the British opium trade by an unnamed "Chinese Minister in London," who in effect hijacks English moral pretensions when he describes the British Empire as a purely financial concern: "Opium is a subject in the discussion of which England and China can never meet on common ground. China views the whole question from a moral standpoint; England from a fiscal. England would sustain a source of revenue in India, while China contends for the lives and prosperity of her people. . . . My sovereign has never desired his empire to thrive upon the lives or infirmities of his subjects."[94] Like Marx, who, in his analysis of British opium monopoly, underlined what he called "the flagrant self-contradiction of the Christianity-canting and civilization-mongering British Government," N. C., the Chinese Minister, and other Chinese contradicted the British Empire's legitimating stories with concrete discussions of British military conquest and economic exploitation.[95]

Chinese anti-opium writers further confronted the willful blind spots in certain English readings of postwar Chinese grievances. English travelers to China often registered local "resentment," noting that the Chinese seemed to hate all foreign "barbarians." "Eyewitness" testimonials, reportage, and fiction about the Chinese in British Asia all tended to abstract and naturalize Chinese hostility toward "foreigners." English writers seemed resigned to the fact of Chinese hostility but a bit bewildered about its possible origins, a question they vaguely attributed to some ancient Chinese character quirk or racial instinct. These witnesses refigured Chinese opposition to British imperialism as a static emblem of Chinese difference, separated from the histories of domination that shaped it. English superiority was so deeply assumed from such a perspective that anything short of manifest Chinese gratitude struck many British observers as irrational or at the very least "inscrutable."[96]

Such obtuseness was willfully self-serving, for it overlooked obvious Chinese opposition to British conquest. The narrative of immigrant worker Lew Chew, a Canton native who traveled to New York via the British colony of Hong Kong, demonstrates the persistence of bitter war memories in late-nineteenth-century China. As he explained in 1903 to a U.S. newspaper reporter, Chew grew up despising the English, whom he called "the red haired, green eyed foreign devils." Chew learned from his grandfather that the English "loved to beat people and to rob and murder. . . . [They] had made wicked war on the Emperor, and by means of their enchantments and spells had defeated his armies and forced him to admit their opium, so that the Chinese might smoke and become weakened and the foreign devils might rob them of their land." And in response to widespread criticisms of Chinese for smoking opium, Chew countered that the effects of alcohol were worse, and that Englishmen "could be seen reeling drunk" through the streets of the British colony at Hong Kong.[97]

Chinese writings published in England similarly contextualized contemporary attitudes toward the British by tracing them back to the war years. A good example is the 1877 article from *Fraser's Magazine* titled "The Foreign Relations of China," written in English by "a Chinese gentleman who has resided two years in London." The essay begins with a series of questions the author has faced in those two years, questions such as "How was it that your nation shuts itself up for ages and centuries?"; "Why don't your people like foreigners to come to China?"; and "Are not your people hostile to foreigners?" These queries are but slightly indirect versions of the implicit question W. E. B. Du Bois recalls at the start of *The Souls of Black Folk*: "How does it feel to be a problem?"[98] In response, the anonymous Chinese writer recounts the military history of the British opium traffic: "For the sake of opium a calamitous war was carried on, which was ended only by a payment of 21 millions of dollars by China. By the accursed drug many thousands of families and millions of people have been ruined, population has been thinned, and crimes have increased in China.... [T]he people of China turn their wrath naturally to the producer, the importer, and the seller of the poisonous drug."[99] The "Chinese gentleman" thus answers self-servingly dense questions about Chinese anger by linking contemporary attitudes to the recent history of the British opium monopoly and the military conquests that made it possible.

Similarly, an 1879 editorial from the Shanghai newspaper *Shen Pao*, reprinted in England, blamed Britain for the postwar spread of opium dens in Chinese ports.[100] In "What the Chinese Really Think of Europeans," an 1871 article for *Fraser's Magazine* reportedly written by "an educated native" of China, the anonymous author complains that the Opium Wars had been disastrous for China because English woolens and cotton cloth drove local textiles out of the market, and "foreign merchants... disseminate[d] poison over the empire in the shape of opium."[101] In his letter to the *London Times*, "N. C." rhetorically prosecutes Great Britain for international war crimes, arguing that the empire is to blame for "the evils and miseries which opium has caused in China.... [N]one who has read a fair account of the opium war in 1841, or is tolerably acquainted with the history... of the opium traffic in China will acquit the English nation of the serious charges of encouraging and fostering the opium traffic, and of compelling, by moral force and coercion, the Chinese Government to admit the drug into China.... England is guilty of national complicity in this pernicious trade." Only when the English people end the opium trade, he argued, would they remove the "stain" from "their national character."[102]

Chinese authors were not alone, for several contemporary English authors, particularly those associated with the SSOT, made similar claims, calling the Opium Wars a "hideous series of massacres" and the opium trade "a great national crime."[103] Together, these anti-opium writings fill in some of the historical blanks produced by casual English claims that the Chinese harbored a seemingly unmotivated hatred of foreigners. This combination of English and Chinese anti-opium writings helped to disseminate Chinese war narratives throughout the late-nineteenth-century English public sphere such that all kinds of printed references to China and opium either explicitly refer or implicitly responded to the two Opium Wars.[104] And as we shall see, the most influential response to the Opium Wars and the mass-mediated conflicts they produced was "the opium den," an imaginary setting that simultaneously denied and recalled memories of war.

THIS IS NOT AN OPIUM DEN

Although they almost never mention the Opium Wars, let alone the larger set of geopolitical relations they helped to engender, opium den narratives nonetheless condensed the recent history of British imperialism in Asia. The literature about London opium dens reproduced in miniature different maps of British Asia that made it imaginatively manageable for English readers. This kind of mapping responds to the particular epistemological challenges posed by the nineteenth-century history of Britain's Asian empire. "Imperialism," according to Fredric Jameson,

> means that a significant structural segment of the economic system as a whole is now located elsewhere, beyond the metropolis, outside of the daily life and existential experience of the home country, in colonies over the water whose own life experience and life world—very different from that of the imperial power—remain unknown and unimaginable for the subjects of the imperial power, whatever social class they may belong to. Such spatial disjunction has as its immediate consequence the inability to grasp the way the system functions as a whole.[105]

As a means for representing British imperialism in Asia, the opium den renders in discrete spatial terms a set of global dynamics that complicate or resist a spatial reduction. Britain's Asian empire was not simply a collection of territories, but also a geographically dispersed, historically sedimented, temporally disjunctive set of relationships. The British force fields that cut across India, Malaysia, and China presumed diverse and changing political regimes (including colonial governments, international treaties, informal alliances, and military power), commercial exchanges (involving staggered or seasonal processes of production and exchange), and fluctuating patterns of mass migration.

Opium den narratives respond to the representational challenges posed by the sum of these forces in a number of ways. Given the difficulties of spatially locating Britain's Asian empire, the London opium den paradoxically becomes a sort of no-place, or a place in process, constantly composed and recomposed by the arrival and departure of Asian migrants; for, as one opium den visitor noted, "These Indians and Chinese are largely a floating population; sailors who come and go: spending their time between Hong-Kong and London—or some other Chinese or Indian port."[106] This "floating population" represents the totality of traffic and trade that helps to constitute British Asia. A missionary among the "Asiatic seamen" of the East End of London claimed that "[t]he opium smoking rooms are the best *Shipping Gazette* I know of; a visit to those places will put me in possession of the news of every arrival from the East."[107] A lithograph and accompanying text in *Illustrated London News* called "The Opium-Smokers" graphically depicts a London opium den as a depot where Chinese sailors wait to ship out. The illustration centers on two reclining Chinese men smoking opium, their faces illuminated by the lamps they use to light their pipes. In the upper-right-hand corner, on the back wall of the den, appears an illustration within the illustration: the opium smoke forms a sort of sea cloud over the image of a ship on a poster that announces in bold letters "WILL SAIL LONDON CEYLON PENANG."[108] In other cases the opium den is itself compared to a ship, as when James Platt writes that it is "similar to the berth of a ship's cabin," or when Conan Doyle's Dr. Watson likens it to "the forecastle of an emigrant ship."[109] Here and elsewhere, the opium den serves as a crossroads or transshipping center that connects England and empire. Such representations performed some of the difficult work of making British Asia comprehensible for English audiences. The cost of such comprehension, however, is the partial evacuation of political and historical content, for the figure of the den as an international depot serves as a suggestive yet empty placeholder for the dense tangle of relations that constitute the British Empire in Asia. Missing is any sense of Britain's controlling interests in Asian trade or the nature of the service that Chinese sailors render the empire. These opium dens occlude, in other words, the unequal relationships that structure British imperialism in Asia.

Prefiguring the ways in which *Broken Blossoms* occludes the Chinese middle passage by transforming the ship into the opium den, magazine writers used the opium den as a figure for the British Empire that imaginatively obliterated historical memories of Chinese resistance. Some writers attempted to fill in this blank space by peopling their opium dens with representatives of various British domains. By selecting and ordering the different "native" representatives of British imperial spheres such as India, Malaysia, and of course China, these authors narrate, in distorted fashion, the economic and political links that define British Asia. In one early, influential English opium narrative, "Lazarus, Lotus-Eating," for instance, an anonymous author claims that "old Yahee's" establishment in Bluegate Fields was patronized by people "from every quarter of the globe," including Chinese, Indians, Malays, "mulattos and Manilla-men."[110] The most common opium den scene, however, includes Chinese and Indians. Depictions of opium dens peopled by Chinese and Indian sailors, here often called "Lascars," include Thomas Archer's *The Pauper, the Thief and the Convict* (1865), Charles Dickens's *The Mystery of Edwin Drood* (1870), Gustave Dore and Blanchard Jerrold's *London: A Pilgrimage* (1872), Rev. George Piercy's "Opium Smoking in London" (1883), J. Randal's "A Chinese Opium Den in East London" (1884), and Charles W. Wood's "In the Night-Watches" (1898).[111] This pairing of Indians and Chinese references and condenses two vital segments of British Asia, the source and market for opium.

A number of texts add Malays to the opium den, implicitly recognizing that British settlements in Malaysia occupied an important geopolitical position midway between India and China. As a result of British expansion into the Malay Peninsula during the second half of the nineteenth century, images of native Malays proliferated in England, where they were represented as an exotic, childlike people prone to irrational fits of violence, often involving a "Malay kriss" or knife, and outbursts called "running amuck."[112] The Malays in opium den narratives also symbolically played the role of Malaysia within Britain's Asian empire. Centrally located in British South Asia, the Straits Settlements were crucial ports that organized relays of capital, commodities, and labor. As if signifying Malaysia's mediating role, opium den Malays almost always appear between a Chinaman and a Lascar, as when a correspondent for the *Morning Advertiser* describes the thirty-odd inhabitants of an East London den as "mostly Chinese, Malays, and Lascars," or when a Christian missionary among the "Asiatic seamen" of the East End claims that "Chinese, Malays, and East Indians alike" frequent the opium dens.[113] In this way opium narratives trace the British imperial triangle that bound together India, Malaysia, and China. Other narratives focus more narrowly on particular segments of the British Asian system, as in stories such as Pearl Fisher's "Opium Smoking in London" (1887) and the anonymous "A Night in an Opium Den" (1891), which describe Chinese and Malay opium smokers; or the Sherlock Holmes story "The Man with the Twisted Lip" (1891), whose opium den, run by a Lascar and a Malay, seems to map traffic between Bengal and Singapore; or finally, the opium den in *The Picture of Dorian Gray* (1891)— peopled by a "half-caste" Indian bartender, a group of menacing Malays, and a repatriated white Englishman returned from Australia.[114] These various groupings represent different strategies for imagining some of the international relationships that composed British Asia.

Opium den narratives thus responded to the challenges of representing forms of British imperialism other than colonization. While the British Asian empire included different kinds of colonies, most notably India and Australia, it ultimately incorporated them into larger imperial systems, where domination took the form not only of direct territorial rule and occupation but also of unequal political or economic relationships. Britain maintained settlements in both Hong Kong and Malaysia, but in neither case were they primarily advance outposts for large-scale English emigration or development; rather, Britain was more interested in these spots as relay points for opium, immigrant labor, and other commodities. Moreover, while colonies and former colonies such as Australia, New Zealand, British Columbia, and the United States were relatively autonomous, they remained economically subordinated to Great Britain. British dominion in Asia was thus guaranteed not only by territorial annexation and control, but also through the orchestration of relationships between different segments of the empire.

In opium den narratives, the various groupings correspond to these sorts of relationships. The close connections between India, Malaysia, and China are represented by the intimacy between Lascars, Malays, and Chinamen as they inhabit the same space and smoke from the same pipe. Motley collections of opium smokers often even share the same beds in opium den stories.[115] The bed where different men of color enjoy their drug is a basic piece of furniture in almost every English opium den story in the period. Although in the next chapter I argue that they support different sexual and other fantasies about cross-racial contact, for now I would emphasize the manner in which representations of "bedfellows" figure the points of contact between distinct imperial sites that commingle and overlap like so many bodies on a mattress.[116]

The truly remarkable accomplishment of this literature, however, is that it deploys the opium den as a figure for British Asia while generally avoiding any direct reference to British interests in the opium trade.[117] This elision is particularly striking in the context of such widespread discussion of the Anglo-Indian opium monopoly. The literature doesn't just ignore British responsibility for the opium trade but actively disavows it. Opium den narratives in effect belittle Chinese criticism of British policy by describing all Chinese speech as meaningless noise, or humorous, garbled attempts to speak English. Chinese discourse is frequently called "chatter" or "jabber," and when transcribed it appears as childlike and comical: "I seboke now forty-two ye-ar... Began at seven tee-een. Was ve-ry ba-ad then... Doctor said I must seboke. So I try seboke..."[118] To many English ears Chinese "pidgin English" sounded silly. James Platt compared it to "monkey language," while the anonymous author of "Reminiscences of a Visit to India and China" wrote that "Chinamen are certainly very funny.... Much of the 'pidgin' English, as their jargon is termed, was quite incomprehensible to me."[119] In contrast to the Chinese anti-opium texts that reiterated Britain's history of opium imperialism, English opium den stories regularly include Chinese characters who, in "broken" English, promote the pleasures of opium: "Have some opium. Opium very good; no bad; no. People tell stories. Smoke opium, live hundred years. Beautiful dreams, happy world."[120] Far from criticizing the opium trade, the Chinese in these writings implicitly absolve Britain by assuming responsibility for the drug's consumption themselves.

The role of white bodies in opium den scenes could also serve to deflect or redirect critiques of British imperialism in Asia. A dozen narratives from the last three decades of the century represent white observers who stand in marked opposition to the Asian inhabitants. Here only Chinese and other South Asians smoke opium, while a visiting author and sometimes a guide merely watch. They may visit, even ask questions, but these writers emphatically draw the line at taking a pipe.[121] Many authors further distance themselves from the scene by repeatedly complaining of the den's disgusting smells. In this way, white expressions of racial disgust deny English intimacy with imperial interests in Asia by constructing the Chinese as absolutely foreign to English sensibilities. By depicting encounters with the Chinese as viscerally disturbing, profoundly exotic experiences, English observers symbolically recoil from direct participation in the imperial system the opium den represents. The distance that some English writers insisted upon between themselves and the Asian subjects of their narratives thus partially displaced the many imperial mediations between the two.[122] This English fascination with the absolute difference between whites and nonwhites diverted attention away from the unequal economic and political relations that hierarchically bound them together.

In the remaining twenty-odd narratives in my sample, racial distinctions break down as English people take to the pipe.[123] Unlike the writers who maintain a safe distance during their visits, the authors of these stories depict white opium den patrons as having become danger-ously intimate with the Chinese and other Asians. Over time, such in-timacy leaves a racial stain that both physically and morally colors the white opium den patron in the eyes of other English observers. Albert Woolf, for instance, calls them "English blackguards" in his eyewitness account "In an Opium Den" (1868).[124] Similarly, in "The Man with the Twisted Lip," Dr. Watson travels to a den called "The Gold Bar" to res-cue Mr. Isa Whitney (whitey?) who, with his "yellow, pasty face" and "drooping lids," resembles the Asian customers that surround him. Or, as Whitney tells Watson, "I'm all off colour."[125] Like its "eyewitness" ana-logues, "The Man with the Twisted Lip" in fact twists the British opium monopoly in Asia into an Asian-dominated trade that threatens to "en-slave" English bodies. It is as though the Chinese had used opium as a means for invading England and snatching away its people—and not the other way around.

The English women who appear in these articles or stories seem es-pecially prone to Asian capture. In most cases, the Chinese opium den proprietor has an English (or sometimes Irish) wife, usually a haggard and disheveled woman who has sunk almost as low as possible.[126] The most despicable den inhabitants, however, are the prostitutes, some-times seduced into opium slavery by predatory Chinamen. As Pearl Fisher lamented, visitors to the dens are sure to "discover some women (English girls, alas!) smoking opium, and ministering to the worst vices of the Chinamen.... They are girls, English girls, fallen—and sadly fallen—and they too smoke opium."[127] White women are here con-structed as especially vulnerable to the pleasures of opium, while their addiction and sexual relations with Chinese men are represented as an unprecedented tragedy. Thomas Archer describes the effects on white women of their intimacy with men of color in the following opium den scene: "The two wretched women who are cooking some rice at a scanty fire are English, but so degraded, even below the degradation of such a neighborhood, that they answer only with ghastly grins and a cringing paucity of words which seem to be borrowed from their [Chinese] com-panions, and to indicate the relinquishment of their last claim to the recognition of their old [white] associates."[128] According to these repre-sentations, cohabitation with opium-smoking Asian men caused cer-tain women to shed their whiteness and assume a degraded new "Ori-ental" visage. By making whites—especially women—the people who ultimately pay for the opium trade, this set of narratives imaginatively

inverts the ruthlessly hierarchical relations that defined British dominion in Asia. Whereas historically Britain had used military force to promote opium traffic into China, these stories depict the Chinese as the
source of a contagious vice that threatens English or "Anglo-Saxon"
racial integrity.[129] By retroactively seeming to justify extreme punitive
measures like the Opium Wars and the unequal trade relations they
enforced, the imaginary Chinese threat to white women helped to partly
eclipse criticism of British imperialism.

Of all the English opium den narratives, *The Mystery of Edwin Drood*
(1870), Charles Dickens's last, unfinished novel, remains the most influential atlas of British South Asia. After 1870, both fictional and non-
fictional opium den writings elaborated generic conventions established
by *Edwin Drood*.[130] About a year before the first installment of the novel
was serialized in 1870, Dickens visited an East End opium den with his
U.S. editor, James Fields.[131] As the sun rises in the first chapter of *Edwin
Drood*, one of the novel's protagonists, John Jasper, slowly awakes from
a narcotic sleep and finds himself in a mean and ragged opium den.
Jasper, the villain of the piece, harbors seemingly murderous intentions
toward his nephew, and leads a double life divided between a country
cathedral, where he serves as choirmaster, and an East London opium
den. But we know none of this in the beginning, for the story starts in
a fuzzy, befuddling way. In the first paragraph, we enter Jasper's head, as
it were, and read his opium-addled thoughts. As he gropes his way to
consciousness, Jasper hallucinates in the distance the tower of his cathedral back home: "How can the ancient English Cathedral town be here!
The well-known massive gray square tower of its old Cathedral?" Pointedly disrupting this hallucination is a second one that momentarily up-
stages the cathedral: "There is no spike of rusty iron in the air, between
the eye and [the tower], from any point of the real prospect. What is the
spike that intervenes, and who has set it up?" The sight of this perplex-
ing spike initiates a caravan of "oriental" spectacles.

> Maybe it is set up by the Sultan's orders for the impaling of a horde of
> Turkish robbers, one by one. It is so, for cymbals clash, and the Sultan
> goes by to his palace in long procession. Ten thousand scimitars flash in
> the sunlight, and thrice ten thousand dancing-girls strew flowers. Then,
> follow white elephants caparisoned in countless gorgeous colours, and
> infinite in number and attendants.

When the vision of the cathedral tower persists, "and still no writhing figure is on the rusty spike," a new and definitive explanation strikes him: "Stay! Is the spike so low a thing as the rusty spike on the top of a post of an old bedstead that has tumbled all awry?"

The first sentence of the next paragraph pulls us out of Jasper's thoughts as an omniscient, third-person narrative voice takes over. "Shaking from head to foot, the man whose scattered consciousness has thus fantastically pieced itself together, at length rises," the narrator announces, from an "unseemly bed" that he shares with "a Chinaman, a Lascar, and a haggard woman." As he rises from the bed, Jasper notices that the woman, who we later learn is the den's proprietor, "Princess Puffer," "has opium-smoked herself into a strange likeness of the Chinaman." Jasper listens to the woman's "mutterings" but declares them "Unintelligible!" Although her speech is garbled, Princess Puffer's "body language" exerts a strange power over Jasper: "As he watches the spasmodic shoots and darts that break out of her face and limbs, like fitful lightning out of a dark sky, some contagion in them seizes upon him." This odd convulsion forces Jasper to withdraw to a nearby chair "until he has got the better of this unclean spirit of imitation." With new composure he returns to the bed, "pounces on the Chinaman," and "seiz[es] him with both hands by the throat." When the Chinaman "resists, gasps and protests," his attacker once again says "Unintelligible!" Jasper next turns from the Chinese sailor with his "incoherent jargon" to the Lascar, whom he drags onto the floor. The Lascar "draws a phantom knife" before finally sinking back into opium oblivion. The "chattering and clattering" continues, but "with some reassured nodding of his head and a gloomy smile" Jasper simply repeats his mantra, "unintelligible!" Jasper finally makes his exit, and in the chapter's last paragraph he has returned to Cloisterdom and resumed his duties as choirmaster.

The presence of the Chinaman and the Lascar indicates that the opium den in *Edwin Drood* is located somewhere on the ideological map of British Asia, where the drug is both produced and marketed. And yet Dickens distances England from the opium trade. While the novel's first paragraph locates the English reader in the mind of an opium addict, in the second paragraph an omniscient narrator who observes the action from a distance takes control of the story. Like the visitors I described earlier who remain aloof from the opium den scene, this shift in narrative perspective symbolically detaches the English from the opium trade. Britain's role in the trade thus remains "unintelligible." The Chinaman's unintelligibility takes on further meaning given Chinese critiques of British imperialism. Although he "resists" and "protests" against Jasper's attack, the Chinamen is ultimately choked quiet. In this way, Dickens tacitly references Chinese opposition to the opium trade, but ultimately reduces it to muffled "gasps" and "incoherent jargon."

The translation of Chinese opposition into "chatter and clatter" enables Dickens to disavow British responsibility for the opium trade. In an ironic twist of imperial relations, England and China switch places, such that the Chinese become the source of opium addiction and white people its victims. Princess Puffer, for example, "has opium-smoked herself into a strange likeness of the Chinaman," even though the trajectory of the drug trade from British India to China might suggest a very different scenario, in which the Chinaman smokes himself into a likeness of the princess. By naturalizing the association between opium and the Chinese, Dickens squeezes out of the picture any direct representation of British opium interests. Here and in numerous other narratives, the fear that a "degrading Chinese habit" will penetrate England and racially debase its white inhabitants effectively inverts critical accounts of British responsibility for the opium trade.[132]

That these imperial reversals and denials were deemed necessary, however, indicates that Dickens and his English readers were consumed by the violent history of imperial conquest in Asia. In particular, the popularity of Dickens's opium den narrative partly rests on his dramatic memorialization of related imperial conflicts during the middle decades of the nineteenth century, most notably the Indian revolts and the two Opium Wars, but also the sporadic Chinese emigrant mutinies, riots, and rebellions described earlier. The novel in fact begins with the imagined spectacle of "Oriental" aggression, including a spike for impaling prisoners and an army of "ten thousand scimitars." The threat of violence that these visions imply seems to motivate Jasper's preemptive attack upon the Chinaman and the Lascar, and he thus reenacts numerous imperial battles. This scene, moreover, repeats official justifications for British wars in Asia, but with a crucial, undercutting difference. In each case, government officials disavowed Britain's responsibility for initiating conflict by claiming that imperial armies merely reacted to prior Indian or Chinese outrages. Similarly, the threat of violence that initiates *Edwin Drood* motivates Jasper's attack on the Chinaman and the Lascar. And yet, in Dickens's version, the "Oriental" threat that precipitates Jasper's outburst is literally a bad dream. Dickens underscores the illusory nature of the Asian threat during Jasper's struggle with the unarmed Lascar, who attempts to defend himself with a "phantom knife." In this way, Dickens inadvertently reveals the ideological distortions that supported British expansion in Asia. Like Jasper, who hallucinates a threat of violence that he then himself enacts, Britain constructed its own imperial aggression as a defensive response to fabricated or exaggerated Indian and Chinese outrages.

The Mystery of Edwin Drood thus illuminates the forms of disavowal that accompanied British imperialism in China. I use the term *disavowal* in the psychoanalytic sense of a defense mechanism in which the subject denies the reality of a traumatic perception. This form of psychic defense is not a rejection of reality pure and simple, but rather a contradictory response in which the subject holds two incompatible beliefs at the same time. Such a subject is split, simultaneously recognizing and denying a perception. In a manner that Freud compares to psychosis, in states of disavowal both denial and recognition "exist side by side... without influencing each other."[133] The same could be said regarding the cultural context that produced opium den narratives. Given the extensive publicity around the Opium Wars and the subsequent trade, it was virtually impossible to avoid recognizing the reality of British conquest in Asia. Opium den literature exists side by side with this knowledge, but it denies the history of conquest by splitting from it. The depiction of Jasper exemplifies this process, for while the Englishman is clearly the aggressor, he acts as though the Chinaman and the Lascar are the threatening ones. Similarly, even though in the words of one historian, "public opinion in England, America, and other countries held the British Government largely responsible for such conditions in China and almost universally condemned the opium traffic," opium den literature condemns the Chinese.[134] Recalling Freud's claim that disavowal is like psychosis, we might conclude that English opium mass culture is truly "hallucinatory," because it simultaneously recognizes and denies British responsibility. And finally, by focusing on the threat the Chinese pose to respectable white people, the mass culture of opium dens inadvertently memorializes the forms of Chinese resistance that it otherwise displaces.

CHAPTER 2

Strange Bedfellows

Opium and the Political Economy of Sexuality

Psychoactive drugs, it has been suggested, are the glue of empires—
particularly if one extends the list of psychoactive drugs beyond
opiates, alcohol, tobacco, tea, coffee, and chocolate to include sugar
and some spices. As commodities, psychoactive drugs are readily used
up, they create their own demand, people will pay far more than their
production costs for them, and they are relatively transportable or at
least their supply can often be controlled. On the other hand . . .
psychoactive drugs can also play their part as empires come unstuck.
—*Robin Room, "Drink, Popular Protest, and*
Government Regulation in Colonial Empires"

Reading representations of opium dens in the context of global political
economy suggests that Western debates over the nature of Chinese labor
were partly anchored in ideas about Chinese sexuality. In late-nineteenth-
century English mass culture, the opium den condensed diverse imperial labor contexts as well as the competing sexual fantasies and ideologies
that the global Chinese presence provoked. Oscar Wilde's influential
queer parable, *The Picture of Dorian Gray*, which was originally serialized in the U.S. magazine *Lippincott's*, provides an apt illustration of the
complicated intersections between sexuality and political economy that
are exposed in many opium den scenes. In one episode the titular hero
anxiously unlocks an ornate cabinet that holds his secret stash of opium.

Between two of the windows stood a large Florentine cabinet, made out of ebony, and inlaid with ivory and blue lapis. He watched it as though it were a thing that could fascinate and make afraid, as though it held something that he longed for and yet almost loathed. His breath quickened. A mad craving came over him. . . . At last he got up from the sofa on which he had been lying, went over to it, and, having unlocked it, touched some hidden spring. A triangular drawer passed slowly out. His fingers moved instinctively towards it, dipped in, and closed on something. It was a small Chinese box of black and gold-dust lacquer, elaborately wrought, the sides patterned with curved waves, and the silken cords hung with round crystals and tassalled in plaited metal threads. He opened it. Inside was a green paste, waxy in lustre, the odour curiously heavy and persistent.[1]

The cabinet—or closet, if you will—of Dorian Gray is already well stocked with the drug, but he nonetheless locks it up again and departs for the opium dens on the quays of East London where docking ships can be seen on the horizon.[2] The craving for opium impels a movement from the fastness of Dorian's home to the edge of the city—and, by extension, the island nation—where England opens out onto the global economy. Indeed, the Chinese opium box decorated with "curved waves" prefigures Dorian's journey to the dockside drug dens, and by extension the passage of opium itself across the sea from Asia to England. As I suggested in chapter 1, the opium den is metonymically related to the immigrant's ship, but here I would also emphasize that Dorian is drawn there because the den represents the forms of queer intimacy associated with male Chinese laborers.

Building upon historian Nayan Shah's rich conceptualization of queer social spaces in his history of Chinese in San Francisco, in this chapter I use the term *queer intimacy* to describe social relations among immigrant Chinese men outside reproductive marriage and in conflict with middle-class Anglo norms. Embracing labor and leisure contexts, queer intimacies cut across bourgeois divisions of private/public and work/leisure. Institutions where numbers of (mostly) Chinese men smoked opium together existed throughout the British Empire wherever Chinese migrant workers clustered. And, as I noted in chapter 1, the trade in opium and the market in Chinese labor were mutually constitutive, each feeding the other. Historically, this nexus of opium and labor is figured in scenes of opium dens where different bodies mix and mingle in great intimacy, seemingly oblivious to the racial, sexual, and class boundaries of bourgeois social space. For these reasons, populations of Chinese men were represented as a perverse menace to the family and the white race in England and other parts of the Anglo world such as Australia and the United States.

This complex concatenation of race, class, and sex hierarchies responded to post–Opium War transformations in the world system that created and sustained a global market in male Chinese labor. The global demand for migrant labor focused on men to the relative exclusion of women, often with the direct support of colonial governments, and this structural exclusion contributed to the construction of Chinese perversity. In a variety of contexts—plantations, mines, and on board ship—Chinese men lived and worked under communal conditions of physical proximity that departed from bourgeois norms of work and home. The organization of labor into all-male groups that ate and slept together deviated from middle-class ideologies of individual self-sufficiency and a gendered division of labor between public and private life.

Focusing on the emergent mass literary culture introduced in chapter 1, here I foreground the imbrication of sexuality with issues of imperial political economy, arguing that discourses positing differences between Chinese and white labor and "standards of living" pivoted around questions of sexuality. Because they were presumed to be "bachelors," Chinese men were said to be able to survive on less than could married white workers. The "white man's standard of living," in other words, was a heteronormative one defined in opposition to Chinese deviance. And, more broadly, the example of Chinese deviance became one of the defining counterpoints for the formation of a reconfigured transnational whiteness. In response to the consequences of the global market in Chinese labor, an emergent English mass culture reworked "Britishness," placing Britain at the heart of an expansive white or Anglo-Saxon empire with branches in Australia, New Zealand, Canada, the United States, and the West Indies. The contrasting example of the Chinese, in other words, reinforced the tendency of British imperialists to identify, in racial terms, with U.S. imperialists. Shared debates over Chinese labor and the problems it posed for "Anglo-Saxons" in England and the United States ultimately supported such transnational racial identifications. More precisely, the perception of racial ties, sharpened by presumed Chinese sexual differences, served to bind Britain to its other white settler colonies. The political and economic affiliations between these "Anglo-Saxon" countries were naturalized as a kind of geopolitical "family feeling" in opposition to the extrafamilial foreignness represented by Chinese bachelor societies. And although Britain and its white settler colonies often clashed over the proper response to the Chinese, most agreed that the Chinese presence was a pressing issue facing whites or "Anglo-Saxons" wherever they might live.[3] Indeed, by framing debates over the Chinese and the future of the empire in terms of what was best for whites as such (and not for England, the United States, or Australia), English writers attempted to quiet dissent by reinforcing allegiances to an international white federation whose "home office," as it were, was somewhere in London. In what follows, I consider sexuality and the political economy of empire in a host of English magazines, paying particular attention to representations of opium dens and the Chinese in works by Wilde and Rudyard Kipling.

At first glance Wilde and Kipling might seem to be so antithetical as to defy comparison. Peter Brooker and Peter Widdowson isolate two strands of thought in turn-of-the-century England—"art for art's sake" and "art for Empire's sake," represented by Wilde and Kipling, respectively.[4] Despite their differences, however, both were important figures in the development of English mass culture and the Chinese presence shapes the work of both in important ways. I thus interpret works by Wilde and Kipling in relation to the larger body of discourses about Chinese sexuality that circulated in popular periodicals, a horizon of meaning that remains largely invisible when their texts are considered in abstraction from their participation in an emergent mass culture.

Both writers also represent various forms of queer intimacy in the opium den. Wilde's texts, especially, make visible the kinds of conflicted erotic fantasies concerning China and the Chinese that accompanied the expansion of the international market in Chinese labor. The opium den scene in *Dorian Gray,* combined with accounts of Wilde's visit to an opium den in San Francisco's Chinatown and his popular public lectures on Asian art, suggest that the British use of Chinese labor was often figured as a homoerotic master-servant relationship. Moreover, Wilde makes explicit the imperial homoerotics that remain implicit in the work of Kipling, who was also a member of the colonial middle class. Early in his career, Kipling wrote a series of short stories and travel articles for an Anglo-Indian newspaper that partly focused on opium dens in Calcutta, Hong Kong, and San Francisco. Read together, the work of these two authors brings into relief the contradictory forms of homoerotic attraction and repulsion that characterized a variety of popular literary and other reactions to the centrality of male Chinese workers in British life; for if Wilde suggests that forms of homoerotic affect helped to support and extend British imperialism in Asia, Kipling's texts reveal that the prominence of Chinese laborers in British Asia also generated homosexual panics. These racialized homosexual panics, I argue, are partly responses to histories of British imperial warfare in Asia and fears of violent Chinese retribution. By focusing on Wilde, a key focus for queer literary studies, and Kipling, an important reference point in postcolonial studies, I hope to bring together discussions of sexuality, race, and empire that have too often occurred in relative isolation from one another.[5]

The Social Life of Things and the Sexuality of Imperial Labor Relations

Although today Wilde is remembered as an aesthete, in the late nineteenth century he was an active participant in an emergent Anglophone mass culture. As we shall see, he edited the English mass magazine *Woman's World,* and, as I have noted, *Dorian Gray* was originally serialized in a U.S. mass circulation magazine. In addition, in the early 1880s Wilde contracted with a promoter to launch highly popular lecture tours of England, Canada, and the United States. These tours were in fact early "media events," in which Wilde gave numerous interviews to newspapers and magazines, and even staged scenes for the benefit of observing journalists. He also had himself photographed and was in turn the subject of numerous newspaper sketches and caricatures.

Throughout his career, Wilde promoted various forms of non-Western ornamentation, particularly from Asia. Wilde and others in the Aesthetic Movement did much to change English and U.S. tastes in this regard. According to an 1895 commentator, "aesthetes" like Wilde stimulated consumer interest in "curios" and "knickknacks" from "India, China, Japan and elsewhere."[6] To the audiences he addressed during his lecture tours Wilde often recommended forms of non-European ornamentation (including Middle Eastern water jugs and embroidery, Japanese vases and matting, Turkish hat racks, and rugs from Persia and China) as design models.[7] Under Wilde's editorship, *Woman's World* published more than thirty essays dealing with aspects of so-called exotic cultures and their ornaments. These articles, too numerous to name, include references to Eastern macramé and wallpaper designs; Persian, Egyptian, and Indian appliqués; South African ostrich feathers for fans; South American perfume bottles; Egyptian and Indian shoes; and Egyptian, Turkish, and Persian bridal costumes. All of these *Woman's World* essays either explicitly or implicitly suggest that non-European ornaments should serve as fashion inspirations for middle-class English women.

Wilde further suggested that European designers had been influenced in important ways by examples of non-Western ornament. In his *Woman's World* review of Alan Cole's translation of Ernest Lefébure's *History of Embroidery and Lace,* for instance, Wilde discussed the beneficent influence of Eastern designs on European lace making.[8] In "The Decay of Lying" (1889), Wilde described the relationship between European design traditions and "Oriental" models in the following way:

> The whole history of [decorative] arts in Europe is the record of the struggle between Orientalism, with its frank rejection of imitation, its love of artistic convention, its dislike of the actual representation of any object in Nature, and our own imitative spirit. Wherever the former has been paramount . . . we have had beautiful and imaginative work. . . . But wherever we have returned to Life and Nature, our work has always become vulgar, common and uninteresting. (*Complete Works*, 978)

Wilde's rejection of mimetic realism makes him sympathetic to "Orientalism." "Oriental" ornament, however, does not represent for Wilde a truly autonomous aesthetic tradition. As he told a U.S. audience, Asian anti-mimeticism lacked the purity of classical restraint and became monstrous in its too absolute distance from nature. True art, Wilde argued, must reconcile Asian abstraction with a Greek-like attention to the natural world.[9] His celebrated Hellenic revival may thus more accurately be called the Hellenic perfecting of "Oriental" aesthetics, in which European artists produce the perfect harmony between Greek particularity and Asian abstraction. Thus, even though Wilde cultivates a taste for Asian art forms, his appreciation of non-Western ornament is paternalistic, subordinating such objects to the greater good of an Aesthetic Empire.[10]

Wilde's interest in so-called exotic ornament implies a hierarchical distinction between, on the one hand, the autonomous, classically derived European fine arts, which, he argued, existed above or beyond the marketplace, and, on the other hand, the supposedly merely ornamental or decorative crafts of the non-European world. For Wilde, non-Western ornament could serve as raw material inspiring the artist-critic, but it could not itself be classified as art. Ironically, the autonomy of great European art—its position beyond the market—depended on the Western artist's use of materials and models imported from other countries. Wilde's true men of culture thus rose above the market and the merely ornamental by appropriating and "improving" non-Western crafts. By actively furnishing his empire with a catalog of tasteful foreign objects— by helping to promote and institutionalize the taste for what he viewed as exotica—Wilde reformulated but substantially reconfirmed an imperial division of labor between British subjects and non-European objects. Borrowing a phrase from Frantz Fanon, who was writing in a related context, we could say that in Wilde's theories, "the other only comes on the stage to furnish it."[11] The hierarchy Wilde constructs between Western art and Oriental ornament is the aesthetic corollary to an emergent international division of labor between white and Chinese labor. In other words, Wilde's aesthetic theories partly replicated the terms of an imperial political economy that depended on the subordination of migrant workers.

Wilde's aesthetic division of labor bears comparison to similar developments in contemporary commodity culture. Just as Wilde limits Oriental ornament to the role of serving Western consumers, in advertising and packaging for tea the Chinese are constructed as fantasy servants. The consumption of Chinese products such as tea and other goods was manifestly linked to the employment of Chinese labor. Advertisers often promoted tea, for instance, with images of the Chinese laborers who produced it. Chinese workers were represented in store windows and on countless tea packages. The anonymous author of the magazine article "Curiosities of Commerce and Trade: The Tea Trade" (1880) notes that most tea consumed by the English came in packages that "everybody is familiar" with, "wooden boxes, covered with oily-looking paper, enigmatical inscriptions, and curious pictures of natives of the Celestial Empire."[12] Such images were so common that they preconditioned the English vision of the Chinese and served as points of reference for narrating "exotic" encounters for English audiences. The Rev. W. H. Gamble of the London Baptist Missionary Society wrote in 1866 that some of the Trinidad Chinese "have the very long, thin moustache which is to be seen represented in the images of mandarins on view in tea-shop windows."[13] The anonymous author of the sketch "A Day with an East-End Photographer" (1891) similarly remarks that the China-man in London "looks for all the world like the Chinaman of the willow-pattern plate in the window of the teashop."[14] These familiar fabrications of Chinese workers both reflected and reproduced English attitudes about the production costs of tea, for each package came to represent, in highly concentrated form, vast quantities of Chinese labor. As W. J. Gordon wrote in an essay about trade for the mass magazine the *Leisure Hour,* "No trade seems to be more firmly established than that in tea, and yet its very existence depends on the cheapest of labour. To produce a pound of tea costs the labour of one man for a day; take it at its wholesale price, knock off the duty, and you need not trouble about the shipper's profit to see how very little the labourer must earn, and what a very little extra would cause a storm in the tea-cup."[15] Like Gordon's ratio of 1 laborer = 1 pound of tea, the tea label "Chinaman" is a shorthand figure for the labor that the tea package represents. So English consumers in some sense recognized that when they sipped their tea they also consumed "cheap" Chinese labor.

Which is not to say that tea labels accurately reflected the labor con-ditions faced by Chinese workers. On the contrary, tea advertisements depicted them in idealized, imperialist fashion, as fantasy servants. A good example is an 1886 advertisement for London's Ellis Davies and Co. Teas. Here a somber Chinese figure holds aloft a banner that an-nounces in bold letters "ED & Co's Pure Teas." This image converts the Chinese emigrant into a personal servant on a colonial model. The banner resembles both the sail of an emigrant ship and the sort of fan that a colonial servant might use to cool his master. The Chinese worker as personal servant or support recalls the Chinese carrying-chairs and rickshaws that commonly conveyed English people throughout British Asia. Finally, the long pole supporting the banner suggests a gardening hoe or other agricultural tool used in tending tea.

A leaflet dated 1887 for the grocer W. Davies contains another fan-tasy of Chinese labor, the domestic servant who serves tea. A male Chi-nese figure offers a tray to "John Bull," the popular personification of the British Empire, who rests on top of a box of tea covered with crudely simulated Chinese characters. The scene is ostensibly set in an English grocery store but could just as well be on a British plantation. It repre-sents as desirable a hierarchical service relationship here marked in pos-ture and pose: the Chinese figure is bent slightly at the waist as he offers the tea and focuses on serving John Bull, who sits at ease looking directly at the viewer while affirming, "Yes, I Quite Enjoy It!" As the John Bull character "hails" the British consumer, his seeming look of recognition predicts a potential customer who takes vicarious pleasure in the prospect of being served.

Related fantasies are at play in an 1890 advertisement for "United Kingdom Tea Company's Teas," which pictures a young woman asleep in her sitting room, surrounded by elves and tiny "Chinamen" who are busy making tea. In the foreground a cluster of small Chinese figures use a rope to hoist a package of United Kingdom tea onto the sitting-room table. Like both the fairy tale about elves who finish the cobbler's work while he sleeps and imperial fantasies about Chinese labor as personal servants, these mini-beings do the work of reproducing domesticity while the lady of the house rests. Packaged tea promises, in other words, to bring the symbolic comforts of cheap colonial labor into the bourgeois English interior. All three tea companies sold their product by reimagining the Chinese labor that produced it as the support for an imperial lifestyle that the consumption of tea supposedly made possible. Depictions of the Chinese as domestic and agricultural laborers further reiterated the discursive and practical British construction of the Chinese worker's "racial aptitude" for those kinds of jobs. As G. R. Cole explained to the readers of *Fraser's*, "[the Chinaman] is by nature well suited for discharging such household duties as washing, cooking, house-cleaning, and is an admirable nurse." There would be no outcry in the colonies, he concludes, if the Chinese were restricted to household work and other forms of personal service.[16] This is actually what late-nineteenth-century white Australians attempted to accomplish by praising farm and service laborers while legally and extralegally harassing workers who ventured into fields such as mining or furniture manufacture, which were considered white men's work.[17] Similarly, by reproducing fantasies of colonial labor, tea packages promoted ideologies that would limit Chinese to jobs producing colonial goods or in service, where they would not compete with white workers.

In other cases, commodity ads represented Chinese workers negatively, as the defining opposite of the white labor that supposedly produced the product in question. During the final three decades of the nineteenth century in San Francisco, some goods such as cigars, shoes, and boots were packaged and advertised as white-made—and expressly not Chinese-made. In conjunction with boycotts of Chinese-made articles, craft associations packaged their products with "white labels" or "white stamps," and supplied businessmen with placards that demonstrated their support for the white worker's boycott of Chinese labor. The label glued to the box of one California cigar brand, according to Alexander Saxton, reads: "The cigars herein contained are made by WHITE MEN." Shoes and boots were similarly stamped "White Labor" and advertised in anti-Chinese publications. All of these efforts at what Saxton calls "product differentiation" sold the desirability of white labor in opposition to Chinese labor.[18]

In English and Australian examples, white labor's parasitic dependence on a negative image of the Chinese worker is even more obvious. In the 1880s, Chinese in Australia entered the colonial labor market as gardeners, laborers, launderers, craftsmen, and domestic servants. But they were generally limited to relatively narrow, menial specializations that did not compete with whites. While white settlers praised Chinese farmworkers and domestic servants, "those in skilled or semi-skilled occupations were harassed—like earlier Chinese miners—and were legally disadvantaged or excluded from employment." To further limit Chinese labor competition, this time on the side not of production but of consumption, Australian governments in the 1880s passed several laws stipulating that Chinese-manufactured furniture be "'ignominiously branded' Chinese-made."[19] White Australians attempted to reproduce a stratified labor market by "racializing" certain commodities, contrasting the "white" and "Chinese" character of the labor that produced them. English advertisements for a product called "Matchless Metal Polish" in the *Pall Mall Magazine* similarly mark the commodity's origin in white labor by incorporating the contrasting image of a Chinese worker. The copy reads: "No Labour Is Required When Using Matchless Metal Polish. British-All-Through." The intruding presence to the left of a conventional "Chinaman"—with round hat, queue, and an opium pipe—brings into relief the slogan that promotes the product's whiteness by implying that it required no Chinese labor. Just as anti-Chinese campaigns in Canada, Australia, and the United States all detailed the supposed dangers of Chinese opium smoking, this advertisement implies that the consumer can avoid supporting that bad habit only by buying goods that are "British-All-Through." Here and elsewhere, manufacturers responded to the presence of Chinese workers by employing fabricated "Chinamen" as means for representing the desirability of white-made goods.

These two different kinds of commodity "packages"—on the one hand, ads such as "No [Chinese] Labor Matchless Metal Polish" that sell white in preference to Chinese labor, and, on the other, those like "ED and Co's Pure Teas" that promote a limited kind of Chinese labor—directly refer to the racialization of male Chinese labor. In the first case, images of the Chinese were used to promote white male manufacturing or craft labor, and in the second Chinese men appear to confirm their "proper place" as servants and field hands. In neither situation is labor rendered completely "abstract," for both sorts of ads bear the traces of what Lisa Lowe calls "the social production of 'difference,' of restrictive particularity and illegitimacy marked by race, nation, geographical origins, and gender."[20] My reading of racialization and late-nineteenth-century commodity aesthetics partly revises Marx's famous discussion of commodity fetishism in *Capital.* A commodity is "a mysterious thing," Marx writes, "simply because in it the social character of men's labor appears to them as an objective character stamped upon the product of that labor; because the relation of the producers to the sum total of their own labor is presented to them as a social relation, existing not between themselves, but between the products of their labor." The "social character" of labor appears as a relationship among the products of labor because, according to Marx, the commodity form equates and homogenizes different kinds of work, and therefore passes as the objective expression of human labor as such: "[W]henever, by an exchange, we equate as values our different products, by that very act, we also equate, as human labor, the different kinds of labor expended upon them."[21] By contrast, the advertisements just described do not equate different kinds of labor, but rather distinguish between the white and Chinese labor that the respective commodities represented. And although commodities do not reflect without mediation the concrete "truth" of labor relations, they do trace in broad outlines the racialized divisions of labor between white and Chinese that subtended British imperialism.

Thus, like Wilde's theories concerning the relative value of "Oriental" ornaments, fin-de-siècle consumer culture responded to ongoing debates about the advantages and disadvantages of Chinese labor. On the one hand, white unions of sailors and washerwomen agitated for restrictions on Chinese immigration to England.[22] Some members of the English press warned of the coming "contest of the cheap races over the dear" and the prospect of an England overrun with Chinese. Chinese emigration had initiated a potentially apocalyptic race war, it was argued, pitting a lower against a higher "standard of living."[23] Similar arguments against Chinese labor were made in California, Canada, and

Australia. Many others, however, actively promoted the exploitation of Chinese labor. In the pages of English magazines such as *All the Year Round, Belgravia, Fraser's Magazine,* and the *Nineteenth Century,* writers praised the productivity of Chinese workers. For instance, as G. R. Cole writes in "The Chinaman Abroad" (1878), an essay for *Fraser's,* "It cannot be denied that so lithe and easily supported an individual is capable of rendering great service in our colonies, where labour of all kinds is in such great demand." He concludes that "many of my countrymen would welcome" the Chinese workers into "our own coal mines and factories, or domesticated in English homes," just as "many of our countrymen in the colonies rely entirely on the Chinaman's assistance for the conduct of their business as well as their domestic comfort."[24] The editors of *All the Year Round* concurred, commending Cole's "thoughtful paper" and arguing that although U.S. and Australian workers hate him "because he works for lower wages," the Chinese emigrant is a "temperate, hard-working creature."[25] Edmund Mitchell's 1894 magazine essay "The Chinaman Abroad" (1894) draws on his observations of Chinese workers throughout Britain and British Asia, including India, Hong Kong, Australia, and the East End of London. Mitchell's Chinese worker possesses "[u]ntiring industry, patience, and perseverance, extreme thrift, the inborn habit and faculty of saving a little day by day, however scanty his earnings." For these reasons, Mitchell concludes that anyone familiar with Australia or the Pacific coast of the United States must "admit that it would be to the great advantage of mankind if the gates swung inwards for the welcome, instead of standing as barriers for the exclusion, of Chinese immigrants."[26]

Like the opponents of Chinese emigration, these authors naturalize the "cheapness" of Chinese labor but evaluate it positively. Most of the compliments bestowed on these workers serve to rationalize low wages, suggesting that the Chinese can reproduce their labor power at a very low rate because they are "easily supported," "easily managed," "thrifty," and demonstrate "the inborn habit and faculty of saving a little day by day, however scanty [their] earnings." Here low wages are the "natural" result of an inborn Chinese ability to live inexpensively and not an effect of an unequal capitalist world economy dominated by Britain. In other words, these authors welcome the opportunity for capitalists to exploit "cheap" labor. Indeed, they often write from the perspective of employers who use the prospect of Chinese labor as a club to discipline white workers and keep wages low. As Cole claims, "in these days, when frequent strikes and wordy meetings among the labouring classes show the unhealthy state of the labour market," so-called cheap Chinese labor looks more and more attractive. "[L]et our artisans beware," he warns, "lest, presuming on their power to extort higher and higher wages by placing their employers on the horns of a dilemma, they go just a little too far, and induce a combination among their employers which may result in their work being quietly taken out of their hands by the supple fingers and more easily contented mind of John Chinaman."[27] These images of the Chinese as inherently tractable workers inverted representations that positioned them as unfairly prodigious rivals of white workers.

Further countering the arguments of the anti-Chinese side, those in favor of the English exploitation of Chinese workers dilated on their desirability in sexually charged terms: the emergent English mass media often focused on the working bodies of Chinese men. The anonymous author of an essay in *All the Year Round* titled "A Street Scene in Foochow," for instance, writes that Chinese workmen are delightfully "naked, save with a girth around the loins" (1881, 130). Similarly, writing about Malaysia in the popular middle-class magazine *Belgravia,* F. Thorold Dickson notes that "The sight which first strikes the newly-landed [English] civilian is that of Chinese carpenters swarming by the dozen over the roofs of houses in the course of building, the body naked from the waist upwards, the long pigtail or queue... tightly coiled round the clean-shaven pate, the whole attitude denoting untiring industry and activity." Of Chinese tin miners he further writes that "[a]s they struggle along upon the swaying planks... bending and straining beneath the double force of weight and motion, their loins girt with a pair of short, loose cotton drawers, their broad backs and sturdy shoulders, bare and streaming with perspiration, they offer a fair example of manliness and endurance."[28] Here the desirability of Chinese workers is partly indexed by the naked power and masculine beauty of their bodies; as part of an effort to promote the benefits of employing Chinese workers, English authors sometimes yoked sexuality to political economy by focusing on the physical attractiveness of their laboring bodies when viewed from the relatively close-up, privileged perspective of the master. Assessments of Chinese labor, in other words, often presuppose the scopophilia of master-servant relations, in which the English observer freely looks at Chinese workers who do not return the gaze.

The pleasures of Chinese labor: illustration from "Qwee," *Pall Mall Magazine,* May 1895.

The homoerotics of imperial service relations involving Chinese men are perhaps most striking in magazine fiction. A short story called "Qwee," serialized in an 1895 edition of a popular English magazine, provides a good example. The story revolves around an intense relationship between an English employer, Captain Blake, and his Chinese servant, "Qwee." The story begins at a Santa Barbara, California, hotel where a group of "Anglo-Saxon" guests are discussing the virtues of Chinese labor. The guests all agree that as long as they are excluded from jobs where they might compete with whites, Chinese men make excellent servants. Indeed, the hero of the story, Captain Blake "wish[ed] to secure a good Chinese servant" and therefore "took many opportunities of watching" Qwee, a servant at the hotel. Blake ultimately employs Qwee and together they travel to the British Columbian outback, where the Chinese servant becomes extravagantly attached to his master. The narrator even claims that Qwee was like a "husband" to Blake. When not attending to the Captain, Qwee discovers gold and lovingly agrees to share it with his employer: "Qwee soon seized an opportunity to take Blake aside, and said, looking at him most affectionately, 'I not

tell others—tell you: we have lots more [gold]—all for you and me...
I love you.'" In the end, when Qwee apparently dies of an unnamed
disease, Captain Blake even sees his loyal servant's ghostly shade, as if to
signify that "a poor Chinese boy, attached to his master" was thinking
of him at the end.

Wilde's aesthetic theories, I would argue, helped make explicit a
homoerotics of empire that in other contexts was often naturalized or
overlooked. In the first place, his passionate advocacy of non-Western
ornamentation often made such objects appear as phallic synecdoches
for desirable racialized bodies. The hero of *Dorian Gray*, for instance,
collects a variety of such objects, exotic musical instruments that "he
loved to touch and try":

> He had the mysterious *furuparis* of the Rio Negro Indians, that women
> are not allowed to look at, and that even youths may not see till they
> have been subjected to fasting and scourging...; the long *clarín* of the
> Mexicans, into which the performer does not blow, but through which
> he inhales the air;... the *teponazili*, that has two vibrating tongues of
> wood, and is beaten with sticks that are smeared with an elastic gum
> obtained from the milky juice of plants; [and] the *yotl*-bells of the Aztecs,
> that are hung like grapes. (*Complete Works*, 107)

Here Dorian's exotic musical instruments seem like strange sex toys
that, when played, recall homoerotic sex acts. The *furuparis* that women
may not see, combined with the *yotl*-bells that are "hung like grapes"
suggest comparison to male genitals, while the Mexican *clarín* that performers suck on and the *teponazili* with its "vibrating tongues" and
"milky juice" both suggest fellatio.

Elsewhere Wilde made more explicit the connection between beautiful exotic things and beautiful, exotic male bodies. As part of a lecture
tour of the United States he encountered a group of San Francisco aesthetes who invited him to tea, where he was struck by their beautiful
Chinese servant, a man who served tea wearing an elaborately embroi-
dered robe. Wilde was also attracted to a group of Chinese workers
that he observed drinking tea out of delicate porcelain cups. As he told
his U.S. audiences:

> When I was in San Francisco, I used to visit the Chinese theaters for
> their rich dresses, and the Chinese restaurants on account of the beau-

tiful tea they made there. I saw rough Chinese navvies [ditch diggers], who did work that the ordinary Californian rightly might be disgusted with and refuse to do, sitting there drinking their tea out of tiny porcelain cups, which might be mistaken for the petals of a white rose, and handling them with care, fully appreciating the influence of their beauty.[29]

The "rough" Chinese navvies recall the sort of "rough trade" that Wilde supposedly fancied, the street boys of London. And the lovely cups that they gently hold like roses suggest an aestheticized Chinese phallus that attracts Wilde's gaze. In these ways, his intense admiration for Chinese things and Chinese men, combined with his own "queerness," served to underline the forms of homoerotic attraction and repulsion that were also reproduced, sometimes in more muted forms, throughout Anglophone mass culture.

The mass cultural construction of the "queer" Chinese worker is particularly evident in the Orientalist caricatures of Wilde that circulated in England and the United States. Because of assumptions about Wilde's sexual deviancy, he was often represented as Chinese, suggesting that in the late nineteenth century, Chinese workers had become synonymous with perversity. In an apparent parody of Wilde's rough navvies holding flower-like teacups, one 1882 U.S. lithograph pictured Wilde as a cartoon "Chinaman" with a long queue and moustache, flanked by "Oriental vases" of the sort he championed and holding his trademark sunflower (but apparently with rats for petals). The caption reads: "No likee to callee me Johnnee, callee me Oscar." Following U.S. publications, English periodicals similarly linked Wilde with the Chinese. In a satiric review of a London Chinese restaurant published in the *Illustrated Sporting and Dramatic News* for 9 August 1894, for instance, a reviewer expressed his disappointment that the restaurant did not serve roasted dog and concluded that "even the spectacle of Oscar the Irreproachable seated on the terrace...fails to lure us further." The accompanying sketch, captioned "Oscar in China," depicts Wilde smoking, teacup in hand, as a Chinese waiter looks on.[30] Once again Wilde is represented as disturbingly close to the Chinese, and the suggestion that the Chinese eat dogs hints at the possibility that his "Oriental" proclivities involve tabooed, unspeakable acts. In all of these cases, the joke at Wilde's expense assumes an audience that is already well acquainted with representations of Chinese "perversity" and the pleasures of employing the

E. B. Duval, "No likee to callee me Johnnee, callee me Oscar," color lithograph, 1882. Reproduced with permission of the William Andrews Clark Memorial Library, University of California, Los Angeles.

services of Chinese workers. But by framing Wilde in this way, such caricatures represent as extreme and exceptional an imperial homoerotics that was in fact much more common.

Popular images of opium dens support this claim with their indirect yet suggestive depictions of the dangers and pleasures of possible intimacy with Chinese workingmen. This in part explains why caricaturists referenced Wilde's well-publicized taste for opium. In a caricature of Wilde printed in the 18 May 1893 *Oxford Magazine* and captioned "The New Culture," Max Beerbohm represented him holding a hookah for an "Oriental" genie.[31] Similarly, a drawing titled "A Voluptuary" in the 14 July 1894 issue of the English magazine *Pick-Me-Up* pictures Wilde as a presumed "Chinaman." The sketch depicts him resting indolently in his chair, smoking one of his opium-laced cigarettes, and proclaiming, "To rise, to take a little opium, to sleep till lunch, and after again to take a little opium and sleep till dinner, *that* is a life of pleasure!" A close examination of Wilde's face reveals cartoonish "Chinese" features— thin, slit-like eyes, and prominent buckteeth. Although I have not encountered a photo of Wilde that exhibits such teeth, caricatures often do.[32] And at least one observer remembered Wilde with the heavy-lidded "almond shaped" eyes "seen sometimes in Orientals."[33] If a taste for opium "Orientalized" the aesthete, this was in part because the drug was embedded within a larger imperial political economy that often made the English directly—or more often imaginatively—"intimate" with Chinese migrant laborers. Thus, as we shall see, the opium den is the scene par excellence where the homoeroticism of empire was staged.

As I suggested at the outset, Dorian's consumption of opium requires him to leave the privacy of his home and to confront his position in a global economy by traveling to the opium dens in the quays of London's East End docks, home to visiting Asian sailors and the Chinese merchants who catered to their needs. Dorian thus finds himself poised on the precarious border of the British Empire, where the silhouettes of incoming and outgoing ships are visible on the horizon (*Complete Works,* 142–43). Situated in this way, the opium den enables Wilde to reflect upon the powerful yet vulnerable solidity of the empire in the face of global Chinese migration. The den's inhabitants, in fact, represent some of the circuits of British Asian trade and labor migration described in chapter 1, including an Indian "half-caste in a ragged turban," and a group of Malay sailors "crouching by a little charcoal stove playing with bone counters and showing their white teeth as they chattered" (ibid.).

A VOLUPTUARY.

" To rise, to take a little opium, to sleep till lunch, and after again to take a little opium and sleep till dinner, *that* is a life of pleasure !"

"A Voluptuary," from the 14 July 1894 edition of the magazine *Pick-Me-Up*. "To rise, to take a little opium, to sleep till lunch, and after again to take a little opium and sleep till dinner, *that* is a life of pleasure!" Reproduced with permission of the William Andrews Clark Memorial Library, University of California, Los Angeles.

Moreover, the Malays with their white "bone counters" recall the Chinese navvies with their white porcelain cups that Wilde encountered in San Francisco. Ultimately, Dorian climbs a staircase "leading to a darkened chamber" where "the heavy odour of opium met him . . . and his nostrils quivered with pleasure." Finally, he "looked around at the grotesque things that lay in such fantastic postures on the ragged mattresses. The twisted limbs, the gaping mouths, the staring lustreless eyes, fascinated him. He knew in what strange heavens they were suffering and what dull hells were teaching them the secret of some new joy" (*Complete Works*, 143). In this way, Wilde called attention to the "open secret" of British imperialism: the fact that it often depended on homoerotic fantasies about the laboring Chinese male body.

WHEN EMPIRES FALL APART: HOMOSEXUAL PANIC AND FANTASIES OF CHINESE RETRIBUTION

Accounts of the opium trade often recall in miniature the Opium Wars and contiguous imperial conflicts in Asia. Many authors in fact seem to reenact these battles in new contexts. In *A Cruise in an Opium Clipper*, for instance, Captain Lindsay Anderson re-creates the Opium Wars in Formosa (Taiwan). Published in 1891, the captain's memoirs look back on his efforts to extend the opium trade in 1859, immediately following both the second Opium War and the Indian rebellions. Recruited in front of the British consulate at Shanghai, Anderson served as third officer on board the *Eamont*, an opium clipper that sailed to ports in Malaysia, Japan, China, Hong Kong, and ultimately Formosa. When the *Eamont's* crew discovers the mutilated bodies of three Dutch sailors on a Formosan beach, they spend four hours burning and looting a randomly selected village. "In the heat of passion . . . it was decided to burn the village down as the only means of avenging the murders." The sailor excuses the looting by arguing that theft unavoidably accompanies all warfare: "War is the same all the world over, whether miniature as this or on a large scale." Indeed, as I suggested in chapter 1, British looting was notorious in Asia, especially during the second Opium War and the sacking of the emperor's summer palace. Anderson concludes that "no one seemed to have a feeling of regret for the many thus rendered homeless in the accomplishment of vengeance. . . . All seemed to agree that it was a dire act of necessity to take summary vengeance on the miscreants, as a salutary lesson in civilization." This lesson amounts to a tutorial in imperial white supremacy, or, as Anderson puts it, the villagers "knew now . . .

that the white man was a being not to be trifled with, and to be re-spected."[34] Here the English Captain Anderson subsumes himself and the dead Dutch sailors within the larger category of "white man."

English opium den visitors similarly engaged the Chinese and other Asians in mock battle, symbolically vanquishing threats to the British Empire. The anonymous author of "Opium-Smoking in Bluegate Fields" (1870) is a good example. After consulting both *Edwin Drood* and the police, the writer and a friend decide to visit an opium den. "Armed" with a stout stick, the two men travel to a court ominously "blocked up at the end by a dead wall," where they find a den run by a Chinese man called "Osee." As they prepare to ascend the stairs, the author hesitates for a moment as he reconsiders the risks involved. "All the policemen had told us that we should find Lascars as the chief fre-quenters of these dens, and Lascars have always been associated in my mind with very sharp knives." His passage into the den only reinforces these fears: "The stairs were so steep that we had almost to hold our heads back as we ascended them, and with a rather vivid anticipation of savages, steel, and blood, they—our heads—emerged very carefully from the hole in the floor which admitted visitors." This odd use of the third person "they" distances the men's heads from their bodies, as if they had been decapitated.[35] While the Indian "mutinies" and Opium Wars are perhaps the most obvious models for such mock battles, opium den representations condensed a host of imperial hot spots in Asia. Britain was fiercely competitive with other European powers in South and Southeast Asia, most notably the Dutch in Borneo and Java and the French in Vietnam. After 1860, moreover, British imperial forces were deployed to quell rebellions or riots in Afghanistan, British Burma (now Myanmar), and Malaysia.[36] Ultimately, however, the author of "Opium-Smoking in Bluegate Fields" emerges from the opium den in one piece, and the implied threat of attack becomes more thrilling than terrifying. In such works, opium dens peopled by sinister Chinamen, Lascars, and Malays increasingly represent an excitingly dangerous Asian landscape where writers (and, by extension, their audiences) become in-timate with the enemies of empire before ultimately mastering them.

As previously noted, a central concern in the Anglo world was the fear that British imperialism in Asia might "blow back" to England and its white settler colonies in the form of Chinese immigration. Observers in England, Australia, British Columbia, and California projected global, apocalyptic struggle between white societies and a rising horde of bestial yellow beings. Inverting the logic of immigration proponents, who focused on the economic attractiveness of Chinese labor, those who would restrict immigration pointed to the supposedly deviant sexuality of Chinese men. And while it was argued that all-male immigrant groups were perverse, they were particularly feared as sodomites. Recalling the phrase "the love that dare not speak its name," F. Thorold Dickson wrote in *Belgravia* that "the lowest of the Chinese indulge in some nameless vices."[37] Other writers, particularly in Australia, were sometimes less circumspect. In the late 1850s, it was often argued that Chinese immigrants were particularly addicted to homosexual practices.[38] Chinese sexuality, according to an 1857 story in an Australian paper, the *Bendigo Advertiser,* was "a gross violation of every principle of morality and to the last degree insulting to our manhood."[39] Chinese homosexuality was often seen as partly a result of demographic patterns favoring male migration. According to 1855 Parliamentary Papers, for example, "The form of depravity which is to be anticipated from a purely male emigration already exists among the Chinese, and we can scarcely doubt that the absence of females would ultimately accumulate an amount of vice which would be intolerable."[40]

The English panic over Chinese sodomy reached a high point between 1905 and 1906, when Parliament investigated sexual practices in the Transvaal mines. The resulting report argued that male prostitution and male "marriages" were common among Chinese miners. While numerous witnesses claimed they were certain such practices existed, they confessed that Chinese sodomy was impossible to detect. Nonetheless, the prime minister concluded that such evils "were certain to arise where the ordinary social conditions were so commonly inverted."[41] Two witnesses, Rev. F. Alexander and Mr. Leopold Luyt, further charged that the Chinese were "teaching" sodomy to black Africans. The report's author, J. A. S. Bucknill, concluded that 6–7 percent of the Chinese workers were "bugger-boys." As a result of the hearings, several Chinese theaters were closed and a few dozen Chinese were repatriated.[42] Moreover, England's general election of 1905 partly turned on the Chinese question in the Transvaal. Unionist candidates discovered that many blamed them for the Chinese presence in the mines. As a result, their speeches were interrupted by anti-Chinese slogans, and their opponents distributed anti-Chinese cartoons and posters.[43]

In the early writings of Rudyard Kipling, fears of Chinese sodomy and Chinese labor coalesce in the opium den. As a young journalist in

India working for the Lahore *Civil and Military Gazette* and the Alla-habad *Pioneer,* Kipling published a number of texts about opium pro-duction and consumption. His first published short story, "The Gate of the Hundred Sorrows" (1884), concerns a Chinese opium den in Lahore. Four years later Kipling reported on his visits to Indian and Chinese opium dens in Calcutta. In the same year he published "In An Opium Factory," an essay about his tour of an opium processing plant near Benares. Finally, as part of a set of 1889 travel letters for the *Pioneer,* Kipling wrote of his trip to an opium den in San Francisco's Chinatown. All of these texts were subsequently collected and republished in India, England, and the United States.[44] Elsewhere, Kipling evidenced his knowledge of and support for Britain's opium policies, particularly as they contributed to Indian revenues.[45]

Kipling's opium texts reiterate themes and tropes familiar in the larger body of magazine writings that I have discussed in Part I. The opium den in "The Gate of the Hundred Sorrows," for example, con-stitutes an imaginary map of Anglo India. The tale's narrator, Gabral Misquitta, is a Eurasian addict who frequents a den run by a Chinese immigrant from Calcutta, Fung-Tching. Fung-Tching's other customers include his nephew, Tsing-ling, "two Baboos" or Bengali clerks, an "En-glish loafer" ("MacSomebody, I think"), another Eurasian from Madras, a "half-caste woman," and two men "from the North" ("Persians or Afghans or something"). "The Gate of the Hundred Sorrows" thus con-tains a virtual ethnographic diorama of Lahore urban "underworlds," at least as Kipling understood them. In the hot summer months before publishing his first story, Kipling took opium and wandered through Lahore at night. As he wrote in his autobiography, *Something of Myself,* "Often the night got into my head . . . and I would wander till dawn in all manner of odd places—liquor-shops, gambling and opium dens."[46] For all its "local color," however, the story also sketches some of the larger geopolitical coordinates of British India. Its characters come from the borders or frontiers of the Raj—Lahore and the Afghan frontier in the north, Bengal and Calcutta to the east, and Madras on the south-east coast. Furthermore, as in the London dens, the Chinese proprietor of Lahore's Gate marks the links between the Indian empire and China, yet makes the Chinese responsible for the opium trade.

While "The Gate of the Hundred Sorrows" echoes the cartographic strategies of narratives set in London, Kipling's opium writings take some unique twists and turns, itineraries that originate in British India.

Kipling's travel reports for the *Pioneer* concerning opium and the Chinese enable him to redescribe an Anglo-Indian subjectivity—formed in the clubs and other provincial institutions of Anglo-Indian station life—as an international, transpacific white personhood. Traveling west from Calcutta to London in 1889, Kipling stopped in Burma, Malaysia, Hong Kong, China, Japan, California, and British Columbia before continuing across the United States to the Atlantic coast. On this trip "Kipling began to see," in the words of his biographer, Charles Carrington, "that British India was not the center of the [imperial] system, not the normal pattern of British expansion."[47] One continuity between India and other sites in the Asia-Pacific empire, however, was the presence of British military or police forces. The writer's newspaper years in India were flanked by important military engagements: the Second Afghan War of 1881 (obliquely referenced in "The Gate" by the Persian and Afghan characters from the northern frontier) and the conquest of Burma, 1885–87. Britain deemed Burma, which was located between India and Malaysia, an important buffer against an expanding French presence in nearby Vietnam and a valuable source of timber and rubies. Britain had occupied lower Burma since 1853 but moved to annex upper Burma in 1885. Local guerrilla resistance, however, turned annexation into a protracted and bloody colonial war.[48]

Kipling memorializes this war on the Burmese leg of his trip when he wistfully recalls all the Englishmen who died in the conquest of Burma. On the steamer to Rangoon he is pleased to see the large number of soldiers from his home region in the Punjab on their way to "serve the Queen" in Burma. Similarly, at Penang he meets a Sikh soldier who polices the local Chinese and Kipling notes that "I cheered myself with the thought that India . . . was not so far off, after all." War stories seem to comfort Kipling, making the young Anglo-Indian feel at home throughout British Asia. He leaves an English club in Penang refreshed, his head filled with "stories of battle, murder, and sudden death." Military considerations such as the relative strength or weakness of British fortifications in places like Singapore or Hong Kong help bind together an otherwise episodic and disjointed set of reflections into a more or less coherent vision of Britain's Asian empire.[49]

The prime targets of Kipling's martial aggression are Chinese emigrants in British Asia. The Chinese in the Straits Settlements of Malaysia, for instance, lead him to ponder the possible military threat posed by China. "What will happen," he wonders, "when China really wakes up, runs a line from Shanghai to Lhassa, starts another line of imperial Yellow Flag immigrant steamers, and really works and controls her own gun-factories and arsenals?" The "enemy" has already advanced into British Penang, whose Chinese population Kipling calls "the first army corps on the march of the Mongol. The scouts are at Calcutta, and a flying column at Rangoon. Here begins the main body, some hundred thousand strong." In the form of secret societies this "army" poses a serious threat to British control of the Straits Settlements. Kipling describes a recent riot in which Singapore "was entirely at the mercy of the Chinese" until British forces reestablished order. The Malay Peninsula, he argues, needs more troops to keep it "out of alien hands." He concludes that even Hong Kong, with its formidable fortifications, remains vulnerable to attack from Canton. Without vigilance, "the time is coming when there will be no European gentlemen—nothing but yellow people with black hearts."[50]

Indeed, the Chinese terrify the future poet laureate of empire. He repeatedly notes that they fill him with fear: "the faces of the Chinese frightened me"; "the mere mob was terrifying"; "Watch the yellow faces that glare at you . . . and you will be afraid, as I was afraid!"[51] This terror helps explain why, after a short tour of Canton, Kipling tells his companion "I want to get under the guns of Hong-Kong. Phew! . . . I was wearied of these rats in their pit—wearied and scared and sullen." On the way back to his ship he passes a battlefield and sees "rusty English guns spiked and abandoned after the [second opium] war."[52] Ironically, even though the British decisively defeated the Chinese, Kipling reads the rusted guns as evidence that the empire is at risk. He seems to suggest that the Opium Wars are not really over, but must instead be waged again and again.

These imaginary military plans are driven by an imperial monomania. As Kipling claims over and over, he despises the Chinese. Although at times he provides a minimalist rationalization for his racism (the Chinese are immoral, they have no souls, they resemble pigs), in most cases even the crudest of explanations is deemed unnecessary:

> I could quite understand after a couple of hours in [the Penang] Chinatown why the lower-caste Anglo-Saxon hates the Celestial.

> I hated the Chinaman before; I hated him doubly as I choked for breath in his seething streets.

> I hate Chinamen.[53]

When he finally reaches China, Kipling's hatred assumes genocidal proportions:

> Now I understand why the civilized European of Irish extraction kills the Chinaman in America. It is justifiable to kill him. It would be quite right to wipe the city of Canton off the face of the earth, and to exterminate all the people who ran away from the shelling. The Chinaman ought not to count.... This people ought to be killed off because they are unlike any people I ever met before.[54]

Racist invective is common in Kipling's prose, and yet he reserves some of his strongest, most unequivocal expressions of fear and loathing for the Chinese. Why do the Chinese mobilize such intense affect in Kipling?

This question can be answered in a number of ways. In the first place, Kipling greets "the Chinese problem" in British Asia as a welcome distraction from conflicts within India. At the start of his journalistic career, the Raj had only recently established a tenuous peace along the northern frontier when a new political threat seemed to emerge from within—forms of Indian nationalism represented by the Indian National Congress. The Indian National Congress, established in 1885, directly challenged the status quo in India by calling for an end to the "arbitrary personal rule" of British soldiers and civil servants. For Kipling, who believed that "the natives" were too childlike to rule themselves, the Congress was at best laughable and at worst deeply dangerous. He said as much in his journalism and, as John A. McClure and Edward Said both note, Kipling excluded the nationalists from the vision of India he would compose in *Kim*. As McClure concludes, "In order to paint a picture of a harmonious India reconciled to imperial rule Kipling has no alternative but to exclude the Indian nationalists entirely.... Indeed, all of Kim's enemies come from beyond the border of British India. Within these borders, all is amity."[55] Similar desires for a strife-free India are at play even earlier, I would argue, in Kipling's writings about the Chinese in other parts of British Asia. Kipling thus eclipses conflicts within the subcontinent by suggesting that the greater threat to imperial rule lies outside of India, among the Chinese. The Chinese in effect enable him to rethink British imperialism in extra-Indian terms.

As a discursive field, "the Chinese question" gave the British Empire coherence, and helped to link it ideologically to the other emerging "Anglo-Saxon" empire, the United States. The presence of Chinese in places such as Calcutta, Singapore, and Hong Kong served to thread together different forms of empire. As objects of imperial policing in diverse locations, the presence of the Chinese prompted the ideological construction of a white or Anglo-Saxon imperial power that subsumed vast regions of Asia. Shared debates over the proper administration of Chinese emigration in the British white-settler colonies of Australia, New Zealand, and British Columbia, on the one hand, and in the United States, on the other, supported ideologies of an international, transpacific white supremacy that was articulated in opposition to the Chinese. In the second half of the nineteenth century, writers in both British and U.S. territories posited a common racial identity that bridged the gap between the two realms. On the British side, writers described white Americans, Australians, New Zealanders, and Canadians as England's stepchildren. According to Paul B. Rich, an "Anglo-Saxon racial ideal led some imperial advocates to stress the common ties of 'blood' with the United States, and so making it a natural ally for Britain as rival European powers like France and Germany had begun to challenge British imperial pre-eminence by the 1880s." The terms *white* or *Anglo-Saxon,* he concludes, provided "the ideological buttress with the colonies of white settlement and with the United States."[56] According to Sucheta Mazumdar, at the end of the nineteenth century a "grotesque symbiosis" emerged in which the "[a]postles of British imperialism turned avidly to cheer on the Americans" in the Caribbean and Pacific. As she reminds us, Kipling wrote "The White Man's Burden" to celebrate U.S. imperialism in the Philippines.[57]

Similarly, Reginald Horsman argues that in the United States the dream of an "Anglo-Saxon" alliance between the U.S. and British empires was common after mid-century, even though it never supplanted notions of a distinctly "American" manifest destiny or checked critiques of British tyranny. In support of this claim, Horsman cites examples concerning Asia that are particularly relevant to the present argument. John Gordon Bennett of the *New York Herald* celebrated Britain's attack on China during the first Opium War "not as a victory for British imperialism, but a triumph for the Anglo-Saxons," including Americans. Similarly, in 1856 Rep. Lemual Evans of Texas dreamed of the day when "the two great branches of the Anglo-Saxon stock, the one pressing from the bay of Bengal, and the other from the golden gulf of California, would meet in some beautiful group of sunny isles in the Pacific ocean, and together clasp their united hands in love and peace around the globe."[58] Such dreams were partly based on common, albeit sometimes competitive, British and U.S. interests in Asia, especially China. Numerous U.S. ships participated in the opium trade and, as Marx noted, the United States had large financial stakes in the commodity circuits that Britain initiated in China.[59] As if recalling that the racial ideologies linking Britain and the United States emerged out of shared investments in the Opium Wars and the subsequent development of Asian commerce, Kipling and other visitors discovered a particularly powerful version of transpacific whiteness in the opium dens of San Francisco's Chinatown.

English and American tourists alike were irresistibly drawn to the opium dens of Chinatown. The English M.P. Henry Hussey Vivian, for example, found Chinatown much more interesting than the rest of San Francisco. After describing for eleven pages a tour of Chinatown that included a stop at an opium den, he writes: "I do not know that I need to say much of the City of San Francisco itself," and quickly brings his narrative to a close.[60] The Englishwoman Iza Duffus Hardy begins an account of her opium den visit by claiming that it is "the duty of every tourist in San Francisco" to see Chinatown.[61] Despite his hatred and fear of the Chinese in the earlier portions of his trip, Kipling himself visited San Francisco's Chinatown twice during his brief stay. Many U.S. tourists shared this enthusiasm. In his travel guide to U.S. cities, Captain Willard Glazier claimed that "the Chinese Quarter... has become famous the world over" and that "it is a locality which no stranger should fail to see."[62] Glazier's advice seems unnecessary, for, as Hardy explains, English and American tourists were "ubiquitous" in Chinatown.[63]

As I have suggested, the opium dens of San Francisco's Chinatown enabled English and U.S. tourists in part to affirm their common whiteness by confronting Chinese difference. Despite their distinct nationalities, all tourists in Chinatown became white. Hardy, for example, claims that she cannot tell the difference between visitors from London and those from New York.[64] Similarly, in W. H. Gleadell's "Night Scenes in Chinatown, San Francisco," an essay he wrote for an English magazine, distinctions between the United States and England are displaced by the more striking opposition between "the white man" and "the Mongol." Recalling their English counterparts, U.S. writers also constructed a transnational whiteness in opposition to Chinese opium smokers. In his 1881 *Harper's Weekly* exposé of opium dens in New York and San Francisco, Dr. H. H. Kane equates Dickens's fictional English opium addict with the real Americans supposedly menaced by Chinese opium:

> It was supposed at the time when the "Mystery of Edwin Drood" first made its appearance that the character of an English opium-smoker was purely the outcome of Dickens's fertile imagination. Who would then have predicted that in a few years' time the number of white men indulging in this Eastern vice would be counted by the thousand? . . . Such however is the case. At a low estimate there are in this country, to-day, from three to five thousand Americans, male and female, smoking opium once or twice daily.[65]

Here the shared danger of an "Eastern vice" foregrounds the white racial identity linking England and America. Similarly, although Kipling often notes differences between Americans and the English or Anglo Indians, such distinctions pale before his assertions of a larger international whiteness. At the dock in San Francisco, Kipling is struck by the fact that "I passed into a city of three hundred thousand white men. Think of it! Three hundred thousand white men and women gathered in one spot."[66] And recall how in China Kipling claims to understand the Irish-American's hatred, suggesting that a common racial disposition links him to these other men. It is as though a mutual hatred of the Chinese serves to definitively "whiten" two groups of people, the Irish and the Anglo-Indians, who have historically been on the margins of whiteness.

Kipling records his first brush with Chinese San Francisco only a few paragraphs later. On the way to his hotel, he sees a policeman "supporting a Chinaman who had been stabbed in the eye and was bleeding like a pig."[67] His next, more substantial encounter occurs when a new acquaintance takes him on a tour of Chinatown.[68] Despite the "filth and squalor"—not to mention his avowed hatred of the Chinese—he returns alone for a second visit because "I wanted to know how deep in the earth the Pig-tail had taken root." He thus chooses a particular tenement house and begins to "burrow down" into the cellar: "Downstairs I crawled past Chinamen in bunks, opium-smokers, brothels, and gambling hells, till I reached the second cellar." Here he stops to admire the building's fortifications, noting that "In time of trouble that house could be razed to the ground by the mob, and yet hide all its inhabitants in brick-walled and wooden-beamed subterranean galleries, strengthened with iron-framed doors and gates." Passing on to a third, opium-smoke-filled cellar, he finds a group of Chinese and someone who looks Eurasian (but turns out to be Mexican) playing poker. A dispute breaks out at the table, and the "Eurasian" shoots a Chinese player in the stomach. As the dying man coughs and falls over, Kipling writes that "all the tides of intense fear, hitherto held back by intenser curiosity, swept over my soul. . . . It was possible that the Chinamen would mistake me for the Mexican—everything horrible seemed possible just then." Kipling bolts up the stairs on "trembling" legs until he reaches the surface and experiences a final rush of terrified excitement: "I dared not run, and for the life of me I could not walk. I must have effected a compromise, for I remember the light of a street lamp showed the shadow of one half-skipping—caracoling along the pavements in what seemed to be an ecstasy of suppressed happiness. But it was fear—deadly fear. Fear compounded of past knowledge of the Oriental—only other white man—available witness—three stories underground—and the cough of the Chinaman now some forty feet under my clattering boot-heels."

"Only other white man." Kipling reconfirms his whiteness in China-town, but the presence, moreover, of a treacherous armed "Eurasian" in the subterranean den recalls the "black hole of Calcutta," or more recently the Sepoy rebels. As a Chinese fort, however, Kipling's "celestial" cellar also references the Opium Wars. This last association is particularly striking given his recent visit to the walled city of Canton, where Kipling saw the abandoned British guns of the second Opium War. His wounded and maimed Chinese figures—the poker player with the hole in his belly, the man in police custody "bleeding like a pig"—recall both the English atrocities of that war and Kipling's own sadistic investment in imaginatively repeating them.[69] Kipling here re-creates these imperial wars, symbolically risking his skin by confronting the enemies of empire and reemerging in one piece. The dangerous fun of his visit to an opium den and poker parlor thus serves as a precursor to the "great game" of empire that Kipling's most famous hero plays with such adolescent zest in *Kim*.[70]

Kipling's representation of opium den inhabitants as enemy soldiers almost completely overwhelms the other, more common role of the Chinese as workers. Or, more precisely, he cannot register Chinese labor as anything other than a military or police problem. Kipling describes the threatening "army" of Chinese that he hates so much in Malaysia as a troop of workers: "some of them sending block-tin to

Singapur, some driving fine carriages, others making shoes, chairs, clothes, and every other thing that a large town desires."[71] The use of military terms to describe labor reveals that in many imperial contexts the two fields overlapped; that is, military force helped to (re)produce and control the labor market at the time of the two Opium Wars and later during Chinese riots, mutinies, and plantation rebellions. Kipling himself described the use of military power to put down Chinese disturbances in the port of Singapore, and he further recalls such conflicts in San Francisco with his description of a policeman who escorts a bleeding Chinese man.

For Kipling, however, the revelation that the labor market in British Asia was a battlefield merely fed his fantasies of reenacting imperial combat. He describes the seemingly prodigious labor power of the Chinese as a secret weapon in their war against whites: "These people work and spread. . . . They pack close and eat everything and they can live on nothing. . . . They will overwhelm the world."[72] What he finds so upsetting is the seeming ability of Chinese emigrants to reproduce their labor power at a cheaper rate, and hence for lower wages, than other workers. The Chinese status as "cheap labor," Kipling claims, results from their innate disposition, what he calls their "devil-born capacity for doing more work than they ought."[73] By fetishizing Chinese labor power as some kind of racialized deviancy or freak of nature, Kipling simultaneously disavows the historical inequalities at the heart of the global economy and feeds the fear and loathing of the Chinese that sustained his rituals of mock battle and white reinforcement.

What is more, Kipling's hatred of the Chinese is overdetermined by discourses linking them to abject forms of sexuality. In this regard, the subterranean opium den represents a fantasy space of anal eroticism. Moreover, in Kipling's account this "anal" Chinese cellar has been deeply penetrated by the Chinese themselves, who the Anglo-Indian writer compares to a "pig-tail," an image that combines phallic and anal connotations. Finally, the implied comparison with the "black hole of Calcutta" further suggests that the opium den is a homoerotic space. Such references in part explain the fact that Kipling's fear seems to mimic sexual pleasure and dread. As he notes, he experienced competing waves of intense curiosity and foreboding. His fear, in fact, "seemed to be an ecstasy of suppressed happiness" over the prospect that "everything horrible seemed possible just then." And although the direct referent of this phrase concerns the possibility that he might be murdered, it also recalls circuitous statements about Chinese homosexuality, as when English observers accused the Chinese of "nameless vices," or of "a gross violation of every principle of morality and to the last degree insulting to our manhood." This reading places Kipling's intense hatred of the Chinese in a new light, suggesting that it is in part the expression of a racialized homosexual panic. According to Sedgwick, such panics are characteristic of "homosocial" societies that promote intense, affective relationships between men that stop short of same-sex desire. Homosocial societies, in other words, anxiously strive to police the border between homosocial and homosexual relationships, or between competitive male friendships and male-male sex. In my reading, Kipling participates in such policing by endeavoring to convert possible homoerotic desires into murderous homosocial battles between white and Chinese men. And finally, the opium writings of Wilde and Kipling further indicate that historically, English homosociality was embedded in the larger political economy of British imperialism in Asia.

Part II

Marijuana

CHAPTER 3

Anarchy in the USA

The Mexican Revolution, Labor Radicalism, and the Criminalization of Marijuana

Although the Mexican Revolution is conventionally dated to 1910–20, the complex histories of upheaval that the term marks exceed those temporal limits and extend throughout the twentieth century. Indeed, the next three chapters suggest that the historical preconditions for the present "War on Drugs" include Mexican revolutionary struggles and border rebellions as well as the socialist and anarchist labor discourses and practices that fanned out across the U.S. Southwest in their wake. Revolutionary and postrevolutionary Mexican immigration to the United States spurred marijuana criminalization in the 1930s and immigration continues to shape drug enforcement policies along the U.S.–Mexico border. In order to historicize the contemporary militarization of the border and the War on Drugs, then, we must revisit the Mexican Revolution.

Recently, scholars of Mexican history have called for studies of U.S. intervention in the revolution in ways that complicate or challenge the tendency to treat it as a discrete event sharply delimited by temporal and national borders. Daniel Nugent, the editor of *Rural Revolt in Mexico: U.S. Intervention and the Domain of Subaltern Politics,* argues that North American capitalists, colonists, and military forces have intervened in Mexico for more than a century, and that many rebellions in Mexico have directly opposed them.[1] A number of the volume's contributors support the claim that historically, Mexican rebellions have responded to, and in some cases directly opposed, U.S. imperialisms. John H. Coatsworth suggests, for instance, that U.S. intervention in

Mexico influenced the revolution in a number of ways: revolutionary peasant traditions were forged through prior nineteenth-century struggles against U.S. imperialism such as the Texas War of 1836–37 and the U.S. invasion of 1846–48; U.S. investments in Mexican agriculture helped to produce economic conditions that encouraged rebellion; and finally, the very "transformation of the U.S.-Mexican frontier into a border region capable of supplying and sustaining revolutionary armies" helped to make the revolution possible.[2] Similarly, John Mason Hart argues that U.S. investments in agriculture and especially mining fueled rebellions in northern Mexico that often took markedly nationalist and anti-imperialist forms.[3] And Rubén Osorio concludes on the basis of Pancho Villa's manifestos and letters that his attacks on the United States were partly guided by an anti-imperial ideology.[4]

Although U.S. interventions were an important part of the Mexican Revolution, Mexican immigrant "interventions" played an equally significant role in U.S. history, especially during the 1930s, the decade that I consider in this chapter and the next two. Partly shaped by U.S. imperialism, the Mexican Revolution in turn helped to reshape the United States in that it encouraged many Mexicans to go north. Revolutionary and postrevolutionary Mexican immigrant workers changed U.S. life in a number of ways. First, they helped to transform the U.S. political economy, including capitalist enterprises, labor markets, and labor organizations. In this context, I emphasize the impact of the numerous strikes in the mines, agricultural fields, and food-processing industries in the U.S. Southwest during the Depression, for Mexican immigrants, many of whom were influenced by revolutionary ideas and tactics, played prominent roles in these labor actions.

Second, Mexican immigrants inspired diverse representations in modernist and mass-produced art, including literature, painting, photography, film, and music. Paraphrasing the title of Helen Delpar's cultural history of the early decades of the twentieth century, in these years there was in the United States an enormous "vogue" for many "things Mexican," particularly folk performance traditions such as music, costume, and dance; handicrafts and murals; and all kinds of romantic, pastoral representations of rural Mexican life.[5] As a fresh set of dramatic historical events, moreover, the Mexican Revolution fascinated early-twentieth-century U.S. audiences. In the next chapter, I analyze in greater detail the influence of the Mexican presence in southern California on the popularity of early musical recordings and Hollywood films about the revolution. In the present chapter, however, I examine the modernist and mass-produced representations of Mexican labor in New Mexico that emerged in response to the revolution. Taken together, the fashion for things Mexican in the United States constituted a vast "image repertoire" of Anglo-American responses to Mexican immigrants, especially workers, in the wake of the revolution.[6] In contrast, Mexican immigrant workers in the United States used strikes, political theater, and musical performances in order to construct an oppositional repertoire of revolutionary images. At the same time, they used the mass media in similar ways, appropriating newspapers, photography, and musical recordings in the service of oppositional countermemory and action.

Finally, the revolution also significantly affected the course of U.S. politics, because the presence of new Mexican immigrants triggered state discourses and practices regarding U.S. citizenship, border control, and local and state police power. In their efforts to police the border and prevent the revolution from spilling over into the United States, officials developed a potent combination of anticommunist and anti-drug discourses. The criminalization of Mexican workers as marijuana smugglers and users in the 1930s suggests that the postrevolutionary Mexican presence in the United States provoked interrelated wars on marijuana and immigrant labor that continue to inform the contemporary war on drugs.

Here I propose to tell a part of that story by considering the effects of the Mexican Revolution on cultural production, labor relations, and drug enforcement in 1930s New Mexico. During the Depression in New Mexico, the local tourist economy largely depended on efforts by both artists and the state to contain postrevolutionary Mexican labor radicalism. Drawing upon revolutionary ideology and practice, Mexicans in New Mexico organized militant local chapters of the United Mine Workers, as well as the allied union of small landed farmers, agricultural workers, and unemployed railroad workers and miners called the League of Spanish-Speaking Workers. The strikes and other actions of such groups sparked a variety of responses that alternated between, on the one hand, a dread of rebellious, drug-smuggling Mexicans, and on the other hand, a utopian longing for a pastoral, precapitalist world without labor radicalism.

Representations of Mexican labor from the famous tourist centers and artist colonies of northern New Mexico generally pathologized rebellious

Mexicans and pastoralized docile ones. Although New Mexican art colonists deployed pastoral representations as part of a critique of mass culture and contemporary capitalist relations of production, many of their works actually resemble the vast body of mass-produced images of the U.S. Southwest, most notably the ephemeral yet ubiquitous visual culture associated with the regional tourist industries. In this way modernists were influenced by and in turn helped to influence an emerging Southwestern mass culture. Constructing romantic images of premodern Mexican laborers, both modernists and mass culture elided actual working conditions as well as the Mexican labor activists who persistently challenged those conditions. From such a perspective, the premodern pastoral Mexican worker became the telos or ideal by which contemporary Mexican labor radicalism was ideologically organized, judged, and policed. Such imagery ultimately helped to support a complementary penal colony in which Mexican workers who refused the pastoral ideal, or for whom this ideal was unavailable, were harshly disciplined by employers and the state.

Which is to say that representations of Mexicans are problematic not simply because they are inaccurate stereotypes, but rather because they had larger consequences in the world. Depictions of Mexican labor in effect constituted the cultural component of state discourses and practices. In order to promote tourism, the modern basis of the New Mexican economy, the state promoted idealized images of local labor relations while at the same time aggressively working to suppress labor organizing. State officials represented working-class Mexican men as threats to law and order in ways that complemented plans to make New Mexico safe for tourism and to police the local supply of "cheap," nonunion labor. Recalling the revolutionary context, Mexicans were simultaneously depicted as "bolsheviks" and "dope fiends." In fact, as applied to Mexicans, dominant U.S. discourses of antilabor red-baiting and marijuana criminalization are lasting legacies of the revolutionary period. As we shall see, these attempts to construct and contain Mexican male criminality were also part of a larger state strategy for promoting the new gendered division of labor that tourism seemed to require. Put another way, the criminalization of Mexican *men* tended by contrast to naturalize or normalize the tourist economy's dependence on the labor of Mexican *women*.

Although in this chapter I investigate dominant economic, cultural, and political discourses, I am especially interested in them as reactions to subaltern agency. Building on my previous discussion of Chinese immigrants during and after the Opium Wars, I attempt to trace the shaping presence of the postrevolutionary Mexican diaspora in U.S. culture and society. How have the movements and mobilizations of Mexican immigrants—including drug smugglers, revolutionaries, anarchists, and labor activists—influenced the intertwined histories of state power, capitalism, and the mass media in the modern United States? How have forms of Mexican resistance shaped cultural production or provoked responses from capitalists and the state? And how have Mexican immigrants worked within and against the terms of dominant institutions? To address this last question, I conclude by analyzing Mexican migrant uses of popular culture and modern mass media to contest their criminalization as communists and drug addicts. I thus suggest that the war on drugs in the 1930s also generated a struggle over mass culture that anticipates the contemporary drug war/media war nexus described in the Introduction.

BORDER BURROS

Although contemporary observers often treat drug smuggling across the U.S.–Mexican border as a novel fact of (post)modern life, the traffic in contraband is as old as the border itself. As soon as the border was redrawn at the conclusion of the U.S.–Mexican War in 1848, Mexicans and Indians took advantage of the arbitrary division, opportunistically crossing the border in one direction to raid and trade for horses, captives, and guns, and then recrossing into another national space to escape capture. Sometimes in collaboration, often in competition, Mexicans, Comanches, Apaches, and other Indians in the second half of the nineteenth century might, for example, attack a settlement in Arizona, New Mexico, or Texas, and then flee into the northern Mexican states of Sonora, Chihuahua, and Coahuila—or vice versa.[7] The postwar expansion of the new territory of Anglo-American political and economic modernity was, from the start, shadowed by a contraband traffic that undermined it.

These nineteenth-century *contrabandistas* thus did not simply cross the border—they used it to their advantage by making it a tool in their illicit trade. Indian and Mexican raiders and traders used the border in order to transgress state sovereignty and evade state market regulations and police powers. They thus operated in the interstices between the differently modernizing U.S. and Mexican states. These *contrabandistas* were so effective that they became a source of international conflict, starting with negotiations over the Treaty of Guadalupe Hidalgo in 1848, when Mexican officials insisted that the United States take responsibility for Indian raids into Mexico launched from U.S. territory. On the U.S. side, such conflicts culminated in the late 1860s, when federal officials claimed that Mexicans and Indians used Mexican territory as a base from which to launch attacks on Texas, and as a safe haven to return to, beyond the control of U.S. justice. Revolutionary upheaval, however, gave new impetus to the contraband trade. The production and distribution of marijuana and other drugs was in fact a significant source of employment for poor Mexicans on both sides of the border at a time when the revolution had disrupted many other economic activities. During the early decades of the twentieth century, large supplies of the drug were transported to the United States through border towns and major cities.[8] One of the most important of these contraband corridors was located along the Rio Grande, where New Mexico, Texas, and the Mexican state of Chihuahua meet. Following the Rio Grande, revolutionary-era narcotics traffic moved through Columbus, New Mexico, and the linked border towns of El Paso and Ciudad Juárez. This traffic employed hundreds of Mexicans in El Paso alone who worked as smugglers of liquor, cocaine, morphine, opium, and marijuana. Smugglers were drawn from the "working-class barrios of border towns" and organized around collaborative, geographically dispersed labor networks within the informal sectors of the transborder economy.[9] "Rank-and-file" members of loosely organized "contraband rings" smuggled drugs and bootleg alcohol from Juárez to El Paso, where the contraband was then transported by burro across the deserts of southern New Mexico and on to a variety of points north, west, and east. According to the Los Angeles newspaper *La Opinión*, by 1928 hundreds of Mexicans in El Paso were working as smugglers or "mules."[10]

A good example is Francisco Gómez, a Mexican who was living in El Paso when he was interviewed in 1929 for Manuel Gamio's study *The Life Story of the Mexican Immigrant*. Gómez told an interviewer that he alternated between jobs in borderland mines and agricultural fields, on the one hand, and smuggling contraband from Mexico to New Mexico, on the other. Recalling nineteenth-century *contrabandistas* who attempted to manipulate the border to their own advantage, Gómez crossed and recrossed the border in order to evade the U.S. draft during World War I and to escape from police officials who attempted to arrest him for smuggling. During one such escape Gómez even took part in a gun battle with U.S. rangers.[11] For U.S. officials, the work of Mexican smugglers epitomized the dangers of radicalized Mexican immigrant workers. The image of the *contrabandista*, in other words, served to organize and mediate discourses concerning Mexican labor as such. The drug smuggler's burro, in particular, would become symbolically central to Anglo-Americans, who produced a large number of images of other Mexican occupations also involving burros, such as farming, wood vending, and small-trade caravans. Similarly, as organized groups of Mexican workers, drug-smuggling associations or "contraband rings" suggested comparisons to radical Mexican labor unions. Furthermore, officials treated organized drug traffic between Old and New Mexico as a kind of criminal violence that overlapped with border banditry, "bolshevism," and ultimately the forms of labor radicalism that the Mexican Revolution inspired. This was partly because smugglers not only transported drugs from Mexico to the United States, but also moved weapons in the other direction.[12] The activist and 1930s radio personality Josefina Fierro, for example, remembers that her mother, a Mexican revolutionary,[13] used to smuggle guns from the United States to Mexico by hiding them in her daughter's baby carriage.[14] Because gun running and drug smuggling sometimes coincided, many Anglo-Americans treated marijuana traffic as an aspect of the revolution. Like gunrunning and so-called border banditry, drug smuggling became a privileged example of alleged Mexican tendencies toward lawlessness and revolutionary violence.

In fact, drugs on the border first appeared as a pressing U.S. problem during General John Pershing's punitive expedition in pursuit of Pancho Villa (1916–17), when it was estimated that thousands of the general's soldiers used narcotics while in Mexico. Also in the wake of Villa's attack, U.S. customs officials and the military aggressively endeavored to interdict traffic passing through Columbus, New Mexico, by illegally stopping and searching all trains and cars from Mexico and searching local private homes. As F. Arturo Rosales suggests, in the 1910s and 1920s "liquor and drug wars" involving competing smugglers and U.S. police powers "rivaled the border battles fought by political factions during the revolution." These contraband wars left numerous smugglers and border agents dead.[15] Throughout the Southwest, the police, border agents, and vigilante groups, including the Ku Klux Klan, increasingly targeted not only Mexican traffickers but also casual marijuana users for arrest, deportation, and beatings.[16] Coinciding with the period of Mexican revolutionary border battles, the (official and unofficial) war on drugs was part of an anxious U.S. counterinsurgency campaign whose ideologies and tactics deeply colored the state's subsequent efforts to contain Mexican labor radicals.

ART COLONIALISM AND MASS CULTURE

The contemporary practice of calling drug smugglers "mules" and "burros" goes back to the Mexican revolutionary and postrevolutionary period, when drug traffickers were named after the beasts of burden they used to transport contraband into the United States.[17] Curiously, after the revolution, the burro also became one of the most popular props in U.S. representations of Mexico and Mexicans. In all sorts of painting, photography, and commercial art, these burros, I would argue, bear the traces of revolutionary upheaval. Indeed, popular representations of burros could be seen as counterrevolutionary revisions of the Mexican *contrabandista*. Responding to the threat of revolution and rebellion condensed by the figure of the drug-smuggling burro, artists and tourists in New Mexico focused their attention instead upon fantasies of better-behaved beasts of burden. In the artist colonies and vacation centers of northern New Mexico, the burro became a figure for a romanticized Mexican worker, a fetish that disavowed postrevolutionary Mexican resistance to dominant Anglo-American labor relations.[18] The art colonists of northern New Mexico transformed the *contrabandista* burro of the revolutionary years into a sort of mascot, in other words, for the kinds of neocolonial Mexican service that both artists and the tourist industry imagined as attractive alternatives to modern capitalist labor relations in the rest of the country.

In the midst of strikes, red-baiting, police repression, and aggressive drug enforcement during the 1920s and 1930s, artists and producers of mass culture in New Mexico were seemingly obsessed with burros. As we shall see, starting roughly in the last decade of the nineteenth century, burros became a favorite photographic subject, while in the twentieth century they became a staple of picture postcards.[19] Postcards from the first third of the century often focus on burros bearing all sorts of burdens, but especially wood for sale. Singly and in bunches, with human drivers or by themselves, wood-laden burros were photographed, drawn, and painted for hundreds—perhaps thousands—of picture postcards. And despite the disdain of many art colonists for "standardized"

Early-twentieth-century postcard depicting burros.

mass culture, they embraced imagery that by 1900 was already a well-established staple of tourist kitsch.[20] Like other visitors to Santa Fe, Willa Cather wrote to Mary Austin on La Fonda Hotel stationery featuring a drawing of a Mexican man driving a wood-laden burro.[21] In her 1927 novel *Death Comes for the Archbishop*, Cather even incorporated a set piece concerning two beautiful burros, Angelica and Contento.[22] Burros are omnipresent in New Mexican literature: artist colony fixture Frank Applegate published several stories about the animals; Austin included a sketch of a Mexican man and his burro as the frontispiece to her *The Land of Journeys' Ending;* and Peggy Pond Church authored an illustrated children's book called *The Burro of Angelitos*.[23] Burros were particularly prominent in regional poetry. In her influential collection *Red Earth: Poems of New Mexico* (1921), Alice Corbin Henderson included a poem titled "Pedro Montoya of Arroyo Hondo," about a Mexican man and the burros he employs to vend wood,[24] while a number of the poems in *The Turquoise Trail: An Anthology of New Mexico Poetry,* compiled by Corbin Henderson in 1928, focus on burros and their humans.[25] Regional poet Lynn Riggs even produced a short tourist-promotion film called *A Day in Santa Fe* (1932) that was advertised in local papers as "featuring the Santa Fe burro."[26]

Representations of wood-bearing burros document, however fancifully, something important about the history of labor relations in New

Early-twentieth-century picture postcard of burros with Mexican drivers.

Mexico. In the late nineteenth and early twentieth centuries, many Mexicans made their living by harvesting wood and transporting it by burro to Santa Fe, where it was sold in the Plaza. To many Anglos, this seemed a picturesquely exotic or primitive practice, and so postcards, ads, and literature repeatedly figured wood-laden burros. But by 1920 or so such burros had already become something of an anachronism as Mexicans increasingly lost communal wood-gathering land to Anglo speculators and federal parks, and as more people in Santa Fe turned to coal, natural gas, and electricity to heat their homes. In such a context the burro bears not only wood but also nostalgic desires for forms of fuel that predate or sidestep the kinds of labor conflict that had come to characterize the local production of electricity in southern New Mexico, but especially the mining of coal near Santa Fe.

In an attempt to escape from mainstream U.S. culture—variously called "Babbitry," mass "standardization," or commercialization—refugees from the East and Midwest looked to New Mexico for alternative ways of life. After relocating to the state, painters who in the East had represented realist urban scenes instead painted colorful landscapes peopled with Mexican farmers and goatherds.[27] Such paintings include Victor Higgins's portrait of a Mexican goatherd called "The Widower" (1926); W. Herbert Dunton's "Pastor de Cabras" (1926); E. Martin Hennings, "The Goatherder" (1925); and John Sloan's "Threshing Floor,

Goats, Santa Fe, 1924 and 1945."[28] Fiction and poetry set in New Mexico represented similar scenes as in stories by Mary Austin about goat herding and cheese making in the village of Cuesta La Plata and Alice Corbin Henderson's poem about a shepherd, "Juan Quintana."[29] Writers and painters also idealized preindustrial forms of handicraft production, as in Austin and Applegate's manuscript, illustrated with Ansel Adams photos, about New Mexican artisans; Burt G. Phillips's painting *The Santero* (ca. 1930); and Ernest L. Blumenschein's painting of a Mexican artisan, *The Plasterer* (1921).[30] Reflecting artist colony disdain for mass production, Father Latour in Cather's *Death Comes for the Archbishop* is charmed by the carved *santos* he finds in Agua Secreta. As Cather writes, "[t]he wooden figures of the saints, found in even the poorest Mexican houses, always interested him. . . . They were much more to his taste than the factory-made plaster images in his mission churches in Ohio."[31] Many artists and writers were dedicated to preserving and promoting all kinds of Mexican handicrafts, including furniture; decorative tin, leather, and ironwork; embroidery, rugs, and weaving. To that end, in 1929 a number of colonists incorporated "The Spanish Colonial Arts Society," an organization that strove to "revive" New Mexican crafts by purchasing historic works and offering cash prizes for the best new productions.[32] During the Depression, a variety of government programs, including those sponsored by the Works Projects Administration (WPA), embraced the handicraft revival as a solution to the problem of Mexican unemployment in the state. As a result, by 1940 twenty-four government-sponsored craft schools were established in New Mexico.

Although Anglo handicraft proponents had good intentions, their plans tended to reproduce a racialized split in the local labor market, such that while whites were offered industrial or commercial job training, Mexicans were exclusively tracked into low-paying craft work. The average pay for such work was so low—about fifteen cents an hour— that most Mexicans avoided it whenever other employment options were available.[33] In contrast, art colonists tended to believe that Mexicans were naturally suited to craft work and the low standard of living it presupposed. Despite the obvious evidence to the contrary represented by the Mexican Revolution and postrevolutionary forms of labor activism, Mexicans were often figured as simple folk content to live at a subsistence level. As Corbin Henderson concludes in her poem about the wood vender, "Pedro Montoya of Arroyo Hondo— / If I envied any, I'd envy him! / With a burro to ride and a burro to drive, / There is hardly a man so rich alive."[34] Echoing Corbin Henderson, Austin argued that as a race Mexicans were characterized by "a type of holy poverty" and "have wantlessness for their inheritance." According to Austin, "The Mexican peon, once his pride of race is appeased by temples and pageants and general civic ostentation, wraps his *serape* around him and lies down on the ground to sleep. He makes a few necessary utensils, and makes them beautifully, pots, fabrics, baskets. The people release themselves in songs and dancing, in the making of pottery and manners; but the satisfaction is in the making, not the owning."[35] Austin seems nostalgic for a world before, as it were, the advent of modern capitalism, when "making" was more important than "owning." In her account, the artistic powers of the Mexican peon represent a critical alternative to a world of standardized mass production. Austin's emphasis on the Mexican's ability to make things "beautifully" is perhaps an improvement over contemporaneous accounts that focus on the squalor and ugliness of Mexican life. And yet the resemblance of Austin's picturesquely poor but happy Mexicans to the singing, dancing, "darkies" of Southern plantation iconography should make us question the critical force of art-colony nostalgia. Unhappy with the modern world, art colonists like Austin did not respond with calls for structural change but instead launched ultimately conservative programs for preserving "traditional" ways of life that centrally include the paternalist forms of servitude that have been historically associated with images of the hacienda and the plantation.

Indeed, the barefoot, straw hat–wearing Mexican boy with his burro recalls the similarly attired plantation "pickaninny." Revising the claims of George Rawick and David Roediger concerning white representations of blacks in the rural South, I would argue that "all of the old habits and styles of life so recently discarded by whites in the process of adopting capitalist values came to be fastened" onto Mexican workers, or in some cases their burro proxies. "The separation of work from the rest of life, the bridling of sexuality, the loss of contact with nature, the timing of labor by clocks rather than by sun and season, the injunction to save by postponing gratification"—in both modernist and mass cultural images, Mexican workers such as the wood vender were depicted as picturesque and exotic exceptions to these capitalist disciplines.[36] Such images promised Anglos a vacation from capitalist discipline by projecting idealized fantasies of Mexican service. Burros bore not only

Anglo mercantilist, Mexican driver, and burros "packed with everything imaginable" outside warehouse (ca. early twentieth century). Image 666 in Ilfeld Photograph Collection, New Mexico State Records Center and Archives, Santa Fe, New Mexico.

nostalgic longings for an older, "precapitalist" way of life but also fantasies about contemporary opportunities for exercising neocolonial power. If in 1930s New Mexico the wood vender and his burro were fast disappearing, in other words, his image continued to promote the kinds of neocolonial service relationships that helped to make Santa Fe and Taos such attractive destinations for artists and tourists alike.

The real counterparts of the shepherds featured in literature and paintings owned neither land nor herds, but instead leased both from large livestock concerns. The resulting form of livestock "sharecropping" effectively bound shepherds in debt to leasing companies. In 1935, for example, after thirty-five years under a sharecropping contract with the appropriately named "Bond Company," sheepherder Amarante Serna remained in debt and therefore tied to the company.[37] Even closer to artists' homes and studios, Mexicans served as day laborers, servants, cooks, and maids within a dual-wage service economy. In 1931, unskilled Mexican labor cost $2.50 to $3.00 a day, and skilled labor was valued at $6.00 to $9.00 a day—roughly two dollars less than the respective rates for white labor.[38] Art colonists often hired labor at these racialized rates to work in their homes as gardeners, handymen, cooks, maids, and washerwomen. And in many cases these same workers sat as models for painters and served as sources of folktales and songs for writers.[39] Pastoral representations of contented Mexican laborers thus not only obscured the struggles of organized labor in the mines and fields, as well as the state's brutal police response, as we shall see, but also romanticized nonindustrial, nonunion forms of neocolonial servitude.

Artist colony pastorals and picture postcards naturalized such servitude by obscuring its origin in human labor. Mexican workers were often compared to the livestock they tended, for example.[40] Frank Applegate even went so far as to posit a "profound, racially inherited understanding" between Mexicans and their burros.[41] More often, modernist and commercial artists naturalized Mexican labor by focusing exclusively on the burro half of the "burro plus Mexican" labor unit. The burro in the short artist colony film *A Day in Santa Fe,* for instance, travels from the mountains to Santa Fe alone, without a human driver, and delivers wood to buyers who place money in a box that he carries on his back. Like one-half of a souvenir "Burro and Mexican Boy" salt-and-pepper set, the burro is all that remains to represent the work of harvesting, transporting, and selling wood. *A Day in Santa Fe* is not unique in this regard, for numerous picture postcards depict wood-bearing burros by themselves, floating in odd isolation from human drivers. These magically autonomous beasts of burden work like fetishes that simultaneously mark and "disappear" human labor. Or, more precisely, in these postcards labor reappeared in the form of a pastoral image that effectively naturalized the conditions of Mexican servitude that they indirectly represented. In all of these ways, artist-colony pastorals about Mexican labor constituted a prophylactic "structure of feeling" that implicitly defended Anglo-Americans against the threat of revolutionary violence and labor radicalism by obsessively promoting fantasies of conflict-free service. As a conspicuous legacy of the recent history of revolution and rebellion, in other words, the cultural and political challenges posed by New Mexican labor activism helped to shape diverse art-colony and tourist representations in the 1930s.

As we shall see, historically, these pastoral images of docile Mexican workers were juxtaposed to representations of threatening and unruly Mexicans from the contemporaneous war on drugs. Together, these representations comprised the dominant ideological terms that practically regulated labor relations in early-twentieth-century New Mexico. Departing from analyses that condemn stereotypes without considering the concrete effects of their circulation, I argue that such imagery directly and indirectly supported state efforts to contain Mexican labor radicalism. Recalling modernist and mass cultural strategies, the state aggressively promoted a pastoral, conflict-free ideal for the employment of Mexicans even as it pathologized rebellious Mexicans. The state in fact often reasserted the differences between these two visions as a means of social control, such that official representations of rebellious Mexican workers were wielded as a sort of weapon to help define, police, and hopefully reproduce a more pliable labor pool. And although the art colonies were not a direct arm of the state, after the revolution regional modernists, producers of mass culture, and the agents of the state nonetheless jointly shaped discourses and practices concerning Mexican labor.

AX-MURDERING MARIJUANA FIEND ATTACKS ART COLONY

The two modes of representing Mexicans just described converge in particularly revealing ways in the remarkable career of Santa Fe art colonist and tourism promoter Ina Sizer Cassidy. Working from her rehabbed adobe home on Canyon Road, Cassidy sold Indian and Mexican artifacts and crafts, edited the "Art and Literature" page of the *Santa Fe New Mexican,* and wrote a regular arts column for *New Mexico Magazine.* In addition to other official appointments, Cassidy was also the state director for the Federal Writers' Project (FWP). As director she supervised research for *New Mexico: Guide to the Colorful State,* a work that she hoped would make New Mexico "accessible to the traveler."[42] On the one hand, Cassidy was typical of art colonists who promoted a pastoral vision of New Mexico that largely avoided direct reference to the region's labor conflicts. Under her direction, for example, FWP publications featured numerous representations of burros and their Mexicans,[43] and, like many of her contemporaries, she had herself photographed with a burro and its Mexican tender.[44] On the other hand, as an enthusiastic member of the local chapter of the Daughters of the American Revolution (DAR), Cassidy probably shared some of the views of the state officials who used anticommunist ideologies to police Mexican labor radicals. The Santa Fe chapter of the DAR, for example, officially endorsed the teargassing of Mexican labor activists suspected of being "communists."[45] And in 1950, when Cassidy served as her chapter's official historian, the group unanimously passed resolutions in support of both federal immigration quotas and the House Committee on Un-American Activities. It also urged Congress to publish and distribute a pamphlet called *100 Things You Should Know about Communism*.[46]

The tourist guide that Cassidy helped to produce, however, muted such reactionary sentiments in favor of familiar forms of pastoralism, including a photo captioned "Wood Hauler with Burros."[47] Although strikes and state oppression were dramatic facts of everyday life in New Mexico, in a chapter titled "Industry, Commerce, and Labor" the guide notes that "The growth of industry and commerce has not been extensive enough to affect greatly the essential economic and social aspects of the native people, who are naturally agricultural and pastoral" (90–91). Despite evidence to the contrary, the guide incredibly concludes that Spanish-speaking workers lacked the "knowledge" and "articulate leadership" (91–92) necessary for labor organizing. In subsequent editions, the chapter's title was changed from "Industry, Commerce, and Labor" to "Industry, Commerce, and Science," and all references to labor were deleted.[48]

Similarly, the guide mostly sidesteps the marijuana "problem" and its connection to labor issues. The word is mentioned once, in a chapter about New Mexico's contributions to American English, where the guide defines marijuana simply as an "herb of the hemp family intoxicating in its effect when smoked" (115). In one other spot the text vaguely references public concerns over marijuana traffic and migrant labor when it reminds the reader that as a "border state" New Mexico is "faced with the familiar border problems of smuggling, illicit immigration and the like." The next sentence, however, brushes aside such problems by instead stressing the exhilarating pleasures of cross-cultural mixing: "The exchange of spiritual and other influences is always in process—a condition which adds an interesting international flavor to the scene" (4). *New Mexico: A Guide to a Colorful State* elides the forms of economic inequality that supported tourism by instead elaborating examples of cultural exchange. While official antidrug discourses attempted to make the Mexican laborer appear before the law—to construct him as visible to the policing gaze of the state—the FWP guide strives to dissolve the potentially rebellious worker and leave only a trace.

In her unpublished short story about Mexican marijuana use, "The Smoke of a Thousand Dreams," however, Cassidy articulated some of the conflicts and contradictions that the *Guide* attempted to mute. The story is set in the northern New Mexican village of Chimayo, on the heavily touristed "high road" from Santa Fe to Taos. Chimayo was famous among artists and tourists for a number of reasons: for its fine woven blankets, its beautiful adobe church (restored in the 1930s with the help of Mary Austin and Frank Applegate), and its uniquely tasty chile, all of which receive glowing mention in *New Mexico: Guide to a Colorful State*. The *Guide* describes Chimayo in pastoral terms: "In the fall when the shimmering gold of the cottonwoods contrasts with strings of scarlet chile that drape the houses, the harvesting of crops is carried on, and grain is threshed on primitive threshing floors with goats and horses tramping it out" (298). This view of the harvest, particularly the strings of drying red chile hanging from the walls of adobe houses, recalls numerous picture postcards, and chile plays an important role in Cassidy's story.

The tale concerns Feliz Pavo, a Mexican sheepherder and wood vender, complete with a burro, and his wife, Marietta. Although by local standards the couple is prosperous, Marietta is dissatisfied with their diet and demands red meat. One day while on his way to the local butcher, Pavo sees a stranger who offers him a suspicious cigarette. Under the drug's influence Pavo begins to suffer delusions of grandeur, believing that the governor has appointed him mayor. Before leaving to meet the governor, Pavo maniacally resolves to hang strings of chiles to dry from the walls of their adobe house, even though Marietta tells him there is none. He quickly grabs an ax and starts shouting for more chile. Finally, Pavo runs at his wife with an upraised ax and shouts: "Red meat is it you want? I bring you the red meat." The next day a neighbor comes to visit Pavo and discovers "hanging on a bare space among the chile, long red hair attached to the head of a woman! 'It was the marijuana, the smoke of a thousand dreams,' whispered the neighbors."[49]

This image of an ax-murdering marijuana fiend hacking through the pastoral picture condenses a host of Anglo-American concerns and obsessions about Mexican labor in the wake of the Mexican Revolution. From one angle, "The Smoke of a Thousand Dreams" figures Anglo-American fears of revolutionary violence that Mexican immigration to the United States helped to provoke. Because the story incorporates into a New Mexican pastoral a character drawn from sensational antimarijuana discourses, "The Smoke of a Thousand Dreams" also references counterrevolutionary campaigns to police Mexican workers by criminalizing marijuana. Cassidy's tale indirectly registers what art-colony

H-4462   A MEXICAN HOME, NEW MEXICO

Early-twentieth-century picture postcard, "A Mexican Home, New Mexico."

pastorals generally tried to deny: the fact that romanticized forms of service coexisted alongside the heavy-handed deployment of state police power. More precisely, the tale reminds us that the picturesque representations of burros, chiles, and adobe that tended to naturalize servitude all depended on the violent state repression and criminalization of Mexican laborers—in other words, the artist colony depended on a penal colony. In these ways, "The Smoke of a Thousand Dreams" remains as the phobic trace of the neocolonial labor relations at the center of the New Mexican tourist industries and artist colonies.

Land of Disenchantment: Mexican Labor, Marijuana Criminalization, and the Tourist State

Although contemporary corporate prisons and prison labor have recently attracted critical attention, the longer history of such developments is sometimes overlooked. Historically, in New Mexico, as in other parts of the United States, state police power has been directly and indirectly imbricated with capitalist interests. Before the New Deal, the New Mexican state penitentiary in Santa Fe routinely rented inmates, most of them Mexicans, to local farmers.[50] As an indirect subsidy to the burgeoning tourist industries of New Mexico, Mexican prisoners were also employed to build and maintain roads.[51] Inmates further supported the largest brick factory in the West, a facility that supplied bricks for state and commercial uses, including in popular tourist institutions like the La Fonda Hotel on the Santa Fe Plaza.[52] Under the New Deal, however, the deliberately fuzzy line between prisons and capitalism was redrawn, at least on paper. In 1934, the federal government effectively outlawed the use of prison labor in competition with nonprison labor. After 1934, in other words, the state was to be the sole consumer of the goods and services that inmates produced. Thus, during the second half of the 1930s, New Mexican prisoners made bricks only for new prison buildings or other state structures such as public schools. However, even after the New Deal's ban on the commercial use of prison labor, police powers continued to directly and indirectly support commercial agriculture, mining companies, and tourist industries by controlling local labor activism.

During the Depression, federal and state officials aggressively policed Mexican labor as part of a larger effort to promote tourism in New Mexico.[53] In the 1930s, federal efforts led to the routing of Route 66 through the heart of tourist attractions in northern New Mexico, as well as to the composition of *New Mexico: A Guide to the Colorful State.*[54] At the local level, Governor Clyde Tingley spearheaded tourist promotion by creating the New Mexico State Tourist Bureau in 1935.[55] As its director Joseph Bursey explained, the Bureau was like a Chamber of Commerce, publicizing the state's "resources" to tourists and possible investors in mining, agriculture, and livestock.[56] Tourism also contributed directly to state spending power by generating sales and gas tax revenues.[57] This combination of financial interests convinced federal and state officials to dramatically expand New Mexico's economic dependence on tourism during the 1930s. Such officials often promoted cheap, pliable Mexican labor as one of the state's greatest "resources." New Mexico was often publicized, for example, as an exotic escape from class conflict in other parts of the United States. Both the state and commercial enterprises thus attempted to make New Mexico attractive to visitors by in effect promoting pastoral visions that recall the power of similar art-colony imagery.[58] And, as my discussion of the *Guide* suggests, in some cases government officials collaborated with artists in order to depict the state as a sort of preserve of natural beauty and cheap labor, unmarred by organized protest.

The response of many Mexicans to low wages and horrible working conditions, however, threatened this image. Conflicts in the village of Madrid are a case in point. A short drive from Santa Fe, Madrid's annual

Christmas display attracted more than a hundred thousand visitors a year.[59] The main employer in Madrid, the Albuquerque and Cerrillos Coal Company, sponsored the display, but the miners themselves were required to mount the show and contribute 2 percent of their wages to pay for the lights.[60] Madrid's Christmas display, argues Richard Melzer, was part of a self-conscious strategy to contain labor activism by keeping workers safely occupied while not in the mines. Moreover, like the state's tourist promotions, "the firm was preoccupied with the town's image because it realized that if labor troubles ever plagued Madrid it would be extremely beneficial to have the public's sympathy on the company's side. Newspaper reporters, politicians and labor review boards might remember Madrid as a peaceful, patriotic and unified town where trouble could be caused only by outside radicals who were intent on destroying everything that was still good in America."[61]

The labor struggles in Madrid were perceptively represented by Margaret McKittrick, a member of the Santa Fe artist colony who in 1935 worked with local miners to compose a photo exposé of working conditions called "Lights over Madrid, New Mexico." A rare example of cross-cultural collaboration, the photos represent the potential of an alternative regional modernism to critically foreground labor exploitation. The collections contrasted a photo of soaring angels mounted high atop telephone poles to a close-up shot of "scrip," the currency the company used to advance credit to its workers. Miners were paid by the tons of coal they produced, but the company routinely deducted more than half of their wages to pay for work supplies, rent for deplorable shacks, and coal for home use. Many miners were forced to draw scrip against future wages and redeem the tokens in the company store. Company president Oscar Huber pursued this practice because he believed that personal debt increased productivity and bound workers to the mines. As a result, according to Melzer, "a system of industrial debt peonage developed."[62] By juxtaposing photos of the Christmas display and scrip, McKittrick and her worker-collaborators thus suggested that the angelic image of flight and free movement literally depended on the control and immobilization of Mexican miners. The photo exposé makes a similar point with a photo captioned "The New Bethlehem." In the center of the photo is a portion of the Christmas display, a large model of Bethlehem framed on one side by a miner's decrepit wooden shack and on the other by a primitive privy. Here the picturesque "little town of Bethlehem" rubs up against the reality of the company town's wretched living arrangements. Poor housing, combined with low wages and dangerous working conditions, led the miners of Madrid to strike in 1936.[63]

The Madrid workers were not alone, for throughout the 1930s Mexican miners launched strikes and other forms of protest at or near major stops on state promotional maps. In 1933, Mexican coal miners walked out of mines in Gallup, a town also famous in the tourist literature for its annual "Inter-tribal Indian Ceremonials." Two years later, Gallup once again drew national attention as the site of a bloody clash between Mexican workers and the police that left two people dead. In 1936, Mexican miners at Terrero, less than twenty miles from Santa Fe, went on strike. There were similar strikes in the mines of Dawson, north of Taos, and at the El Paso Electric Company to the south.[64] The League of Spanish-Speaking Workers was also active in the area. Inspired by Mexican anarchists and revolutionaries and founded with Industrial Workers of the World (IWW) help in the beet fields of southern Colorado in 1928, the League had more than eight thousand members in Santa Fe, Gallup, Las Vegas, and numerous smaller villages.[65] In 1935, the union protested against attempts by the governor of Colorado to establish a border blockade against migrant farmworkers entering the state from New Mexico. Similarly, the union helped to defeat a 1935 criminal syndication bill that would have made it even harder to organize workers. And although it had agricultural origins, La Liga actively supported striking miners in Gallup, Madrid, and Terrero, and also organized miners and others to press the state for expanded relief spending and increased taxes on large landowners. Mexican labor activism of this sort threatened to spoil the state's publicity campaigns and to scare off potential tourists and investors.

Management, state officials, and many of their public supporters agreed that as dangerous "outside agitators" and "alien communists," these striking Mexican workers called for a remorseless police response.[66] In each case, members of the state militia served as strikebreakers, beating, teargassing, arresting, and in some cases killing Mexican workers.[67] The governor regularly deployed the militia to break strikes, as he did during the Madrid and Terrero actions.[68] One year later, in 1937, Tingley called in the state police to "disperse" a union delegation of men, women, and children who had occupied his Santa Fe office and demanded jobs, relief, and increased taxes on the rich. The police teargassed the protesters and arrested eight. That evening the League distributed fliers calling for a mass protest meeting the next day in the Santa Fe Plaza, a favorite destination for tourists as well. Under the boldly lettered heading "GASSED!!! BECAUSE THEY WERE HUNGRY! BECAUSE THEY ASKED FOR WORK!" the flyer declares that "Tingley is a friend of the rich, a servant of the big landowners. He serves his masters well—with tear-gas and arrests!"[69]

As the public response to the League's sit-down strike reveals, in practice anticommunist discourse was gendered and racialized, for it was implied that the term *communist* was a euphemism for a dangerous class of Mexican men. When the Associated Press wire service reported Tingley's actions against a group that he told reporters were "communists," his office was flooded with letters of support, including notes of commendation from the Santa Fe Chamber of Commerce and from Ward Hicks, president of the advertising firm that handled the state's tourism promotions.[70] Although women were often directly involved in union actions, including the sit-down strike in the governor's office, by describing the dangers posed by Mexican workers in terms implicitly coded as conventionally masculine, critics constructed wage work and labor activism as exclusively male endeavors. Tingley's supporters further used language drawn from the lexicon of racial disgust and military conflict to describe strikers, calling them a "lawless, un-American gang" of "dirty" "varmints," domineering "invaders," and "roughneck" "communists." By contrast, supporters applauded the governor's "intestinal courage" and "firm" "stand" in defense of national "dignity," while several letter writers commended Tingley for compelling the upstart "aliens" to "respect" American "law and order." As if rewriting scenes from *The Birth of a Nation,* these letter writers, I would argue, imagined the governor as a white knight who protected U.S. "dignity" from the racial and sexual threat posed by dangerous brown men. Such fantasies corresponded to a larger environment of racial terror that often rivaled Jim Crow. State police efforts to "clean up" "alien communists" were buttressed both by heavy-handed private security forces and self-described anticommunist vigilante groups who dressed in white sheets and hoods.[71] As F. O. Matthiessen wrote after witnessing state and vigilante efforts to bust New Mexican unions, "more and more the term Communist is being applied, vaguely but with harmful results, to the slightest divergence [of Mexican labor organizations] from Republican or Democratic party politics."[72]

Although contemporary Mexican labor activism was its most immediate cause, the "red scare" of the 1930s was also a legacy of the Mexican
revolutionary struggles along the border from about 1910 to 1920. During these years, U.S. papers reported on anti-American sentiment in
Mexico and the threat to U.S. lives and property posed by what New
Mexican state senator Albert Bacon Fall called "wild Bolshevists."[73] As
Alan Knight has argued, the United States repeatedly intervened in
Mexico in an effort to "deradicalize" the revolution by checking agrar-
ian land reform and the nationalization of oil and railroads—policies
that threatened U.S. investments.[74] The fear that the revolution represented Mexican labor's attack on U.S. capital led Fall to propose the
invasion of Mexico in 1913.[75] The urgency of this demand for U.S. military intervention may in part have stemmed from the concern that, as a
border state, New Mexico was acutely vulnerable to revolutionary movements. New Mexican statehood was postponed for more than sixty
years after it was first made a U.S territory in 1851. With a large population of often rebellious Indians and Mexicans, New Mexico was, in
effect, deemed not white enough for incorporation as a state until
1912.[76] At the beginning of the Mexican Revolution, then, the territory
was only newly and insecurely affixed to the United States, and Mexican "bolshevism," it was feared, threatened to unfix it.

The border conflicts that characterized the years immediately following statehood further fueled fears that New Mexico might become
engulfed in revolutionary violence against capitalism and private property. The U.S.–Mexican border zone was an important site for the production and dissemination of revolutionary ideology and practice directed
at state-supported capitalisms on both sides of the border.[77] Although
many critics called them "communists" or "bolsheviks," the diverse group
of guerrilla fighters, saboteurs, labor organizers, and strikers that made
up the borderland revolutionary forces had a variety of known and un-
known interests and ideologies in mind. However, anarcho-syndicalist
discourses and practices seem to have been especially compelling to
border Mexicans.[78] Anarcho-syndicalists called for the formation of
international proletarian solidarities in order to launch a millennial war
against state-sponsored capitalism; they attacked private property and
the state's protection of it; they promoted governance from below, including calls for direct action such as general strikes, industrial sabotage,
and violent confrontation; and they encouraged the collective ownership of property and a mutual aid ethic.[79] Unlike communists, who

strove to destroy capitalism by seizing state power, anarcho-syndicalists argued that because state power inevitably supported capitalist exploitation, workers should oppose the state with labor unions as alternative units of social organization. Their critique of state territorial sovereignty and promotion of international alliances would have been attractive to Mexicans, whose interests often crossed national borders and clashed with state efforts to police them. Moreover, anarcho-syndicalist constructions of the union or party as a means for engaging in clandestine guerrilla warfare and sabotage were tactically well suited to the conditions of poor Mexican workers with meager resources for fighting and organizing. For similar reasons, an ethical emphasis on communalism and mutual aid resonated with Mexicans, particularly immigrants, who had long organized *mutualistas* to support neighbors in need.

Working-class Mexicans remobilized such discourses and practices in a variety of forms. The most important anarcho-syndicalist organization in the U.S. Southwest was the Partido Liberal Mexicano (PLM). The party was cofounded by Ricardo Flores Magón, a Mexican critic of the Díaz regime who attempted to foment revolution while in exile along the border, first in Los Angeles and then in San Antonio. Starting in 1910, the PLM publication, *La Regeneración,* edited by Magón and with a circulation of more than twenty-five thousand throughout the borderlands, was dedicated to revolution in Mexico and, increasingly, to anarcho-syndicalist approaches to the labor problems of Mexican workers in the United States. The radical revolutionary turn by PLM members toward labor conditions in the United States was most dramatically signified by a document called the "El Plan de San Diego," named for the town in south Texas where it was supposedly signed. In the words of Emilio Zamora, the document called for the formation of "an anarcho-syndicalist order in revolutionary alliance with oppressed peoples throughout the Americas."[80] More specifically, the document proposed a revolutionary coalition of Mexicans, blacks, and Japanese in order to fight "Yankee tyranny"; the execution of all Anglo males over the age of sixteen; the establishment of independent republics in the Southwestern states, including New Mexico, that were taken from Mexico by "North American imperialism"; and finally, the collectivization of all private property.

In hundreds of incidents between 1915 and 1916 in the lower Rio Grande Valley of south Texas, Plan adherents called "los sediciosos" tore up railroad tracks, burned bridges, sabotaged irrigation pumps, raided ranches, and skirmished with U.S. Army units and Texas Ranger patrols. In these years, the valley was "a virtual war zone" where Mexican revolutionary, anti-imperial attacks on Texas were met by a ruthless counterinsurgency that combined white nativist vigilantes, the Texas Rangers, and various state militias.[81]

At the same time that these anarchist rebellions raged in Texas, Pancho Villa threatened to bring his wing of the Mexican Revolution to New Mexico. In 1916, Villistas executed eighteen U.S. mining engineers in the adjacent Mexican state of Chihuahua, and in the same year another group attacked the U.S.-owned International Mining Company, robbed the company store, and kidnapped the superintendent, the company doctor, and several employees.[82] Most spectacularly, in March of that year Villa's forces raided the town of Columbus, New Mexico. The raiders, who themselves suffered more than two hundred casualties, killed eighteen U.S. soldiers and civilians, wounded many others, looted several merchants, and proceeded to reduce much of the town's business district to rubble. Images of the destruction circulated in U.S. papers and as popular postcards, including one captioned "Ruins of Commercial Hotel, Columbus, N.M., in which 6 Americans were killed and their bodies cremated."[83] More than twenty years later, the raid was still a raw memory for local Anglos, as Federal Writers' Project workers discovered when they interviewed them about Villa.[84] Framed as bandits and bolshevists, Mexican revolutionaries were criminalized as communists in ways that foreshadowed and shaped subsequent reactions to Mexican labor radicals during the Great Depression.

The connection that many Anglos made between the Mexican Revolution and New Mexican labor activism was partly justified by the fact that the revolution influenced many of the Mexicans who migrated to the U.S. Southwest to work in the mines and fields. During the revolution, different kinds of direct action—including guerrilla raids, sabotage, and strikes—were integrally connected, composed of similar leaders, overlapping rank-and-file constituencies, and radical ideologies. Revolutionary forces, particularly in the north, included large numbers of agricultural workers and miners—jobs that in the United States were increasingly occupied by radicalized, postrevolutionary Mexican immigrants.[85] By the time of the Depression, after the brutally successful U.S. military offensive against border rebellions and the end of the revolution, many Mexican immigrants to the United States stopped calling for armed rebellion but preserved elements of anarchist ideologies and practices, transforming them for new contexts. Historians of Los Angeles and south Texas have shown that many borderland anarchists active in the 1910s became Southwestern labor organizers in subsequent decades, and I would argue that northern New Mexican labor organizations suggest similar continuities.[86] The League of Spanish-Speaking Workers' occupation of Governor Tingley's office, for example, combined elements of anarcho-syndicalist discourses and practices, including militant direct action against the state, attacks on private property, and a communal ethic represented by demands for the redistribution of wealth through taxation and relief.

Although some League activists were New Mexican natives, others were recent immigrants from northern Mexico who had participated in revolutionary struggles. Born in the northern state of Chihuahua, League leader Jesús Pallares joined Madero's revolutionary forces as a young man and fought for four years before getting wounded and mustering out in 1915. Shortly thereafter he legally immigrated to New Mexico where he worked as a miner at most of the state's labor hot spots, including Dawson (where he went on strike with anarchist coworkers), Gallup, and finally Madrid, where in 1934 he founded and served as vice president of the local chapter of the United Mine Workers (UMW), a union that organized four strikes over the following two years. The same year that he helped establish the UMW in Madrid, Pallares also joined the League and helped to mount successful protests against antiunion legislation. Eventually, he was evicted from company housing in Madrid (a common strikebreaking practice, dramatically represented in the 1950 film *The Salt of the Earth*, about a miners' strike in New Mexico), jailed by a federal immigration inspector, and charged with "communist" activity. In a confidential letter to the federal secretary of labor, Governor Tingley argued that because the League was "the New Mexican branch of the Communist organization," their leader should be immediately deported. Tingley's wish was granted in 1936, when the INS deported Pallares for supposedly advocating the violent overthrow of the U.S. government.[87]

This kind of red-baiting was one strategy among many for gaining control over the legacies of the Mexican Revolution in the United States. In order to justify state intervention in labor disputes during the Depression, both management and the state pathologized Mexican laborers, reinterpreting Mexican resistance as a sign that certain brown bodies were inherently "anarchic" and in need of discipline. A good example is the criminalization of marijuana, a labor-control tactic that overlapped with red-baiting by similarly focusing on brown bodies out of control. In the years immediately following the revolution, nearly every state west of the Mississippi passed laws regulating marijuana. And in 1937 New Mexico was among a group of western states that successfully pressured the federal government to consider a national law, the Marihuana Tax Act of 1937.[88] The resulting criminalization of marijuana in effect gave the state additional power to police Mexican immigrants and labor activists.

The hearings for the act indicate that it was specifically directed at Mexican workers.[89] As if to reinforce the drug's popular link to Mexicans, witnesses generally used the Spanish *marijuana* rather than the Latin word *cannabis,* which, along with "Indian hemp," was the preferred term in the influential and often cited late-nineteenth-century British imperial investigation into the weed's uses among workers in India. Experts in the 1930s translated prior, British-colonial usage into Spanish, as it were, in response to a related yet distinct labor context in the U.S. Southwest. Witnesses for marijuana criminalization repeatedly explained that the legally designated term *marijuana* was a *Mexican* Spanish word. Dr. W. C. Woodward, legislative counsel for the American Medical Association, even compared it to an illegal alien by arguing that "the term 'marihuana' is a mongrel word that has crept into this country over the Mexican border."[90]

During five days of testimony, several influential themes of marijuana discourse emerged: the drug was a Mexican import now well established in the U.S. Southwest; marijuana use was especially common among male laborers, who became murderers and rapists after smoking it; Mexican marijuana dealers sold the drug to white schoolchildren; and finally, marijuana was spreading from the Southwest to the rest of the nation.[91] Marijuana supposedly removed inhibitions and unleashed the most primitive physical impulses. Or, as the FBI warned, the marijuana user "becomes a fiend with savage or 'cave man' tendencies."[92] In the case of migrant laborers, according to the hearings, the drug thus exaggerated or perverted the "natural" characteristics of Mexicans, the primitive, impulsive, childish, and yet hardworking people imaginatively projected by employers and tourist promotions.[93] The prodigious reserves of energy expended in acts of drug-induced violence supposedly subtracted from the sum of productive labor, and so, according to this calculus, the marijuana fiend became a deranged and useless farm or mining machine. Moreover, in an effort to substantiate the threat that marijuana posed to the United States, witnesses testified to the remarkable productivity of Mexican growers in the Southwest, who reportedly cultivated tons of the drug every year.[94] This kind of illicit agricultural work, witnesses implied, represented potentially valuable, yet ultimately misdirected or wasted, labor power. Before both the law and the boss, then, the male Mexican worker was only visible as a physical manifestation of force, either for labor, criminal commerce, or random acts of violence. Because the hearings positioned Mexican men as powerful, yet potentially unruly, reserves of labor power, they seemed to justify state support for union busting and the intimidation of workers.

The history of marijuana criminalization indicates the close relationship between state and capitalist methods for controlling Mexican workingmen. In each context, Mexicans were constructed as valuable, yet volatile, concentrations of physical force that had to be disciplined and regulated. Both employers and the police posited Mexican men as targets of what Michel Foucault called "biopower." Foucault defined two, related kinds of biopower. The first centers on "the body as a machine . . . [and] its integration into systems of efficient and economic controls." The second focuses on "the species body . . . as the basis of the biological processes," including "propagation, births and mortality, the level of health, life expectancy and longevity." With the term *biopower,* Foucault referred to a variety of techniques for "the subjugation of bodies and the control of populations." He concluded that these two forms of biopower were indispensable to the development of capitalism, which "would not have been possible without the controlled insertion of bodies into the machinery of production and the adjustment of the phenomena of population to economic processes. . . . [Capitalism] had to have methods of power capable of optimizing forces, aptitudes, and life in general without at the same time making them more difficult to govern."[95] Elsewhere, Foucault reminded us, as Aihwa Ong has written, "that some forms of modern power cannot be attributed directly to the reproduction of capitalist relations and labor power."[96] Here, however, he suggests that while the deployment of biopower functioned to discipline bodies and control populations across various social fields, such techniques were particularly suitable for managing labor. Such was the case in 1930s New Mexico, where deployments of biopower by capitalists, the state, and modernists converged over Mexican bodies. In each of these interrelated discursive spheres, images of rebellious or anarchic

Mexicans justified draconian efforts to discipline workers while pastoral images of pliable Mexicans suggested dominant idealizations of subjugated bodies and controlled populations.

Recalling artistic representations and official discourses that implicitly positioned Mexican rebels as threats to racial and sexual purity, the federal marijuana hearings constructed Mexican men as the polymorphously perverse, consolidating other to institutionalized white, heteronormative patriarchy. Ruled by animal impulses, the Mexican migrant of the hearings threatened to violate all sexual prohibitions. Not only was he deemed a rapist, but it was also suggested that the Mexican migrant "seduced" girls and boys with marijuana. Witnesses for the state obsessively returned to seemingly pedophilic scenarios in which Mexican men offered marijuana to white schoolchildren. They tried to provoke forms of visceral disgust when they implied, for example, that Mexican marijuana smoking "spreads" like a sexually transmitted disease. Some witnesses even gave Mexican marijuana a sort of phallic agency by describing the drug's "invasion" or "penetration" of the nation.[97] In these ways, the antimarijuana hearings, like anticommunist rhetoric, constructed Mexican workers as violent brown male bodies out of control. The construction of Mexican men as sexually transgressive or abnormal not only masculinized and demonized Mexican labor activism but also served, by contrast, to legitimate and normalize Anglo masculinity.

The masculinization and sexual pathologization of Mexican workers has added implications for the representation of Mexican women. The masculine focus of anticommunist and antidrug discourses made Mexican men hypervisible while at the same time obscuring the work and activism of Mexican women. This preoccupation with male workers partially reflected middle-class Anglo-American notions of separate spheres that the work of Mexican women contradicted. Although women did not usually work in the mines or on the railroad, they nonetheless engaged in forms of labor that made Mexican male wage labor possible and that many Anglo-Americans coded as "male." In the small, rural villages of the Rio Grande Valley, women performed work in the home cooking, cleaning, and caring for children, but also outside, working the fields, tending animals, harvesting crops, and selling farm products. Much of this work was subsistence production; however, women also produced goods for the market, including many kinds of produce, but especially chile. The area's most important commercial crop, chile was produced through a system of sharecropping. Three large mercantile companies advanced seeds to small growers and, after harvest, paid for the produce by extending company store credits to farmers. In these stores, subsistence goods bought on credit cost about 10 percent more than already inflated cash prices. The result was forms of debt bondage that centrally involved the women who contributed most of the labor that went into chile production, including sowing, thinning, weeding, cultivating, and picking the chile; stacking, sorting, and stringing it to dry; and in some cases marketing it to local merchants. At harvesttime, chile production served as an important source of wage labor for village women, who earned about a dollar a day during the two- to three-week season.[98] Such female labor vanishes, however, in state discourses that focus solely on male workers, or in picture postcards or stories depicting the finished product of stringed chiles.

In addition to harvesting and marketing chile, women increasingly worked for wages as maids and cooks, often servicing the artist colonies and the burgeoning tourist industry. Rachel Sánchez Olivas, for example, recalls that as a girl growing up in a small New Mexican village, she worked in the house and on the farm in order to help her parents, who grew alfalfa and chile, but who also worked at the Fred Harvey and Hilton Hotels in nearby Albuquerque. Reflecting on her different daily tasks in a 1980s interview, Sánchez Olivas noted that such work turned her into a "tomboy" and she concluded that "I was a boy and I was a girl."[99] Rosaura Sánchez's analysis of gender politics in nineteenth-century California is apt here, for she notes that, as in New Mexico, labor relations on small *Californio* farms disturbed dominant assumptions about gender difference. Many Mexican and European visitors, according to Sánchez, were struck by the fact that women not only performed tasks traditionally assigned to women, such as weaving, sewing, and cheese making, but also those coded as male, such as tending livestock and cutting wood. These observers were surprised to see women "dressed like men," performing "male" jobs, riding horses, and even handling rifles. Although, as Sánchez argues, we must avoid romanticizing such gender relations, because within them women were still subjected to patriarchal domination, it remains the case that in nineteenth-century California, as in 1930s New Mexico, "gender discourses were more fluid and ambiguous" than in middle-class Anglo-European contexts.[100] The seemingly contradictory nature of village gender and labor relations generated both practical difficulties and conceptual dissonances for state representatives committed to the logic of separate spheres. State Home

Improvement Agents sent to the villages to "educate" Mexican women in hygiene and home economy were flabbergasted at their inability to convince villagers that the plastering of home exteriors, work that traditionally fell to groups of women, was in fact more appropriate work for men.[101]

The foregrounding of Mexican men in red-baiting and antimarijuana discourses responded to such contradictions by refocusing the gendered division of labor that unevenly supported a regional economy newly restructured around tourism. An obsession with the Mexican worker as distinctly male in his potential criminality and sexual perversity helped to phobically redraw the gender distinctions that village labor relations blurred. By isolating Mexican men, moreover, as the source of labor problems in the Southwest, union busting and drug enforcement discourses rendered the exploitation of "feminized" forms of service labor unproblematic. Although state representatives incessantly rehearsed the dangers posed by a potentially violent and perverse male workforce, they treated the employment of Mexican women as maids and cooks as unremarkable and normal. According to Sarah Deutsch, New Deal job programs tended to channel Mexican women into domestic work by training them in sewing, cooking, and cleaning.[102] At the same time as the state and its supporters loudly demanded the use of police power to control male workers, they quietly encouraged women to work as "domestic" servants for households and hotels. Pastoral images of docile, domesticated beasts of burden thus also represent, in displaced forms, Anglo-American desires for tractable "feminized" labor.

The preceding comparison of male and female labor indicates that in 1930s New Mexico biopower—the various techniques for "the subjugation of bodies and the control of populations"—included the reproduction not only of race and class but also of gender differences. This meant that dominant labor disciplines helped to structure local social space along lines of class, race, and gender. Biopower domains included a number of differently configured work sites: the mines, worked mostly by men; the agricultural fields, which included men and male-headed family work units; the tourist industry, which particularly targeted Mexican women; and the state penitentiary system, which was largely aimed at Mexican men. As a space of enforced labor built by prisoner-workers, the infamous New Mexico state penitentiary concretely instantiated official policies of labor discipline built on the criminalization of Mexican men. In 1932, construction was completed on a new penitentiary building that could house twenty-four women and, if necessary, could expand to hold twice that many. Prison officials planned at most, then, for only fifty female prisoners, and even this modest figure would prove too large, for although between 1931 and 1940 the pen held roughly between five hundred and 650 male prisoners, it never housed more than about a dozen female inmates. The majority of male prisoners, moreover, were of Mexican descent.

The prison often served as a holding pen for male labor organizers and strikers, many of whom were ultimately turned over to the INS for deportation.[103] By implicitly targeting Mexican workingmen, antidrug laws complemented the explicit criminalization of Mexican labor activism. Side by side with labor leaders, the state penitentiary held notable numbers of working-class Mexican American men who were charged with drug possession. Between 1930 and 1939, fifty-three of these prisoners appear on penitentiary induction sheets, and only four are listed as "American" under "Nationality." Prison officials list the remaining prisoners' nationality as "Mexican," even though the vast majority were born in the United States.[104] Recalling the phrase "alien communist," the official language of imprisonment constituted "Mexicans," regardless of citizenship, as "un-American." Just as the term *communism* was used in New Mexico not simply to describe party affiliation but as a code word for supposedly inferior and threatening racial others, in local penal discourses the term *Mexican* designated race and class, not citizenship. Moreover, arrests and convictions of "Mexican" workers for marijuana possession were most concentrated during the years of, and in the areas with, the highest levels of labor organization and action.[105] And, not surprisingly, given their reputation as labor radicals, miners often received the highest sentences.[106] By constructing and then punishing "communists" and "dope fiends," state police powers imposed criminalized race, class, and gender identities onto working-class Mexican men.

The concrete arrangements of prison life doubled and reinforced what David Montejano calls the dense "web of labor control" that confronted many Mexican workers on the outside. In the context of 1930s Texas, he notes that employers and the state worked in concert to "immobilize" and "guard" Mexican agricultural workers. The police routinely arrested migrant workers for vagrancy and then gave them the option of working off the fine by picking cotton for local farmers. According to Montejano, "such 'convict labor' was routinely guarded by armed deputies while working cotton. To complement this method of recruiting labor a 'pass system' was instituted to prevent unauthorized pickers from leaving the county."[107] A similar set of power relations governed workers in New Mexico, where employers and the state imposed interlocking forms of labor discipline. Mexican workers were vulnerable to diverse forms of state identification and surveillance. As we have seen, labor organizers were subject to red-baiting investigation and punishment at the hands of federal immigration officials and local sheriffs—not to mention private security forces and vigilante groups.

Once convicted of a crime, a carceral gaze illuminated the bodies of Mexican men. State penitentiary induction forms exhaustively taxonomized brown male bodies by including mug shots, sex, age, build, height, weight, hair color, eye color, complexion, and even hat and shoe sizes. Finally, the forms included front and back sketches of male bodies that prison officials used to note identifying marks such as scars and tattoos. After this initiation into prison visibility, Mexicans workers were inserted into forms of labor discipline that replicated conditions on the outside. Prisoners were organized into guarded gangs for work on the penitentiary farm, in the brick factory, or at some other task.[108] And, as on the outside, drug enforcement functioned as a means to control the penitentiary's mostly Mexican labor force. Just three months before Governor Tingley called in the state police to teargas and imprison League members, he received a report on a "Special Investigation of Narcotics and Weapons at the State Penitentiary," in which witnesses testified to the need for tighter controls on marijuana traffic inside, particularly in the brickyard, where the majority of employed prisoners worked.[109] As this sequence of events suggests, in many cases the penitentiary functioned as a testing ground for forms of labor discipline and surveillance that the state would subsequently adopt in its dealings with organized labor. The incarceration of Mexican workers, whether for striking, marijuana possession, or other crimes such as "vagrancy," created an environment that made it easier to manage labor, particularly during the Depression, when both unemployment and anti-immigrant sentiment ran high. The pathologization of Mexican labor further supported the governor's attempts to restructure the local economy around tourism. Officials who pathologized brown labor indirectly supported the tourist industry by endeavoring through intimidation and force to reproduce a "malleable" workforce, and thereby prevent strikes that might scare off potential visitors. When such measures failed, and strikes and other labor actions occurred anyway, Governor Tingley could reassure potential tourists that New Mexico was a patriotic, law-and-order state by spectacularly punishing Mexican "communists."

Moreover, this history of combined state, capitalists, and cultural efforts to police Mexican dissent foreshadows the development of the state-sponsored privatization of the war on drugs in contemporary New Mexico. In the 1950s, the existing state penitentiary buildings were torn down, and its prisoner-made bricks were recycled in order to build a local tourist institution, "Maria's New Mexican Kitchen." The fruits of prison labor can still be seen there, on a wall that serves as the backdrop for the restaurant's tortilla maker, a Mexican woman enclosed in a glass booth so that patrons can enjoy the spectacle of her labor. Prison officials found it more difficult, however, to find a home for the old pen's records, which bounced from agency to agency before finally landing at the New Mexico State Records Center and Archives around 1980, the same year as the infamous state pen riot, one of the bloodiest in U.S. history. The prison's records remain uncataloged, however; with limited labor and other resources, documents concerning private property such as land, mineral, and water rights have a higher priority.

Recalling the prison officials who attempted to dispose of the institution's historical records, contemporary state politicians have suppressed the past by representing corporate prisons and prison labor as a brave new world of cost-effective corrections. In a public ceremony in 1998, Republican governor Gary Johnson ritually padlocked the "antiquated" main unit of the state pen, proclaiming that he was thereby "closing an era and turning towards a better future in Corrections." With the governor's active support, the state had recently contracted with the Wackenhut Corporation to run two prisons. According to the governor, these private prisons "offer New Mexicans a better product [and] better service at a reduced cost."[110] But how new and improved was this product? Inmates at the private prison in Santa Rosa provided one answer when they rioted on 31 August 1999—the first anniversary of the governor's speech. And although the governor supported marijuana decriminalization, since the opening of private prisons, convictions for drug trafficking and possession have more than doubled.[111] According to official sources, during the 1990s the majority of prisoners in the state were "Hispanics" who worked as day laborers before their convictions.[112] Behind bars, inmates now do similar work. In 1999, prison furniture makers, garment sewers, cobblers, broom makers, and other workers generated a record $5 million in sales. A New Mexico Corrections Industries products and services catalog is even available on the Web.[113]

Although these contemporary examples of prison privatization and prison labor suggest continuities with the 1930s, conditions have not remained static. On the contrary, at different times and places in the twentieth century, the blurry boundary between state and capitalist interests was constantly redrawn, and the particular composition of public and private forces in a given police context thus changed over time. Such changes further respond to new demographics. In the 1930s, for instance, a post–Mexican revolutionary diaspora provoked a reorganization of the state and commercial forces that composed the dominant "bloc" of police power. But while contemporary New Mexican prisons react to different (albeit related) demographics, they deal with them in some familiar ways. Whereas in the 1930s the state pen focused on Mexican men, today the prison system includes increasing numbers of Mexican women. In a part of the state pen that Governor Johnson did not close, for example, male and female inmates work in a telemarketing program to promote tourism and investment in New Mexico.[114] And at the New Mexico Women's Correctional Facility in Grants, which is run by the Corrections Corporation of America, inmates make microfilm and microfiche for the state of New Mexico, which ultimately sponsors the State Records Center and Archive, where I researched much of this chapter.[115]

MEDIA MEXICANS

With this brief sketch of the contemporary prison-industrial complex in mind, I would like to conclude by returning to Mexican labor activism of the 1930s, for therein lies not only an alternative history of police power in New Mexico, but also an archive of strategies for countering criminalization that may suggest useful models for critical political engagements in the present. Amid state, capitalist, and artistic campaigns to police them, Mexican workers took direct action to oppose their criminalization as communists and dope fiends. In petitions to Governor Tingley, League of Spanish-Speaking Workers members protested the deportation of union leader Jesús Pallares as well as other Mexican workers and activists.[116] Mexican workers engaged, moreover, in forms of public protest directed against what I have called the New Mexican penal colony. When a 1935 criminal-syndication state bill threatened to make it illegal to advocate "any change in industrial ownership," seven hundred members of the League helped to defeat it by marching to the state capitol with protest signs in English and Spanish and by occupying the senate galleries.[117] Similarly, in 1935, amid crowds of visiting tourists on the Plaza, the Santa Fe chapter of the League organized a May Day celebration in solidarity with the international proletariat and billed as a protest against the "terrorization of the foreign-born by deportations" and "the rising menace of fascism."[118] The interruption of this May Day celebration into a prominent tourist setting can in part be read as an indirect protest against the powerful pastoral images I have described. At the same time as they implicitly attacked the pastoral ideals that were used to control Mexican workers, these and other League protests also responded to the increasing state criminalization of labor. Whereas the state wielded the law to punish labor organizing, Mexican activists reappropriated legal discourse so as to charge the powerful with forms of criminality, as when League members protested their arrest by arguing that the deployment of police against strikers was an unlawful violation of civil liberties or that the police should instead investigate wealthy tax evaders.[119] And while dominant forces concentrated on male labor activists, union fliers and petitions repeatedly underlined the participation of women in strikes and other protests. By countering hegemonic representations of Mexican labor, League members challenged images of themselves as either pliable, pastoral workers or violent, animalistic criminals.

More precisely, Mexican activists engaged in a multimedia guerrilla war against dominant modes of representing Mexican labor. Working-class Mexicans insistently attempted to seize texts, images, and songs for their own purposes, engaging in practical and symbolic struggles over social position, identity, and self-determination.[120] Because state hegemony depended, among other things, on the manipulation of texts, including legal discourses, government hearings, and the press, Mexican activists also entered into the struggle over representation. If in official discourses Mexican workers were described as dangerous communists and drug addicts, the members of La Liga countered with letters, petitions, and posters representing themselves as a harassed people fighting for food and justice. The League also attempted to grab local, national, and international press publicity when, for example, its members occupied the governor's office. In this endeavor they were largely successful, for a number of people from across the country drew upon accounts of the occupation in their local papers in order to telegraph their condemnation of the governor's response.[121] Similarly, press publicity partly motivated the League's occupation of the state senate chambers in protest of an antilabor bill. In both cases, "direct action" can be read as a form of militant political theater whose imagined audience includes mass-media print communities.

Labor radicals engaged in similar struggles over visual—especially photographic—representation. State-supported labor systems centrally included forms of surveillance that disciplined workers and prisoners alike. But while the state criminalized Mexican workers with countless penitentiary mug shots and diagrams of defining physical features, union members circulated alternative photos of unjustly jailed activists, such as the image of La Liga organizer Juan Ochoa that graces a petition the group sent to the governor. We can further read the willingness of Mexican miners in Madrid to be photographed (or have their substandard company housing photographed) by Margaret McKittrick as a similar effort to oppose state and company imaging techniques. In each case, Mexican workers attempted to intervene in the dominant politics of the visible by entering into the production and circulation of photographic images. Such multimediated actions were directed not only at the state, but also at both mass and modernist cultural productions. League representations of Mexican workers as hungry and harassed activists for justice were directly opposed to a wide range of dominant representations, such as the picture postcards, paintings, poems, and stories I have analyzed.

In sometimes less direct, less obvious ways, Mexicans have also used music to contest dominant representations. Combining "live" performances and reproduction on records, Mexican musicians critically reflected upon the role of the state in disciplining Mexican workers in the United States. Mexican *corridos* recorded in the 1930s partly focus on the migrant laborers' dealings with border patrol or other police agents, both when entering the United States and when being deported. Mexican songs about marijuana smuggling and smoking similarly bring into focus the interaction between Mexican immigrants and state police powers. Although labor unions did not organize specific actions against the criminalization of marijuana, the popular culture of Mexican workers contains critical perspectives on state policies of contraband control.

In his analysis of early-twentieth-century *corridos* about Mexican smugglers, Américo Paredes has argued that the smuggler "was seen as an extension of the hero of intercultural conflict" because he defied U.S. border authorities, and, by extension, the hegemony of an Anglo-American criminal justice system in the Southwest.[122] In an essay titled "The Theme of Drug Smuggling in the Mexican Corrido," María Herrera-Sobek applies Paredes's ideas to her own analysis of songs from the 1960s and 1970s.[123] By analyzing the *corrido* smuggler as someone who opposes U.S. border police, Paredes and Herrera-Sobek suggest the centrality of Mexican engagements with U.S. border control within Mexican immigrant popular cultures. Songs about marijuana, moreover, that were popular among Mexicans in the United States during the early twentieth century lead us back to the revolutionary border rebellions that helped to provoke the "drug war" of the 1930s.

"La Cucaracha" is a song of the Mexican Revolution that seemingly promotes both border rebellion and marijuana. In distinct but related forms, including live performances, commercial recordings, sheet music, and Hollywood film, "La Cucaracha" entertained, for different reasons, both Mexican and non-Mexican listeners in the United States. In chapter 5 I analyze in greater detail the intercultural contest over "La Cucaracha" in particular and Mexican uses of modern media in general. Drug wars provoke media wars, and the conflict between dominant and subaltern uses of the song illuminates the more general, formative engagement of postrevolutionary Mexican immigrants with contemporary U.S. media. I want to close this chapter, however, by introducing the song and some of the questions it raises.

"La Cucaracha" is closely associated with revolutionary leader Pancho Villa. Reportedly a favorite among Villista forces, who supposedly performed it after successful campaigns, "La Cucaracha" humorously yet sympathetically focuses on the lowly cockroach, a figure for Villa's soldiers, who, the song suggests, cannot keep marching because they have no more marijuana to smoke. "La Cucaracha" was, in particular, a favorite song among Mexicans in 1930s New Mexico. In a 1937 collection of local folk songs, New Mexican folklorist and WPA researcher Aurora Lucero-White included both "Mexican" and "New Mexican" versions of the song.[124] Like other popular songs from the period, "La Cucaracha" promotes the sustaining, even revolutionary, pleasures of the drug. In the song "Marijuana, La Soldadera," written at the time of the revolution but recorded in 1929, the drug is even used as a figure for a brave female soldier of the same name. "Marijuana" initially goes to war with her beloved, Juan, in order to cook his meals. In the end, however, she proves "braver than her Juan" ("más valiente que su Juan"), and when he dies in battle, Marijuana takes up his rifle and joins the fight. As a result she is promoted to the rank of sergeant.[125] Other songs like "La Marijuana," written and recorded around 1930, in the middle of the Mexican marijuana scare, contradict antidrug campaigns by enjoining listeners to smoke.[126]

As a song that implicitly celebrates the exploits of Villa's marijuana-smoking soldiers, "La Cucaracha" belongs to a larger group of *corridos* that glorify Villa's violation of U.S. law when he illegally crossed the border in order to attack Columbus, New Mexico. As Paredes notes in his discussion of smuggling, "the laws that prohibited uninterrupted traffic across the river were mainly those of the U.S., and the Borderer's experience had not made him love or respect Anglo law."[127] Popular sympathy with the smuggler's violations of Anglo law also extended to Villa, and a number of *corridos* celebrate his evasion of the U.S. military force led by General Pershing that was sent into Mexico to apprehend him after the attack on Columbus. In one *corrido,* Villa appears as a sort of revolutionary trickster who eludes his pursuers and magically turns gringo technology against U.S. forces. Villa here disguises himself as an American soldier and laughs in Pershing's face. He also paints stars on a U.S. flag that he then uses to trick the air force into landing so that he can capture their planes. In one of these planes Villa flies over U.S. soldiers and waves "good-bye." Finally, he hangs a number of Americans from telegraph poles, and the remaining soldiers shamefully retreat to the United States.[128] The *corrido* thus reverses, in carnivalesque fashion, hierarchies between the United States and Mexico, such that a lone Mexican from the peon class triumphs over seemingly superior forces, and even turns the emblems of Yankee modernity—the airplane and the telegraph pole—against U.S. power.

Trickster sentiments also animated performances of "La Cucaracha" in 1930s New Mexico, for that song similarly inverts social hierarchies by celebrating the common revolutionary soldier, the marijuana-smoking cockroach. At a time when Anglo-American authorities were using Mexican revolutionary history in order to criminalize labor activists as "alien communists," "La Cucaracha" served as a counternarrative that reasserted a subaltern view of revolutionary justice and an implicit critique of U.S. discourses of (inter)national law and order. In response to state-sponsored efforts to red-bait labor activists and use marijuana criminalization as a mode of labor control, Mexican immigrants symbolically opposed such practices by appropriating a song that forthrightly linked marijuana smoking to revolution. And conversely, the song suggests that contemporary antimarijuana laws were deployed precisely to block radical change. The local popularity of "La Cucaracha" represents, I would argue, a critique from below of the politics of criminalization in 1930s New Mexico and beyond.

By appropriating modern media technologies and entering into struggles over mass cultural representations, Mexicans resisted criminalizing discourses that would consign them to prison, as well as pastoralizing forms of representation that would ideologically imprison them in a premodern world. Thus, although I have stressed the use of anarchist tactics, that is not to say that strikes and similar forms of protest are "direct actions" in the sense of being unmediated by or unrelated to culture. As Aihwa Ong has noted in a related context, "the daily practices of workers in defending themselves against various modes of control are also struggles over cultural meanings, values, and goals."[129] Following Ong, I would argue that as a social formation, Mexican protest activities cut across the neat divisions that characterize conventional accounts of modernity. As David Lloyd and Lisa Lowe note, "within modernity, the sphere of culture is defined by its separation from the economic and the political within the general differentiation of spheres that constitute 'society.'"[130] By disrespecting the boundaries between the political, the economic, and the cultural, Mexican activists in the 1930s rebelled against dominant understandings of "the modern," and changed the very terms of their engagement with it.

In the next chapter, I return to the complex, overlapping relations among the political, the economic, and the cultural that the early-twentieth-century war on drugs makes visible, but in a new context—Los Angeles during the formative period of Hollywood film production. Whereas here I have argued that critical attention to drug enforcement and police power in New Mexico reveals subaltern opposition to a power bloc composed of the state and the artist colony, in the following two chapters I focus on the war on drugs against Mexican immigrants in 1920s and 1930s Los Angeles, exploring a set of historical discourses and practices that, among other things, suggests the mutually sustaining relationships that have historically linked police power and the emergence of Hollywood cinema. Moreover, the alliance between Hollywood and the police was a response not only to conventional forms of Mexican protest, but also to cucaracha-style interventions in dominant mass media.

CHAPTER 4

LAPD, the Movie

Hollywood, the Police, and the Drug War against Mexican Immigrants

A brief sketch of the life of Anthony Quinn will provide an apt preview for this chapter, because the actor experienced firsthand the ways in which Hollywood and the police have criminalized Mexicans. Quinn begins his 1972 autobiography *The Original Sin* with an account of his first visit to a psychiatrist.[1] The doctor is also a fan and starts the session by showing Quinn a manila folder full of the star's press clippings. When he reads in one clipping that Quinn was born in Mexico during the revolution and that both his parents fought with Villa, the doctor confesses, "I'm afraid all I know about the Mexican Revolution is what I saw in the picture *Viva Villa*, with Wallace Beery." As the doctor continues reading the newspaper's account of Quinn's lineage, the conversation shifts from Hollywood revolutionaries to Hollywood Indians:

"It goes on to say here that your father was an Irish adventurer and your mother an Aztec princess."

I had to laugh out loud.

He looked up. "Why do you laugh? Isn't it true?"

"My father was part Irish, that part is true. But I was laughing at the Indian princess crap."

"My wife and I thought it was very romantic when we read it."

"I guess that's what Paramount Pictures publicity wanted you to feel. They didn't think it was romantic enough for my mother to be plain Mexican."

"Why was that?"

"What the hell, Doc, you live in Los Angeles. You know what most people here feel about Mexicans."

"I don't. I've only been here a couple of years, Tony. May I call you Tony?"

The question about Mexicans irritated me. He had begun to look like a red-necked Texan already.

"Sure, if I can call you by your first name."

He roared with laughter. "You can call me anything you want— and that isn't all you're going to call me before you're through."

"Well, being a Mexican in southern California is not exactly an open sesame. For years they used to have signs at dance halls and restaurants: 'No Mexicans allowed.' Mexicans were lazy, thieves, greasy; they were either zoot-suiters or Pachuchos, marijuana smokers."

"Did you ever smoke marijuana, Tony?"

"No, I never did."

He made some marks on a piece of paper.[2]

Perhaps combining elements from the Pocahontas and Ramona myths—themselves favorite film subjects—the studio fabricated a romantic royal lineage for Quinn that displaced the more complicated, seemingly contradictory, life history of a Hollywood star with subaltern origins. His father, Francisco, was half Irish and Mexican, but his mother, Manuela, was not an Aztec at all (let alone a "princess"), but a poor, half Tarahumara Indian. Both parents did indeed fight with Villa, and during that time Manuela became pregnant with Anthony. She then left the army but reunited with Francisco in 1917 in El Paso, where young Quinn saw his first motion picture, a silent Hollywood film starring Spanish actor Antonio Moreno, a popular "Latin lover" of the day. Like many other Mexican immigrants of the period, both of Quinn's parents worked on the railroad. When he was still a child, his family was recruited to pick walnuts in San Jose, but when they stepped off the train they discovered that they had been employed as scabs to break a strike of Mexican workers. According to Quinn, his parents, who were "outraged over the duplicity of the landowners," refused to play that role. For the next several years the family picked grapes in northern California and lemons and oranges in southern California. Later in life, when his first wife, Katherine, the adopted daughter of Cecil B. DeMille, remarked that Santa Barbara reminded her of horse rides with childhood friends, Quinn responded that the same area reminded him of "the indignity of earning a living on your knees."[3] In the 1920s his family finally settled in East Los Angeles, where Francisco landed a job with Selig Studios, first as a grip and then as a cameraman filming stock footage of animals for Hollywood pictures. Francisco became friends with Douglas Fairbanks, Rudolph Valentino, and the previously mentioned Moreno. Every weekend, ten-year-old Anthony accompanied his father to the studio to watch the production of a jungle picture or a western. Roughly a decade later, Quinn's future father-in-law, DeMille, hired the part Tarahumara actor to play a Cheyenne brave in *The Plainsman,* starring Gary Cooper (more on Cooper later).[4]

Quinn's Mexican revolutionary origins profoundly shaped his life in Hollywood. In 1972, he approvingly quoted his mother's recollections of the revolution and the critique of exploitation that it inspired: "We were just poor people fighting for our stomachs. . . . Everybody felt courage now. All the resentment they had been swallowing for years now came out. Things could be different. Maybe it wasn't God's law that some people should starve while others had plenty. Maybe the man who plants the lettuce can also eat the salad."[5] Quinn ultimately adopted his parents' perspective on the revolution: "Everyone saw the revolution through his own circumstance, and Villa's suggested a class struggle. That is how I came to see it too, filtered through the eyes of my father. By 1913, when Villa allied with Emiliano Zapata in Mexico City, he spoke with the voice of the working man, and my father listened."[6]

Quinn seemed to hear a similar voice, for in the 1940s he became involved in leftist politics in Los Angeles. He used his new celebrity to raise money for the "Sleepy Lagoon" defendants, a group of young Mexican men or *pachucos* who were wrongly accused of murder. The trial, a prelude to the infamous "Zoot Suit Riots," was part of an influential constellation of dominant ideas and practices in Los Angeles that criminalized Mexicans. Or, as Quinn explained to his psychiatrist, Mexicans in southern California were often perceived as "thieves," "zoot-suiters," *pachuchos,* and "marijuana smokers." Quinn's efforts on behalf of the Sleepy Lagoon defendants were partly motivated, he wrote, by a post-revolutionary sense of obligation: he was asked to help by the grandmother of one of the accused, a woman who had kept Manuela Quinn and her new baby boy from starving during the revolution. His public support for the Sleepy Lagoon defendants, according to Quinn, "[a]lmost cost me my career. . . . I was accused of being a communist, and a knee-jerk Mexican."[7] By the mid-1940s, the actor's presumed proximity to *pachuco* "crime," combined with his close friendships with blacklisted actors and writers such as John Howard Lawson, earned Quinn a place on the studios' "gray list of actors tabbed as communist sympathizers."[8] As we saw in the last chapter, in the postrevolutionary U.S. Southwest, the term *communist* was often used as a label for politicized Mexican immigrants. Both in theory and in practice, official forms of anticommunism have often been directed at Mexicans and other stigmatized groups, particularly those involved in antiracist struggles. According to Jon Lewis, the U.S. House Committee on Un-American Activities hearings of 1947 tended to conflate communism with Jewishness, unionism, and antiracism.[9] During their testimony to the committee, Lewis explains, several of the Hollywood witnesses focused on the anti-Semitism and racism that animated the hearings. One of Quinn's friends, John Howard Lawson, denounced the proceedings as an "attack [on] Negroes, Jews, and other minorities."[10] As Lawson's testimony and Quinn's narrative both suggest, anticommunism included a set of ideologies and practices directed at policing people of color and antiracist movements.

It is the details of such a life story, I would argue, that the studio attempted to efface with its scenario about the "Aztec princess" in Anthony Quinn's past. Although the actor reasoned that Paramount invented this "romantic" heritage in order to distance him from any association with Mexican criminality, in practice the studio combined both sets of associations in its construction of his early star image, which oscillated between the romantic "noble savage" *and* the dangerous racialized criminal. Or, in Carol Lombard's formulation, the actor was typecast as an "Indian," "a Mexican," and a "hoodlum."[11] In a number of films from the 1930s and early 1940s, Quinn was repeatedly cast as an Indian. In addition to his role as a Cheyenne warrior in *The Plainsman* (1936), he also played Crazy Horse in *They Died with Their Boots On* (1941) and Yellow Hand in *Buffalo Bill* (1944). Quinn was proud of his Mexican Indian background but he objected to the stereotypical roles he was offered. He was even more troubled, however, by his roles as criminals. In *Night Waitress* (RKO, 1936) and *Sworn Enemy* (MGM, 1936), two of his earliest film roles, the actor played small parts as gangsters; in the prison drama *Parole* (Universal, 1936), he was cast as an inmate; in *Tip Off Girls* (1938), Quinn played the leader of a truck hijacking ring; in the comedy *Thieves Fall Out* (Warner, 1941) he once again played a gangster; and finally, he played an ex-con in *Larceny, Inc.*

(Warner, 1942). By the mid-1940s, Quinn began to feel that the criminal component of his screen image had overwhelmed the noble savage, such that even his own father-in-law and onetime director, Cecil B. DeMille, could only see him as a "Mexican bandit."[12] Near the ehd of the decade, the actor briefly left Hollywood for Broadway, in part because of red-baiting, but also because of what we might call, borrowing a phrase from contemporary police discourse, the practice of "racial profiling" in film. As Quinn's reference to the stock figure of the "Mexican bandit" suggests, in the wake of revolutionary upheaval in the first decades of the twentieth century, both Hollywood and the police increasingly cast Mexican immigrants in narratives of crime and punishment.

Both Hollywood red-baiting and racial profiling were, in effect, responses not only to Quinn's revolutionary trajectory, but also to the vast number of similar postrevolutionary Mexican immigrants to Los Angeles who, though they did not usually enter into filmmaking, shared the actor's experiences of displacement, labor, and criminalization in early-twentieth-century California. During and after the revolution, over a million Mexicans immigrated to the United States, particularly to Los Angeles, and they often brought along radical ideas and practices. Largely excluded from jobs in film production, Mexican workers were nonetheless a major source of the unskilled labor that, starting in the 1920s, supported the larger southern California economy, and, by extension, a film industry that indirectly depended on the region's low labor costs.

As in chapter 3, where I examined the interrelationships among immigrant labor, police power, and the famous modernist art colonies in New Mexico during the first three decades of the twentieth century, in the following two chapters I describe how in the same years the Mexican presence in Los Angeles prompted the formation of a mutually reinforcing set of relationships between state police powers and the film industry. The next chapter concerns the history of film production in Los Angeles, and the manner in which Hollywood filmmakers incorporated aspects of police ideology and practice in an attempt to materially and imaginatively police the Mexican immigrants in their midst. The focus of the present chapter, however, is on the police and their influential interventions in an emergent southern California mass media. The Los Angeles Police Department (LAPD) and other law enforcement officials attempted to use the media in order to promote police work in general, but particularly when it targeted Mexicans. These LAPD "media events" drew in part on conventions from Hollywood. The police, in other words, mobilized film plots and visual strategies to represent Mexican criminality, and, by extension, the necessity for aggressive drug enforcement. One of the most (in)famous modern urban police forces in the world, the LAPD has historically built its power base by policing Mexican immigrants and by using new mass media to publicize and promote its anti-Mexican efforts. Combined with the preceding chapter's analysis of New Mexican contexts, moreover, these interrelated histories of Hollywood and the police suggest that the revolutionary Mexican presence in the Southwest constituted an unprecedented crisis or rupture within and against U.S. modernity.

At about the same time as the studios were consolidating their power in southern California, judges, legislators, and policemen increasingly turned their attention to Mexican immigrants and the threat they posed to dominant power relations in the region. Lawyers and judges joined members of the Chamber of Commerce in calling for an aggressive attack on Mexican crime, while legislators passed new laws that criminalized strikes and labor organizing, and held hearings on the dangers of Mexican criminality in southern California. Finally, the LAPD served local business interests by breaking strikes, arresting protesters, confiscating radical literature, and enforcing laws aimed at managing the "reserve army" of workers whose existence helped keep wages low.

The history of drug criminalization in particular reveals how the police enforced capitalist interests by focusing on Mexican labor. Starting roughly in the mid-1920s and extending into the late 1940s and after, dominant groups in L.A. regarded Mexicans as potential "reds" and dangerous drug smugglers and users, particularly of marijuana. The image of Mexicans that Quinn confronted—the lazy, thieving marijuana smoker—indicated that, if not correctly managed and policed, Mexicans who, when tractable, constituted one of the greatest boons to the regional economy, could instead become the enemies of both capital and the state. Drug criminalization, in other words, was a means not of excluding Mexicans from the labor market but of incorporating them into it as disciplined, subordinated workers. Building upon the last chapter's analysis of drug enforcement in New Mexico as a form of biopower aimed at managing Mexican labor, I will suggest that historically, drug enforcement represents a central strand in the web of social controls that the state mobilized to police Mexicans, including not only a host of vice and vagrancy laws, but also (as Quinn reminds us) legally sanctioned and enforced segregation in housing, parks, restaurants, and, of course, movie theaters.

In the late 1920s and 1930s, police in L.A. mobilized media such as radio to reach a mass audience with their own, self-promotional versions of drug enforcement. The *Los Angeles Times* is particularly important in my account because it mediated the mutually reinforcing relationship between state and film-industry efforts to control Mexicans. Newspapers like the *Los Angeles Times* largely featured stories on crime and entertainment, often blurring the line between the two. At the same time that the reviews and ads in the paper's entertainment section regularly referred to Hollywood crime dramas, the "news" portions resembled forms of entertainment like film. In what follows, then, I pay particular attention to police press releases published in the newspaper and newspaper movie reviews because the daily paper helps make visible the overlapping political and representational projects of Hollywood and the LAPD. Which is not to say that Hollywood and the police worked in explicit and direct concert with one another, or that all of their interests and actions always coincided. On the contrary, the film studios and the LAPD remained relatively autonomous institutions with distinct agendas. This was in part because the two had different structural relationships to the dominant capitalist powers in early-twentieth-century southern California. The studios, in other words, had an ambivalent, sometimes competitive relationship with the more powerful group of real estate speculators and other businessmen that the police in effect served. Hollywood and the police nonetheless cultivated practical, material ties with one another. And when it came to the Mexican presence in the region, the two sets of institutions shared an interest in the management of immigrant laborers. For distinct yet related reasons, filmmakers and the LAPD both benefited, in other words, from a political economy dependent on the enforced docility of Mexican immigrant workers. As a result, the police and the film studios became laboratories, as it were, for the creation of influential ideas and practices aimed at containing the Mexican presence in Los Angeles.

The police endeavored to "hail" a white, middle-class constituency, in ways that paralleled Hollywood's efforts to engage film audiences. Symbolically trading Mexican bodies back and forth between themselves, Hollywood and the police produced similar representations of Mexicans as hypersexual and perverse. In the 1920s and 1930s, the LAPD elaborated in theory and practice a model of Mexican criminality that was in many ways based on conceptions of Mexican sexuality familiar from film. Represented as a sign or symptom of a more general Mexican sexual deviancy, the spectacle of Mexican drug crimes emerged as a popular police "media event" for at least two seemingly contrary, yet ultimately complementary, reasons. First, police news reports about Mexican drug crime reinforced projections of Mexican deviancy and therefore invested drug enforcement with the ideological urgency associated with drives to police Mexican threats to Anglo-American sexual norms. At the same time, however, the premise that drug crimes indexed Mexican depravity in turn worked to invest drug enforcement with the intensities and excitements of ostensibly prohibited sexual fantasies and desires. Police press releases concerning their drug enforcement efforts against Mexicans invited readers to simultaneously take erotic pleasure in fantasies of sexual transgression and in the punishment of such transgressions. This double address recalls the similarly ambivalent spectacles of Mexican criminality in film. Moreover, through a combination of text and image, police press releases generated miniature narratives that resembled silent films and their intertitles. As Hollywood perfected a new visual language and a set of narrative techniques, police press releases increasingly mimicked them. Following the dominant arc of U.S. film history, the police constructed criminal spaces or "settings"; reproduced visual (and verbal) "close-ups" of heroic drug enforcement agents; and deployed images of drugs and drug paraphernalia like film "props" that linked Mexican characters to crime. The police, in other words, borrowed Hollywood techniques for generating the diegetic illusion, the fantasy that the film represents a compelling world unto itself, imaginatively segregated from the larger social realities surrounding it. Just as film spectators colloquially report getting "caught up" in the fictional world of the film, police reports invited readers to lose themselves in scenarios of Mexican criminality in abstraction from the larger political-economic relations that dominated the southern California border zone. Borrowing Giuliana Bruno's provocative phrase from her reconstruction of early-twentieth-century Neapolitan cinema, in what follows I argue that the often fragmentary and uneven records represented by police media events and films from the late 1920s and early 1930s constitute a sort of "ruined map" of dominant power relations in Mexican Los Angeles.

NARCOTIC WAR HELP INVOKED

Judge Fricke Shows Danger to Every Citizen...

Pictures of the havoc wrought by drug addicts were presented to City Club members yesterday by Superior Judge Fricke, president, and W. J. Herwig, general superintendent of the Narcotic Research Association.

"When we consider the fact that in the Pacific Coast States there are more than 800 drug addicts, in addition to the more than 10,000 Mexican users of marihuana, and that each addict is an actual or potential criminal, we cannot longer refuse to recognize that we have before us a gigantic social problem," said Fricke.

Los Angeles Times, 13 February 1930, sec. 2, 2

SEE...

HARRY CAREY's *Navajos*

in a Hair Raising

WILD WEST SHOW

Every Sunday Afternoon

Four Miles North of Saugus

TRADING POST—FREE SWIMMING POOL

Eat at the Navahogan

Advertisement on the inside cover of Judge Fricke's pamphlet *American Citizenship and Law,* containing "a treatise upon Americanism," 1927.

If a movie had been made about the life of Charles W. Fricke, it might have starred Gary Cooper. Fricke was a superior court judge in Los Angeles from the 1920s to the 1940s, and before that he was a professional criminologist, district attorney, and an LAPD instructor who wrote several frequently reprinted manuals concerning the law and its enforcement. And in addition to bearing a vague resemblance to Cooper—himself the son of a judge—Fricke also shared some of the actor's conservative politics. During the Hollywood antired campaigns of the 1940s and 1950s, Cooper, along with other industry conservatives such as Walt Disney, King Vidor, and Sam Wood, formed the Motion Picture Alliance for the Preservation of American Ideals (MPA) in 1944 in order to "uphold the American way of life" and to "drown out the highly vocal, lunatic fringe of dissidents" in Hollywood.[13] Cooper and other members of the MPA actively cooperated with investigators for the House

Committee on Un-American Activities by testifying as "friendly" witnesses and in some cases identifying suspected communists in the film industry.[14] Several years later, shortly after the release of *High Noon* (1952), in which Cooper famously starred as a frontier lawman, the MPA helped to block the exhibition of *Salt of the Earth* (1954), a film made by blacklisted Hollywood filmmakers and working-class Mexicans about a contemporary mining strike in New Mexico.[15] Recalling the red-baiting of Quinn for his activism against police racism in Los Angeles, the MPA tended to brand antiracist, pro-labor films like *Salt of the Earth* as "communist."

The origins of Gary Cooper's Hollywood politics can be traced to an even earlier moment, however. Cooper began an affair in 1929 with Lupe Vélez, his costar in *The Wolf Song*, in which he played a fur trapper who kidnaps and marries a young Mexican woman named Lola Salazar. In a highly publicized breakup a few years later, Cooper reportedly ended the relationship because his mother objected to her son marrying a Mexican Catholic.[16] Afterwards, the two stars' lives would take dramatically different turns. Along with fellow Mexican performers Dolores Del Rio and Ramón Novarro, Vélez was falsely accused of being a communist.[17] Cooper, on the other hand, helped to establish and publicize a paramilitary organization aimed at suppressing communism. In a 1935 exposé in the *Nation,* Carey McWilliams reported that Cooper was one of the founders of a military order named "The Hollywood Hussars," whose members engaged in armed military drills and wore costumes that resembled U.S. cavalry uniforms during the western Indian wars. The group promised to "uphold and protect the principles and ideals of true Americanism" against the threat of alien subversion. As one of the group's newspaper ads noted, membership was limited to "American citizens of excellent character and of social and financial standing." Members included not only former military officers but also an L.A. county sheriff, Chief James E. Davis of the LAPD, and two superior court judges who, as McWilliams points out, had many occasions for passing judgment in cases involving "the rights of workers and organizers charged with violating California's numerous laws for the maintenance of the status quo."[18]

According to McWilliams, Cooper's Hollywood Hussars had two primary aims. The first was to counteract the spread of "radicalism" in the film industry as represented by a handful of liberal stars, notably including the Mexican actress Dolores Del Rio. The group's second goal was to gain positive media attention for the use of private and public police power to protect business interests and silence dissent.

> [The Hussars] are designed to advertise the charms of fascist organization to the American public. Through the publicity medium of the industry, the most powerful propaganda machine in America, these gaudy units sponsored by popular and well-known stars, can be advertised to millions of Americans as the latest and snappiest fascist models. It is even rumored that a motion picture will be made, presenting the Hollywood Hussars in the act of suppressing a radical uprising in California. All these groups have volunteered their services to the authorities in "case of trouble." They constitute a threat and a warning. Nor should the business aspects be overlooked.... [T]here can be little question of the identity of the forces that are giving the Hussars their moral support. The meetings of the organization are held in the Hollywood Chamber of Commerce.[19]

Here McWilliams is less worried about the Hollywood Hussars as direct agents of vigilantism than about the reactionary ideas and practices that they were able to publicize in the media. Along with the celebrity members of other local paramilitary groups such as the Light Horse Cavalry and the California Esquadrille, stars such as Cooper and his fellow Hussars served, according to McWilliams, as the public relations face of fascism in the mass media.[20] And, as he argued in a pamphlet from the same year, fascist Hollywood was part of a larger social formation in 1930s Los Angeles that included reactionary institutions such as the Friends of New Germany, the Silver Shirts, the American Nationalist Party, and the Aryan Book Store.[21]

Although not, to my knowledge, a Hollywood Hussar, Judge Charles S. Fricke and many other officials in the war on drugs in the 1920s and 1930s shared many of the group's political positions, including an exclusionary model of "Americanism"; a pronounced suspicion of noncitizens; a fervent antiradicalism; and an avid support for dominant capitalist property and labor relations. And, like the Hussars, Judge Fricke's Narcotic Research Association (NRA) was headquartered in the Los Angeles Chamber of Commerce building. As a judge, an antidrug crusader, and a lecturer at the LAPD Training School, Fricke helped preside over a conservative criminal justice system that particularly targeted Mexicans. During the late 1920s and early 1930s, Mexicans were disproportionately arrested for and convicted of a variety of crimes, but particularly those involving drugs. The judge referenced and attempted to legitimate these racialized arrest rates when he ominously warned the elite members of the City Club about the "gigantic social problem" posed by a veritable army of ten thousand Mexican marijuana addicts. Within such a context, we might expect that Fricke dispensed a particularly harsh brand of justice to the Mexicans unlucky enough to end up in his courtroom. Indeed, this would turn out to be the case a decade and a half later, for at about the same time as Cooper and the Motion Picture Alliance for the Preservation of American Ideals were busy attacking communism and promoting "Americanism" in the film industry, Judge Fricke was presiding over the Sleepy Lagoon murder trial (1942). As historian Edward J. Escobar has noted, during the trial Fricke, who had a reputation for being anti-Mexican, "proceeded to brazenly violate the defendants' legal rights" in ways that would ultimately lead their conviction to be overturned on appeal.[22] Combined with the Zoot Suit Riots, the Sleepy Lagoon case was a massive media event that helped to further fortify the dominant image of Mexicans as criminals and drug addicts.

Finally, like Gary Cooper, Judge Fricke was adept at using the media to publicize his conservative ideas. Famous for playing the "strong, silent" type of the Anglo cowboy or lawman, Cooper was a sort of walking advertisement for the conservative law-and-order "Americanism" that his political organizations promoted. Similarly, Fricke used his position as both L.A. superior court judge and president of the NRA to help publicize and promote drug enforcement directed at Mexicans. Along with similar groups like the International Narcotics Education Association, Fricke's organization promoted annual "Narcotics Education Weeks" and other events in which they lectured schools, members of civic organizations, and church groups concerning the dangers of drugs.[23] Through such efforts, the organization gained promotional newspaper exposure for its cause; the *Los Angeles Times,* for instance, reported on the NRA's annual banquets at the Chamber of Commerce building. According to the *Times* in 1929, Judge Fricke's fellow NRA officer W. J. Herwig addressed the audience of more than two hundred members and distinguished guests including the mayors of Los Angeles, Pasadena, Glendale, and Long Beach. Suggesting the extent to which drug enforcement functioned as a form of "biopower" for the policing of working bodies, Herwig warned the powerful businessmen and politicians about the army of ten thousand criminal addicts who made the "narcotic evil . . .

almost as much of an industrial menace as it long has been a social menace." Herwig was seconded by Capt. Harry S. Seager of LAPD's famed narcotics squad, who asserted that "Dope and crime go hand in hand."[24] Prominent members of the LAPD like Captain Seager were not only direct participants in the war on drugs that disproportionately targeted Mexicans but were also active in the various efforts to publicize and promote it in print media and other contexts. As this section's second epigraph further suggests, the work of promoting police power overlapped with the business of making movies. The ad for Harry Carey's Wild West theme park is only the first of many film-related ads inside Judge Fricke's pamphlet, *American Citizenship and Law*. It also includes glossy, full-page photos of actors and actresses, a full-page endorsement from movie cowboy Tom Mix, a full-page ad for a series of Fox westerns, and one for Max Sennett comedies.[25] The inclusion of movie ads in a work on criminal justice is a telling indication of the mutually sustaining ways in which Hollywood and the police influenced one another.

According to Mike Davis, the broad outline of dominant power relations in 1920s and 1930s Los Angeles looked like a pyramid. At the top were the business interests represented by the Merchants and Manufacturers Association, most notably the *Los Angeles Times* empire. This group ruled Los Angeles as "a de facto dictatorship," relying on the LAPD's infamous "Red Squad" to keep "dissent off the streets and radicals in jail." Next came "the social base of this authoritarian regime," a middle strata largely composed of "the great influx of Middle Western babbitry between 1900 and 1925—one of the great internal migrations of American history." Together these two levels represented "the political supremacy of militant Protestantism," as well as the forms of white supremacy that limited (while not eliminating) the emergent political power of many Jewish studio heads. "For the half century between the Spanish-American and Korean wars," according to Davis, the *Times* dynasty and its allies presided "over one of the most centralized—indeed, militarized—municipal power-structures in the United States. They erected the open shop on the bones of labor, expelled pioneer Jews from the social register, and looted the region through one great real-estate syndication after another."[26] Nonetheless, in spite of the anti-Semitism of L.A.'s ruling elite, Jewish studio moguls, like their gentile counterparts, were generally political conservatives who often shared the antilabor, law-and-order attitudes of the *Times* crowd.[27] As Lary May argues, film producers moved to Los Angeles in search of cheap, nonunion labor and as part of an effort to identify their product with the supposedly "American" values of this famous antilabor bastion.[28]

At the bottom of the power structure were the Mexican workers who arrived in massive numbers during and after the revolution and who provided "the new WASP ascendancy" with "its essential economic support."[29] Indeed, L.A.'s twentieth-century economic growth was driven primarily by real estate development and secondarily through agriculture, and Mexicans were the predominant source of inexpensive labor in both cases.[30] In addition to harvesting and canning crops and working as unskilled labor in various aspects of construction, thousands of Mexicans were employed as members of railroad section or extra gangs.[31] The *corrido* "El Lavaplatos" (The dishwasher, ca. 1930), by Pedro J. González, describes these kinds of work, as well as dishwashing, in a brief, first-person immigrant narrative.

> I dreamed in my youth of being a movie star
> And one of those days I come to visit Hollywood.
> One day very desperate because of so much revolution
> I came over to this side without paying the immigration.
> What a fast one, what a fast one, I crossed without paying anything.

The immigrant persona of the song then describes the difficulties of working on a railroad section gang; harvesting tomatoes and beets ("Oh what work, and so poorly paid, for going on one's knees"); and finally ends by describing cement work:

> When I had nothing I had to work with cement.
> Oh what torment, oh what torment, is that famous cement.
> Toss some gravel and sand in the cement mixer,
> Fifty cents an hour until the whistle blows.
> Four or more of us strained at that famous pulley.
> And I, how could I stand it, I was better off washing dishes.
> How repentant, how repentant, I am for having come.[32]

As the song suggests, such difficult and poorly paid work was the underside of "tinsel town" and the dream of being a star, for the exploitation of "cheap," unorganized Mexican labor in Los Angeles was the precondition for capitalist development in southern California, including in the film industry.

The employment of Mexicans to fuel development required the heavy-handed use of police power to manage workers and thereby maximize profits.[33] Indeed, Escobar argues that historically, one of the LAPD's central reasons for being was to police Mexicans. Starting as early as the 1880s, according to Escobar, the department developed "an unsavory reputation for corruption and brutality," a reputation that in the twentieth century was increasingly earned at the expense of Mexicans.[34] Police control over workers was integral to growth strategies for Los Angeles in the late nineteenth and early twentieth centuries. Early on, capitalists decided that in order to compete with San Francisco, which had an excellent port and hence an economic edge, they would need to build Los Angeles on cheap wages. Thus, in contrast to San Francisco's strong (albeit white-supremacist) union tradition, Los Angeles became one of the most antiunion cities in the country. Subservient to local business interests, the LAPD and other police powers effectively propped up the low-wage economy by helping to regulate the local labor market.[35] Simply put, the LAPD managed labor relations by disproportionately arresting Mexicans for a host of crimes.[36] Fluctuations in capitalist demands for cheap labor help to account for the perennial police campaigns against the "Mexican problem" in southern California between 1907 and 1940. The police helped to control seasonal labor markets by arresting "vagrants" and compelling them to work in the fields; or conversely by arresting workers in the slack winter months after the harvest.[37] Moreover, employers kept wages low by overrecruiting workers, thus maintaining a "reserve army" of the unemployed, and the police were often called upon to control these "surplus" workers.[38] In addition, the LAPD mounted counterinsurgency campaigns that combined strikebreaking, the confiscation of "subversive" literature, and the infiltration and sabotage of labor unions and radical organizations.[39]

Recalling the postrevolutionary New Mexican context analyzed in chapter 3, these policing practices partly emerged in response to the prospect of the Mexican Revolution spilling over the border.[40] These fears of mass rebellions against U.S. capitalism and the state provided many of the ideological resources for the LAPD's repressive response to the radical Mexican presence in Los Angeles, most notably the anarchist Magón brothers and their organization, the Partido Liberal Mexicano (PLM), a history I shall return to. In particular, the infamous LAPD "Red Squad" that Davis mentions was a highly repressive reaction to the postrevolutionary Mexican presence in southern California. As the name implies, the Red Squad was a special police unit dedicated to repressing communism, anarchism, and any other radical threat to the status quo.[41] In addition to breaking up "subversive" meetings and strikes by beating and arresting labor unionists and other agitators, the group collected intelligence information on reported communists, anarchists, radicals, and immigrants. Overlapping with the Hollywood Hussars, the Red Squad kept shared information with German and Italian fascists and provided pistol permits and gold badges to a number of Hollywood film directors, executives, and actors. In exchange, film people promised to aid the LAPD's "War on Reds," and serve as deputies in the event of a communist uprising.[42] During the 1930s, the Red Squad's war on radicalism was often waged against Mexicans, as when the unit helped repatriate Mexican immigrants or break Mexican strikes.[43] Police campaigns against supposed "reds" were further supplemented by vigilante actions in which members of the American Legion or the Ku Klux Klan violently attacked and disrupted meetings of leftist groups.[44]

Complementing the Red Squad was the department's Narcotics Squad. Starting in 1926, the head of the LAPD was James E. Davis, a member of the Hollywood Hussars whom one contemporary described as a "bitterly anti-labor man who saw Communist influence behind every telephone pole."[45] As chief of police, Davis greatly increased the Narcotics Squad's size and extended its activities.[46] During the late 1920s and early 1930s, the Narcotic Committee of the California State Legislature repeatedly praised the Narcotics Squad as a model of "efficient" drug enforcement.[47] Such praise effectively meant that the police did a good job of targeting Mexicans. In the geographical imaginary of official reports on drugs in California between 1926 and 1932, San Francisco was associated with opium and the Chinese, while Los Angeles was linked to marijuana and Mexicans. Or, as the 1932 report of the State Narcotic Committee put it, "[O]ur narcotic problem in California is intensified by the Chinese in the north and the Mexicans to the south. The large percentage of opium used in northern California and the marijuana used in Los Angeles is evidence of this fact."[48] As a result of this focus on controlling Mexicans in southern California, in the late 1920s and early 1930s, the LAPD arrested Mexicans for drug crimes at an alarming rate. Although the Mexican population in early-twentieth-century Los Angeles probably constituted less than 10 percent of the population, it made up almost 40 percent of those arrested for drug crimes, particularly those involving marijuana.[49]

This criminalization of Mexicans for marijuana is consistent with the bigger picture of police harassment of Mexicans, and yet drug criminalization still stands out. In fact, among the various official forms of "biopower" that targeted Mexicans, drug criminalization occupied a privileged, ideologically central position in the reproduction of police power. More precisely, the focus on Mexicans as drug criminals historically served as a popular and compelling way of promoting police power as such. In the early twentieth century, the LAPD's reputation was deeply tarnished and in need of a dramatic promotional makeover. The department's budgets and appropriations depended on its ability to serve dominant interests and promote the image of Los Angeles as a place "where law and order reigned supreme." Yet police participation in gambling and prostitution in the 1920s and 1930s set off a series of scandals and calls for reform.[50] To project a semblance of legitimacy in the face of graft and scandal, the department increasingly tried to bolster its reputation by promoting its activities before a public accustomed to vaudeville and the movies. A good example is the semiannual police inspection and departmental review at the L.A. Coliseum. According to a 1933 story in the *Times,* all "citizens, their families and friends" were invited to the Coliseum, where "every form of police activity will be illustrated" by 2,500 participating officers. As part of its effort to attract an audience, the LAPD announced that it would demonstrate an "exotic" form of Japanese self-defense called jujitsu. The *Times* story announcing the event was even illustrated with a photo of an officer using a jujitsu move to disarm a criminal.[51] During these years, the police went to extreme lengths to bolster their reputation. The Santa Monica police, for instance, formed a chorus and dance troupe to entertain local clubs. According to the *Times,* the group, managed by Chief Clarence Web, performed in striped prison uniforms. The story was illustrated with a photo of the chorus performing one of its most popular numbers, a dance called the "Lockstep Jazz," which the story describes in this way:

> The shuffling, jazzy movement, executed in prison lockstep, with the dancers wearing costumes that dazzle the eye, with their shimmying, undulating bars and stripes, has made such a big hit here that, following a first performance before Santa Monica Rotarians, the "Cops' Chorus" has been deluged with offers of engagements by other clubs and organizations. Not only do they shake a mean limb (of the law) but they have their own orchestra and stellar soloists.[52]

Both of these stories evidence the close working relationship between the LAPD and the *Times*. As Davis and Escobar state, historically the department has served the ruling elite, and in the 1920s and early 1930s that meant working for the *Times* empire of Harrison Chandler and his business associates. Thus, when it came to advertising police power, it was often hard to tell where the police stopped and the mass media began.

An examination of news reports concerning Mexicans arrested for marijuana possession and traffic in the period supports this last claim. Indeed, drug enforcement directed at Mexicans would prove to be one of the LAPD's most popular "media events." During these years the department collaborated with the *Times* in order to use Mexican arrests as an advertisement for the value and efficiency of police work as such. Suggesting comparisons with forms of antiunion red-baiting in which Mexicans were criminalized en masse, in their public pronouncements both the police and news reporters focused on narcotics cases involving mass arrests of suspected drug peddlers. The fact that drug enforcement was directed at controlling Mexican workers was indirectly registered when the police referred to suspected drug traffickers in the same terms they used for Mexican labor organizations, such as "mobs," "bandits," and large criminal "rings."[53] And, more generally, the press and the police described the drug trade in terms that recall "legitimate" forms of agricultural labor. In 1928, the LAPD reported that it had arrested a husband-and-wife team who seemingly alternated between conventional agricultural work and marijuana cultivation. According to the police, the couple attempted to sell marijuana in Los Angeles that they had grown while harvesting beets in Wyoming.[54] Mexicans, moreover, were often arrested for supposedly working entire "farms" or "ranches" of marijuana.[55] As quoted in the *Times,* the police claimed that they had apprehended a group of Mexicans for growing two tons of the drug—"enough marijuana to make half of Los Angeles dizzy." The officers, who told reporters that the weed resembled alfalfa, used two "hay wagons" to transport it to the police station.[56] These kinds of news-mediated police reports promoted dominant claims that, while potentially valuable as cheap labor, Mexicans needed to be carefully managed in order to prevent a potential turn from legal to illegal forms of farm labor.

In addition to advertising the need for police power to manage Mexicans, police reports in the *Times* often puffed the department's efficient and professional response to Mexican drug crimes. Under headlines such as "Another Held in Drug Round-Up," "Marihuana Haul

Made in Drug Raid," "Drug Traffic Struck Blow," and "'Strong-Arm Mob' Believed Broken by Arrests," the paper and the police repeatedly emphasized the size and frequency of "big busts" involving large numbers of arrests and large amounts of marijuana.[57] Similarly, police officers routinely claimed to have detected one of *the* major sources of narcotics in Los Angeles.[58] In one of the most sensational cases, the LAPD, working in conjunction with federal narcotics agents, foiled a "huge Mexican dope-smuggling ring" made up of two Mexican women and several white men, including a prominent Venice churchman and financier. As the police told the *Times,* the "gang" was responsible for "flood[ing]" Los Angeles with "narcotics of Mexican origin."[59] One of the arresting officers was Captain Chitwood, the head of the Narcotics Squad, who had previously used the *Times* as a forum for boasting that the unit was "the best narcotic squad in the United States."[60] Police Chief Davis also used the press to promote his successful response to the Mexican drug problem in Los Angeles. In conjunction with a story about the Narcotics Squad arrest of a Mexican for selling marijuana, Davis told the *Times* that although drug addiction was a major cause of crime, drug crimes were at their lowest level in L.A. history thanks to his own expansion of the Narcotics Squad's activities.[61] Here Chief Davis seems to justify the ongoing need for police power to combat Mexican crime while at the same time lionizing the department's triumphs.

How, one might wonder, did drug enforcement directed at Mexicans become such an important aspect of police public relations? Press coverage suggests that news stories about Mexicans and marijuana served to anchor or organize a variety of race- and gender-marked sexual fantasies that in effect helped to make drug enforcement erotically compelling for mass audiences. In the first case, police press reports tended to represent Mexican women in ways that suggested their sexual availability. If we compare press coverage to actual arrest rates, a striking imbalance emerges, for although Mexican women are underrepresented in drug arrest statistics, they nonetheless played a prominent role in police reports. County jail records for 1926 and 1927, for example, suggest that although in general Mexican women were disproportionately arrested for prostitution and other sex crimes, none were arrested for violating drug laws.[62] Which is not to say that Mexican women were never arrested for drug crimes; police reports often focused on them. Rather, revising Peter Stallybrass and Allon White's influential formulation, I would argue that although Mexican women were marginal to actual law enforcement practice, they were nonetheless symbolically central to the early-twentieth-century war on drugs.[63]

Between 1927 and 1934, Mexican women constituted a significant presence in police press reports that served to promote local drug enforcement efforts. And although it may never be known how many of these women actually used or trafficked in marijuana, the LAPD's history of corruption should make us skeptical. Such skepticism is supported by news reports suggesting that it was police practice to arrest everyone in a house where drugs were found. In one case, police reported arresting all the inhabitants of a "Marijuana Ranch," including a fifty-three-year-old mother and her fourteen-year-old daughter.[64] Other cases in which a lone Mexican woman was arrested in a house with a group of men may also suggest the LAPD's belief in guilt by association, indicating that Mexicans were sometimes criminalized as a group, irrespective of gender.[65] And yet gender remains key to understanding the ideological significance of the women in drug enforcement reports. Such reports intimated that Mexican women who consorted with large groups of Mexican men in marijuana "dens" were "loose" and sexually deviant, for no "respectable" woman would keep such company. Further, some stories seem to suggest that even Mexican marriage was a form of deviancy or a partnership in crime, as in the case mentioned earlier of the Mexican couple that grew and harvested marijuana together.

The most dramatic example of a drug enforcement media event linking drugs and Mexican women's sexuality was the 1932 news report on the department's bust of a "huge Mexican dope-smuggling ring." In the *Times* version, the members of this so-called gang appear to be mixed in terms of race and gender, including Fredrick Grant White of Venice, Adela Garcia of Nogales, Mexico, Mrs. J. J. Baca, "member of a prominent Southern California family," and Thomas Cox and A. C. Costello of Los Angeles. Their arrest at their Los Angeles headquarters was the culmination of an eight-month investigation by the LAPD into the Mexican narcotics that had "flooded" Los Angeles. Focusing on Nogales "as the port of entry," the police determined that

> the Garcia woman was the "runner." They assert she made trips back and forth across the border on certain days carrying twenty-five ounces each trip concealed in a vest worn securely beneath her clothes. She made the trips until she had accumulated 500 ounces of dope, and then "ran" the contraband into Los Angeles. The officers say they trailed her

to the asserted headquarters. . . . According to the officers, White headed the ring, while Cox was the investigator of prospective purchasers, Costello and Mrs. Baca made the necessary wholesale connections in Mexico, and the Garcia woman was the runner.[66]

Although Mr. White supposedly headed the ring, both the police investigation and the newspaper story that promoted it centered on "the runner," "the Garcia woman." Indeed, I would argue that the report eroticizes her in ways that shore up police power.

The photo and caption that accompanied the story highlight the manner in which sexual titillation was mobilized in support of police power. The photo featured three narcotics officers handling "the Garcia woman's" dirty laundry, as it were, the unique undergarment she reportedly wore in order to run drugs from Sonora to southern California. Captioned "Woman Runner Uses Special Girdle," the photo shows three narcotics officers holding the criminal underwear stretched out between them in order to display its secret, supposedly dope-filled inner pockets. The officers thus offered to share with the reader their own seemingly intimate access to Garcia's "special girdle." The title above the photo—"Nogales Reported Point of Entry"—was also sexually suggestive, promising readers a point of entry into the inner workings of a Mexican drug "ring," and by extension symbolic access to Miss Garcia's body. Finally, the large headline above the story as a whole completed the fantasy of sexual access to Mexican women: "F. G. White, Former Venice Churchman, Trapped in Asserted Dope-Smuggling Ring." Here a sexualized Mexican woman seems to stand in for the drug ring that trapped Mr. White, the organization's putative head. In this way, the story plays upon fantasies of miscegenation between white men and Mexican women. Within such police-sponsored fantasies, Gracia may be a dangerous "trap," like some exotic *vagina dentata,* but in the hands of trained police she is reduced to a titillating but safe display.

These media events, in which the police publicized their effectiveness by offering their audiences the spectacle of Mexican women's sexuality, invite comparison to a body of Hollywood film narratives from the same period. As film critics such as Nick Browne, Miriam Hansen, Ana M. López, and Ella Shohat have shown, depictions of romantic relationships have been carefully segregated in Hollywood films.[67] All of these authors, however, emphasize that there are significant exceptions to this rule. As Browne states, in the history of U.S. film, an absolute prohibition against marriage and sexual relations between white women and men of color was "paired by contrast with the frequently actualized relation between a nonwhite female with a white male."[68] I will return to the white woman/man of color couple, but first I want to focus on the second half of Browne's equation in order to argue that numerous silent and early sound films made sexualized Latin American women, and especially Mexican women, erotically available to Anglo heroes.[69] Here I have in the mind the "cantina girl," an influential film character from the 1920s and 1930s who served as a precursor to the sorts of characters played by Rita Hayworth and Carmen Miranda in the 1940s.[70]

The numerous films featuring Mexican "cantina girls" who fall in love with Anglo-American heroes bring into relief the dominant sexual fantasies about Mexican women that also animated LAPD media events. Both Hollywood and the police, in other words, represented Mexican women as exotic and possibly decadent, potentially criminal, and, most important, sexually available. Or, more precisely, Mexican women were not only represented as desirable but ultimately as desiring white male authority. The character of the Mexican cantina girl usually works for a living as a singer and/or a dancer in a bar or nightclub. With her revealing costumes, sensuous performances, and potentially untrustworthy ways, the cantina girl projects an aura of sexual abandon that, while titillating, stops just short of "looseness" or "prostitution." And in each case, the sexy Mexican cantina girl falls in love with an Anglo-American hero, often pointedly choosing him over a Mexican suitor.[71] Early in her Hollywood career, Dolores Del Rio seemed to specialize in such roles. In RKO's *Girl of the Rio* (1932), she starred as Dolores, a beautiful young Mexican woman who sings in a sleazy border-town bordello. Dolores's true love is an Anglo-American named Johnny Powell, whom she ultimately chooses over a Mexican admirer, the vain, leering, menacing Don Tostado (Leo Carrillo), who wants her for his mistress. In such films, cantina girls fall for Anglos in part because the Mexican alternatives are so thoroughly lampooned and vilified. It is thus not surprising that the Mexican government found Carrillo's Don Tostado so offensive that it banned the film.[72] If Del Rio was Hollywood's favorite cantina girl, Carrillo was preferred for roles as the brutish and buffoonish Mexican foil in romances involving Mexican women and white men.[73]

While such films construct Mexican men as romantically unappealing, they often suggest that Mexican women are inherently attracted to white men, and fall for even the most unlikely white wooers.[74] The

Armida as a "cantina girl" in *Border Café* (1937).

romantic lead in *Girl of the Rio,* Johnny Powell, inexplicably works as a card dealer in a seedy border-town casino. Similarly, in *Border Café* (RKO, 1937), a Mexican cantina singer named Dominga (played by Mexican actress Armida) falls for one of the most unattractive romantic leads in early Hollywood history—Keith Whitney (John Beal), the spoiled, perpetually drunken, self-loathing son of a U.S. senator. By the end of the film, however, Whitney (whitey?) dries out, reconciles with his father the senator, and helps to stop a cattle-rustling gang. In this way, the film suggests that Whitney's most appealing feature is his relation to state power and the rule of law. The film thus indirectly promotes the supposed desirability of white police power to a Mexican character whose real-world analogues might have less reason to love the police.[75]

The ideological subtext of *Border Café* is made explicit in films where the cantina girl falls in love with an Anglo policeman. In *Lasca of the Rio Grande* (Paramount, 1931), the title character is a sensuous Mexican dancer who runs a Rio Grande gambling house. At the beginning of the film, she flirts with a local ranch owner named Don José (once again played by Carrillo), but by the end she has fallen in love with a Texas Ranger. Although historically the Rangers' reputation for racist brutality has earned them the fear and loathing of many Mexicans, in the end

Lasca sacrifices her own life in order to save her beloved Ranger from Don José's jealous rage.[76] Perhaps the most notable example of a film promoting Mexican love of the police is the film *Air Police* (Sono Art–World Wide Pictures, 1931), which focuses on airborne border patrol agents, Jerry and Andy, who fly to Mexico disguised as smugglers in order to break up a Mexican drug ring. While working undercover at a Mexican cantina, the two officers fall in love with a dancer named Dolores. When the smugglers discover Andy's true identity, however, they kill him, and at first Jerry thinks that Dolores has conspired with Pascal, the leader of the smugglers, to murder his friend. But when Pascal captures Jerry, Dolores comes to the rescue. Once Jerry dispatches the evil Pascal, she explains that she had nothing to do with Andy's death and the two characters end the film in an embrace.[77] As indirect reflections on official efforts to manage Mexican workers, these films try to legitimate police power by suggesting that Mexican workingwomen found it desirable.

Like the police report concerning Garcia, the Mexican drug runner with the criminal underwear, such Hollywood films made police work erotically compelling by imbuing it with taboo interracial sexual fantasies. The desirability of police power, moreover, was deployed to obscure and therefore naturalize heavy-handed efforts to police Mexican women's sexuality at a historical moment in which more and more women were entering the local labor market, often in such seasonal work as harvesting or canning, but also increasingly in service positions as maids, cooks, waitresses, and taxi dancers.[78] As the preceding discussion of police reports suggests, the LAPD not only used constructions of Mexican women's sexuality to promote police work but also sometimes used drug laws to target women living in suspiciously "nontraditional" households. Similarly, it used adultery laws and local ordinances requiring lodging houses to register with the city in order to arrest Mexican men and women living together outside of state-sanctioned wedlock.[79] And although police records indicate that Mexican women were, like men, disproportionately arrested for assault and vagrancy, the preceding example indicates that in general women were most vulnerable to prosecution for so-called crimes against morality, including prostitution and other sex crimes.[80] Both police reports about Mexican drug crimes and films focusing on cantina girls reinforce the criminalization of Mexican women as sexually voracious and "loose."

Such representations register the increasing presence in the local economy of Mexicana wageworkers, including those in new commercial leisure and entertainment sectors such as bars, dance halls, and, of course, Hollywood.[81] Starting in the 1910s and 1920s, both southern California film industries and the police presupposed a wage-labor economy that was increasingly dependent not only on Mexican immigrant men but also on women. Mexican actresses such as Vélez and Hayworth (originally Margarita Cansino) in fact began their careers as versions of the cantina girl, dancing in Mexican theaters and nightclubs. And although only a handful of Mexican women actually became film actresses, as independent wage earners they often served as models for women working in more mundane occupations in which they sometimes enjoyed a small taste of financial independence.

Equally important as possible models for Mexican workingwomen were the early-twentieth-century Mexican revolutionaries who lived in Los Angeles. Local Mexican anarchists, many of them women such as María Talavera and Teresa Arteaga, called for a redistribution of wealth from rich to poor, but also from men to women. They further criticized the marriage contract as a capitalist institution that oppressed women, and excoriated the church's tyranny over sexuality, including restrictions on birth control and divorce.[82] These ideas may have appealed to immigrant women who earned their own wages and lived outside the direct control of patriarchal families, or at least aspired to. In the theaters and dance halls of L.A., Mexican women attempted to actualize anarchist demands for female economic and sexual autonomy. Several women interviewed in the late 1920s for Manuel Gamio's *Life Story of the Mexican Immigrant,* for example, reported that they came to the United States after a divorce, and several decided to begin a new life by attempting to work as film actresses, singers, or dancers. Others took jobs as taxi dancers and lived in their own apartments, engaged in premarital sex, practiced birth control, and earned enough to pay for visits to nightclubs and the movies.[83] Although we should avoid romanticizing the lives of such women who, despite their earnings, often continued to live in desperate poverty, wage labor enabled them to claim a thin but important margin of independence.

Such women participated in forms of "queer intimacy" living and working in ways that contradicted white middle-class heterosexual norms.[84] A good example is "Isobel Sandoval," who was interviewed for Gamio's study. The interviewer first met twenty-five-year-old Isobel at a Mexican dance hall in Los Angeles called "Club Latino," where she worked as a taxi dancer. After a night of dancing and a postwork outing to a local bar, the interviewer joined Isobel and a party of her friends at the young woman's apartment, where the interview was conducted. Married at eighteen and divorced three years later, at the time of the interview she shared lodgings with two working-class men, whom she affectionately calls Ponchito and Gustavito. As she explains, she uses her wages to support two children who live in San Francisco. Here is her account:

> Some years ago I worked in the theatre. I sang couplets and danced Spanish dances and the *jarabe tapatío*. I have traveled almost everywhere in California working in the Mexican theatres and thus have earned my living. Since more than a year ago, perhaps two, I have worked in the dance halls, almost always the "Latino," and I have succeeded in making something sometimes. Almost always I make some $25 or $30 a week, sometimes I make more. I have lived with girl friends of mine, we have had apartments together, but I have convinced myself that it is better to live alone or with friends like Ponchito and Gustavito. I am absolutely free, if I wish I come to sleep and if I don't I don't . . . We three help each other when we have money, while with the girl friends one cannot do that way, because after a while jealousies and differences spring up and they don't like this or that, and there never lacks a reason over which to quarrel. Many girls think that Gustavito is my lover because they see that we live in the same house and that we like each other a lot. . . . But although it wouldn't make any difference, that isn't so. Gustavito likes me a lot because I have taken care of him, when he hasn't had either friends or money. Then I have been for him more than a sister, and he has been the same to me. It doesn't make any difference either to him nor to me what is said about us. After all we know what people are like.[85]

Let me speculate concerning the aspects of Isobel's story that depart from dominant heterosexual norms. It is tempting to imagine Ponchito and Gustavito as early-twentieth-century *jotos* or "queers" and Isobel as a "fag hag."[86] Isobel's use of the diminutives "Ponchito" and "Gustavito" for "Pancho" and "Gustavo" recalls not only sibling contexts, but also, I would argue, queer naming practices. In this way, we might think of the titles "Ponchito" and "Gustavito" as the two men's *joto* names. The slippage between sibling and queen identities is further suggested by Isobel's claim that "I have been for him [Gustavito], more than a sister, and he has been the same to me." Reading this statement as an expression of queer intimacy, I would suggest that Isobel and Gustavito have constructed an alternative "family" made up of male and female "sisters." I find encouragement for this interpretation in what the interviewer's unpublished notes tell us about the apartment's layout: Isobel has her own room, while the two men share a Murphy bed in the living room.[87] The published version of Isobel's story, however, omits all reference to sleeping arrangements in the apartment. Thus, although we cannot discern for certain the actual sexual practices of its inhabitants, it remains clear that Isobel's household departs in significant ways from the norm.

Although not necessarily typical of workingwomen at the time, economically independent, sexually autonomous women like Isobel contradicted dominant, Anglo models of female virtue and monogamous heterosexuality. And this threat to dominant forms of sexuality partly explains why working-class Mexican women were the objects of intense concern for both the police and Hollywood. Both groups, moreover, endeavored to promote and profit from sexualized images of Mexican women while at the same time serving to police Mexican sexuality. Or, more precisely, both Hollywood and the police used constructions of Mexican women's sexuality as a means for practically and ideologically latching onto bodies and populations in order to better control them. The LAPD used titillating representations of Mexican women in order to promote ongoing efforts to police them, particularly for drug and other vice crimes. Similarly, Hollywood representations of the cantina girl exploited assumptions about the inherent hypersexuality of Mexican women while at the same time promoting a highly restricted, carceral ideal of female virtue.

Girl of the Rio, for example, promotes a fantasy of hot Mexicana sexuality tamed by the love of whiteness. The Anglo hero, Johnny Powell, begins the film by enthusing to his fellow card dealer, Bill, about the Mexican girl he loves. When Bill asks why such a great girl is working at a Tijuana brothel called the Purple Pigeon, Johnny answers that Dolores is different, a "white ribbon girl," meaning a virgin. "They all are when they begin," Bill replies, a reminder of police discourses and practices that constructed working-class Mexican women as irresistibly prone to prostitution and other sex crimes. And although this does not turn out to be true of Dolores, in the brothel where she works she is constantly compared with the prostitutes. In an early scene at the Purple Pigeon, the prostitutes and Dolores take turns entertaining Don Tostado, the former with fawning compliments and sexual innuendo and the latter with a passionate rendition of a song called "Querida." In a subsequent scene, set in her dressing room at the brothel, the film eroticizes Dolores's scantily clad body with close-ups of hips and legs that in effect decompose her into fetishistic part objects. When Tostado pressures her to become his mistress, however, she resists by insisting that she is a "good girl." And although she proves to be extremely passionate about Johnny Powell, the fact that she directs her desire exclusively at the Anglo hero serves in the end to chasten and domesticate her charismatic sexuality. When Tostado threatens to murder her beloved unless she becomes his mistress, Dolores agrees to go away with him in order to save her Johnny, but vows to take poison rather than submit to the Don's desire. She is prevented from taking the poison but still escapes a "fate worse than death," and ultimately saves Johnny from Tostado's firing squad. Together the lovers ride off into the sunlight of a new day. In this way, the film safely diverts what it represents as the rushing current of the Mexican woman's sexuality into a narrow, Anglo-defined and -directed circuit. Here the construction of the cantina girl as hypersexual becomes the basis for reimagining Mexican women in restricted terms that ultimately legitimate white supremacy.

As figures for Mexican women wageworkers, both the LAPD's female drug criminals and Hollywood's cantina girl made explicit the extent to which the eroticization of Mexican women became one means of policing their labor. Similarly, both Hollywood and the police also projected models of Mexican male sexuality as a means for policing brown bodies, but with some important differences. Many U.S. films, most famously *Birth of a Nation,* were preoccupied with the supposed dangers of the black rapist, but police records indicate that given L.A.'s large Mexican population, the more immediate local concern was working-class Mexican men. According to LAPD records for 1927 and 1928, Mexican men were disproportionately arrested for a variety of sex crimes, and in some cases the disproportion was particularly glaring, such that while roughly one out of every ten persons in L.A. at the time was Mexican, one out of every four men arrested for rape and almost half of those charged with pandering were Mexican men.[88] The assumption that Mexican men were sexually voracious and physically violent permeated a wide range of official police discourses and practices directed at Mexicans, but especially drug enforcement. The linking of drug crimes to Mexican male sexuality had multiple effects. The presumption that Mexican men were potentially perverse bodies out of control partly served to "explain" Mexican criminality and therefore to justify police efforts to contain it. At the same time, the association of sex and drugs helped to promote police actions by imbuing drug enforcement with tabooed erotic fantasies. In other words, although police power was directed at policing Mexican men and enforcing the ban on their sexual relations with white women, police representations of drug crimes nonetheless exploited fantasies of such supposedly forbidden congress in order to advertise drug enforcement and make it erotically compelling. And finally, the police often drew their representations of sex, drugs, and Mexicans from Hollywood's repertoire of images.

In chapter 3, I suggested that in the federal marijuana hearings, witnesses often described the act of producing and selling marijuana as if it were a form of predatory Mexican sexual aggression that threatened to violate white women and children. Local officials in southern California made similar equations, as when a state narcotics agent reported that marijuana grown in the agricultural fields of the Imperial Valley represented a greater threat to "schoolchildren" than any other drug.[89] Similarly, in a 1934 speech to the L.A. County Federation of Women's Clubs, reported by the *Times,* Captain Chitwood of the Narcotics Squad ominously declared, "I would rather have one of my children suddenly killed tomorrow than to hear that he had become addicted to the use of narcotics," perhaps echoing Dolores's claim in *Girl of the Rio* that being forced to have sex with a Mexican man is a fate worse than death.[90] One of the most striking examples of the mobilization of fantasies about Mexican sexuality in order to justify and promote police power is an LAPD news report, mentioned earlier, about the arrest of three Mexicans for growing and selling "enough marihuana to 'to make half of Los Angeles dizzy.'" The report is arrestingly illustrated with the "cheesecake" photograph of a young, apparently white woman posed with the "evidence." Captioned "Miss Mary Fiesel and Marihuana," the photo depicts the young woman reclining on a "bale" of the weed, her legs in prominent view beneath the long, leafy marijuana stems that rest on her lap. From under her flapper curls Miss Fiesel looks down with a smile at the marijuana stem she holds in her hands. The long marijuana stems function as props that metonymically represent a transgressive Mexican masculinity in titillating proximity to a white woman. The accompanying newsprint underlines this reading, describing the drug in related phallic (or tumescent) terms, claiming that the "marihuana weed" produces "seed pods for smoking" and that two of the Mexican men arrested had "more than 100 cans of the smokable seed." This amalgamation of seed-producing marihuana stalks and the seductively posed Miss Fiesel indirectly references fantasies about transgressive sexual relations between white women and Mexican men. Thus, although sexual congress between the two was officially prohibited, police reports subtly promoted drug enforcement by flirting with such tabooed fantasies. And allusions to the violent perversity of Mexican sexuality effectively obscured the origins of drug enforcement in capitalist demands for labor discipline and control.

Such police news reports bear comparison to sensational "exploitation" films such as the low-budget movie *Marihuana: Weed with Roots in Hell* (1936).[91] Its director, Dwain Esper, made other cheap shockers such as *Narcotic* (1933), *Maniac* (1934), and *The Narcotic Story* (ca. 1935), and served as the distributor for the infamous *Reefer Madness* (1937). *Marihuana* opens in a roadhouse as two Latin drug dealers—Tony Montello and Nick—prepare to seduce a tipsy group of white teens into smoking the weed.[92] Effusively friendly and inviting, Tony and Nick convince the youngsters to attend a beach party, but the party becomes an orgy after the dark men give the kids marijuana, leading white girls to strip, dance, spoon, skinny-dip, and have sex on the beach. As a result, one young white woman drowns, and the film's female protagonist, Burma, is impregnated by her white boyfriend, Dick. Soon Dick starts to work for Tony and Nick, helping to smuggle marijuana into the United States, when he is suddenly killed in a shootout between smugglers and the police. With Dick dead, Tony persuades Burma to give up her baby for adoption and join him in a life of crime. She quickly becomes an addict, and aggressively sells marijuana to other young white people in order to hook them on heroin. Burma's fatal scheme, however, involves kidnapping her respectable sister's child, a little girl who turns out to be the daughter Burma had previously given up for adoption. After learning this news, Burma returns to the apartment where Nick and Tony are holding the girl. As she steps out of the elevator, "double-exposed effigies of Nick and Tony" appear on either side of her, repeating the enticements that first drew her into addiction, crime, and disgrace ("If you listen to me you're going to make a lot of money," etc.).[93] She opens the apartment door and discovers the police questioning her accomplices. Burma falls to the floor as Nick and Tony rush to her side to

Lobby card for *Marihuana: Weed with Roots in Hell* (1936).

catch her. The camera cuts to a shot of the apartment's bedroom door, through which her daughter is briefly visible before it slams shut. The film's final shots show handfuls of marijuana cigarettes sprinkled on the floor around Burma's crumpled body.

Marihuana, in my reading, is a race-mixing melodrama in which Latin drug dealers hook white kids on dope, targeting in particular a young blond schoolgirl, Burma, whom they seduce into a life of crime and sexual "disgrace." The film represents narcotics as racialized part-objects, framing hypodermic needles and marijuana cigarettes as phallic signs of her symbolic violation by Tony and Nick. The drug here serves as a metonym for Latin men, while scenarios of marijuana smoking represent proxies for fantasies and fears of brown men having sex with or raping white women. The closing scenes of the film support this interpretation. As Burma weaves through the apartment hallway, the ghostly, superimposed images of Tony and Nick are followed by a shot of the dazed young woman stopping to insert a needle in her arm. Inside the apartment, the door slams on her daughter, signifying that Burma has severed all familial relationships and other ties to the respectable white, heterosexual world at the moment when she falls into the arms of the two Latin gangsters and joints scatter on the floor at her feet. An unwed mother, outside the circle of Anglo-American civility, Burma is caught between menacing brown men.

Marihuana: Weed with Roots in Hell is part of a genre of similar cheap films, including not only the previously mentioned *Narcotic* and *Reefer Madness*, but also *The Pace That Kills* (1935), *Assassin of Youth* (1937), *Paroled from the Big House* (1938), and *Wages of Sin* (1938), in which the drug drags young white characters into violence and perversion. And although such films were marginal to the main current of film production, *Marihuana*'s representation of Latinos recalls earlier images from a genre of silent westerns called "greaser" films. As in the federal hearings for a national law to criminalize marijuana, in these films Mexican men are violent and lascivious drug addicts and smugglers.[94] Beginning in 1922, however, Hollywood was forced by an emergent postrevolutionary Mexican government to significantly revise, while not totally abandoning, this genre. In that year, Mexico threatened to exclude all titles by any company that exhibited films offensive to Mexican national dignity anywhere in the world. Unable or unwilling to lose the lucrative Mexican market, the studios and their self-appointed industry censors attempted, often unsuccessfully, to make films that appealed primarily to a U.S. audience while at least not overtly offending Mexican national censors. The results were films that preserved elements of Mexican criminality from the "greaser" tradition and subsequent exploitation films but recast them in slightly more subtle and indirect ways.

In the 1930s, the Mexican actor Leo Carrillo specialized in these newly revised greaser roles. As the libidinous villain of *Girl of the Rio,* for instance, Carrillo's Don Tostado recalls the silent Mexican heavies. And though not expressly described as a "dope fiend," he constantly drinks and smokes. Or, as his name implies, Tostado is perpetually high or "toasted," making him an indirect representation of the Mexican marijuana menace of LAPD crime reports. Carrillo's most infamous role, however, was in *Viva Villa* (1934), in which he played the Mexican general's impulsively violent and vain sidekick, named Sierra. As played by Wallace Beery, Villa is himself a primal, aggressive character, while Sierra represents the extension of the general's most extreme impulses and desires. Taken together, these two characters are so sadistic that a writer for the *Nation* titled his review of the film "The Marquis de Villa."[95]

A prime example of Villa's sexual sadism occurs during the last third of the film when Villa threatens to rape one of his benefactors, Teresa

(Fay Wray), a wealthy Spanish Creole. Villa occupies her hacienda, and as his soldiers raid the pantry and fondle the female servants, Sierra is charged with locating Teresa and bringing her to the revolutionary's darkened room, where he drunkenly tells her, "I only know how to make love one way. If I see an angel I got to make love that way, I got to grab hard." When he pulls her to him for a bruising kiss, Teresa breaks away, produces a gun, and shoots him in the hand. Villa quickly disarms her, and then Sierra enters and shoots her. Although displaced in time and space, such scenes of rapaciousness recall dominant police models of Mexican male sexuality. In particular, the scene rehearses taboo fantasies about sex between Mexican men and white women like the upper-class Spanish woman Teresa. The character's whiteness would have been reinforced by Wray's star image, which was closely tied to her immediately previous role as the blonde white woman menaced by King Kong.

Further, the Mexican men in *Viva Villa* condense a host of "perverse" sexual fantasies, including those involving homosexuality. Both Villa and Sierra are humorously represented as vain and narcissistic in ways that have historically been coded as "feminine" or homosexual. These comic intimations of the two men's perversity are more grimly represented in the film's torture scene, in which Villa revenges himself upon his rival, General Pascal, in ways that suggest anal rape. Previously, Pascal had publicly humiliated Villa by making him beg for his life, and then he executed Villa's beloved Francisco Madero, the short-lived president of Mexico. The subsequent scene of Villa's revenge begins with the general recounting his degradation at the hands of one man, and the declaration of his intense, frightening love for another. At the outset, the general sloppily eats an apple and recalls for Pascal that prior scene of humiliation. "Maybe I love somebody at that time," Villa tells his prisoner. "A little fella with a beard. Love make you frightened. Maybe you love somebody. Gotta wife, kids?" The camera then cuts to a close-up of ants crawling over a rotting orange, and Villa nonchalantly notes that the insects like honey even better. In his hands he holds a long, thin, round jar of honey from "the same place that I crawled on my knees. Maybe you like some?" Pascal responds in horror, "No, Pancho, that's not the way," but Villa insists, "that's my way" (recalling his earlier claim to Teresa that "I only know how to make love one way"?), and then dips his fingers in the jar and smears it on Pascal's face. Villa orders his men to rub the honey everywhere—"put it on his ears, his eyes, his nose, his mouth, put it everyplace on him, everyplace." Off camera, Pascal is apparently staked over an anthill, and his groans and screams serve as the sound track to a surreal montage of Villa sitting down to gnaw on a rib, a close-up of ants crawling all over the empty honey jar, a long shot of vultures in a tree, and a return to the general tearing meat from a bone. Oscillating between extreme states of masculine humiliation, desire, and homicidal rage, this odd scenario between Mexican men recalls the paranoid gothic novels analyzed by Eve Sedgwick, in which violent homosocial intensities reference and displace publicly prohibited homosexual desires.[96]

Indeed, the production history of *Viva Villa* suggests that in dominant U.S. representations, Mexico and Mexicans were sometimes the reservoir for fantasies about a racialized homosocial sadism. In many respects, in fact, *Viva Villa* is indebted to the gangster film, a genre characterized by the kinds of violent homosocial intensities just described. The writer and initial director of *Viva Villa*, Ben Hecht and Howard Hawks, respectively, had previously produced *Scarface*, which is also about a violent and sadistic Latin gangster.[97] Hawks seemed to see Mexico and Mexicans through the lens of gangster films about crime in the United States. He told an interviewer years after finishing the picture:

> When we went down to Mexico to make *Viva Villa* they had some sort of gangsters down there, and I was taken to meet the man who shot Villa. . . . They all carried guns, so I carried a gun. I used to be a damn good shot with a revolver. I took the gun out and shot at a tin can and made it roll along the ground. Shot again and made it keep on going, put the gun back. That was all luck, you know. Oh, golly, they looked at me—they weren't going to start anything if I could shoot *that* way.[98]

Here Hawks takes obvious pleasure in the potentially dangerous friction between himself and Mexican "gangsters." As the interview continues, his reminiscences assume a pronouncedly homoerotic tone. In one instance, the director describes a Mexican man dressed in a "pink leather suit" (!) who, upon recognizing the director of *Scarface*, luridly offers to shoot another man while Hawks watches.[99] Next Hawks describes the Mexican extras: "We had the soldiers and the peons, we would search them all two or three times, and they'd whittle wooden bullets, which, if you put a gun close enough to somebody, would go into his stomach. And they would stick bullets up their rectums and pull 'em out and shoot somebody."[100] This strange image of rectal

Mexican bullets penetrating other men in the stomach suggests that we might productively rethink the conventions of Mexico westerns—including firing squads, "mano y mano" showdowns, and "Mexican stand-offs"—as constituting violent, racialized fantasies of sex between men.

C. L. R. James's suggestive remarks concerning the new forms of violence and aggression he detected in U.S. mass culture after 1929, particularly the cycle of gangster films, provide a useful model for interpreting representations of Mexican men. In *American Civilization* (ca. 1950), James argued that after the stock-market crash, "the whole popular so-called entertainment world began its turn to violence, sadism, cruelty, [and] the release of aggression." In implicit disagreement with an emergent Frankfurt School interpretation of U.S. mass culture, James stresses that post-crash mass audiences were not simply the passive victims of a culture industry. Such a view, he concludes, imagines that the mass of people are "dumb slaves"—"a conception totally unhistorical." Instead, James insists that "the mass decides what it will see" and filmmakers are "in violent competition with each other for the mass to approve what they produce."[101]

Why did Depression-era audiences make films about violence, sadism, cruelty, and aggression so popular? According to James, the Depression was merely the immediate (albeit devastating) indication of an even larger contradiction in the history of capitalist democracy in the United States. Simply put, although U.S. democracy was historically built on ideologies of individual freedom for white males, capitalism continually undermined the material basis for even these limited forms of autonomy.

> In such a society, the individual demands an esthetic compensation in the contemplation of free individuals who go out into the world and settle their problems by free activity and individualistic methods. In these perpetual isolated wars free individuals are pitted against free individuals, live grandly and boldly. . . . In the end, "crime does not pay" but for an hour and a half highly skilled actors and a huge organization of production and distribution have given to many millions a sense of active living, and in the bloodshed, the violence, the freedom from restraint to allow pent-up feelings free play, they have released the bitterness, hate, fear and sadism which simmer just below the surface.[102]

Here the gangster is vicariously appealing because, on the one hand, he acts out utopian longings for freedom and agency, and, on the other, he embodies disappointment and rage over the material barriers to the real-

ization of individual autonomy. According to James, the mass popularity of the gangster film leads in two, contradictory directions—a potentially democratic rebellion against the authority of capitalism and the
state, and a "totalitarian" embrace of fascist populism and the strong
man of action.

Viva Villa exemplifies both of these directions. On the one hand, as
a sort of Mexican revolutionary Robin Hood who flouts aristocratic
authority and takes what he wants, the character of Villa was vicariously
appealing to Depression-era audiences as a figure of rebellion against capitalism and the state.[103] This partly explains why some reviewers seemed
to see Villa as a democratic freedom fighter. A reviewer for the *Motion
Picture Daily* sympathetically wrote that the film represents "the heart
cry of an oppressed people...galloping like an army of Paul Reveres
across the countryside."[104] Moreover, as a figure of "perverse" desire, the
"Marquis de Villa" may have been attractive because he represented dissident erotic affects and practices, allowing viewers to vicariously rebel
against dominant sexual prohibitions. *Viva Villa* ultimately contains these
potentially radical democratic impulses, however, not only because, as
James would have it, "crime does not pay" and in the end Villa must
die, but also because the film promotes the arbitrary use of force in response to social contradictions. And in this regard Villa and his sidekick
Sierra are a sort of "bad cop"/"worse cop" team that suggests, in displaced
fashion, the excesses of the LAPD.

In other words, to the extent that Anglo-Americans took vicarious
pleasure in the violent and perverse exploits of such characters, it is
partly because they enjoyed the sexual sadism associated with proto-
fascist police power while at the same time disavowing such pleasure by
projecting it onto Mexican men. The comparison with fascism is apt in
this context, because MGM proudly publicized the fact that the film's
star, Wallace Beery, was awarded a gold medal for his performance from
Italy's National Fascist Association of Motion Picture and Theatrical
Industries.[105] As the drug war waged against Mexicans makes particularly apparent, the LAPD, like Hollywood, also learned how to exploit
the erotic appeal of police power. The ideological significance of the
department's mass-media dissemination of eroticized drug enforcement
scenarios was thus overdetermined. In the first place, police propaganda
represented supposed drug crimes as the expression of a distinctly Mexican sexual pathology that called for forceful police action. In the second
place, however, police reports promoted drug enforcement efforts by

exploiting fantasies of the very same sorts of hypersexuality that the police supposedly worked to contain. In the end, the sexual sadism and perversity associated with Mexicans radiated outward, bathing police power in an erotic brown glow.

Thus far, I have focused on the ways in which police reports concerning Mexican drug crimes implicitly reproduced popular film conventions. The details of film plots are revealing in part because, as Carl Gutiérrez-Jones has shown, narrative is central to U.S. legal ideologies, particularly with regard to the criminalization of Mexicans in the U.S. Southwest.[106] And yet, a comparative analysis of police narratives and Hollywood plots alone cannot capture the formal similarities between the two kinds of storytelling. Filmmakers had at their disposal new technologies for generating narratives, including the use of constructed settings, costumes, props, lighting, sound, editing, and camera angles. Together, these techniques were used to persuade audiences to suspend their disbelief and accept the "diegetic illusion," whereby the film world is apprehended as its own distinct reality, perceptually segregated from the immediate context of film exhibition and, by extension, from the larger social context.[107] For its part, the LAPD adopted some of the representational techniques of film. Like Hollywood filmmakers, the police strove to invent a new set of representational techniques—a new visual language—for telling their tales of Mexican criminality.

In order to generate sympathy and support for the LAPD drug war, the department increasingly mobilized mass-media visual technology such as the newspaper camera. Whereas police reports published in the *Los Angeles Times* never include photos of Mexicans arrested for drugs, they often picture the arresting officers, as in the photo described earlier in which the police hold up the drug-smuggling girdle. Such photos function like "close-ups" that focus on brave officers and make them available as points of identification for newspaper readers or "viewers." Virtual close-ups of policemen and other officials were part of a larger effort to use the mass media to generate positive publicity for the police by personalizing law enforcement, much the way filmmakers use close-ups to produce the illusion of psychological depth and complexity. Suggesting the need for positive publicity, a *Times* story headlined "How Can We Halt Rising Flood of Crime Here?" featured the anti-Mexican drug warrior Judge Charles W. Fricke, who argued that the number one cause of crime was a "lack of respect for our penal laws." As if to "personalize" his point of view, Fricke's remarks were illustrated with a "head shot" of the jurist.[108] The *Times,* moreover, often used visual language to describe law enforcement speeches and police actions. The paper, for example, described Fricke's antidrug speech to the L.A. City Club as if it were a cinematic spectacle, noting that the Judge "*Shows* [the] Danger to Every Citizen," and that he presented "*pictures* of the havoc wrought by drug addicts" to his audience.[109] Finally, as representatives of the panoptic gaze of the law, the police were seemingly aligned with the gaze of the film camera, as in headlines such as "Official Eye on Hemp Growers."[110] In all of these ways, the police used visual techniques reminiscent of filmmaking in order to represent themselves as the heroic protagonists in what I call "LAPD, the Movie." Whereas published police reports focus on images of the police in virtual close-ups, supposed Mexican drug criminals are represented by what might be called evidentiary "props," including not only marijuana stalks and bales, but also related forms of drug remnants and paraphernalia such as burned matches, marijuana cigarette butts or "roaches," and the tobacco tins supposedly used to package the weed for sale.[111] In Hollywood films, props are often used to "anchor" characters in particular meaning, such that a Mexican character's whip or branding iron signifies uniquely Mexican forms of sexual sadism. Similarly, the drug-related props found in police reports effectively link Mexican "characters" to drug crimes.

Ultimately, these different ways of visualizing the police and Mexican drug criminals contributed to the formation of a drug-war "mis-en-scène" that imaginatively abstracted drug enforcement from its larger social contexts. Although, as I have argued, drug enforcement responded to capitalist needs for a compliant labor force, mass-mediated police reports imply that Mexican drug use and traffic constitutes its own self-enclosed criminal underworld, cut off from larger economic interests. Rather than depicting drug enforcement as an arm of labor discipline, in other words, the police attempted to reinforce a sort of "diegetic illusion" whereby a constructed world of inherent Mexican criminality gains its persuasive power by perceptually segregating police work from the political economy that historically informed it. Here, then, we see some of the preconditions for more recent developments, in which the contemporary U.S. war on drugs has become a mass-media spectacle unto itself, separated from the larger political and economic interests that provide its impetus in the first place.

Which is not to suggest that mass media are completely colonized by the state, for one of the central arguments of *Drug Wars* is that the media play an active role in the war on drugs. Similarly, in the 1930s, Hollywood did more than passively serve as a source of visual strategies that the police then elaborated; rather, while remaining relatively autonomous from the state, filmmakers were nonetheless agents in the war on drugs that targeted Mexicans. As the next chapter shows, films incorporated Mexican songs, particularly those about drugs, in highly contained and segregated ways, suggesting that such music served as the imaginary proxy for the Mexicans targeted by the police. Moreover, the incorporation of Mexican music was matched by renewed efforts to assimilate Mexican audiences as disciplined spectators. The inclusion of Mexican music in early sound films, in other words, can partly be read as an attempt to draw Mexican audiences into the diegetic illusion and inculcate in them the norms of the so-called classical mode of Hollywood spectatorship, whereby the viewer sits attentively and quietly focused on a central narrative film to the relative exclusion of side distractions such as live musical performances. Hollywood's war on drugs, however, entangled the industry in a series of conflicts with Mexican cultural workers and audiences over the legitimate uses of sound: Hollywood's efforts to police Mexicans partly focused on insurgent Mexican radio performers who inspired not disciplined spectatorship but mass protest movements. The participation of filmmakers in forms of symbolic police work was also a reaction to unruly Mexican performers and audiences who disobeyed Hollywood spectatorial norms by screening films with live musical performance and encouraging audible audience participation. By confounding the policing of spectatorship such audiences indirectly opposed the mass-mediated use of sound to police Mexican workers.

CHAPTER 5

La Cucaracha in Babylon
Mexican Music and Hollywood's Sonic War on Drugs

In chapter 4, I concluded that LAPD drug enforcement efforts borrowed narrative strategies and representational techniques from Hollywood. This chapter suggests that, in response to the Mexican presence in Los Angeles, Hollywood studios mobilized the police and policing practices in order to segregate the industry from the increasingly Mexican social space that surrounded it. Coinciding with the rise of Mexican immigration to southern California in the 1920s, film companies promoted ties with local law enforcement and formed their own private police forces. These Hollywood police departments served and protected huge, self-enclosed film factories that, recalling other local factories and the many "whites only" neighborhoods in Los Angeles, largely barred Mexicans. Although Mexican workers were generally excluded from jobs in film production, however, Hollywood films often made use of Mexican themes, settings, and especially music. Just as the state worked to integrate Mexicans into the local economy as carefully policed workers, so filmmakers sought to integrate "Mexicanness" as a marginalized or subordinated aspect of film plots, settings, and sound tracks.

With the advent of synchronized sound in the late 1920s, Hollywood often turned to Mexico and Mexicans in search of material to showcase the new technology, but it faced the problem of how to incorporate popular Mexican music in a manner that did not seem to support or encourage Mexican criminality. This was a particularly pressing issue because one of the most popular film songs from the 1930s was "La Cucaracha."

As I noted in chapter 3, "La Cucaracha" was a Mexican revolutionary song, associated with Pancho Villa, that frankly celebrated revolt and marijuana in the figure of "la cucaracha," the revolutionary subaltern who only marches when he has marijuana to smoke. Although today the song is a well-known example of musical kitsch, non-Mexican audiences in the 1930s seemingly greeted it as a sensational novelty when it was reproduced on records, sheet music, and in numerous shorts, cartoons, and films, most notably *Viva Villa* (MGM, 1934). The song's contemporary status as a cliché testifies to the film industry's obsession with the postrevolutionary Mexican diaspora that surrounded it. The incorporation of "La Cucaracha" both exposes and conceals the fact that many films set in revolutionary and postrevolutionary Mexico, the U.S.–Mexican border zone, or the nineteenth-century "frontier" were also, in a displaced sense, about the policing of Mexicans in Los Angeles. Depression-era filmmakers, in other words, filtered "La Cucaracha" through the history of local, national, and international police discourses and practices. The various formal and informal efforts by filmmakers and industry watchdogs to censor or rewrite "La Cucaracha" represent contradictory attempts to imaginatively police sounds of subaltern dissent. For this reason, we might say that in the 1930s and after, Hollywood film was part of a mass culture of counter Mexican insurgency.

Instances of Mexican insurgency in modern Los Angeles include not only strikes and protests but also attempts to intervene in a highly policed mass media in order to criticize the combined power of capitalism and the state. Crisscrossed by various forms of police power, communications and entertainment media were, in the early decades of the twentieth century, tense fields of political conflict. During the revolution, the Magón brothers, the famous Mexican anarchists introduced in chapter 3, were arrested and tried in Los Angeles for publishing a supposedly "obscene" newspaper, and the resulting media circus set the tone for subsequent mass-media struggles between Mexican insurgents and dominant, reactionary forces. Moreover, in the 1930s, activists and local media celebrities such as Pedro J. González and Josefina Fierro drew upon revolutionary traditions in order to oppose the criminalization of Mexicans in the mass media; instead, they used the airwaves to criticize the arbitrary use of police power. Starting in the late 1920s, González, who had fought with Villa in the revolution, hosted a popular Spanish-language radio show on a Los Angeles station, and during the Depression he used it to condemn the use of police power to deport or "repatriate" local Mexicans. Once a favorite musical performer of the police and other city officials, González was arrested and wrongly convicted on trumped-up charges of statutory rape, thus demonstrating the tight police controls that Mexicans confronted in the media. In addition to organizing protests against police abuse and the segregation of public places, including movie theaters, Fierro similarly used her weekly radio show to oppose Mexican criminalization. She also cultivated connections to Hollywood in order to rally filmmakers around Mexican immigrant causes and to influence movie depictions of Mexicans. In these ways, Mexicans such as Fierro, González, and a host of anonymous immigrants indirectly left their mark on a movie industry that worked hard to exclude them.

As the stories of Fierro and González suggest, the history of modern sound technologies overlapped with the local history of police power, including the drug war that targeted Mexican immigrants in the 1920s and 1930s (discussed in chapter 4). Modern sound reproduction included the interrelated phonographic, broadcasting, and movie industries that developed during years of intense struggle involving the postrevolutionary Mexican presence in southern California. Mexicans and Anglo-Americans at the time were in conflict and competition over how to use new forms of audio mass media. Struggles over sound technologies occurred not only in contexts of production, as in Fierro's and González's insurgent uses of radio, but also in the settings of sound reception, such as the Mexican movie theaters of Los Angeles. Mexican audiences and movie programmers appropriated early sound films in ways that contradicted emergent Hollywood norms of exhibition and spectatorship. As a rejoinder, the studios attempted to incorporate music into films so as to displace or exclude the musicians and other performers who generally accompanied sound films in a variety of different movie houses, but particularly in Mexican theaters. While Hollywood endeavored to contain Mexican music by subordinating it within its films, Mexicans often subordinated sound films to the pleasures and interests of larger musical variety shows. Mexican variety shows reframed films with alternative sound tracks that addressed immigrant histories and thereby contradicted the principal trajectory of Hollywood film in the direction of increasingly standardized and "Americanized" deployments of sound. Divergent Mexican uses bring into relief the extent to which dominant film sound exercised a sort of ideological police power that was aimed at symbolically containing Mexican music as well as Mexican dissent.

This chapter also counters the tendency in U.S. film studies to ignore the Mexican presence in Los Angeles and its significance for the emergence of Hollywood film industries and other mass media. When I first began thinking about this topic, it seemed reasonable to expect that early Hollywood film production must have in some way been affected by the mass of new Mexican immigrants in their midst—how could it be otherwise? I thus anticipated finding a significant body of scholarship on "the Mexican question" in Hollywood, but I was surprised to discover that while one could fill a cineplex with critical works that consider the role of European immigrants in the history of film, there was not a single book or essay on the Mexican presence in and around Hollywood and its consequences for film production. As such scholars as Nick Browne, Jane M. Gaines, and Ella Shohat have all shown, film critics have generally marginalized the role of race in the history of U.S. film.[1] And although there are a handful of essays that focus on the careers of Mexican stars, a few on "images of" Mexicans in early film, and a small number that consider Hollywood's sway over Mexican immigrants, no study exists concerning the formative role of Mexican immigrants in the history of silent and early sound film.[2]

The postrevolutionary Mexican diaspora in southern California shaped the emergence and then global hegemony of Hollywood in a number of ways. The Mexican presence was formative for aspects of film production and exhibition, and local Mexican populations helped to shape all sorts of film narratives, but especially westerns and musicals. Furthermore, the industry viewed films about the "Mexican question" through the lens of the local police state. In other words, Hollywood's interest in depictions of Mexican violence, revolt, and criminality was a symbolic rejoinder to the Mexican anarchists and other radicals in modern Los Angeles who were some of the most visible critics and targets of local police powers. Mexican radicals were highly visible political actors and propagandists in modern L.A. who, as we shall see, launched protests and strikes, but also published newspapers, produced radio shows, and reappropriated Hollywood films for alternative entertainments. Combined with direct acts of rebellion, interventions by Mexican radicals into an emergent mass culture ultimately generated largely repressive responses from a film industry increasingly committed to civic law and order.

As a highly capitalized mode of entertainment that ideologically hails and viscerally engages audiences, Hollywood film exerts a powerful influence over mass audiences. My analysis of the 1930s war on drugs, however, helps make visible the formidable influence and agency of Mexican immigrants in the U.S. mass media. As noted in the preceding chapter, the mass-mediated war on drugs, including in films, was a direct response to the presence and actions of Mexican immigrant workers in Los Angeles. Because their movements and actions often motivated or provoked film productions, Mexican workers were in effect coproducers of southern California film culture. Moreover, in order to avoid reifying dominant representations by taking their ideological aspirations as accomplished facts, we must also consider what various audiences actually did with films. Mexican audiences in Los Angeles reinterpreted them in subaltern ways, recontaining films in variety formats that represented immigrant perspectives on dominant power relations. Finally, the manner in which they recontextualized films had a formative effect on the industry, for Mexican appropriations of Hollywood films ultimately shaped the kinds of movies that were made.

MEXICAN MOVIES WOUND AMERICANS
Animosity, perhaps engendered over the strained relations between the United States and Mexico, gave too realistic a complexion to the battle scene staged yesterday by the Monrovia Feature Film Company on the San Gabriel Wash, about two miles from El Monte. Frank Hanners of Monrovia was shot in the right eye with a blank cartridge and John Algers of Los Angeles had his right thigh pierced by a lance, both weapons being wielded by Mexicans in "Gen. Pio Pico's Army." . . .

Included in "Pico's army" was a large number of Mexicans, and some instances of rough handling of them by men in the "Commodore Stockton forces" apparently resulted in bad blood. About 800 men were engaged on both sides and the "battle" was fought on the same ground where the original engagement occurred and which resulted in the termination of Mexican rule in California at the beginning of the Mexican war.

The Monrovia company is filming a ten-reel historical photoplay entitled "The Daughter of the Don."
Los Angeles Times, 3 June 1916, sec. 1, 7

In this news story, the staging of a U.S.–Mexican war battle for *The Daughter of the Don* opens the wounds of other, even more immediate conflicts resulting from the extension of the Mexican Revolution into southern California. The phrase "strained relations between the United States and Mexico" obliquely refers to the revolution's threat to U.S. investments and, more locally, to the presence in Los Angeles of radical Mexican groups such as the Partido Liberal Mexicano (PLM). The same edition of the *Los Angeles Times,* for instance, reported on another kind of media battle, the ongoing trial of the Magóns for publishing their anarchist newspaper, *La Regeneración.*[3] Anticipating the "rough handling" the Mexican extras received from the fictional U.S. military forces, a few months earlier the *Times* had reported on the brothers' arrest "in which Enrique was severely beaten." Emphasizing its support for the way the police handled the arrest, and perhaps registering a certain vicarious pleasure in reviewing the beating, the *Times* editors captioned the photograph of the "notorious anarchist" with the note "The bandage on Enrique's head marks the impact of a revolver-butt when he resisted arrest." Together, the brothers were charged with unlawfully using the U.S. mail to distribute "obscene, lewd, lascivious, or indecent" material. In a significant revision of the term's conventional sexual meanings, the state successfully argued that *La Regeneración* was "indecent" because it supposedly incited arson, murder, and assassination.[4] The Magóns' attempt to use the media to disseminate radical information, combined with their critique of marriage and their cohabitation with female partners on their L.A. "commune," led to the redefinition of their publication as a sex crime in ways that foreshadow the subsequent criminalization of Mexican sexuality.[5] Their Los Angeles trials, moreover, became spectacular media events in which the *Times* worried over the brothers' abilities to mobilize masses of Mexican supporters in the downtown plaza and at the courthouse.[6] It may very well be that the invective of the *Times,* the police, and prosecutors against *La Regeneración* and the Magóns spilled over onto the mock battlefield in *The Daughter of the Don.* At any rate, these two interrelated sets of news stories suggest that from its earliest inception, the southern California mass media constituted a field of conflict intimately shaped by revolutionary histories.

Certain Mexican media workers in the 1920s and 1930s seem to have approached their work as a form of Mexican revolutionary anti-imperialism by other means. A good example is Josefina Fierro, a Los Angeles radio personality, community activist, and future leader of the first national civil rights organization for Latinos in the United States, El Congreso de Pueblos de Hablan Español (Congress of Spanish-

Speaking Peoples).[7] Fierro was quite literally a daughter of the Mexican Revolution. Her grandfather had been executed for his opposition to the Díaz regime, while her father and uncles took part in the Magonista revolt in Baja.[8] And, like Anthony Quinn's parents, Fierro's father fought with Villa. One of her earliest memories concerns her mother, also a Magonista, who used Fierro's baby buggy to smuggle arms into Mexico from the United States. Born in Mexicali in 1914, she moved with her family to Arizona when she was about ten years old, before finally settling in southern California a few years later. Living in Los Angeles in the early 1920s, mother and daughter renewed their revolutionary associations by seeking the aid of local radicals. Fierro remembers seeing IWW slogans such as "Save Mooney, Save the Scottsboro Boys" on the walls of one meeting place on Western Avenue. Early in life, Fierro imbibed from her Magonista mother radical views on religion, capitalism, racism, sexism, and fascism. Her mother forbade her children from using racial slurs against African Americans and the Chinese, and she refused to wait on her son, leading Fierro to remark, "She made me feel that we were equal." What is more, "She taught me what she knew about capitalism and socialism. At that time, she thought socialism was the best," and yet Fierro's mother was quick to argue that the Soviets were closer to fascism than socialism.

In addition to revolutionary politics, cultural production was a vital part of Fierro's early years. "All my life," she recalled, "I was always around music and entertainment." In 1923 or 1924, she and her mother bought a lot in East Los Angeles—because of restrictive covenants, one of a limited number of places Mexicans could own houses. At the time, as Fierro recalls, East L.A. was already a veritable "Mexican town." It was there that she learned Mexican songs from her mother, who played piano and guitar, and her uncle Benito, who was a composer. As she remembers, "All the old songs just knocked me out." And in these years, the life of the neighborhood children, according to Fierro, was centered on the Mexican theater at First and Main.

Around 1926, Fierro and her mother traveled north to pick cotton in the San Joaquin Valley. Her mother eventually opened a small restaurant and, with the connivance of the local sheriff, sold bootleg to other workers. During the next several years, Fierro fell in love with the movies and learned some hard lessons about racism in California. She remembers that as a teenager she would often pump the organ at the local movie theater in order to see films for free. When there were no movies, Fierro's mother and grandmother would rent out the theater and "put on a complete Mexican show," performing, for example, songs from the early musical version of *Ramona* (1928), starring Dolores Del Rio. She also remembers getting in a "fight" at the movies once when her mother refused to sit in the section of the theater reserved for Filipinos, Mexicans, and blacks. When the former revolutionary refused to give up her seat, the management relented but then banned them from the theater after that. Her mother constantly reminded her of this incident and, as an adult, Fierro would return to the theater leading a group of protesters.

After graduating from Madera High in 1933, Fierro went to live with her aunt, Gloria Amador, who was singing in a Mexican nightclub near Fairfax Avenue. According to Fierro, she attended classes at UCLA by day, and visited nightclubs like the Trocadero, the Coconut Grove, La Bamba, and El Serape by night where she watched the floor shows and studied between acts. It was at one of the clubs where her aunt sang that Fierro met her first husband, John Bright, a leftist screenwriter who was eventually blacklisted. During these years, she enjoyed L.A.'s cosmopolitan, interethnic nightlife by visiting black and Latino nightclubs, socializing with musicians like Duke Ellington, dancing tangos and rumbas, and talking about movies and politics with Hollywood liberals such as Anthony Quinn, Katherine DeMille, Dalton Trumbo, and Orson Welles. According to Fierro, many Mexican musicians worked in Los Angeles nightclubs and "tried to get into pictures." In fact, her own brother became an actor and had a small part in Mae West's *She Done Him Wrong* (1937).[9]

By day, however, Fierro used her Hollywood contacts to enter into local and state politics, first by working with the Motion Picture Democratic Committee (MPDC), a group that organized liberals in Hollywood in support of left-leaning candidates for Congress and governor. With help and funding from the MPDC and the Mexican consul, in 1934 Fierro founded the Mexican Defense Committee (MDC), a precursor to El Congreso, dedicated to fighting discrimination against Mexicans. In both groups she continued to cultivate the financial support and publicity help of leftist Hollywood. Anthony Quinn raised money and support for El Congreso and Dolores Del Rio attended its first meeting in 1939. According to Fierro, she worked with the group because she felt that it was important for Anglos "to know about the Mexican people that lived there with them because it was originally our state, we lived there before they got there, it was our land had been taken away from

Josefina Fierro's twenty-first birthday party at La Bamba. Courtesy of the
Department of Special Collections, Stanford University Libraries.

us, and they knew nothing about us." As a result, she and one of El
Congreso's other founders, Luisa Moreno, spoke to the Screen Actors
Guild and other Hollywood groups about anti-Mexican discrimination
in Los Angeles, including in segregated movie theaters.[10] In these years
she was close to leftist filmmakers, such as the future members of the
Hollywood Ten, including Herbert Biberman, the director of *Salt of the
Earth*. Throughout the 1930s and 1940s she lobbied filmmakers to avoid
scenarios "where Mexicans are the only *bandidos* and Mexicans are
always the bad guy."[11]

Combining mass-media interventions with more conventional forms
of political action, Fierro's life and work make visible the multifarious
ways in which police power saturated social space in Mexican L.A.,
especially with regard to the use of police power to manage Mexican
bodies and populations. Recalling her mother's fight over segregated
movie seating in the San Joaquin Valley, Fierro's group, the MDC,
protested segregation in southern California parks, swimming pools,
and movie theaters. And as her recollections concerning restrictive
covenants further suggest, the segregation of public space complemented

Fierro (left, with cigarette) and members of the Hollywood Ten in Mexico City. Courtesy of the Department of Special Collections, Stanford University Libraries.

patterns of legally sanctioned residential segregation. So fiercely did Anglo property owners seek to safeguard such segregation that they occasionally took vigilante action, as in the contemporary news story in which three residents of Burbank threatened to bomb a fourth who had sold property to Mexicans.[12] In addition, MDC actions make visible the segregation of work spaces, particularly at local sites of industrial production. Fierro recalls that in the 1930s Mexicans in Los Angeles were concentrated in agriculture and largely excluded from trade unions and jobs in manufacturing and retail sales. In response, the MDC organized successful boycotts against companies that did not hire Mexicans, including the Eastside Brewery, General Mills, and numerous drugstores.

Most of Fierro's work with the MDC, however, involved organizing criminal defenses for Mexicans wrongly accused of crimes and protesting cases of police misconduct, including the killing of seven Mexicans. One of the most famous examples of such activism involved her work with the Sleepy Lagoon Defense Fund, dedicated to freeing the group of young Mexican men wrongly accused of the so-called Sleepy Lagoon murders. And, recalling the police targeting of Mexican workingwomen, members of the MDC, including Fierro, made citizens' arrests of several police officers who had detained Mexican waitresses on fabricated charges of prostitution and then offered to release them in exchange for sexual favors. (In contrast to the police reports and Hollywood films analyzed in the last chapter that depicted Mexican women as hypersexual, in this case it was the officers of the LAPD who were sexual predators.)

Finally, Fierro organized a mass protest against LAPD and INS "repatriation" of Mexicans and Mexican Americans. Between 1929 and 1932, more than 365,000 Mexican immigrants and Mexican Americans were forced or strongly encouraged to leave the United States as part of a larger effort to reduce welfare rolls and free up jobs for white U.S. citizens. These repatriation drives began in Los Angeles before spreading to other parts of the Southwest and Middle West. From 1931 to 1933, for instance, 3,492 Mexicans boarded repatriation trains leaving from San Bernadino.[13] In response, Fierro organized a counter caravan of three thousand people—almost as many as those deported—who traveled from Los Angeles to Sacramento in order to surround the state capitol in protest against repatriation.

In all of these campaigns, Fierro mobilized the relatively new medium of radio as a weapon of protest. As she explains, she hosted a local Spanish-language radio show that was "strictly politics." Fierro's radio promotion of the march on the capitol helped to make it a mass action that mobilized thousands of people. She also used the radio to organize mass boycotts, like the one that forced the East Side Brewery to hire forty Mexicans and pay for a year of radio time. In these ways, Fierro reappropriated the radio as a technology for generating insurgent forms of "biopower" that were mobilized in opposition to state police forces, for, as she quickly discovered, the radio was a powerful way to communicate with and mobilize working-class Mexicans, many of whom came from nonliterate, oral cultures in rural villages of Mexico. Particularly well suited to the entertainment and informational needs of such people, new sound technology such as phonographs and radios were owned in large numbers by many working-class Mexicans, as Manuel Gamio found in his 1928 study.[14] Mexican Los Angeles thus anticipated the contemporary interface between subaltern populations and postmodern mass media recently analyzed by John Beverley, among others. Beverley argued in 1999 that "the tremendous growth in the last thirty or forty years in the audiovisual mass media" has produced a "mutation of the Latin American public sphere" that tends to undermine a historically hegemonic construction of value, or what he calls, following José

Joaquín Brunner, a "'cultured' vision of culture": "Populations formerly immersed in the primarily oral, iconographic world of rural popular culture can pass, in the process of becoming proletarianized and/or urbanized, directly from that culture to the culture of the media... without going through print culture."[15] A similar situation existed in Los Angeles as early as the late 1920s, when, according to George J. Sánchez, competition in the broadcasting industry led marginally profitable stations to increasingly sell radio time to Spanish-language broadcasters. Such broadcasts included news, political commentary, and advertisements but were "dominated by 'traditional' music from the Mexican countryside, rather than the orchestral, more 'refined' sounds of the Mexican capital and other large urban centers." As Sánchez further notes, these programs appealed "to the thousands of working-class Mexican immigrants within the reach of the station's radio signal" in part because radio, "unlike *La Opinión* and other periodicals," reached them "whether or not they could read."[16] Given L.A.'s early emergence as a mass-media center, and given the increasing, albeit limited and uneven, Mexican access to the means of radio broadcasting and reception, early-twentieth-century Mexican immigrants combined popular and mass cultural orientations and practices that have only fairly recently come to characterize the Latin American public spheres described by Beverley, in which subaltern populations engage modernity via a media culture that bypasses literacy and, more broadly, an elitist, "cultured" view of culture.

Pedro J. González discovered the power of radio to mobilize working-class Mexicans when, after announcing during his 4 A.M. radio broadcasts that two hundred workers were needed in the downtown plaza later that morning, he was subsequently stunned to discover that more than six hundred workers, armed with picks and axes, had answered his call.[17] When he arrived at the plaza after his broadcast, González found a mass of job seekers but also about twenty LAPD paddy wagons full of Mexicans. Starting in the second half of the 1920s, González worked as a longshoreman in San Pedro before making recordings as a singer and musician for Columbia Records. A few years later he began to broadcast radio *revistas* or musical variety shows on Station KELW in Burbank, an area where racists had used the threat of bombings in order to enforce anti-Mexican segregation. Nonetheless, González was able to buy airtime early in the morning in a slot that had proven unprofitable for English-language programs but that attracted a ready audience among early-rising Mexican workers. Thousands of avid fans listened to his show on the radio and as part of the studio audience. A short drive from Universal City, González's Burbank studio was also close to the citrus groves where many of his listeners worked, and they came out in force for his live broadcasts. According to the radio personality,

> In San Fernando there were lemon packing houses where more than 500 ladies would work and other young people, you know, packing and picking and so on. So these people were so close to Burbank, they would surprise me and I would get there about ten to four in the morning and then at four, just ready to open the station, there was two or three trucks full of young girls and boys, just waiting for me. I had an incredible audience at that time of day.[18]

While much of Anglo Los Angeles slept, Mexican immigrant workers constituted new, mass-mediated public spheres. Together with the Burbank Theater, a venue that alternated between Hollywood films and live Mexican *revistas,* González's broadcasts anchored a small media center in Burbank that catered to immigrant workers. He also organized his own live, theatrical versions of the radio *revistas.* González productions like *Locura de Radio* (The madness of radio) at the Teatro Hidalgo competed for the attention of Mexican audiences with both Hollywood and Mexican films at Teatro Bonito and Teatro Electrico.[19] Like Fierro, González socialized with Mexican stars such as Del Rio and Ramón Novarro, and he even worked briefly as an extra in *Viva Villa.*[20] González was also a "crossover" success whose variety shows were popular in Anglo-American theaters and at private parties thrown by the ruling elite of Los Angeles, including the mayor, the district attorney, and the chief of police. With this unique combination of audiences González was one of the most well known public figures in all of Los Angeles.

González's first encounter with new communications technology, however, occurred more than a decade earlier, when as an adolescent he worked as a telegraph operator for Pancho Villa. A schoolmate of Enrique Magón and an early reader of *La Regeneración,* González was eventually conscripted by Villa and during his service he joined in the famous raid on Columbus, New Mexico; involuntarily appeared in a silent film of a firing-squad execution; and narrowly escaped execution himself. And he received and transmitted telegraphic messages for Villa, using communications technology as a weapon in guerrilla warfare. Revolutionary forces used the telegraph to send messages over great distances in order to mobilize faraway troops or to warn them of an advancing enemy. By quickly crossing the distance between different villages near the telegraphic line, the new communications technology rendered space radically fungible. Years later, González found that radio similarly traversed vastly different spaces and thereby violated the segregation of social space that prevailed in Los Angeles. In his account, the massive police response to the hundreds of Mexicans who answered his radio request for workers was prompted by angry phone calls from white Angelenos who charged that the broadcast had disturbed the peace in their neighborhoods. L.A. district attorney Buron Fitts grabbed González by the arm in the plaza that day, and angrily explained that the police had received numerous calls from people complaining about the early-morning sound of Spanish-language radio. Just as restrictive covenants in Los Angeles helped to fortify what George Lipsitz calls a "possessive investment in whiteness," the complaining callers presumed that there existed a related "sound covenant" that they called upon the LAPD to enforce.[21]

In addition to transgressing such sonic segregation, González's broadcasts mobilized working-class Mexicans in ways that violated the segregation of regional residential space. He remembered, for example, that on the way to the plaza many Mexicans asked Anglos in adjacent neighborhoods for tools: "When the American person would give them the axe in the garage he would see that there was maybe 20 Mexican people with axes on their shoulders and they would wonder, 'What's going on?' But this was happening in San Fernando, San Gabriel, El Monte, and there in L.A. All over the place."[22] In response to the unprecedented way in which the broadcast had made space radically fungible, the DA publicly reminded white Los Angeles that González had been a telegraph operator for Villa and ominously wondered aloud, "What if he starts telling all the Mexicans—not [just] here but all over, in Arizona or whatever, New Mexico and all these other states—what if he tells them, 'Rise up with a bottle of gas...and start burning all the Americans' houses.'"[23] Although his broadcasts never included such an incendiary call, González did inveigh against the Depression-era repatriation of Mexicans and he also helped raise money for defense against deportations. As Sánchez observes, "the potential power generated by this mass appeal was so substantial that it not only threatened the cultural hegemony of the Mexican middle class in Los Angeles but also worried local Anglo American officials" like the DA, who targeted the radio personality for arrest in 1934 on fabricated charges of statutory

rape.[24] His conviction, imprisonment, and then deportation on falsi-
fied sex charges was the culmination of years of state harassment in
which social workers and the police had also falsely charged the radio
celebrity with sex crimes simply for driving his daughters and her class-
mates to school.[25]

Even during his trial, however, González continued to draw huge
Mexican crowds, and the Spanish-language press gave it extensive coverage in an effort to attract Mexican readers. The coverage of the trial in
La Opinión combined bold headlines ("PEDRO J. GONZALEZ ARESTADO!";
"PEDRO J. GONZALEZ, CULPABLE, I A 50 ANOS EN SAN QUINTIN!")
with narrative photo sequences (González and his family entering the
court; crowds lining up to get into the courtroom; González with the
bailiff; González listening to the prosecution's summation) in ways that
recall both Hollywood films and the emergent Mexican film and *foto-
novela* culture.[26] The trial, in fact, competed for the attention of *La
Opinión*'s readers with ads for both Mexican and U.S. films such as *Revolution, La Sombra de Pancho Villa, Police Car Seventeen, Contrabando,*
and *Lone Cowboy.*[27]

As González's career suggests, in the 1930s sound technology was an
increasingly volatile target and tool of police power. According to Mike
Davis, in the 1920s, shortly before the LAPD began to target González,
it "pioneered the replacement of the flatfoot or mounted officer with
the radio patrol car—the beginning of dispersed, mechanized policing."[28]
In the 1930s, the department further initiated plans for individual officers
to wear "miniature radio receiving set[s] . . . whenever they are assigned
to blockade duty in a round-up of thugs or gangsters."[29] The police also
used radio broadcasts to disseminate police views on crime and to stimulate public support.[30] Deploying different sound technologies, Hollywood joined in this struggle to police the Los Angeles "soundscape."
Film studios revised and adopted certain police functions by resegregat-
ing film production onto studio soundstages where it was isolated from
the newly criminalized Mexican spaces that Fierro and González reached
with their broadcasts. By thus separating the process of production from
Mexican work sites and neighborhoods, the studios similarly distinguished
sound films from Mexican radio broadcasts and recordings. Although
today we think of film as a distinct medium, historically sound movies
overlapped with radio and records in ways that made it difficult to
cleanly divide them. In the late 1920s and early 1930s, sound films, for
instance, were often imagined on the model of radio broadcasts, as in

RKO's famous radio tower logo, and early examples often resembled popular radio variety formats.[31] At the same time, Hollywood viewed radio as a competitive rival for audience attention, particularly during the Depression.[32] I would add, however, that in Los Angeles the border skirmishes between film and radio assumed a racialized character, such that Hollywood strove to make sound films a "respectable" form of entertainment for white members of the middle class by implicitly opposing them to Mexican radio shows, with their audience of presumed "criminals." The studio system with its new infrastructure for making sound pictures served in part as a material and ideological barricade against the Mexican presence in southern California.

Before around 1915, Carey McWilliams writes, the respectable members of Los Angeles, at the time still "a self-righteous and pious community," maintained their distance from the budding film industry. Because it was assumed that movie people were not fit for respectable society, they were segregated like moral "lepers." Apartment buildings and houses often bore signs that read "No Dogs or Actors Allowed." Similarly, in response to the new industry, Hollywood residents forced the city of Los Angeles to enact zoning ordinances that restricted film studios to prescribed areas.[33] After 1915, however, the film industry was consolidated and generally accepted in southern California, in large part because of its major contribution to the local economy.[34] But the industry's new stature was endangered during its "purple period," which began in 1922 with the infamous Fatty Arbuckle rape and murder case and included a number of high-profile drug scandals. One of the most sensational drug-related scandals concerned the 1922 murder of Paramount director and president of the Motion Picture Directors Association, William Desmond Taylor. Although the murder was never solved, the investigation revealed his affairs with young starlets and speculation spread in local and national newspapers about the existence of a "drug cult," presided over by a Chinese man, in which Taylor and others dressed in kimonos and performed "unmanly acts."[35] One popular theory was that Taylor had actually been engaged in an effort to keep drug dealers out of the industry and was therefore killed by a Mexican "drug ring."[36] Indeed, in the flurry of news stories about vice and immorality in Hollywood that followed the Taylor murder, Mexico and Mexicans were repeatedly invoked as the source of drugs in and around Hollywood. An unnamed star told a reporter about a "drug orgy" of picture people in Mexico.[37] Reporters further wrote of a "Mexican-American ring," and one quoted a Los Angeles narcotics agent as saying that "it's the Mexicans and negroes who bother us."[38] The same reporter emphasized the Mexican origins of marijuana, as well as the adverse consequences of smoking it:

> In certain published accounts of high jinks in Hollywood marijuana is mentioned as one of the drugs consumed by the insatiate performers. Marijuana is Indian hemp, sometimes called Mexican weed.... The Mexicans mix the dried leaves with tobacco and smoke them in cigarettes. The effect is inflammatory stimulation. The marijuana excites the nerves, deadens fear, turns a coward into a swashbuckler, [and] accentuates evil propensities.[39]

Equally sensational were the revelations concerning the drug addiction, medical commitment, and untimely death in 1923 of Wallace Reed, a popular leading man for Jesse L. Lasky's Famous Players who specialized in roles as "strong-jawed, all-American figures."[40] Even a red-blooded American hero, it seemed, could not withstand the foreign pleasures of imported narcotics.[41] This kind of bad publicity over drug and sex scandals, combined with demands by politicians and religious groups for the censorship of films, revived middle-class WASP opposition to the film industry in southern California.

The film studios took a number of steps to shore up the industry's crumbling respectability and hence profitability. First, the industry dramatically changed the way it occupied space in Los Angeles. In a massive and material way, film producers largely withdrew from their increasingly Mexican surroundings and into big, self-contained studios with largely all-white workforces. Whereas Spanish-language radio broadcasters used sound technology to traverse regional space, Hollywood's deployment of sound precipitated the withdrawal of film production into massive industrial gated communities. With newly insulated, double-walled soundproof studios, location shooting was greatly reduced as Hollywood became an "indoor industry." Tourists and other visitors were unwelcome in the newly enclosed and soundproof studios that one contemporary observer compared to a "windowless jail."[42] "Acquiring social respectability with the introduction of sound, the movies proceeded to wall the industry off from the rest of the community."[43] Thus, at the same time that sound technology attracted audiences and therefore helped the industry rebound from the economic effects of recent scandals, it also enabled the studios to isolate a largely white filmmaking "community" from the criminalized social spaces of southern California. "Occupying from thirty to forty acres of land," and relatively self-sufficient and contained, the studio became a "walled town," complete with "its own office buildings; its factories (the stages); its theaters and projection rooms; its laboratories, dressmaking shops, blacksmith shops, machine shops, wardrobes, restaurants, dressing rooms, lumber sheds; greenhouses; scene docks; electrical plant; garages; and planing mills."[44] With names like "Universal City" and "Fox Movietone City," the studios resembled exclusive, incorporated municipalities.[45]

In addition to employing on- and off-duty policemen to control strikes and Pinkerton detectives to collect information on radical influences in movie unions, the major studios also had their own police forces.[46] Situated in the San Fernando Valley near both Burbank, where González would broadcast, and the citrus groves that his Mexican audiences picked, "Universal City" employed its own police department. On the day the studio was opened, in fact, its chief of police was chosen to hand founder Carl Laemmle a gold key to the "new municipality."[47] Similarly, the Warner Brothers police helped to guard the studio's new sound equipment before its use in the film *Don Juan* (1926), starring John Barrymore as the Latin lover. As Jack Warner wrote, "there was trouble all over Hollywood in 1926, and I had a tip that some of the hotheads were planning to wreck our Vitaphone equipment when it reached the freight yards from New York." Warner employed the studio police chief and a captain from the Los Angeles sheriff's office, each with loaded shotguns, to patrol the freight yard while the recording equipment and giant speakers were unloaded. According to Warner, "*Don Juan* made its California debut without any open violence."[48] One year later, as if to underline the fact that the deployment of sound technology entailed the policing of Mexicans, the first sound effect in Warner's *Old San Francisco* (1927) was a gunshot that kills a Mexican patriarch.[49] Here the police shotguns used to guard Vitaphone seem to morph into the audio apparatus, suggesting that sound was becoming a symbolic weapon partly aimed at Mexicans.

These forms of studio police power protected largely white communities of as many as three thousand employees from the Mexican presence in L.A. According to Scott Greer, the various motion-picture unions were "Jim Crow" organizations that excluded people of color.[50] This was evident to African American actors Ossie Davis and Ruby Dee when they first came to Los Angeles in the early 1940s. They were dismayed to see that, with the exception of a handful of performers, their studio was "an all-white world" with virtually no people of color working as technicians, grips, electricians, prop people, makeup artists, wardrobe assistants, or hairdressers.[51] Studio segregation was complemented not only by the segregation of film exhibition, but also by the residential segregation of those who worked in the industry. Before sound, film actors and actresses were a fairly common sight on the streets of Los Angeles or on nearby locations. Because the earliest microphones were not only heavy and hard to move but also "omnidirectional" such that they "picked up noise indiscriminately," however, the stars of early sound films withdrew from the surrounding city to the enclosed soundstages, where their voices (and other sounds) could be isolated and more intelligibly recorded.[52] At about the same time, stars, directors, and producers increasingly secluded themselves in new celebrity enclaves like the Hollywood Hills, Bel-Air, Beverly Hills, Brentwood, Santa Monica, and parts of the San Fernando Valley. Dispersed over large parts of the L.A. region, motion-picture people patronized the same restaurants and stores and lived apart in their own self-enclosed worlds.[53] As Lary May notes, celebrity homes were situated "in the farthest reaches of this suburban city, removed from ethnic groups and business centers." The new residential geography of the film industry served to free film stars "from any nearby reminders of social responsibility" by isolating them in exclusive neighborhoods supposedly protected against vice.[54] To be sure, such exclusiveness was in large part driven by a desire to isolate industry insiders and celebrities from and elevate them over the mass of nonpicture people, yet Hollywood's self-segregation was also in some measure part of a larger, racialized response on the part of regional elites to the insurgent Mexican presence in conflict-ridden southern California.

The Film Production Code of 1930 represented a more familiar Hollywood response to scandal (and, I would suggest, to the Mexican presence). Although the code is best remembered for restricting representations of sex and crime, I want to focus more on two of its less well known prescriptions that together served to police film responses to the local war on drugs. As part of an effort to disassociate film production from drugs, the industry's Production Code Administration (PCA) attempted to enforce the commandment "ILLEGAL DRUG TRAFFIC must never be presented. Because of its evil consequences, the drug traffic should never be presented in any form. The existence of the trade should not be brought to the attention of audiences."[55] At the same time, under the heading "National feelings," the code stipulated that "the just rights, history, and feelings of any nation are entitled to consideration and respectful treatment," "the use of the Flag shall be consistently respectful" and "[t]he history, institutions, prominent people and citizenry of other nations shall be represented fairly."[56] Although broadly stated, the last stipulation responded in part to a recent, highly publicized incident in which Hollywood grossly insulted the Mexican flag. Before it was even completed, *Viva Villa* had offended audiences in Mexico when, during a local parade, the actor Lee Tracy went out onto his hotel balcony and urinated on a Mexican flag in front of the building. The Mexican press was outraged and called for a ban on all MGM films.[57] Tracy was quickly fired, the controversy was smoothed over, and the film was ultimately screened in Mexico City.[58] But the incident shows that in practice, the code's rules concerning nationality were in large part directed at preserving access to Mexico, one of Hollywood's largest foreign markets.[59] The industry dominated the Mexican film market throughout the 1930s, but Mexico threatened Hollywood's hegemony not only by banning films about Mexican bandits but also by taxing U.S. imports in order to fund a domestic film industry.[60] Hollywood further feared that English-language sound films might prove unattractive to Spanish speakers, and that there was a movement in Mexico to promote Spanish films and ban English ones.[61] This situation marks one of the key differences between Hollywood, with its global financial concerns, and the Los Angeles police, who generally disregarded the responses of Mexican audiences to *their* media events.

In combination, these two sections of the code tended to discourage direct references to the war on drugs involving Anglo-American police and Mexican drug smugglers. Although the police newspaper reports analyzed in chapter 4 might have suggested such plots, industry rules limiting the representations of both drugs and Mexicans would have made it difficult to film them and receive the PCA's seal of approval. Which is not to say that films never broached the topic, for the producers of low-budget "exploitation" movies such as *Marihuana: Weed with Roots in Hell* did not even bother to submit them to the PCA. The code had a greater degree of influence over mainstream filmmakers, often forcing them to resort to ingenious forms of indirect suggestion or telling displacement. The code's enforcer, Joseph Breen, seemingly identified with the "G-men" and other police who fought the narcotic menace, but he insisted that films about them should be carefully handled so as to avoid direct reference to drugs. In a letter to the producers of *The Traitor* (Majestic/Puritan, 1936), a film about a Texas Ranger (Tim McCoy) who goes undercover to bust a drug-smuggling ring led by Chicago gangsters and Mexicans, Breen wrote: "On account of the original Code, under which the Production code operates saying, in the paragraph regarding 'crimes against the law': 'Illegal drug traffic must never be presented,' we request that all of these references to 'the stuff' be played down as much as possible, and in Scene 339, the underlined word in Smoky's speech: 'You bust up the biggest *narcotic* ring in the country,' be eliminated."[62] Similarly, in 1940, Breen wrote to producers at Republic that

> because of the insidious effects of this drug and its ready accessibility, it has been the established policy of the industry to make no reference whatever to marihuana in our pictures. This viewpoint has been repeatedly urged upon us, not only by the Treasury Department of the United States which is engaged in a superhuman effort to stamp out the use of marihuana, but by a number of international governmental groups engaged in a crusade against the use of such drugs.[63]

In these cases, the PCA head called on the combined authority of "superhuman" federal agents and a global antidrug campaign in order to censor explicit references to drugs; but at the same time he encouraged Hollywood to simply substitute circumlocutions and render drug plots implicit.

In cases such as RKO's *Border G-Man,* the code not only encouraged filmmakers to address the drug war in indirect or allusive ways, but also to obscure the role of Mexicans within it.[64] This movie concerns a Justice Department investigator, Jim Galloway, who is sent to Texas to foil a gang—Louis Rankin, Rita Browning, and "Smoky" Joslin—that plans to smuggle weapons to an unnamed South American country. Here gun smuggling seems like a substitute for drug smuggling, particularly given that one member of the gang is called "Smoky" and that the Justice Department detective discovers the contraband weapons hidden inside bales of hay, recalling the Mexicans captured by the LAPD with "bales" of marijuana (see chapter 4). Indeed, a whole series of films from the 1930s focusing on crime along the U.S.–Mexican border, including movies about gun smuggling, cattle rustling, and banditry, beg to be read as indirect reflections on the local war on drugs.[65] *Border G-Man* further illustrates a second common strategy of indirection or displacement, in which characters from South America partly serve as stand-ins for Mexicans. Another example is *Flirting with Fate,* a film that stars Leo Carrillo as "Sancho Ramirez," a bandit from Paraguay who bears a striking resemblance to the actor's many Mexican characters.[66] As a consequence of code restrictions, references to the Mexican presence in L.A. and the drug war it ignited were not localized in films "about" drugs but were instead disseminated across a range of other kinds of plots and genres.

One seemingly unlikely home for drug-war references was the sound track. In the 1930s and 1940s, the Production Code Administration turned its attention to "La Cucaracha," the Mexican revolutionary song that promoted the pleasures of marijuana. Perhaps because the song refers to both marijuana and Mexicans, it was singled out by PCA head Joseph Breen, who objected to its use in an otherwise wholesome Gene Autry picture called *Rancho Grande* (1940) and in the frothy musical comedy *La Conga Nights.* In the case of the latter, Breen wrote to an executive at Universal: "The first verse submitted is not acceptable by reason of its reference to Marihuana. As you know, it is a fixed policy of the industry in pictures, for obvious reasons. For your information, this same lyric has been submitted to us recently by several other studios, and we have had to turn it down on the same grounds mentioned above."[67] Here Breen acknowledges the fact that in its contemporary context, "La Cucaracha" inevitably brought the war on drugs to mind. Notwithstanding his claim of "zero tolerance" for the song, however, the PCA allowed Hollywood to repeatedly use "La Cucaracha." Between 1931 and 1946, it was used in ten feature films, including *Viva Villa,* and several shorts, most notably the Oscar-winning color musical named after the song.[68] "La Cucaracha" was a popular cultural phenomenon not only in film but also on records, radio, and sheet music. Following the success of the song in *Viva Villa,* even Louis Armstrong recorded it in 1935.[69] At the same time, "La Cucaracha" was a staple of commercial songbooks from the 1930s.[70] It was further disseminated in the form of sheet music, much of which was published to advertise or capitalize on films such as *Viva Villa.*[71] The song even inspired a dance of the same name.[72] Why, we might wonder, was "La Cucaracha" so popular?

One reason for the song's appeal was its indirect association with Mexican criminality as represented by the police. Recalling the ways in which Mexican criminality was sexualized and even eroticized in police drug enforcement discourse, in Hollywood films "La Cucaracha" carried fantasies of Mexican sexual passion and violence. For many Anglos, Mexican music was an exotic commercial entertainment, and part of its appeal was its presumed expression of extreme forms of sexual excitement. As Pedro J. González explained, at the private parties of the powerful in Los Angeles, he and his band, Los Madrugadores, were called upon to provide the musical accompaniment to all sorts of taboo excitements, as if Mexican music, along with liquor, were the social lubricants that enabled Anglos to experience the forms of abandon that they associated with Mexicans.[73] During Prohibition, González and his group were asked to perform at alcohol-fueled parties, attended by the mayor, the chief of police, and the DA who would ultimately prosecute him. The radio personality's experiences with the L.A. elite in such contexts were overdetermined by the larger contemporary Anglo-American exoticization and commercialization of Mexican folk music in night-clubs, records, and movie theaters. During the late 1920s and early 1930s, dominant mass media codified the supposedly "exotic" qualities of Mexican music in ways that would become commonplace in subsequent decades. From such a condescending perspective, Mexican music was, like "the blues," the rough and raw entertainment of rural "colored" folk, full of strong, unmediated emotions and impulses. Recalling the pastoral images of Mexican labor and culture analyzed in chapter 3, white audiences constructed Mexican music as a reservoir of the sort of "primitive" vitality that Anglo-American modernity supposedly required its subjects to renounce. In powerful white contexts, however, the supposed primitivism of Mexican music did not function as a critique of Anglo-American modernity; on the contrary, as an entertainment commodity, Mexican music increasingly served as a supplement to the status quo. Bluntly put, Mexican music was an important source of recreation and "release" for politicians and policemen that indirectly sustained their efforts to suppress Mexican dissent.

More precisely, Mexican music represented the kinds of sexual abandon supposedly prohibited in "respectable" Anglo America. As González notes, powerful Anglos frequently asked him to supply their parties with Mexican strippers.[74] The musicians themselves, moreover, were often erotic objects for members of the white audience: "When we'd be at these parties, the wife of some important man would grab one of the Madrugadores." But "something worse happened to me," González claimed, for once the mayor's drunken wife followed him to the bathroom and attempted to kiss and embrace him.[75] The Anglo eroticization of Mexican music further helps explain why the audiences at these parties were particularly attracted to raucous *rancheras*—songs of rural Mexico focusing on extreme states of love and loss and replete with *gritos,* piercingly high-pitched shouts. According to González, "the American people would go crazy" when the performers would "go 'youpee' . . . They really liked that 'whoopee' stuff."[76] Anglos may have been attracted to the sound of the *gritos* because they suggested and provoked sexual excitement. This reading is supported by González's translation of the *grito* as "whoopee," the contemporary slang term for sexual intercourse, "making whoopee."[77]

The association of Mexican music with fantasies of Mexican sexuality is further suggested by a scene from *The Day of the Locust,* Nathaniel West's dark modernist novel set in 1930s Hollywood. The scene concerns another drunken party accompanied by Mexican music, involving Tod Hackett, a Hollywood set and costume designer, Faye Greener, a pretty young white woman with dreams of stardom, her boyfriend Earle Shoop, a cowboy who "worked occasionally in horse operas," and the cowboy's Mexican friend, Miguel.[78] Earle and Miguel live in a sort of hobo camp, and together they throw a rough dinner party for Tod and Faye, involving lots of drinking, smoking, and Mexican music. "Toffee-colored with large Armenian eyes," "pouting black lips," a head of "tight, ordered curls," and wearing a "long-haired sweater, called a 'gorilla,'" Miguel exudes a sort of animal sexuality aptly represented by his fighting cocks, "Villa" and "Zapata."[79] After dinner, they smoke and drink tequila until Miguel begins to sing a "revolutionary" song. When Faye joins in, the song comes to represent a symbolic form of miscegenation and a possible prelude to actual interracial sex:

> Their voices touched in the thin, still air to form a minor chord and it was as though their bodies had touched. The song was transformed again. The melody remained the same, but the rhythm broke and its beat became ragged. It was a rumba now. . . . [Faye] took a long pull at the jug and stood up. She put one hand on each of her buttocks and began to dance. . . . The Mexican stood up, still singing, and joined her in the dance. . . . They met head on, blue-black against pale-gold, and used their heads to pivot, than danced back to back with their buttocks touching, their knees bent and wide apart.[80]

Faye's boyfriend, Earle, reacts ambivalently to this sexualized display. At first he seems to relish the music. "Suddenly he, too, jumped up and began to dance. He did a crude hoe-down. He leaped into the air and knocked his heels together. He whooped." Nonetheless, "he couldn't become part of their dance." Apparently enraged over his exclusion, the cowboy uses a big stick to club Miguel on the head.[81] In this way, the scene suggests the intense, conflicted associations that Mexican music carried for Anglo listeners. Resonating with the period police reports discussed in chapter 4, in other words, the music condensed sex and violence, desire and the billy club. Anglo characterizations of Mexican music resembled the white image of jazz that Michael Rogin analyzes in *Blackface, White Noise,* in which the music's seeming "libidinal charac-ter... flirted with transgression along not just gender lines (sexual plea-sure for respectable women) but also racial ones."[82] West partly conflates stereotypes of Mexican and African sexualities when he "blackens" Miguel, describing him with black lips, curly black hair, and "blue-black" skin partly covered by a furry "gorilla" sweater.

As further suggested by Armstrong's "rough," rumba version of "La Cucaracha," both jazz and Mexican "folk" music shared rhythmic and other features that many white Americans coded as hypersexual. The ambivalent sexuality that many Anglos associated with Mexican music was further reinforced by the song's references to marijuana, sung again and again in film sound tracks from the 1930s and 1940s. These drug references subtly infuse films with the set of race and sex fantasies that have historically clustered around drug enforcement. In *Viva Villa,* for instance, "La Cucaracha" was interspersed between sexually suggestive and sadistic scenes that served to associated the song with extreme states of intoxication and sexual incitement, as film reviewers obliquely sug-gested. One reviewer wrote that "Pancho Villa marches again to the *mad* music of 'La cucaracha,'" and another compared the sound track to the "heart cry" of Mexican people "thumping in rhythmic crescendo."[83] More critically, in his review for the *Nation,* William Tracy wrote that *Viva Villa* was a "vigorously sustained assault on the eye and the ear," a "super-spectacle" that "assailed" the viewer with "teeming images of sound and shape."[84] Here the sound of "La Cucaracha" is likened to a sonic assault that in Tracy's account is the appropriate sound track to the film's scenes of sadism.

However, perhaps the best example of a film that uses the song to evoke the sex and drug fantasies reminiscent of contemporary police discourses is the RKO musical *La Cucaracha*. A short, *La Cucaracha* was still influential, winning an Academy Award and stimulating audience interest and thus studio investment in Technicolor musicals. The film focuses on Chapita (Steffi Duna), a young woman who works in a Mexican cantina, and her lover, Pancho (Don Alvarado), a dancer there. As it begins, Chapita learns that a famous Mexico City theatrical promoter (Paul Porcasi) will visit the cantina that night, and Pancho plans to leave her to become a star on the national stage. Soon thereafter, Chapita confronts him backstage, they quarrel, and when Pancho dismisses her as nothing but a "cockroach," she vows to get revenge. As Pancho and his partner begin to perform what is announced as "our national dance" (the *jarape tapatío,* or "Mexican hat dance"), Chapita leads a group of patrons in a rendition of "La Cucaracha" that interrupts the pair. Although she adds new verses in English, Chapita repeatedly sings the chorus in Spanish, complete with marijuana references. Enraged, Pancho lunges at her and the attempted attack turns into a stylized dance, to the tune of "La Cucaracha," that mimics a physical fight: the pair alternatively advance toward one another and then retreat, with Pancho holding his hand outstretched as if ready to choke Chapita. At the song's conclusion, Pancho chases her backstage, which is lit in an angry, Technicolor red, where he threatens to kill her. His rage is interrupted, however, by the impresario, who is so impressed with their new dance that he offers the couple a job performing it on the "national" stage. This offer reconciles the fighting Mexican couple, and the film ends happily.

While remaining consistent with Production Code norms, *La Cucaracha* nonetheless broadly hints at the existence of Mexican sexuality and drug criminality. As a generic "cantina girl," Chapita is presumably hypersexual, and we learn in the very first scene that Pancho is a womanizer. The fact that he is a Mexican dancer, moreover, makes his sexuality further suspect because it places him in the tradition of Valentino, the "Latin lover." As Miriam Hansen argues, Valentino's career was marked by the "stigmata" of "sexual ambiguity" and "erotic ethnicity."[85] His Italian origins, which in the nativist United States could suggest a disturbing proximity to African blackness, combined with his status as an erotic object for female (and gay male) fans, tended to link Valentino, in Hansen's account, to a host of abjected or pathologized qualities including "effeminacy," homosexuality, and all manner of "deviant" sexuality.[86]

La Cucaracha visually quotes an especially homoerotic scene from Valentino's *Blood in the Sand* (1922), in which he played a bullfighter who holds an audience in his dressing room with his male "admirers" before each performance. As these men look on, we see Valentino's manservant dress him in bullfighting drag, starting with his slippers and climaxing with the wrapping of a long sash around his waist.[87] In a similar scene backstage at the cantina, Pancho argues with his manservant while the latter dresses him. At first Pancho angrily denounces Chapita for thinking that she has a claim on him, but when his manservant adds his own disparaging remark about her, the dancer becomes outraged and defends her. In the midst of this quarrel between men, the manservant wraps a red sash around Pancho's waist in ways that showcase his legs and buttocks, encased in skin-tight toreador pants. At the same time, I would suggest, Valentino's sexual "deviancy" is also wrapped around Pancho, who was in fact played by one of Valentino's minor competitors, the Mexican actor Don Alvarado. Pancho is thus represented as at some distance from normative, Anglo-American masculinity—a vain, flashily dressed dancer who objectifies himself for others. When Chapita enters the dressing room, she calls him a vain "peacock," which results in an angry masculine protest in which he scorns her as a mere "cockroach." Here Pancho seems to protest too much; the film suggests that his virility is in question as it turns him into a sort of "male impersonator." The more he asserts his masculine independence by proclaiming a preference for the company of men, including not only the manservant but also the impresario, the more "queer" he seems.[88]

The odd dance that Pancho and Chapita perform suggests deviant sexuality of another sort as well. To the extent that paired dancers in Hollywood musicals represent heterosexual couplings,[89] and the dance substitutes for acts of sexual intercourse, then Pancho and Chapita's "cucaracha" dance represents rough sex, if not rape. This interpretation is reinforced by the way the sound track music changes when the dance starts, from a slow, guitar-accompanied version of "La Cucaracha" to an up-tempo, "rumba fox-trot" arrangement played by an orchestra.[90] With its "rough," syncopated rhythm, this version of the song may have suggested intense, primitive sexuality to many Anglo listeners and is thus an apt accompaniment to the Mexican couple's violently erotic dance number. Finally, the suggestion of Mexican deviancy is sealed by the film's references to marijuana, not only directly, in the lyrics of "La

Cucaracha," but also indirectly, in the cigarette smoke that permeates the film. Indeed, in three different publicity photos, the three main characters are all shown with cigarettes in their hands. Even more strikingly, one publicity photo shows the Mexican orchestra that supposedly plays "La Cucaracha" in the film, and most of the musicians are shown smoking.[91] Given industry norms that restricted representations of drug use, cigarette smoking in a Mexican setting could be seen as a substitute for marijuana. The way in which cigarette smoke could stand in for marijuana is nicely illustrated by one sheet music rendering of "La Cucaracha" that includes the Spanish lyrics about marijuana but claims that the song concerns "a tobacco addict." Its cover illustration, moreover, is reminiscent of antimarijuana discourses in which the drug unleashes sexual desire in Mexican men, for it depicts a Mexican peon smoking a cigarette and, like a comic-strip thought bubble, the cloud of smoke above his head contains the image of female legs in heels, stockings, and garter.[92]

As in police reports, however, *La Cucaracha* flirts with suggestions of Mexican sex and drug deviancy in ways that ultimately reinforce and justify police practices. By rejoining the couple in the end, the film narrative extricates Pancho from his prior, homoerotic context and splices him into a symbolic heterosexual marriage. The ending further normalizes Chapita by transforming her from a "loose" cantina girl into a potentially respectable woman, paired off with Pancho. The intimations of deviancy that pervade the film give way to a comedic resolution that symbolically polices Mexican gender and sex relations.[93] Indeed, both the film and related sheet music use "La Cucaracha" to suggest Mexican deviancy while at the same time "translating" Spanish lyrics about marijuana and the Mexican Revolution into English lyrics about heterosexual love and lawful marriage. In one case, for example, the song's famous chorus, "La Cucaracha, La Cucaracha, / Ya no puede caminar / Porque no tiene, porque le falta, / Marihuana que fumar" is paired with "American lyrics" like "La Cucaracha, La Cucaracha, / You're love's sweetest melody / La Cucaracha, La Cucaracha / Soon our wedding march you'll be."[94] Here a song that has been associated with revolution, sex, and drugs is re-formed and domesticated as a wedding march. By raising suggestions of Mexican deviancy and then ultimately containing them with an implied marriage, the makers of *La Cucaracha* seem to justify the contemporary policing of Mexicans before finally positing their own, sym-

Publicity still from *La Cucaracha*. Courtesy of the Academy of Motion Picture Arts and Science.

bolic form of narrative police power by ushering the couple into hetero-sexual normalcy at the film's conclusion.

The dance's representation as a distinctly Mexican nationalist per-formance further polices the couple by phantasmatically segregating them from the film's primarily Anglo-American audiences. Although Chapita's rendition of "La Cucaracha" initially interrupts Pancho's per-formance of the Mexican "national dance," together they create a new dance, destined for the nation's capital. The filmmakers thus contain the couple's excesses within a Mexican-nationalist frame partly in order to preempt possible Mexican objections, but also because it served to imaginatively distance the Mexican couple from the United States. For white southern California, in other words, this Mexican-nationalist frame served as a form of symbolic police power that imaginatively repatriated immigrant Mexicans back to Mexico. *La Cucaracha* con-stituted an Anglo-American wish-fulfillment fantasy—a setting in which Mexican characters perform for white audiences but nonetheless main-tain a carefully controlled distance. Contained within a self-enclosed Mexican scene, Pancho and Chapita represent white longings for Mexi-

Marijuana and Mexican sexuality: "La Cucaracha" sheet music (1937).

cans who "know their place," workers who do their jobs and stay in their own neighborhoods.

Finally, the very ways in which *La Cucaracha* deployed new film technologies suggest their policing functions. Its use of color, for example, visually reinforced the film's markedly Mexican setting. Mexican characters and scenes were submitted to a new color process that was limited to blues, greens, and reds—a visual palette historically deemed ill suited for filming "white" skin and contexts but supposedly conducive to rendering colorful Mexican scenes and "dark" skin.[95] The three-color process thus visually heightened the Mexican difference from Anglo-Americans by foregrounding elaborate, brightly colored costumes. It also racialized Mexican characters by imparting a reddish hue to their skin. The actors in *La Cucaracha* seem to wear a heavy pancake makeup that gives their skin a red tone on film, an effect that is heightened by red costumes and red lighting. Like Hollywood, police powers in California also saw Mexicans as "red," not only because of their Indian backgrounds but also because of their proclivity for revolutionary or radical action. As Escobar notes, starting in 1924, LAPD arrest records even referred to Mexicans as the "red" race.[96] By making Mexicans similarly "red," *La Cucaracha* visually reinforced the radical otherness of Mexicans to U.S. whites.

In a related fashion, this and other films deployed sound so as to aurally "segregate" Mexicans from white characters and audiences. We can see this in the case of scores commissioned for silent films and ultimately for incorporation into sound pictures. As noted earlier, the first sound effect in *Old San Francisco* was of a gunshot of a Mexican character; but in other portions of the film the score serves to distinguish between "Spanish" Mexicans and other characters. The score, in other words, reproduces racial differences by linking particular themes to particular characters, such that the Irish hero is accompanied by lilting fiddles and harps; the Eurasian villain by an atonal "Oriental" leitmotiv; and the heroine, Señorita Vásquez, by strumming guitar and castanets.[97] *La Cucaracha*, however, takes a different approach to sonic segregation. Whereas contemporary Mexican radio waves traversed the segregated social spaces of white-dominated Los Angeles, *La Cucaracha*'s sound track localized Mexican music within an all-Mexican setting. We might say that Mexican music was increasingly put into film scenes under ideological "police custody," so that white audiences could "overhear" Mexican sounds from the seemingly safe distance afforded by segregated movie theaters.

This domestication and resegregation of Mexican music was partly a response to the dissemination of alternative songs about marijuana that implicitly flouted police power. As noted in chapter 3, in the 1920s and 1930s, Mexicans recorded their own versions of "La Cucaracha" and other songs that disregarded prevailing police controls by enjoining listeners to smoke. For instance, in the song "La Marihuana," recorded around 1930 by Trio Garnica-Ascencio, a Mexican *ranchera* group popular on the variety-show circuit, the singers begin with the imperative "fume y fume" ("smoke and smoke") and end with the lines "marihuana, ya no puedo ni / levanta la cabeza / con los ojos rente colorados y la / boca resca, resca" (Marihuana, I can no longer raise my head / With my eyes so very red and my / mouth so very dry).[98] Somewhat later, the Los Angeles composer and musician Lalo Guerrero would perform and record "Marijuana Boogie," in which "marijuana" is seemingly both the name of a dance and the singer's girlfriend. The song thus uses playful forms of indirection that mark the fact that Mexican music, like other forms of expression, has historically been subjected to various forms of police power. Moreover, like "La Marihuana," "Marijuana Boogie" constructs a utopian party scene that sharply contrasts with the sobrieties and disciplines of the carefully policed social spaces of modern Los Angeles.[99] Further, just as marijuana smoking may have served as a numbing form of consolation, like alcohol, in the face of exploitative labor conditions and the militarization of social space, it may also have served as a sort of psychic consolation that reproduced an aspect of Mexican folk practices in new urban spaces. In all of these ways, Mexican immigrant music about marijuana foregrounds the limitations of the dominant construction of social reality by proposing compensations and projecting alternatives.

As these contrasting musical traditions suggest, the Mexican presence in Los Angeles helped to fracture local mass media into dominant and alternative public spheres. Miriam Hansen has demonstrated that silent films were historically put to different uses in dominant and immigrant contexts. In the dominant arc of the history, both film production and exhibition norms were aimed at constituting particular kinds of respectable, middle-class spectators who focused attentively on a central, narratively coherent feature film. I would highlight in particular two facets of this model. First, it tended to promote a new, normative spectator that eschewed forms of audience participation in favor of sitting quietly focused on the screen. This new audience discipline presupposed that spectators should internalize a form of self-policing while watching a movie. Second, complementing the new middle-class norms of movie-house comportment, film programs were streamlined and refocused so as to reinforce the imaginary autonomy of the fictional film world from its larger production and reception contexts. Over the course of the 1910s and 1920s, according to Hansen, filmmakers strove to produce the "diegetic illusion," whereby the film fiction becomes its own, self-enclosed world.[100] The "suspension of disbelief" necessary for the illusion required newly disciplined spectators who took for granted, according to Hansen, that the fictional world of the film was perceptually segregated from the space of the theater, and more generally, I would add, from the larger surrounding social space of southern California. In Hansen's formulation, new forms of spectator discipline appeared "as the industrial response to the problems posed by the cinema's availability to ethnically diverse, socially unruly, and sexually mixed audience."[101] In other words, by symbolically enclosing films within their own imaginary worlds, separated from the immediate exhibition setting and the larger social context, the middle-class mode of spectatorship served to elevate film and "rescue" it, for example, from immigrant audiences.

As an increasingly important part of the dominant public sphere, then, Hollywood film was in part a reaction formation opposed to the possible uses of film by socially marginalized groups such as Mexicans.[102] In contrast to silent, disciplined, middle-class viewers, Mexican audiences participated in the show. This was in part because, in increasing contrast with white, middle-class theaters, where the focus was on a feature film and additional attractions were kept to a minimum, in the Mexican theaters of L.A. films were incorporated into larger variety-show formats in which programs of Mexican singers, musicians, dancers, and comedians preceded and followed film screenings. Variety performers reframed films in heterogeneous ways by juxtaposing them with nostalgic immigrant songs about rural Mexico; with regional Mexican dances to live musical accompaniment; with *corridos* about the revolution, border rebellion, and Mexican bootleggers and smugglers; with burlesque skits about the pratfalls of immigrant life, including new urban possibilities for sexual encounters, misunderstandings, and double entendres; with boleros and other songs about sexual desire, illicit love, and "loose" women and men; and, of course, with songs about marijuana.[103]

According to Tomás Ybarra-Frausto, the variety-show tradition that Mexicans combined with film screenings had some of its origins in the Mexican Revolution. Such shows "played a crucial role in projecting from the stage the popular base of an emerging national culture" and "functioned as a tribunal for the debate of national issues." Further, with the stock character of the *pelado,* a sort of satirical "underdog" figure, the *revistas* "projected a minority view of prevailing social conditions" that opposed official norms and "criticized and lampooned those in power and their institutions."[104] Similarly, the stock figure of the "insouciant *vedette* (singer-dancer-actress)" further departed from dominant gender norms. "In the United States, suffragettes clamored for judicial and political power while flappers stood up for sexual and personal autonomy. In Mexico (and in Mexican theaters in the U.S.), viable exponents of emerging feminine freedom were the *vedettes,* the audacious singer-dancer-actresses.... With their bold and saucy routines, they questioned sanctified codes of modesty and decorum."[105]

The incorporation of films into Mexican variety shows resituated a medium with pretensions to white, middle-class respectability within a working-class milieu. Mexican variety shows implicitly opposed the "upward mobility" of films by articulating them to vernacular, working-class entertainment traditions. What is more, variety formats "not only inhibited any prolonged absorption into the fictional world on screen, but the alternation of films and nonfilmic acts preserved a perceptual continuum between fictional space and theater space," and, by extension, between theater space and the larger social world of Los Angeles. In contrast to the ideal, middle-class context in which the spectator was perceptually distanced from the action at the front of the theater, Mexican performance traditions, according to Ybarra-Frausto, "bonded the spectators and the spectacle in a nexus of social interaction."[106] The juxtaposition of (both U.S. and Mexican) films with performances by local and regional celebrities, amateur talent contests, and audience singalongs gave Mexican immigrant moviegoing a localized, social dimension that potentially undermined the "diegetic illusion." In contrast to the dominant model of spectatorship that segregated film from larger social conditions, Mexican audiences in Los Angeles instead tended in some measure to integrate the two, connecting film and world. The incorporation of films into Mexican variety shows thus encouraged modes of audience behavior—"a more participatory, sound-intensive form of response, an active sociability, a connection with the other viewer"— that "deviated from middle-class standards of reception."[107]

The historical friction—and in some cases open conflict—between dominant Anglo-American and alternative Mexican public spheres crystallized in part around sound. The mass mediation of sound was a field of cultural and social conflict. Media activists such as Josefina Fierro and Pedro J. González used the radio in directly oppositional ways, in the latter case provoking an extreme police response. And although Mexican variety shows were not oppositional in the same way, they nonetheless represented an alternative to dominant social norms. Mexican film audiences appropriated English-language sound films in ways that largely disregarded or diminished their diegetic illusion or narrative world. The singer Lydia Mendoza provides a striking example. In the 1930s Mendoza performed in the movie and musical variety shows of Mexican Los Angeles and other parts of the U.S. Southwest. The first film she recalls ever seeing was *The Jazz Singer,* a (partly) musical film often remembered as helping to launch sound filmmaking. In her account, the film's English intertitles and song lyrics were meaningless to her, and yet she greatly enjoyed the novelty of sound and the music in particular. Mendoza's memories of her first sound movie suggest that Mexican audiences often ignored film narratives but found pleasures and meanings in films nonetheless. Mexican movie exhibitors in L.A. thus alternated between, on the one hand, Mexican sound movies such as *Alma Mexicana* and *La Llorona,* and, on the other hand, Hollywood talkies, including a variety of films, but especially musical comedies like *Gold Diggers of 1933,* Mae West's *I'm No Angel,* and Eddie Cantor's *Roman Scandals.*[108] Moreover, as I have suggested, exhibitors who catered to Mexican immigrant audiences often packaged Hollywood sound films in ways that subordinated them within larger Mexican variety formats. Rather than imagining that these movies served to assimilate or "Americanize" Mexican spectators, Spanish-language newspaper listings instead suggest that immigrant audiences sometimes annexed Hollywood musicals and other films to popular Mexican entertainments. In numerous newspaper ads, Mexican variety shows, and in some cases Mexican films, upstaged Hollywood films, reducing them to the status of an "added attraction." An ad for Teatro Mexico, for instance, announced a *revista* called *Los Perros de Presa* in large bold letters and then added in smaller type that the show was preceded by a program of unnamed sound films.[109] Similarly, an ad for the Burbank Theatre gave top billing to a "Gran Programa de Vaudeville con Revista de Muñecas Burbank," and subsidiary billing to the English-language films *Massacre* and *Take a Chance.*[110] And as if to transform the plot of the infamous *The Girl of the Rio,* which sexualized and criminalized Mexicans (see chapter 4), the ad for El Teatro Hidalgo listed the film in small type, beneath the larger, bolder type of the main attraction, a musical variety show featuring a Mexican magician called "El Gran Pepet en sus maravillosas

transformaciones."[111] In all of these ways, Mexicans literally and symbolically "redubbed" movies with subaltern sound tracks, folding films
into live shows that responded to local, collective concerns.

In contrast to the Mexican use of sound films as one part of an alternative, immigrant public sphere in 1930s L.A., Hollywood studios at
first attempted to deploy sound technology in order to displace competing forms of entertainment like the musical variety show. Warner
Brothers, for example, pursued the Vitaphone sound system in part as a
cost-saving device for its own theaters, and they in turn promoted it to
other exhibitors by arguing that they would no longer need to hire live
performers.[112] Hollywood filmmakers attempted in effect to block the
reframing of films within variety-show formats by producing what might
be called "virtual *revistas*," sound movies that were meant to subsume
live musical performances.[113] In an effort to attract Spanish-speaking
audiences both in Latin America and in the United States, Hollywood
studios made more than a hundred films in Spanish between 1929 and
1938.[114] And a number of these films seem to mimic the Mexican *revista*.
One of the earliest Vitaphone shorts, for example, was called *Mexican
Tipica Orchestra* (1929), a film of an unnamed Mexican orchestra that
was presumably meant to be shown with a feature film and in lieu of a
live musical performance. In many of these films the studios employed
a small number of Mexican (and other Latin American) writers, musicians, and performers in order to simulate live musical reviews. A good
example is *Charros, Gauchos y Manolas* (1930), also known as *Revista
Musical Cugat*, featuring performances by Xavier Cugat's Orchestra,
Mexican songs and settings, as well as the performance of an erotic
dance by a Mexican woman. In other cases, Hollywood made concur-
rent, Spanish-language versions of its English films. For example, at
Universal City *Dracula* was filmed in English by day, and at night, on
the same sets, it was shot in Spanish, starring the locally popular Mexican performers Carlos Villarias and Lupita Tovar. Similarly, the musical
review called *The King of Jazz* (Universal, 1930), starring Paul Whiteman
and his Orchestra, was concurrently filmed as *El Rey Del Jazz*, starring
Tovar and Mexican actor Martín Garralaga as "maestros de ceremo-
nias" and featuring renditions of "La Paloma" and "Cielito Lindo."[115]
And films such as *La Cucaracha* incorporated performances of the *jarabe
tapatío*, a regional Mexican dance also popular in local Mexican theaters.[116] With such films the studios sought to subsume Mexican music

within the world on the screen, and to in effect preclude the inter-relationships among performance, audience, and the surrounding so-cial terrain that characterized the alternative public spheres of Mexican entertainment.[117]

Nonetheless, Mexican theaters contradicted this trend by combin-ing Hollywood's virtual *revistas* with live musical performances in ways that implicitly responded to the immediate context of police power in Los Angeles. The exhibition of *El Caballero de la Noche* (1932), a Spanish-language musical made by Fox, is a case in point, for El Teatro Hidalgo reframed that film as a carnivalesque, potentially critical rejoinder to the contemporary deployment of police power against Mexicans in Los Angeles. The film was a remake of a Tom Mix vehicle called *Dick Turpin* (1925) that concerns the eighteenth-century English bandit of the same name. The Spanish-language version, however, starred José Mojica, a close friend of Pedro González who was very popular in Los Angeles. As Turpin the singing masked bandit, Mojica may have appealed to Mexi-can audiences as a representative of resistance to police authority. The film begins at a public execution, when a disguised Turpin sings a song, written by Mojica, that mocks the wealthy.[118] As if to underline his status as a social bandit and populist hero, when Count Churlton's guards attempt to apprehend Turpin, the crowd comes to the rescue and helps him escape. On the highway, Turpin robs the count, and then impersonates one of his armed guards to gain access to his castle. Eventually he is discovered and arrested by the count's men. Turpin sings a song on the way to the gallows before being rescued by his side-kick Tom. Finally, Turpin escapes to the arms of Lady Elena, the count's fiancée, and the film ends happily.

In 1934, *El Caballero de la Noche* had an extensive run at Teatro Hidalgo in downtown L.A.[119] Teatro Hidalgo was a good match for the film's populist, antiauthoritarian plot, because it was one of the more working-class film venues in Mexican Los Angeles. Promoted as "El Teatro de la Raza," the Hidalgo advertised its "precios populares." Indeed, in contrast to more "high-toned" theaters such as Teatro California, Teatro Hidalgo was relatively inexpensive and democratic in its seating. Whereas the California charged as much as fifty cents for orchestra seating and twenty-five cents for the balcony, all seats at the Hidalgo were the same price—sometimes as low as ten cents. Admission at non-Mexican theaters was generally more expensive, ranging as high as $1.50

for evening balcony seats at movie palaces such as Grauman's Chinese Theater.[120] In addition, Teatro Hidalgo framed films with events calculated to attract working-class audiences, including *revistas* like González's "Locura de Radio," but also raffles for Mexican immigrant "staples" such as radios and sacks of flour for tortillas.

I would speculate that *El Caballero de la Noche* may have been popular with Mexican audiences in part because it bore a resemblance to their surrounding social world, in which the police protected capitalist labor relations. According to the historian of eighteenth-century London Peter Linebaugh, the story of Dick Turpin on which *El Caballero de la Noche* was loosely based represents a plebeian response to the new "capitalist organization" of the London meat market, and by extension to emergent capitalist labor relations. As Linebaugh observes, the capitalization and centralization of the London meat market excluded many small producers, who often joined bands of highwaymen and poachers that preyed upon the newly privatized estates that supplied the new market. As a legendary social bandit who stole cattle and venison from the rich, Turpin's story reminds us that historically, the extension of capitalist labor relations was not inevitable but instead required the deployment of various kinds of police power. Such an understanding of the relationship between capitalism and the police perhaps in part explains the appeal of *El Caballero de la Noche* for working-class Mexican audiences. Figures like Turpin would have been familiar to Mexicans in the musical traditions described in chapter 3, the narrative ballads or *corridos* about bootleggers and drug smugglers who defy the police.

As this example suggests, the topic of police power has been a central subject of conflict in Los Angeles mass media. In particular, the media was an important public-relations weapon in the early-twentieth-century "drug war" that the LAPD waged against Mexicans. An investigation into alternative, Mexican media responses to police power makes visible the extent to which dominant media like Hollywood films participated in multiple ways in the larger policing of Mexicans in southern California.

Part III

Cocaine

CHAPTER 6

Cocaine Colonialism

Indian Rebellion in South America and the History of Psychoanalysis

Throughout *Drug Wars*, I have argued that the official administration of drug traffic, which has often aimed to manage subaltern labor, has also helped to create subaltern resistance. Part II suggests that U.S. drug control efforts in the 1930s had the goal of controlling potentially rebellious Mexican workers, and yet such measures also provoked Mexican struggles against criminalization. Similarly, Part I contends that the British-controlled monopoly was a means for exploiting Chinese labor, but this system remained haunted by Chinese rebellion. In Part III, the linkages between labor control and subaltern rebellion remain an important focus, for the history of cocaine traffic reveals much about the relationships between imperialism and Indian resistance in the Americas.

In the second half of the nineteenth century, an emergent global market in cocaine depended on and helped to reproduce de facto systems of Indian slavery in Peru.[1] Indian debt peons on large plantations not only grew and harvested coca, but the product of their labor was in turn distributed to others as a means of controlling them and making their labor more profitable. Recalling the British context, where opium was sold to Chinese workers in order to help make them work longer and harder, in South America coca was disseminated to Indians on plantations and in mines for similar reasons. First the Spanish conquerors and later European and creole capitalists discovered that, as a powerful stimulant and appetite suppressant, coca made Indian laborers more valuable by enabling them to work long hours with little food. For this reason, the owners of coca plantations distributed the plant's leaves to the very Indians who produced them.

Before the 1880s, coca consumption was largely limited to South America. After that, however, it became a global commodity that was sold in large quantities by pharmaceutical companies and patent medicine producers. Both kinds of entrepreneurs used modern advertising techniques to promote the drug.[2] "Vin Mariani," a popular wine fortified with coca, was the subject of an aggressive advertising campaign including testimonials from European royalty; two U.S. presidents; writers such as Jules Verne, H. G. Wells, and Alexandre Dumas; the inventor Thomas Edison; the actress Sarah Bernhardt; and even Pope Leo XIII. The success of Vin Mariani inspired a host of other beverages such as Café-Coca Compound, Doctor Don's Kola, Rococola, Inca Cola, Vin des Incas, and, of course, Coca-Cola.[3] The demand for the drug in Europe and the United States led to a massive expansion of the commercial coca industry in Peru.[4] Indeed, around the turn of the century cocaine played a prominent role in an emergent international mass consumer culture.

Among the new cocaine entrepreneurs was the young Sigmund Freud, who promoted the drug to Western doctors and consumers as a pleasurable and beneficial commodity. Between 1884 and 1887, Freud wrote six papers on cocaine. In the first and most significant of these works, "Über Coca" (1884), he enthusiastically recommended the drug as a stimulant, as an aphrodisiac, and as a cure for alcohol and morphine addiction. The essay is, in part, a historical account of the leaf's use among Peruvian Indians, making it Freud's earliest published work of anthropological speculations. One year later, he produced his only published scientific experiment, in which he attempted to record the objective effects of cocaine on measurable quantities of muscular energy. Shortly thereafter, Freud recommended coca to Vienna's physiological and psychiatric societies during two public lectures. These lectures excited great interest in both Europe and the United States. The first volume of the 1885 *British Medical Journal,* for instance, contained sixty-seven separate pieces on cocaine.[5] During this period, Freud recommended cocaine to just about anyone who would listen—colleagues, family, friends, his fiancée, and ultimately the world. He even became a minor advertising celebrity, penning an endorsement of the Parke-Davis Cocaine Preparation.[6]

Freud's promotion of cocaine has received relatively little critical attention. Freud himself was always rather sheepish about his work on coca. In a letter to his first biographer, he dismissed it as a mere hobby.[7] In keeping with this assessment, his cocaine writings were excluded from the *Standard Edition of the Complete Psychological Works of Sigmund Freud.* This oversight was partly addressed in the early 1970s when a popular U.S. press published *The Cocaine Papers.*[8] Perhaps as part of an effort to capitalize on a new interest in drugs and the counterculture, the edition reprinted Freud's scientific papers on cocaine as well as excerpts from works on the drug's contemporary context, not to mention a whimsical piece on the relationships between Freud and Sherlock Holmes. This last topic was also the subject of a popular novel by Nicholas Meyer titled *The Seven-Percent Solution* (1974), in which Freud treats Holmes for cocaine addiction. The novel was ultimately turned into a popular Hollywood film of the same name. Such celebrity, however, overlooked one of the most striking features of Freud's cocaine research—the fact that it presupposed forms of Indian neo-slavery. By contrast, in the late nineteenth century, it was virtually impossible for Freud and his contemporaries to completely ignore the effective dependence of cocaine production on coercive labor systems. Among scientific researchers, this was a well-known fact that was reported on at length, most notably by the Swiss naturalist Johan Jacob Von Tschudi, whose *Travels in Peru* helped to spark European and U.S. interest in the drug.[9]

Freud reacted to this knowledge in ways that foreshadow his subsequent elaboration of the concept of disavowal. As I noted in chapter 1, disavowal is a psychic defense in which two conflicting beliefs are held at once. In such states, according to Freud, both denial and recognition "exist side by side ... without influencing each other." Freud's theory constitutes an apt gloss on his earlier cocaine research, in which he seems to say, "I know that coca is made by virtual slave labor, and yet all the same ..." He does not therefore reject outright the knowledge of actual labor conditions, for its distorted traces are everywhere in his cocaine writings, which, in my reading, constitute a cognitive map of cocaine colonialism in Peru and the forms of labor exploitation that it entailed. Moreover, Freud's work registers Indian resistance to such labor systems. In this way his cocaine papers illustrate a more general claim, elaborated in greater detail in the final chapter, that historically, conflicts over cocaine represent forms of Indian warfare by other means.

Such conflicts, moreover, can ultimately be discerned in Freud's psychoanalytic revisions of his earlier cocaine studies. In the later work, Freud injects concerns related to the conditions of the international pharmaceutical trade into his construction of the analytic subject, allowing the second to displace, by subsuming, the first. In other words, Freud implodes the space of slavery and rebellion into psychological space, reimagining an imperial division of labor in terms of conscious and unconscious topoi. In this way, Freud translates an imperial map into a psychic map that relocates Indian resistance within the shifting boundaries of a polymorphously perverse and "primitive" unconscious.

COCAINE AND INDIAN LABOR

In imperialist imagery, the Indian is inherently lazy. Hegel even elevated such a charge to the level of a philosophical concept. His theory of history valorizes the march of Spirit as active will and reduces the inhabitants of the Americas to the principle of passivity, Spirit's other. In "The Geographical Basis of History," Hegel writes:

> A mild and passionless disposition, want of spirit and a crouching submissiveness toward a Creole, and still more towards a European, are the chief characteristics of the native Americans; and it will be long before the Europeans succeed in producing any feeling of independence in them.... The weakness of the American physique was a chief reason for bringing the Negroes to America, to employ their labor in the work that had to be done in the New World.[10]

Hegel's claim about the substitution of African slaves notwithstanding, in practice the supposed laziness of Indians became the justification for slavery and debt peonage, for if Indians would not work freely, it was reasoned, they must be forced. Such is the logic, for instance, of Sr. A. Larrea, the commander of the Peruvian Naval Station, whose report on Indians of the Amazon was published in a promotional work titled *The Amazon Provinces of Peru as a Field for European Emigration* (1888): "The Quichuan is always submissive to your face but slow to perform; soured by ill-treatment, he will hardly do anything unless compelled. He will do nothing well unless he is treated as a slave. Treat him kindly and you will make him a thief; whip him and he will rise up and thank you, and be your humble servant."[11]

As Larrea's remarks suggest, slavery and other forms of coercion such as debt peonage were common in the Amazon wherever Europeans exercised power.[12] Another author in the same emigration manual, Leonardo Pflucker y Rico, further indicates the central role of coca in the exploitation of Indian labor. In his account, Indians work for seemingly impossible lengths of time in the silver mines—twelve hours a day, seven days a week, plus two to three night shifts a week. Which means, according to Pflucker y Rico, that "they only rest twelve hours out of each twenty-eight hours of work, which appears strange, but can be understood when the natural physique of these men is observed, aided by the use of coca."[13] Coca helped to make such grueling labor regimens possible for several reasons. Its euphoria-inducing properties presumably dulled the pain of brutal working conditions; as a stimulant it energized working bodies; and finally, as an appetite suppressant it enabled Indians to work long hours with little food and hence at a reduced cost. For these reasons, throughout the nineteenth century, employers in the region distributed coca to their Indian laborers and incorporated periodic coca breaks into the work schedule.[14]

The relationship between coca and coercive forms of labor is perhaps best represented in Tschudi's *Travels in Peru*. In a famous passage cited by Freud and others, Tschudi describes the amazing feats of a sixty-two-year-old Indian named Hatun Huamang whom the naturalist employed as a servant and guide.[15] Tschudi employed Huamang for five days and during that time the Indian supposedly consumed only coca and slept only two hours a night. This example led Tschudi to conclude that coca functions as a food substitute and that when used in moderation it is "very conducive to health."[16] Freud references this passage in order to promote the benefits of coca, and yet he takes it out of context, ignoring the role of coca in exploitative labor relations. As Tschudi notes, on the plantations the "poor Indian is kept in a state of slavery by advances of clothing, meat, brandy &c.... The laborer who is set down in the plantation-book as a debtor for ten or twelve dollars, has a good chance of remaining during the rest of his life a tributary slave.... European importations, such as can be purchased at very low prices in the Sierra, are sold at high profits by the owners of plantations to the poor Indians, who have to repay them by long and severe labour."[17] And, as he emphasizes, coca was primarily beneficial in situations where Indians were compelled to work under horrible conditions with inadequate food. Without coca, "the Peruvian Indian, with his spare diet, would be incapable of going through the labor that he now performs.... It is an essential means of preserving the nationality of the Indians, and in some measure mitigating the melancholy fate of that once great race which disease and excessive labor now threaten to destroy."[18] Moreover, although Tschudi argues that the moderate use of coca is harmless, he stresses that in the mines and plantations excess is the rule, which ultimately takes a terrible toll: "An inveterate *coquero,* or coca chewer, is known at the first glance. His unsteady gait, his yellow-coloured skin, his dim and sunken eyes encircled by a purple ring, his quivering lips and his general apathy, all bear witness of the baneful effects of the coca juice when taken in excess."[19] In his zeal to promote cocaine, Freud ignored such claims.

Freud disavows the role of coca in the exploitation of Indian labor by displacing slavery into the distant past of the Spanish Conquest. Following Tschudi, in "Über Coca," Freud begins his history of the drug at the moment "when the Spanish conquerors forced their way into Peru." He notes that "the Spaniards did not initially believe in the marvelous effects of the plant, which they suspected was the work of the devil, mainly because of the role which it played in the religious ceremonial."[20] This attitude only changed, according to Freud, when the Spanish "observed that the Indians could not perform the heavy labor imposed upon them in the mines if they were forbidden to partake of coca" (50). The conquistadors compromised, he concludes, by rationalizing and controlling coca use, distributing leaves at regular intervals in the day and including "coca breaks" (ibid.) in the work schedule. Recalling the Spanish rationalization of Indian coca use, Freud goes on to sing a "song of praise" to a drug that has made notoriously reluctant Indians work and now promises Old World consumers that they can somehow tap into the prodigious vitality of the New World. And yet, by focusing on the sixteenth-century Conquest, he obscures the extent to which forms of virtual Indian slavery continued into the nineteenth century. In this way, he effectively denies that the Spanish Conquest represents the precursor to his own efforts to promote coca. In other words, because most of the world's coca was produced by Indian debt peons, Freud's dream that one day large numbers of people in Europe and the United States would consume the drug suggests that his plans ultimately depended on forms of conquest that would conscript Indians to labor in support of a global cocaine market.

This disavowal of conquest is apparent even in Freud's clinical analysis of coca's effects on Europeans. According to Freud, rather than making Europeans slave masters, cocaine promises the experience of self-mastery:

"One senses an increase of self-control and feels more vigorous and more capable of work. . . . One is simply normal, and soon finds it difficult to believe that one is under the influence of any drug at all." In this analysis, cocaine does not directly add to subjective well-being; instead, it merely mitigates against forces that could depress normal health. In "Über Coca," Freud suggests that the vigor produced by cocaine "is due not so much to direct stimulation as to the disappearance of elements in one's general state of well-being which cause depression. One may assume that the euphoria resulting from good health is also nothing more than the normal condition of a well-nourished cerebral cortex which is not conscious of the organs of the body to which it belongs" (60). Here, cocaine allows normal consciousness to emerge by isolating psyche from body, euphorically elevating the spirits beyond a consciousness of material embodiment. Freud presents the drug as an exotic commodity that enables consumers to enjoy states of heightened normalcy that seemingly free them from their bodies, and, metaphorically, from the larger material conditions in which the production of cocaine was embedded.

This description of cocaine euphoria dovetails with Freud's professional interests and can be read as an advertisement for the unique medical value of cocaine and, by implication, for Freud's own talent. Although a consideration of professional profit motives does not exhaust all possibilities, Freud's writings in this period demonstrate that he consciously calculated the professional benefits of cocaine promotion. Depressed by his relative obscurity and held back by anti-Semitism, Freud hoped that the promotion of this "magical substance" (60) would allow his considerable talents to emerge from the limits of their immediate professional environment. Indeed, Freud's claims regarding cocaine's work-enhancing powers were in part based on his use of the drug. I would argue that in order to transcend stereotypes of the "primitive" Jew, Freud was willing to reify the exploitation of Indian labor on which his projected upward mobility depended.[21] Freud in effect generalized his particular use of Indian cocaine, suggesting that the value distilled from the Other in the form of pharmaceuticals could enable European individuals to abstract themselves from larger political-economic contexts.

At the same time, however, one can detect Freud's tacit recognition that his research depended on conquest in his identification with Spain. As a teenager, Freud took a lively interest in the Spanish language and Spanish culture. In the early 1870s he began studying Spanish with a childhood friend, Eduard Silberstein. We might say that the boys' friendship was partly based on playing "Spaniards and Indians," for in a letter Freud wrote while researching coca he claimed that the two had enjoyed "romantic dreams about Red Indians, Cooper's *Leatherstocking*, and sailor's stories."[22] They read Cervantes together and formed a club they called the Academia Española, which even had its own seal, the gothic letters "AE" under a stylized crown.[23] Both boys adopted Spanish names (Freud's was "Don Cipion") and exchanged numerous letters written in clumsy, schoolboy Spanish. And although Freud often adopted a jocular tone when writing about it, he was nonetheless seriously devoted to the club, even upbraiding his friend for neglecting their studies:

> In my official capacity of M.d.l.A.E. [Member of the Spanish Academy] I must not withhold from you a question of great political significance that has been preoccupying me greatly. At a time when everyone is recognizing the Spanish Republic, the Spanish Academy, an unexcelled model of organization and of such importance to its maternal organism, seems to be turning away from Spain and unmindful of its origins, granting admittance, or rather exclusive dominion, to barbaric customs and foreign sounds even in its official documents.[24]

Here, however humorously, Freud identifies with the Spanish state. He would retain his youthful interest in Spain throughout his life.

Indeed, at the height of his adult career, Freud recalled enough of his boyhood studies to correspond in Spanish with his Spanish translator.[25] Moreover, he sprinkled Spanish words throughout "Über Coca" and cited several Spanish-language sources. And in his letters he seems to identify with the great fictional knight Don Quixote. In a letter from 1884 in which he responds to a request from his fiancée, Martha Bernays, he chivalrously promises that if necessary he will don "armor at once" and then presses her to finish reading *Don Quixote*.[26] In a letter later that year, he compares the requirements in a class he is teaching to "the condition the hero [of *Don Quixote*] makes to all the knights he has conquered."[27] Again, although Freud's tone is humorous, he nonetheless seems to take the Spanish knight quite seriously. As he wrote years later, although *Don Quixote* is the "immortal prototype of every humorous novel," its hero "grows in the author's hands into something more serious than seemed originally intended."[28] And later in life, without a hint of irony, Freud made explicit his identification with the Spanish colonizers, writing, "I am actually not a man of science, not an observer, not an experimenter, not a thinker. I am by temperament nothing but a *conquistador* and adventurer... with all the inquisitiveness, daring, and tenacity characteristic of such a man."[29]

In this way, Freud participated in a larger idealization of the Spanish Empire often referred to as "Spanish Fantasy." While popular interest in the Spanish past has a longer history, going back at least to the 1840s and the publication of W. H. Prescott's widely read histories of Spanish conquest in the Americas, in its late-nineteenth- and early-twentieth-century incarnations "Spanish Fantasy" was indebted to Helen Hunt Jackson's novel of Spanish California, *Ramona*. This last work was published one year after "Über Coca" and was translated into German and Spanish shortly thereafter. As the example of *Ramona* suggests, "Spanish Fantasy" was an international phenomenon. In the U.S. Southwest, buildings were increasingly modeled on Spanish colonial architecture, and civic groups mounted pageants and plays in which Anglo-Americans dressed up as Spanish dons and señoritas. Elsewhere I have suggested that such practices enabled Anglo-Americans to represent themselves as the logical successors to the Spanish Empire in the region.[30] Here I would make a similar claim regarding Freud, who, through his endorsement of cocaine, imagined himself as a sort of heir to the Spanish Empire in Peru.

While working on cocaine, Freud looked up to another man who seemed to embody the qualities he associated with the conquistadors— his mentor, Dr. Ernest Fleischl. As he confided to his fiancée, Freud revered Fleischl as "a thoroughly excellent person in whom nature and education have combined to do their best. Wealthy, skilled in all games and sports, with the stamp of genius in his manly features, good-looking, refined, endowed with many talents and capable of forming an original judgment about most things, he has always been my ideal."[31] Freud could nonetheless also assume an adversarial stance toward Fleischl that recalled the chivalrous battles between Spanish knights that he enjoyed in Cervantes. In the same letter in which he professes his veritable subjection before the superior Fleischl, he also petulantly scorns the "lofty science" his friend both serves and exemplifies. Freud suggests that by chivalrously devoting himself to Martha Bernays rather than to his profession, he finally has an advantage over the man he has so envied. What follows is a masochistic fantasy that finds Freud in Fleischl's sumptuous quarters, daydreaming about his friend stealing his fiancée: "I looked around his room, fell to thinking about my superior friend and it occurred to me how much he could do for a girl like Martha, what a setting he could provide for this jewel." Although Fleischl would be able to take Martha to the Alps, Venice, and Rome, at present Freud could only offer her a life of "hiding and near hopelessness." He concludes that the realization of this fantasy is probable, almost inevitable: "I was compelled painfully to visualize how easy it could be for him— who spends two months of each year in Munich and frequents the most exclusive society—to meet Martha at her uncle's house. And I began wondering what he would think of Martha." Freud finally breaks off this daydream and ends the letter, resolving to assert the rights of romantic conquest: "Can't I too for once have something better than I deserve? Martha remains mine."[32]

Freud's daydream figures Martha as a treasured object that recalls the Spanish silver mines of Peru, as well as his own conquest of coca. In this letter Martha becomes a value counter between professional rivals, a jewel suspended between two masculine settings. In other letters Freud addresses Martha as his "Princess." And although the term is a fairly common endearment with a variety of associations, in the present context it is notable that in "Über Coca" Freud mentions another sort of "Princess"—the Incan "goddess of love" (77) who was represented holding coca leaves in her hand. Similarly, the frontispiece for W. Golden Mortimer's celebrated *History of Coca, the Divine Plant of the Incas* (1901) depicts "Mama Coca," an Indian woman wearing a feathered headdress, "presenting the Divine Plant to the Old World," here personified as a Spanish conquistador.[33] By imagining himself as a Spanish conqueror and the woman he repeatedly claims to "possess" as an Indian, Freud indirectly registers his knowledge of imperial labor relations in the production of coca, which in effect make Indian workers, including women, de facto possessions of the plantation owners.

Such knowledge is further reflected in Freud's discussion of cocaine's value as a food supplement and digestive aid. In "Über Coca," he argues, "there is ample evidence that Indians under the influence of coca can withstand exceptional hardships and perform heavy labor without requiring proper nourishment during that time" (51). And yet when he comes to describe the drug's possible uses by non-Indians he does not recommend it as a food substitute but rather as a cure for indigestion. By way of testimony, he notes, "I have experienced personally how painful symptoms attendant upon large meals—viz., a feeling of pressure and fullness in the stomach, discomfort and disinclination to work—

"Mama Coca Presenting the 'Divine Plant' to the Old World," in W. Golden Mortimer, *History of Coca, the Divine Plant of the Incas* (San Francisco: And/Or Press, 1974), opposite title page.

disappear with eructation following small doses of cocaine. Time and again I have brought such relief to my colleagues; and twice I observed how the nausea resulting from gastronomic excesses responded in a short time to the effects of cocaine, and gave way to a normal desire to eat and a feeling of bodily well-being" (65–66). Whereas Indians used coca to supplement an impoverished plantation diet, Freud here promotes the drug to Europeans as a remedy for overeating. In the move from Indian starvation to white gluttony, Freud produces a cognitive map of the unequal economic relationships between Europe and South America.

Freud further indicates that his own scientific experiments depend on Indian labor by suggesting that they mimic the work of Indian treks. In order to support his claim that coca is an effective tonic, Freud cites the experiments of Sir Robert Christison, who reproduced Indian-like feats of endurance. Christison engaged in various small expeditions— rural hikes and two scalings of Ben Vorlich—in order to verify reports of coca use among the Indians. For a brief period, such experiments were the rage among scientific hobbyists. Sir Clifford Allbut, for example, reportedly took cocaine on walking tours of the Alps in hopes of amazing his companions with his physical prowess.[34] Once again Freud maps unequal economic relations by noting that while coca enables Indians to work under harsh conditions, it promises to enable Europeans to pursue leisure activities and scientific experiments, and, he hopes, career advancement and financial rewards.

Finally, Freud's remarks on the work-stimulating properties of cocaine for European consumers indirectly reference the drug's role in coercive labor systems. His cocaine research is centrally concerned with work value and the values of work; he claims that the drug's main use "will undoubtedly remain that which the Indians have made of it" (63) as a work stimulant. The drug purportedly raises up in humans, in the very center of their being, a readiness for labor. Or, as Freud writes, "the effect of cocaine results from an elevation of the central readiness for work" (116). His calculations concerning this readiness to work resemble, in some respects, a labor theory of value: his experiments focus on metabolic rates and the effect of cocaine on the ratio of food energy to labor output. Freud proposes that the drug represents a metabolic "source of savings." He explains that a "biological system which has absorbed the drug" can amass a "greater store of vital energy which can be converted into work than would have been possible without coca. If we take the amount of work as being constant, the body which has absorbed cocaine should be able to manage with a lower metabolism, which in turn means a smaller intake of food" (68). Indeed, Freud finds that cocaine short-circuits the "normal" homeostasis between food and labor, increasing "the physical capacity of the body for a given short period of time" and allowing the body "to hold strength in reserve to meet further demands" (63). As he asserts again and again, the stimulant functions as a form of nourishment and has a positive impact on the food-to-labor ratio. Recalling the use of coca in the mines and plantations of Peru, Freud in effect suggests that the drug aids in the production of surplus values by allowing workers to reproduce their labor power with less food and hence at a cheaper rate. His theory in effect envisions the Indian as a reserve of labor power that can reproduce itself for nothing, or almost nothing—a few mouthfuls of a drug that literally grows on bushes.

Still, Freud's thinking on the matter remains confused in particularly revealing ways. In his account, cocaine's effects defy categorization as either physiological or psychological. After waffling over the metabolic "source of savings" theory, he tentatively argues that cocaine produces a psychic dividend:

> [T]he human nervous system has an undoubted, if somewhat obscure, influence on the nourishment of tissues; psychological factors can, after all, cause a healthy man to lose weight. . . . The therapeutic quality of coca which we took as our argument at the outset does not, therefore, deserve to be rejected out of hand. The excitation of nerve centers by cocaine can have a favorable effect on the nourishment of the body afflicted by a consumptive condition, even though that influence might well not take the form of a slowing down of metabolism. (69)

While isolating psychological factors, Freud frames his claim by referring to a physiological process—nerve excitation—whose workings remain "obscure." Freud's research thus opens up questions that are irresolvable within the limits of his terms. Does cocaine ease the mind's labor upon the body, or the body's labor upon the mind? Does the drug help the mind to repress any consciousness of the body, or does it make possible the body's elevation of mental functions? Ultimately, the answer is both and neither, for Freud presumes a contradictory subject who is simultaneously conscious beyond bodily limits and yet somehow still connected to a working body. In my reading, this weaving together of elevated psyche and laboring body becomes a fantastic allegory of the unequal relationships between European consumers and Indian producers.

COCAINE AND INDIAN RESISTANCE

Freud's imaginary yoking together of consumers and producers, however, repeatedly threatens to come undone as he confronts the specter of slave revolts. Such possibilities are amply represented in Tschudi's *Travels in Peru.* Tschudi, for instance, describes an unsettling incident in which, while staying in an Indian hut, he inadvertently discovered a large number of muskets: "I, quite unsuspectingly, inquired of the Indian why he thought it requisite to keep so many weapons of defense? He replied, with a sinister frown, that the time would come when he should find them useful."[35] Even more striking in the present context, Tschudi observes that Indian attacks on white and mestizo communities were particularly common around the coca fields. He notes that "the worst enemies" of the coca-producing regions of the Moñtana de Vitoc are the "wild Indians" called the Chunchos. According to the naturalist, since the seventeenth century, the Chunchos had continually attacked the Catholic missions and the local plantations. In 1674, in response to the mission's "oppression of the Indians," there was "a great insurrection" in which "all the whites were massacred." By 1739 the mission was reestablished, only to be destroyed three years later during an Indian insurrection reportedly led by the Incan Atahuallpa, also called Juan Santos. Tschudi reports that the revolt spread throughout the region as Indians destroyed all the missions, burned villages, laid waste to the plantations, and killed 245 Spanish soldiers and twenty-six priests. Continuing Indian resistance precluded Spanish colonization for the next four decades.[36]

After 1784, settlements were again established, and the Chunchos began to work on the plantations in exchange for meat, tools, and other things. "Unfortunately, the plantation owners soon began to take undue advantage of this friendly intercourse, and to charge exorbitant prices for the articles required by the Indians. For a pin or a needle they demanded two days work, for a fishing-hook four, and for a wretched knife, eight, ten, or more."[37] Ultimately, the Indians destroyed the villages in the area and killed many of the settlers. Several years later, a Spanish military governor attempted to subdue the area by converting a Chuncho village into a coca field. This practice of expropriating Indian land for coca production was common in the Andes not only under Spanish rule, but also in the 1880s, when coca production was greatly expanded.[38] But to return to Tschudi's narrative, "the Chunchos continued to harass their neighbors, particularly during the time of the coca harvest, which could not be gathered without military protection." As a result of these attacks, workers and settlers fled and the coca fields "became a waste."[39] Such conflicts continued after Spanish independence, establishing a pattern throughout the region that Tschudi describes as "the alternate rise and decline of cultivation and civilization."[40]

Although Freud read this account of Indian rebellion in the coca fields, he does not directly address such possible side effects, as it were, of his proposal for increased European and U.S. use of the drug. Instead, his writing and career are filled with oblique references to the threat of subaltern revolt. More precisely, in many of his descriptions of cocaine's effects he superimposes fantasies of Indian revolt onto the consumer's body. Although in "Über Coca" he focuses primarily on the drug's power to stimulate labor, he also notes its secondary sexual effects. As noted earlier, he observes that the natives of South America represented their goddess of love with coca leaves in her hand. In the same passage, Freud, who does not "doubt the stimulative effect of coca on the genitalia," concludes that just as the *coquero* is hyperactive, he is also hypersexual. Freud writes that the male *coquero* can perform amazing feats of physical *and* sexual endurance: "When he is faced with a difficult journey, when he takes a woman, or, in general, whenever his strength is more than usually taxed, he increases the customary dose" (51). Indeed, according to Freud, travelers confirmed "that the *coqueros* sustain a high degree of potency right into old age" (73). In a letter he wrote to his fiancée, he suggests that cocaine had a similar effect on his own body, symbolically converting him into a wild Indian with seemingly violent desires: "Woe to you, my Princess, when I shall come. I will kiss you quite red and feed you till you are plump. And if you are forward you shall see who is the stronger, a gentle little girl who doesn't eat enough or a big wild man who has cocaine in his body." Under the influence of cocaine Freud thus becomes a sexual savage who promises to assail Martha with bruising kisses.[41] Similarly, in "Über Coca" he writes that "Among the persons to whom I have given coca, three reported violent sexual excitement. . . . A young writer, who was enabled by treatment with coca to resume his work after a longish illness, gave up using the drug because of the undesirable secondary effects which it had on him" (73). Recalling the Indians described by Tschudi, who violently resisted the labor demands of the coca growers, here the drug's aphrodisiacal properties threaten to subvert the writer's productivity.

Freud would encounter a similar symbolic subversion when Flieschl, the man he idolized, became a cocaine addict or a *coquero*. By the time the two met, Fleischl desperately needed morphine injections to numb the nerve pain associated with an amputated thumb. Soon thereafter, Freud advised him to kick morphine by switching to cocaine. At first cocaine injections seemed to help Fleischl, leading his younger friend to cite him as a cured morphine addict.[42] Disturbing reports of cocaine's effects, however, soon surfaced. Doctors began to suggest that it was an addictive poison and not a universal panacea. Indeed, one researcher blamed Freud for unleashing a plague upon the human race.[43] The dangers of cocaine were made painfully manifest for Freud during his treatment of Fleischl, who began to take enormous doses of the drug. As a result, Fleischl experienced violent delirium tremens, complete with hallucinations of snakes crawling over his body. Freud spent many nights attending to Fleischl during these states of chronic intoxication, prompting him to wonder "if I shall ever in my life experience anything so agitating or exciting" as to defy description.[44] Indeed, Fleischl's pain had a profound effect on Freud. As he wrote to his fiancée, "I love him with an intellectual passion. . . . His destruction will move me as the destruction of a sacred temple would have affected an ancient Greek. I love him not so much as a human being, but as one of Creation's precious achievements. And you needn't be at all jealous."[45] Unfortunately, Freud's platonic ideal eventually died in 1891 of an illness reportedly complicated by his drug use.[46]

The fatal confrontation between ideal Fleischl and Indian cocaine deconstructs Freud's prior claim that the drug divides mind and matter: Fleischl tried to appropriate cocaine therapeutically and it killed him. In this case, the medical division of labor backfires, and the Indian remedy deployed to prolong European life instead shortens it. It is as though coca had invaded the "sacred temple" of Western civilization, recalling the rebellious Indians Tschudi describes who destroyed the Spanish missions and laid waste to fields of cultivation. Fleischl's decline into cocaine addiction, in other words, mimics the decline of colonial civilization engendered by Indian resistance.

Even Fleischl's hallucinations, I would suggest, represent projections of Indian rebellion. Like the insects and other crawling things that figure so prominently in accounts of addiction, his visions of snakes slithering over the surface of his skin rewrites on the body what Michael Taussig has called the phantasmatic "topography" of the jungle in colonialist representations. Taussig cites the example of the white Colombian Joaquín Rocha, who described the Putumayo jungle as a "Dantean" hell filled with the "swarming of infinite vipers and venomous insects."[47] As Taussig explains, in such accounts the horror of the jungle is often paired with descriptions of the horror of Indian savagery, as if the two were interchangeable. The "image of stark opposition and of otherness in the primeval jungle comes forth as the colonially intensified metaphor for the great space of terror and cruelty" constituted by colonial labor relations.[48] Taussig in effect argues that representations of the jungle and savage Indians serve to displace colonial violence. I would add that such imagery—both in travel literature and in medical accounts of cocaine hallucinations—also represents the specter of Indian revolt.

For his part, Freud ultimately adopted images of the devil and the demonic familiar from colonialist representations of Indians to describe the unfortunate effects of cocaine.[49] As Freud himself noted in "Über Coca," before they discovered its power to prop up forms of Indian slavery, the Spanish suspected that coca was "the work of the devil" (50) and that it was used in idolatrous rites. Freud's first essay on the subject was in part dedicated to exorcising such views, and yet three years later, in an essay titled "Craving for and Fear of Cocaine," Freud changed his tune. No doubt with Fleischl's fate in mind, he wrote that the drug could lead to "a rapid physical and moral deterioration, hallucinatory states of agitation similar to delirium tremens, a chronic persecution mania, characterized in my experience by the hallucination of small animals moving in the skin, and cocaine addiction in place of morphine addiction—these were the sad results of trying to cast out the devil by Beelzebub."[50]

PSYCHOANALYSIS AND INDIAN REBELLION

As I noted at the outset, Freud's essays on cocaine are not included in the *Standard Edition* of his complete works. Although the exclusion of the cocaine papers has helped to consolidate the psychoanalytic corpus proper, the sharp cut between discourses is hardly self-evident. On both sides of the divide, we can discern Freud's characteristic yoking of psychology and anthropology, individual development and the development of the species. Despite such similarities, scholars usually relegate the cocaine work to the prehistory of psychoanalysis—the land of chemistry, the nervous system, and the cerebral cortex. In practice, the relative silence concerning the cocaine papers serves to divide Freud's career into two parts, before and after analysis.[51] Such an orientation prevents critics from noting the influence of the cocaine research on subsequent theories. As a pressure point in his entire oeuvre, Freud's cocaine work can also be read as a hinge that mediates between his physiological and his psychological work.[52]

By partly constituting the *coquero*'s vigor and endurance in sexual terms, Freud sets the stage for his future studies in the universal, phylogenetic basis of subjectivity. He will eventually argue that the unconscious contains a psychic inheritance from the primal past—a reserve of primitive, erotic impulses that must be sublimated if the work of civilization is to proceed.[53] Freud's evolutionary assumptions (in effect, the psychoanalytic version of the formula "ontology recapitulates phylogony") place (male) children, hysterics, neurotics, prehistoric men, and contemporary "savages" all on roughly equal developmental planes. These various characters remain rough drafts, immature versions of the ideally sublimated subject, who efficiently converts primal sexual desire into professional and cultural achievement. Freud's libido theory focuses on the transfer of psychic energy between different spheres of consciousness in a manner that recalls his earlier attempts to transform Indian coca into European vitality.[54]

In this way, his writings on sublimation recapitulate the trajectory implicit in his cocaine writings, where he moves from "raw," sexualized Indian custom to more "sublimated" medical uses. In the genealogy I am sketching here, Freud's analytic model of psychic topography represents a revision of his earlier accounts of cocaine's value for European medicine. Beginning roughly in 1895, with his *Project for a Scientific Psychology,* Freud substitutes a psychic map for the geopolitical map implied by the cocaine work; he transforms the space between South America and Europe into psychic spacing, the gap between consciousness and the unconscious.

Freud's cocaine work can thus be read as the first step in the march of Oedipus across the globe, the first step in an attempt to submit all human activity to the sovereign reign of a Psychoanalytic Subject that bears a more than passing resemblance to the Spanish conquistador. Freud's seeming identification with the conquistador as a representative of Western civilization became all the more urgent given European anti-Semitism.

Marianna Torgovnick, for instance, has argued that "anti-Jewish propaganda portrayed Jews in the same terms Freud and his culture routinely used for the primitives. Although he rarely acknowledged its existence, this kind of propaganda...may have motivated Freud's insistent need to see himself and Jews who were like him as civilized beings antithetical to the primitive" (199). According to Torgovnick, this "insistent need" led Freud to argue in 1915 that "the great ruling powers among the white nations" must maintain their power over other peoples (197). Although in 1930 with the publication of *Civilization and Its Discontents,* "the great colonizer of psyches now balked at any unqualified endorsement of the imperial state" and in some measure began to directly question anti-Semitic demagoguery, Torgovnick suggests that Freud nonetheless remained "an apologist for civilization" (198, 201). She concludes that "Freud's picture of himself as a man of science (and the gender is important) allowed him to believe that he wrote from within the system of European civilization; it sustained his sense of himself as European (Roman) citizen rather than Jewish Other" (201). Freud reserved the position of Other, I would argue, for those peoples who were, like the Indian *coquero,* subject to the power of "primitive" desires.

The development of Freud's professional writings describes a circle: he moves from the political-economic context of Indian labor, however disavowed, to the "internal" world of "the primitive" within European individuals, and finally, in his sociological and anthropological speculations, he projects this model of analytic subjectivity back onto social relations. In late Freud, however, this "circle" is broken by the resurgence of the original context of Indian rebellion, this time in the form of a widespread "primitive discontent" at the heart of civilization. As Freud ages, he increasingly (re)turns to his prior preoccupation with Indian resistance in the form of certain group misfirings, or the rage of primitive tribes and urban masses. His final texts focus less on the sovereign subject and more on the forces of Eros and Thanatos that threaten its sovereignty.

Injecting savagery into the Oedipal subject thus remains fraught with risks. We can discern some of these risks even in Freud's early, supposedly "physiological" work. In the cocaine papers, I detect an attempt to internalize the seeds of social discontent. The drug Freud injects into himself and others represents, for him, the distillate or chemical sublation of another race: Freud tends to confuse coca with the people who traditionally use it, often treating the first as a metonym for the second, and vice versa. He opens "Über Coca" by noting that the coca bush, with its "egg-shaped" leaves and "red egg-shaped fruits... provide[s] an indispensable stimulant for some ten million" Indians (49). Watch those eggs—they are also time bombs and alien seedpods. Once Freud injects the Indian Other into the psychoanalytic subject, it acts like a demon seed. In the *Standard Edition,* from roughly the *Three Essays on Sexuality* on, Freud increasingly meditates upon the Other's egg, the seed of primitive instinct in the civilized psyche, the irritating grain of black sand in the oyster. Permutations of this theme—the irreducible unruliness of primitive desires—can be traced through texts such as "Civilized Sexual Morality" (1908), *Totem and Taboo* (1913), *Beyond the Pleasure Principle* (1920), "Group Psychology" (1921), and *Civilization and Its Discontents* (1930). As time passes, Freud's focus becomes less the problem of the Other injected into the Oedipal subject, and more a matter of confronting the unraveling of this model of individual subjectivity in the face of the "primal horde" or "group mind."

The early history of drug enforcement in the United States, where doctors hotly debated Freud's work and the work of others on cocaine, recalls the forms of subaltern rebellion I associate with the cocaine papers. In some Southern states around the turn of the century, it was first argued that black laborers could work longer and harder with cocaine in their blood. Soon, however, U.S. physicians began reporting cases of dangerous black addicts. A 1900 edition of the *Journal of the American Medical Association,* for example, cites reports of "Negroes being addicted" to the dangerous drug. These reports are echoed by the *Philadelphia Medical Journal,* which in 1902 argued that an "alarming growth of the use of cocaine among Mississippi Negroes has suggested medical laws for suppressing the evil." Testifying to Congress in 1910, one Dr. Koch warned that cocaine-using black men posed a dangerous threat to white women. In a 1914 *New York Times* article, as well as in a second essay that year appearing in the *Medical Record,* Dr. E. H. Williams cautioned against a growing "menace" of black cocaine use; he claimed that the drug prompted black men to commit "violent crime[s]" and "unprovoked murders." Dr. Williams even made the incredible claim that cocaine made blacks "more resistant to bullets" and better marksmen. Because of such reports, several Southern police departments changed from .32 to .35 caliber handguns, fearing that otherwise they would not be able to stop "coke-crazed" black men. Such paranoid legends were current during a period rife with lynchings. Between 1900 and 1920, while black masculinity was being forcibly tied to the stereotype of the savage rapist, it was also being imaginatively affixed to cocaine use.[55]

Starting in the 1980s, the functionaries of the war on drugs also identified racial enemies. Indeed, law enforcement officials have relocated geographic areas associated with drug production, sale, and use within the volatile boundaries of unrestrained "primitive" impulse on a mass scale. In my reading, the war on drugs reverses the logical movement of Freud's work—the shift from geopolitical to psychic topographies—by reimposing popular versions of his psychic model onto social space in the form of public policies that produce "dark" and "savage" areas of drug crime: those who deploy antidrug rhetoric in effect retranslate the psychobiographical model back into the drug paradigm. Needless to say, "drug warriors" participate in this discourse without considering the historical relationship between imperialism and notions of drug vice. Recalling Freud, they collapse the social and historical world into notions of individual responsibility. On the domestic front, a writer for *Time* magazine argued that "the worst problems of the black underclass . . . connect directly to black manhood and responsibility." The author lumps together unwed mothers and drug dealers as evidence of a dangerous lack of control among poor blacks.[56] While whites sell most of the cocaine in the United States and represent the majority of its consumers, blacks are the ones who must assume "responsibility" for the drug trade by going to prison. This disproportion has even been institutionalized by the penal code, where those convicted of selling five grams or more of crack cocaine, worth about $125, receive a mandatory five-year term in prison. Yet one must be caught with five hundred grams of powdered cocaine, nearly fifty thousand dollars worth of the upscale version of the drug, in order to receive an equivalent sentence.[57] As police powers constitute inner-city areas as dark underworlds by barricading minority neighborhoods, the public justifications for the drug war become self-fulfilling prophecies.[58]

Further, as I shall suggest in the final chapter, the United States has attempted to export its model of addiction and individual responsibility to Latin America, where it pressures coca-producing countries to suppress the traditional use of coca leaves among Indian peoples. According to John T. Cusack, former chief of staff of the House Select Committee on Narcotics Abuse and Control, one of the highest priorities of such countries should be the eradication of domestic coca use. As he argues, South American nations have an obligation first to themselves and second, of course, to the "developed nations," to squash the pernicious drug. In practice, however, South America officials invoke this obligation as a way to pursue their own internal enemies, particularly tribal peoples. In these ways, the war on drugs has mobilized fears of savage *coqueros* in what amounts to a genocidal drive to criminalize entire families, regions, and peoples.

CHAPTER 7

Drug Wars Are Indian Wars

Frontier Drug Enforcement and the Ends of U.S. Empire

One of the most prescient works on the history of drug wars in the Americas is a remarkable novel called *Almanac of the Dead* by Leslie Marmon Silko. Presupposing more than five hundred years of conflict and spanning the Americas, *Almanac* focuses on the apocalyptic struggle between Euro-American imperialism and indigenous resistance. On one side there are legions of evildoers, including corrupt policemen, judges, government officials, capitalists, arms dealers, and racist killers. On the other side are Yupik shamans, Yaqui smugglers, Mayan rebels, and a multiracial army of the homeless. The role of drug traffic in such struggles is one of the novel's central concerns: *Almanac* contains a host of characters involved in the cocaine trade, including South American drug lords, U.S. military officials, and perhaps most interestingly, a group of Indian drug smugglers based in Tucson. In this way, the novel represents an indigenous form of hemispheric cognitive mapping.

According to Silko, however, when she first started writing the novel in Tucson, she did not envision it as a work about hemispheric geopolitics. As she explained to an interviewer,

> I noticed in Tucson that there was a lot of drug trafficking. In the early 1980s, there were all these activities and rumors in Tucson. So I decided I would make a very short, simple, commercial novel. Something that anyone could read, not political, something that I would call a cops-and-robbers novel about cocaine smuggling.... And then, I started

looking into the police in Tucson, and they were so corrupt, and then, as I started writing I found out that the U.S. government was bringing the cocaine in because they wanted to finance the Contras to fight the Sandinistas. That is common knowledge and yet a big scandal, and the U.S. covered it up. The CIA glutted the cocaine market in the U.S. and brought the price down. They would bring it in with military aircraft. So this was common knowledge in Tucson.[1]

Although she began to write a "simple" piece of crime fiction with a local setting, her investigation into drug enforcement in Tucson ultimately led Silko to a much more ambitious mapping of conflict in the Americas, such as the well-documented collusion she describes between the CIA and the contras.[2] Silko's example suggests the possibility of rereading a variety of contemporary popular cultural forms such as police dramas and action films as reactions to an increasingly militarized, hemispheric war on drugs.[3]

Indeed, Silko notes that her understanding of the new militarization of the border in the 1980s was what prompted her to rethink her planned "cops-and-robbers novel about cocaine smuggling." As she tells it, her inspiration came from a disturbing dream:

> It was so vivid and so horrifying. The dream was triggered by the Air Force helicopters on these small bases behind my house in the Abra Valley. The Air Force base in Tucson does maneuvers over there. I'm afraid to think where I got the intuitions I finally had to write about, like the torture. There are facilities at those bases to train army officers from down south. I had the dream right before I woke up early in the morning. The helicopters were going over my house. In the dream I see them coming very low. And I knew from the dream there would be war, someday, for whatever reason. There was saber rattling by one general at Fort Huachuca in Arizona—*New York* magazine ran a piece about it. He said, "Today we'll take Tegucigalpa and tomorrow Tucson." I cut out the article because I had that dream. He was basically talking about Fort Huachuca in Arizona, and why we were there.[4]

Arizona's Fort Huachuca, it turns out, is an important base of operation for the war on drugs, not only because it is the training ground for both U.S. and Latin American soldiers engaged in drug enforcement, but also because its border location makes it an ideal spot for gathering military intelligence concerning the transborder traffic in drugs and people. The fort is home to the U.S. Army Intelligence School that trains pilots for aerial surveillance operations. Fort Huachuca also teaches military personnel how to operate remote-control "drones," unmanned aerial vehicles that record suspicious movements along the border, sometimes with potentially disastrous consequences, as when three of the car-sized vehicles crashed along the U.S.–Mexico border in the early 1990s.[5]

Military ideology, tactics, weapons, and technologies increasingly came to dominate U.S. domestic and international drug enforcement policies starting around 1984, when President Reagan declared that drugs posed a direct threat to U.S. national security. With their "low-intensity conflict" doctrines, military hardware, and high-tech surveillance and communications equipment, the drug wars of the 1980s and 1990s bore a greater resemblance to military actions than to the U.S. ideal of a civilian police authority that is at least theoretically bound by the rules of due process. In fact, the militarization of drug enforcement largely dispensed with the long-standing U.S. legal distinction between the rules of war and the rule of law. Similarly, Latin American states have often used U.S. drug-war money, military hardware, and training to oppress Indian peoples in their countries without regard for legal safeguards and rights.[6]

But in Silko's account, the antidrug rhetoric used to justify militarization and a disregard for legal protections ultimately conceals the fact that historically the U.S. war on drugs has been waged not simply or only to end drug traffic but also to annex it to state power. The use of drug traffic to support the state is evident in a number of ways. First, the United States has supported drug traffic to finance imperial wars. U.S. participation in the cocaine trade as a means for funding right-wing military proxies such as the contras could be viewed as the refinement and expansion of strategies first deployed during the Vietnam War, in which the United States promoted the heroin trade in order to support anticommunist Hmong forces in Laos.[7] Second, at the same time as it fostered drug traffic internationally, the state used the "drug problem" as an excuse for the criminalization and suppression of domestic dissent, a topic about which Silko has much to teach us. As she suggests, drug criminalization was used in the 1960s and 1970s to suppress radical civil rights organizations. And finally, the United States has indirectly promoted drug consumption as a method for controlling people of color and other dissident subjects. Drugs have been deployed, in other words, as weapons of counterinsurgency that aimed to dissipate or sedate oppositional energies.

Almanac of the Dead historicizes the 1980s war on drugs in relation to one of its formative precursors, the war against the American Indian Movement (AIM) of the early 1970s. U.S. police and intelligence forces not only attempted to contain and neutralize AIM in part by criminalizing its members for drug use and traffic, but also used military tactics against Indian activists that would subsequently be redeployed in the war on drugs. Silko enables us to see how texts by Indian writers and activists such as Mary Crow Dog, Russell Means, and Leonard Peltier anticipate contemporary criticisms of U.S.-sponsored drug wars directed at Indian peoples in Latin America. In *Almanac of the Dead,* Silko makes the history of U.S. counterinsurgency against AIM one backstory, as it were, to her narrative about Yaqui Indian drug and weapons smugglers along the contemporary U.S.–Mexico border. Like native peoples in the United States, the Yaquis have a long history of resistance to state power in Mexico, and together these histories shape Silko's novel. With her comparative stories of different Indian struggles against the state, represented in this chapter primarily by the AIM/Yaqui narrative axis, Silko reterritorializes Indian peoples in ways that radically contradict state projects throughout the Americas. More precisely, taking the war on drugs as one starting point, the novel challenges the extension of state authority over indigenous peoples in Mexico and the United States.

From Drug Dealing to Drug Interdiction: The State and Native Peoples

Several Native American writers and activists have suggested that drug traffic has functioned as a means of social control. Gerald Vizenor has claimed that the drug addiction and trafficking of AIM leader Clyde Bellecourt undermined the oppositional power of the movement.[8] Similarly, in *Lakota Woman,* Mary Crow Dog argues that AIM served as the antidote for the kinds of torpor engendered by the ready availability of drink and drugs in the early 1970s. Before the emergence of the movement, she argues, she and her group of young Indian friends "just drifted from place to place, meeting new people, having a good time. Looking back, a lot was based on drinking and drugs. If you had a lot of dope you were everybody's friend, everybody wanted to know you. If you had a car and good grass, then you were about one of the best guys anybody ever knew. It took me a while to see the emptiness underneath all this frenzied wandering."⁹ Crow Dog notes of her sister, Barbara, that she ultimately "felt burned out, her brain empty. She said she got tired of it, just one trip after the other. She was waiting, waiting for something, for a sign, but she did not know what she was waiting for. And like her, all the other roaming Indian kids were waiting, just as the Ghost Dancers had waited for the drumbeat, the message the eagle was to bring. I was waiting, too. In the meantime I kept traveling" (59). Indeed, the title of the chapter in which she documents those years of drug-induced wandering is "Aimlessness," as if to suggest that drug taking partly blocked the formation of political movements like AIM, filling a vacuum that would soon be displaced by direct political action.

In *Almanac of the Dead,* Silko argues forcefully that the state has used drugs as a weapon of counterinsurgency. That is how, for example, the aristocratic South American drug lord Serlo describes the value of drug traffic for U.S. police powers:

> Enemies of the United States had actually tried to cut off the supply of heroin to the United States near the end of the Vietnam War. During the summer of the disruption of heroin supplies, dozens of U.S. cities had burned night after night. Without cocaine and heroin, the U.S. faced a nightmare as young black and brown people took to the streets to light up white neighborhoods, not crack pipes. Secret U.S. policy was to protect the supply of cocaine. Without cocaine, the U.S. would face riots, looting, even civil war.¹⁰

In a similar vein, although from a very different political perspective, another character, Clinton, argues that the promotion of drug traffic has been an important tool of police power. Clinton is an African American Vietnam veteran who, after returning to the United States, attempts to launch a rebellion of the homeless against the state. Recalling the CIA's use of the heroin trade to finance anticommunist forces in Laos, Clinton draws a more or less direct connection between the Vietnam War and the availability of drugs in U.S. ghettos. According to Clinton, just as the draft helped "solve" the problem of ghetto uprisings in places such as Detroit and Los Angeles by sending disaffected people of color to the front, drug use also functioned as a form of social control: "The poor were tired and sick. They would rather watch TV [than engage in political struggle]. A few were making big money from the others who bought a few minutes of forgetfulness from a pipe or a needle. Illness, dope, and hunger were the white man's allies; only dope stopped young black men from burning white America to the ground" (426). Clinton's partner, the homeless white veteran nicknamed "Rambo," rejects this speech as a "paranoid" conspiracy theory, and some readers might be inclined to agree. Indeed, this was the response of government officials and the mainstream press to allegations that the CIA knowingly flooded minority neighborhoods with cheap crack cocaine in order to fund its Central American campaigns. Maxine Waters, the congressional representative from South Central Los Angeles, launched a probe into such allegations and ultimately held a local meeting in which members of the community confronted the head of the CIA. According to Waters, the agency was complicit in cocaine traffic in South Central.[11] Although Waters's charges were well documented, the mainstream press and government officials roundly rejected them as mere "paranoia." But as Alexander Cockburn and Jeffrey St. Clair conclude, black "paranoia" on this score was amply justified by the history of official efforts to employ drugs against communities of color.[12]

Cockburn and St. Clair document the history of medical experiments conducted first on slaves and ultimately on free blacks. Perhaps the best-known case is the infamous Tuskegee experiments, in which doctors studied the progress of syphilis in black patients when left untreated. Starting in 1932 and continuing for four decades, hundreds of infected black men from Alabama were given placebos so that researchers could observe the effects of the disease. Other forms of treatment were deliberately withheld from the men, resulting in more than a hundred deaths.[13] More often, however, the state experimented on people of color in order to develop a drug of social control.[14] Starting with the end of World War II, various U.S. intelligence agencies searched for a "mind-control" drug that could be used in the Cold War, and they generally conducted their research on African American prisoners. Although the ultimate targets of such experiments were the Soviets and Communist China, they were also aimed at controlling dissident people of color in the United States. A good example is the work of Dr. Louis "Jolly" West, a psychiatrist who presided over the Neuropsychiatric Institute at UCLA and a coworker of CIA chemists researching the utility of LSD as an agent of social control. In the late 1960s and early 1970s, neurologists and psychologists such as West were preoccupied by the kinds of urban violence represented by the riots that Silko references. West's mentor, Dr. Ernest Rodin, had promoted castration as a legitimate weapon in the war against urban unrest. He compared "dumb young males who riot" to cattle and claimed that "the castrated ox will pull his plow" and that "human eunuchs . . . are not given to violence."[15] In the wake of the Watts rebellion, West adopted a similar perspective but instead argued for the use of a sterilizing drug called cyproterone. As he wrote in 1975, "The role of drugs in the exercise of political control is also coming under increasing discussion. . . . Control can be imposed either through prohibition *or supply*."[16] Rather than limiting the political usefulness of drugs to a project of prohibition, West argued that governments should also supply immobilizing drugs as a supplement to the heavy-handed use of police power.

Such histories put the charge of "black paranoia" in a new light. And although researchers have often focused on the African American context, a similar narrative can be constructed for Indians. For instance, another sort of drug—alcohol—has historically been used to control Native peoples. As Silko's Laguna character Sterling notes, during the so-called Apache wars of the 1870s and 1880s, whites profited from the ongoing conflict.

> There was money to made by getting the government contracts to feed all those soldiers. Somebody had to sell them horses to ride. . . . Tucson merchants . . . did not want to see the Apache wars end. So they paid off a whiskey peddler. They sent the whiskey peddler to get Geronimo and his men drunk. The peddler showed Geronimo newspaper headlines from Washington, D.C., and warned Geronimo if he or his men "came in," they'd all be hanged. The newspaper headlines were quotes from U.S. congressmen who wanted Geronimo dead. The Indian Ring in Tucson kept the Apache wars going for years that way. (80)

Sterling's claim is supported both by Geronimo's own narrative as well as the work of historians such as William E. Unrau, who argue that between 1802 and 1892 the trade in alcohol fueled Indian wars.[17]

The use of alcohol to control indigenous peoples finds it contemporary corollary in the use of antidepressants to control Indian inmates. This is one implication of Salish historian Luana Ross's *Inventing the Savage: The Social Construction of Native American Criminality*. Ross quotes the Santee Sioux inmate Eugene Delorme, who suggests that the Washington State Penitentiary uses Thorazine to control Native prisoners:

I'll tell you the big trick they had. They kept everybody on Thorazine, see. They give you Thorazine three, four times a day, and that was guaranteed to keep everybody quiet, in line and just kinda shuffling around like zombies, you know. I took my share of the Thorazine, then after a week or so I started hiding it because I couldn't handle it anymore. When you take Thorazine, well, you can't even think.[18]

Indeed, several of Ross's other Indian informants note that "it is easier to acquire drugs legally inside prisons than it is illegally on the outside." Although this suggests a striking difference between life inside and outside of prison, she notes an important continuity, for many Indians who are prescribed drugs were imprisoned for supposedly violating drug laws. Ross concludes that the prescription of drugs medicalizes Native life experiences, serving not only to control such prisoners but also to pathologize and depoliticize their problems.[19] Given such histories, it requires only a small logical step to conclude that the availability of illegal drugs on Indian reservations and elsewhere in effect constitutes a form of counterinsurgency directed at indigenous peoples. Even if not the result of a coherent and concerted official policy, drug traffic has the considerable added "benefit" to the state of keeping Indians (and others) partly in check.

Official complicity in drug traffic further supports domination by providing occasions for the selective enforcement of drug laws. Recall the case of Dr. West, the medical researcher with CIA ties who recommended the use of drugs to control urban uprisings. As already noted, West advocated a two-pronged approach to social control, in which the state would control dissent both by supplying drugs and through their prohibition. The doctor continued: "The total or even partial prohibition of drugs gives government considerable leverage for other types of control. An example would be the selective application of drug laws . . . against selected components of the population such as members of certain minority groups or political organizations."[20] As Cockburn and St. Clair note, West's remarks anticipate the unequal enforcement of drug laws against African Americans in the 1980s, and a similar case could be made in the Native American context. A recent Justice Department report called *American Indian Crime* indicates that "American Indian confinement towers above [the] national average." According to the report, "the number of American Indians per capita confined in state and federal prisons is about 38% above the national average." On any particular day, the report further notes, approximately one in twenty-five Native peoples over eighteen is under the jurisdiction of the criminal justice system. This rate of Native criminalization is almost two and half times the rate for whites. Finally, the report notes that an important part of the state's response to such statistics is to build more prisons. The Clinton administration's Indian Country Law Enforcement Improvement Initiative, for example, earmarked $34 million for the construction of new correctional facilities.[21]

Such trends are particularly apparent in Arizona, a state with a large Native population and the setting for much of the action in *Almanac.* Although during the 1990s the U.S. prison population doubled, the rate of increase for Arizona was almost twice the national average.[22] According to Arizona Department of Corrections spokesman Michael Arra, because Arizonans have voted for "tougher laws and stiffer sentences," prison has become "a growth industry" in the state, such that "we continue to expect an increase in prison population."[23] The prison population explosion both nationally and in Arizona is largely a result of new drug laws.[24] And the two overlapping social groups most affected are women and people of color. New drug laws have led to a dramatic increase in the number of female inmates in Arizona, while people of color, including American Indians, are disproportionately imprisoned there.[25]

The criminalization of Indian peoples is a prominent topic in writings by Native authors. Russell Means, for instance, argues that in Indian country and the world over "Western civilization" is synonymous with the prison:

> [N]ow that I've traveled over much of the world, I know you can gauge how "civilized" an Indian reservation or native village has become by the number of jails it has and how many indigenous people can be talked into becoming policemen. The best measure of Western civilization is not mathematics or anything that goes with it, not agriculture or political systems or theology or philosophy. "Civilization" to the Western mind is police and jails: They signify law and order.[26]

In a reversal of imperialist intellectual history, Means writes here as an ironic Indian anthropologist whose observations lead him to conclude that the defining accomplishment of Western civilization is the imposition of "law and order" across the globe. Adopting a similarly ironic tone, the Lakota medicine man John (Fire) Lame Deer writes:

A "Warrior" is sworn to protect the safety of all children in the village and give up his life freely.

Teacher, Father, Grandfather, Warrior.

Moments like eating breakfast at the kitchen table, on the way to grandma's house, or getting ready for a brand new day of school are all great opportunities you have to communicate with your children. Take time, pass down the traditions and communicate to our youth that drugs are not a part of our Native cultures. For more information on talking to your kids about drugs, please call 1.800.788.2800.

Communication. The Anti-Drug.
Office of National Drug Control Policy
www.theantidrug.com

Drug warriors: Office of National Drug Control Policy targets Indians.

Before our white brothers came to civilize us we had no jails. Therefore we had no criminals. You can't have criminals without a jail. . . . We had no written law, no attorneys or politicians, therefore we couldn't cheat. We really were in a bad way before the white man came, and I don't know how we managed to get along without the basic things which, we are told, are absolutely necessary to make a civilized society. But now visible progress is everywhere—jails all over the place, and we know these jails are for us Indians.[27]

Undermining the narratives of progress that support state "civilizing" missions, Lame Deer notes that the apex of white civilization for Indians is the construction both of criminality and of jails.

An AIM leader unjustly imprisoned to this day at the federal penitentiary at Leavenworth, Leonard Peltier makes a similar argument. He begins one chapter of his *Prison Writings: My Life Is My Sun Dance* with the epigram "My crime's being an Indian. What's yours?" In the ensuing chapter he writes:

> When you grow up Indian, you quickly learn that the so-called American Dream isn't for you. For you that dream's a nightmare. Ask any Indian kid: you're out just walking across the street of some little off-reservation town and there's this white cop suddenly comes up to you, grabs you by your long hair, pushes you up against a car, frisks you, gives you a couple good jabs with his nightstick, then sends you off with a warning sneer: "Watch yourself, Tonto!" He doesn't do that to white kids, just Indians. You can hear him chuckling with delight as you limp off, clutching your bruised ribs. If you talk smart when they hassle you, off to the slammer you go. Keep these Injuns in their place, you know. . . . So, when you grow up Indian, you don't have to become a criminal, you already *are* a criminal. You never know innocence.[28]

Here Peltier suggests that his unjust criminalization for participating in the occupation of Wounded Knee has deeper roots in the history of violent, illegal U.S. military and police actions against Indian peoples. The FBI wrongfully accused and convicted him of killing one of its agents in a shootout at the Pine Ridge Reservation in South Dakota in 1976, the year of the U.S. Bicentennial.[29] Leading up to the July 4 celebration in fact, the FBI falsely reported to the media that AIM was allied with the Soviet Union and planning to bomb Mount Rushmore. In opposition to the ideological forces of hyperpatriotism that ultimately coalesced around the Bicentennial, the AIM leader participated in the occupation of Wounded Knee and worked to publicize the ongoing history of U.S. military crimes against Indian people represented by the infamous 1890 massacre:

> The American Indian Movement through the years has sought every means possible to bring these crimes against humanity to the attention of the world, hoping that at least some of you would listen and search deep within yourselves for the humanity to demand that the U.S. gov-

ernment stop these crimes. The destruction of our people must stop! . . .
You practice crimes against humanity at the same time that you pi-
ously speak to the rest of the world of human rights! America, when
will you live up to your own principles?[30]

Over the course of his *Prison Writings*, Peltier connects his own imprisonment to prior moments in the history of U.S. military actions against
Indian opposition. In his account, dominant forms of U.S. law and government do not control "crime"; rather, their repressive military actions
against Indian peoples actually produce crimes against international
humanity.

Peltier's claim that the criminalization of Indians is a militarized
form of social control—a punitive means to "keep these Injuns in their
place"—is given a slightly different shape by Mary Crow Dog, who
glosses her own experiences with the police in this way:

> During the years I am describing, in some Western states, the mere
> fact of being Indian and dressing in a certain way provoked the attention
> of the police. It resulted in having one's car stopped for no particular
> reason, in being pulled off the street on the flimsiest excuse, in being
> constantly shadowed and harassed. It works subtly on your mind until
> you start to think that if they keep arresting you anyway you should at
> least give them a good reason for it. (65)

Indeed, Crow Dog further notes that police harassment eventually provoked her to commit crimes such as shoplifting and drug taking. Here
she describes a vicious circle—criminalization generates the very forms
of criminality it is supposedly meant to prevent, which in turn provides
new opportunities for further criminalization. In her account, police
power does not interdict crime but in fact produces it in ways that further
anchor state power. The criminalization of Native peoples thus becomes
a self-fulfilling prophecy that ultimately supports state repression.

The history of drug enforcement practices targeting Native peoples
thus verifies the Foucauldian claim that the law does not work simply
through the prohibition of crime but also through the production of
criminality. The criminalization of peyote is a case in point. Since at
least the early twentieth century, various Native peoples in the United
States have used peyote as a means for accessing sustaining spiritual
visions. According to Mary Crow Dog, peyote rituals have helped to generate pan-Indian identities and political action: "Peyote is a unifier, that

is one of its chief blessings. This unifying force brought tribes together in friendship who had been enemies before, and it helped us in our struggle. I took the peyote road because I took the AIM road. For me they became one path" (101). And she further notes that her husband, an Oglala spiritual leader named Leonard Crow Dog, claimed that peyote represented an important alternative to the medical and legal regimens of social control he encountered in jail: "When he was in jail for having been at Wounded Knee, the prison psychiatrist visited him. . . . Crow Dog told him: 'I don't need you. Peyote, he is my psychiatrist. With the power of this holy herb I could analyze you.' The shrink did not know what to make of it. To a judge, Leonard said: 'Peyote is my lawyer'" (98).

Given its role in the production of pan-Indian political actions, until very recently peyote use was criminalized. Crow Dog notes, for example, that in the 1930s Bureau of Indian Affairs (BIA) police drove her husband's father, Henry Crow Dog, from the South Dakota town of St. Francis for engaging in peyote rituals. She also describes more recent attacks on peyote meetings by the police in Holbrook, Arizona, as well as an incident in which a prison warden confiscated Leonard's bag of sacred tobacco, claiming that it "smells like some hippie drug" (229). It is only fairly recently that Crow Dog and others successfully resisted the criminalization of peyote, and it became legal for licensed members of the Native American Church to cultivate, transport across international borders, and use peyote.

In the preceding discussion, I have focused on the North American context, but the U.S.-sponsored war on drugs has had similar consequences for indigenous peoples throughout the Americas. Like peyote in some parts of the United States, in the Andes coca plays a central role in Indian life.[31] Yet in an attempt to export its own model of addiction, the U.S. government has pressured coca-producing countries to police the traditional use of coca leaves among its indigenous peoples.[32] In practice, however, South American officials use drug-war money and military support to contain indigenous forms of dissent. Although they account for only a minuscule percentage of Colombian coca production, Indian settlements are more likely to be raided than are the big, non-Indian producers.[33] In this way, the U.S. and South American militaries use drug enforcement as an alibi for suppressing dissent.[34] And, according to Marcos Avirama Avirama, a representative of the National Organization of Indigenous Peoples of Colombia, U.S. drug-war money has helped the Colombian military assassinate indigenous leaders.[35] In opposition to such policies, Avirama Avirama's group demands, among other things, government support for shamans who utilize coca leaves.[36]

Nonetheless, if some Indian peoples in South America have found the commercial cultivation of coca attractive, such developments are largely the result of a U.S. drug enforcement policy that funnels money into eradication efforts at the expense of economic development. As Bruce M. Bagley concludes, "U.S. strategy and tactics emphasize repressive action over economic development, civilian institution-building, and multilateral cooperation."[37] Combined with the IMF and World Bank imposition of austerity measures supporting the interests of first-world capitalists, the drug war has helped to make coca one of the few cash crops available to Indian peasants. Far from functioning as an effective form of drug interdiction, in other words, the drug war actually helps to drive the global traffic in cocaine.

WOUNDED KNEE, A REHEARSAL FOR THE WAR ON DRUGS

Once Barb took some acid in a girlfriend's bedroom. There was a huge flag on the wall upside down. The Stars and Stripes hanging upside down used to be an international signal of distress. It was also the American Indian's sign of distress. The Ghost Dancers used to wrap themselves in upside-down flags, dancing that way, crying for a vision until they fell down in a trance. When they came to, they always said that they had been in another world, the world as it was before the white man came, the prairie covered with herds of buffalo and tipi circles full of people who had been killed long ago. The flags which the dancers wore like blankets did not prevent the soldiers from shooting them down. Barb was lying on the bed and the upside-down flag began to work on her mind. She was watching it and it was just rippling up the wall like waves; the stripes and the stars would fall from the flag onto the floor and would scatter into thousands of sprays of light, exploding all over the room. She told me she did not quite know whether it was an old-fashioned vision or just a caricature of one, but she liked it.

—Mary Crow Dog, *Lakota Woman*, 58–59

As I have noted, the state-abetted availability of drugs in Indian communities has done great damage, but in works by Native activists drug use and traffic often serve as formative preludes to political action. Recalling *The Autobiography of Malcolm X,* in which the black leader's account of his early life as a pimp and drug dealer serves as the prologue to his politicized conversion to the Nation of Islam, in his autobiography *Where White Men Fear to Tread,* AIM leader Russell Means includes a chapter called "Dealing" that similarly serves as the introduction to his subsequent life as an activist. While dealing drugs, Means had the first of his many encounters with the police and the criminal justice system, and perhaps began formulating the ideas about the criminalization of Indian peoples that partly guided his involvement with AIM. Similarly, Mary Crow Dog suggests that her years of aimless drug consumption marked an "emptiness" that only AIM could fill. And in the quotation that begins this section, she describes the remarkable acid trip of her sister, Barb, which she describes as a distorted anticipation of the radical visions that would ultimately animate AIM's famous occupation of Wounded Knee, the site where in 1890 a group of Sioux Ghost Dancers were massacred by the U.S. military. Just as the Ghost Dancers incorporated and inverted the symbol of U.S. state power, Crow Dog's sister found in LSD—a drug that the state had hoped to use as a form of mind control—a vision of radical change that AIM ultimately attempted to enact.

Just as AIM originated out of the need to address police brutality and the criminalization of Native peoples, the occupation of Wounded Knee began in part as a response to a miscarriage of justice involving the murder of an Indian man in South Dakota. On 23 January, a non-Indian named David Schitz stabbed to death a young Oglala man named Wesley Bad Heart Bull in the town of Buffalo Gap. In the subsequent trial, Schitz was convicted of second-degree manslaughter for killing the unarmed Indian. Dismayed that Schitz had received a relatively light sentence even though eyewitness testimony revealed that her son was murdered "intentionally and in cold blood," Sarah Bad Heart Bull called upon AIM to intervene. As a result, two hundred AIM members peacefully gathered at the county courthouse in Custer, South Dakota, to demand redress. AIM leaders Dennis Banks, Russell Means, Leonard Crow Dog, and Dennis Hill were allowed inside to talk with officials, but a large contingent of local and state police, supported by FBI "observers," blocked the entrance of others, fired tear gas into the crowd, beat protesters with riot sticks, and arrested twenty-seven. That number included Sarah Bad Heart Bull, who, when she attempted to enter the courthouse in Custer, was beaten on its steps by two police officers, who later accused her of yelling obscenities. (She ultimately served five months in prison while her son's murderer avoided doing any prison time.)[38] Indians who tried to aid her were teargassed and beaten, "a fracas between Indians and police spread through the courthouse," and two police cars were overturned and burned.[39]

The conflict at the Custer County courthouse was part of a larger struggle over the enforcement of treaties. Or, as Means put it, "the primary goal of the American Indian Movement has always been to force the United States to live up to its own laws by meeting the obligations it took on when it signed our treaties" (421). Before the occupation of Wounded Knee, the organization mounted a march on Washington called "The Trail of Broken Treaties." Means and others were particularly interested in enforcing the Fort Laramie Treaty of 1868. As he explains, this treaty

> confirmed that my ancestors' territory extended from the north branch of the Platte River in present-day Nebraska, eastward from Iowa to the Missouri River, and north through the Dakotas, Wyoming, and Montana to Canada. In the center were the Black Hills. Our rights to the *Paha Sapa* were confirmed in a document written in English that clearly stated the treaty could be amended only by the vote of three-fourths of all adult male Lakota. The United States desperately had sought that treaty after it had been defeated in battle after battle. (419)

When gold was discovered in the Black Hills, however, the treaty was routinely violated as white miners descended on Lakota territory, setting the stage for a series of conflicts that culminated in 1890 with the Wounded Knee massacre. In the twentieth century, according to Ward Churchill and Jim Vander Wall, economic speculation led to further expropriation of Indian lands to support agricultural, cattle, logging, and coal industries. The discovery of uranium in the Black Hills in 1952 strengthened U.S. designs on that region. Thus, in addition to leasing national forest land for mining to transnational corporate giants such as Union Carbide, Chevron, and Anaconda/ARCO, the United States launched a uranium mining and milling operation on an abandoned military base near the Pine Ridge Reservation. As a part of this operation, in 1962 the Atomic Energy Commission dumped more than two hundred tons of radioactive waste along Cottonwood Creek, where it ultimately made its way into the water table at Pine Ridge.[40] Peter

Matthiessen concludes that "the presence of F.B.I. observers" during the conflict at the county courthouse "suggested to the Indians that state and government authorities were concerned less with law and order than with the obstacle to Black Hills mining leases that A.I.M. insistence on Indian sovereignty might represent.... Following the Custer riot, the Attorney General assigned 65 U.S. marshals to Pine Ridge: the 'new Indian wars' were underway."[41] In response, members of AIM occupied Wounded Knee and, according to Mary Crow Dog, declared it "a sovereign territory of the independent Oglala Nation" (140).

On the U.S. side, the "new Indian wars" meant that a large, well-equipped army of local, state, and federal police forces was mobilized to defeat AIM. These forces were informally supplemented by local white vigilantes. According to Means, white-supremacist militias even offered to fly a private plane over the occupation site in order to drop a bomb. The United States also received the active support of the local tribal government, presided over by tribal president Dick Wilson. In Matthiessen's words, Wilson was the head of a "U.S. puppet government" that served as a neocolonial proxy for the United States.[42] Supported by the Bureau of Indian Affairs, Wilson served U.S. imperial interests by shoring up an alien system of rule, imposed by the federal government, which displaced preexisting tribal governments.[43] The United States annually invested $24 million in his administration, and this money helped fund the infamous tribal police force.[44] As a result, during these years almost a hundred people—many of them AIM members—were the victims of unsolved murders or suspicious "accidents."[45] When people began to call Wilson's police the "goon squad" because of their violent repression of AIM supporters and other Indians, they countered by wearing the term as an ironic badge of honor, adopting it as the acronym for "Guardians of the Oglala Nation" or GOONS.[46]

Recalling U.S.-supported dictatorships the world over, Wilson maintained state support for his administration by bringing the Cold War to Pine Ridge. After the "Trail of Broken Treaties" march on Washington, Wilson banned AIM on the reservation, incorrectly arguing that it was a communist front group. As Means remembers, Wilson "told the media that the Indians occupying Wounded Knee were tools of a Communist plot designed to destabilize the U.S. government. He claimed that other AIM leaders and I had visited Hanoi and were receiving support from Russia and China, and that only he stood between America and our monstrous alien conspiracy" (276). The references to Hanoi and the Vietnam War are telling, for the official U.S. ideologies and tactics of that war would ultimately reappear at Wounded Knee.

Indeed, to many Indian observers, the federal response to the occupation seemed like a new Indian war filtered through Vietnam. Although it was theoretically a civilian police operation, in practice the U.S. response was more like a military action, complete with Pentagon advisers and hardware. The Pentagon supplied weapons to state forces at Wounded Knee in order to practice operation "Garden Plot," a program of counterinsurgency designed in 1968 as a response to "civil disorders" such as the Watts rebellion.[47] The paramilitary units mobilized at Pine Ridge came equipped with night-vision goggles, armored personnel carriers (APCs), automatic weapons, and "enough ammunition to wipe out every Indian in the Dakotas."[48]

Mary Crow Dog describes the battlefield in this way:

> Elements of the 82nd Airborne were brought in, waiting their turn at nearby Hot Springs—just in case. A 'copter called *Snoopy* suddenly had a sniper in it taking potshots at us. Heavy 50-caliber MGs opened fire on our perimeter. Our telephone lines to the outside world were cut.... Special kill-and-destroy teams were being flown in, with attack dogs and infrared gun scopes which enabled the government sharpshooters to see us in the dark. Trip-wire flares saturated the whole area around us. If we touched the wire a flare would go up bathing the whole landscape in a strange, ghostlike light.... Beyond our perimeter, the scene was right out of a cheap World War I movie. There feds were building themselves regular sandbag positions with stoves and all the comforts of home.... We could hear the rock 'n' roll music drifting in from their bunkers. They wore light blue Day-Glo man-from-Mars jumpsuits or camouflage outfits. Their positions were surrounded by ever-growing mounds of empty shells and beer cans. Their armored cars were fitted out with high-powered strobe searchlights and M-79 grenade launchers. We had little to put up against this sort of war technology. (136)

Crow Dog compares the scene to a "World War I movie," but films and television coverage of Vietnam also come to mind. The rock-and-roll music and party atmosphere, for example, suggest a scene from *Apocalypse Now*. Crow Dog makes a similar point by way of an analysis of another "war movie":

Two years later, seven of us who had all been at the Knee went to see the movie *Billy Jack*. There was a superficial similarity to Wounded Knee—an Indian making a last stand inside a white clapboard church surrounded by a lot of state troopers—but afterward [Leonard] Crow Dog was joking, "That Billy Jack had it easy. He was besieged for only twenty-four hours and there were no heavy MGs or APCs. And he was taken out with just a pair of handcuffs on him while they trussed us up with manacles, leg irons, and waist chains like something out of a medieval torture movie. Yeah, Billy Jack had it easy." (168)

Billy Jack's martial-arts skill would have been a poor match, Crow Dog jokes, for the Vietnam-era military hardware used against AIM. In diverse ways, the war in Vietnam was daily waged at Wounded Knee. Recalling the Vietnamese women who took up arms against the United States, Mary Crow Dog writes that "our women played a major part at Wounded Knee," and "we had two or three pistol-packing mamas swaggering around with six-shooters dangling at their hips, taking their turns on the firing line, swapping lead with the feds" (131). U.S. forces reacted to these women with ideas and tactics drawn from the war against the Vietnamese. Madonna Gilbert, a Lakota member of AIM who participated in the occupation, remembers, for example, that once she and another AIM member named Lorelei Decora "ran into an army of tribal police, sheriffs, U.S. marshals, and FBI" who "were scared shitless" of them. Perhaps influenced by wartime propaganda about both AIM and the Vietnamese, the officers "handcuffed us, threw us in vans, called us 'gooks' and a lot worse—derogatory dirty stuff, you know, because we were women. And that was America's elite with all their war toys—I mean, helicopters, APCs, the whole Vietnam number, blue jump suits, infrared lights, guns everywhere you looked; it was Wounded Knee and the Seventh Cavalry all over again."[49]

The comparison Gilbert draws between nineteenth-century Indian wars and Vietnam is apt, for the "structure of feeling" that animated U.S. attacks on Indian peoples was ultimately exported to Southeast Asia. Richard Slotkin argues, for instance, that the "myth of the frontier" governed the U.S. pursuit of the war in Vietnam, making the My Lai Massacre of 1966 a reenactment of the Wounded Knee Massacre of 1890. Indeed, commenting on the similarities between photos of the two massacres, the Lakota medicine man John (Fire) Lame Deer remarks, "My Lai was hot, and Wounded Knee was icy cold, and that's the only difference."[50] And if the nineteenth-century Indian wars were exported to Vietnam, Gilbert suggests that Vietnam "blew back" to Wounded Knee during the 1973 occupation. Similarly, the state used forms of counterinsurgency against AIM that were straight out of the CIA bag of Cold War dirty tricks. The FBI hired a number of people, most notably Douglas Durham, to infiltrate the movement. As a member of a CIA special-forces team in the late 1950s and early 1960s, Durham received training in demolitions, burglary, and sabotage for use in Guatemala. There he aided a CIA-sponsored army of Cuban counterrevolutionaries, ultimately providing air support for the Bay of Pigs invasion in 1961. In the wake of that disaster, Durham became a policeman in Des Moines, Iowa, where he used the position to cloak his own participation in criminal activity, including bribery, burglary, and prostitution. While a member of the Des Moines force, he allegedly brutally beat his wife, who ultimately died. The police psychiatrist in the ensuing investigation recommended that Durham be institutionalized, arguing that he was a violent schizophrenic who was "unfit for office involving public trust." Fearing bad publicity, in 1964 the Des Moines police department quietly fired Durham, but he reportedly continued to participate in organized crime, including the heroin trade.[51]

In 1973, Durham reappeared at Wounded Knee, but this time as a clandestine employee of the FBI. With black-dyed hair and wearing brown contact lenses, he pretended to be part Chippewa. Durham subsequently joined the Des Moines chapter of AIM and quickly infiltrated the group at Wounded Knee, working closely with AIM founder Dennis Banks and acting as the organization's national security director. In this capacity he aggressively worked to undermine AIM from within not only by embezzling money but also by spreading rumors that various loyal AIM members were FBI informants. As a trusted adviser to Banks, Durham was present at the meetings between lawyers and AIM leaders in preparation for their Wounded Knee trials, and the FBI informant no doubt shared information with the prosecution. At another trial of AIM members, he masqueraded as a psychotherapist and gave damning testimony against the defendants. Durham also supplied much of the disinformation that the FBI would subsequently use to discredit AIM as part of its Counter Intelligence Program (COINTELPRO), including the claim that the organization was planning acts of terrorism during the U.S. Bicentennial celebrations. Within months of being unmasked as an infiltrator, the former FBI operative repeated such unfounded charges during congressional hearings and on a lecture tour sponsored by the John Birch Society.[52] AIM members now believe that Durham was responsible for the death of an Indian woman named Jancita Eagle Deer.[53]

In response to state military attacks, AIM engaged in defensive forms of militarization and counter-countersubversion. If Wounded Knee seemed to repeat Vietnam, this was in part because several of the AIM occupiers were veterans of that war. The war experience of Buddy Lamont, for example, helped him build bunkers at Wounded Knee. And, like many soldiers in Vietnam, Lamont was ultimately killed at Wounded Knee by a sniper. As Crow Dog notes, "Buddy received his honorable discharge from the Marine Corps just about the time a government bullet killed him. He is buried on the hill by the ditch, joining the ghosts of all the other Sioux killed at Wounded Knee" (143). Other veterans, according to Means, were put in charge of the occupation security force, while still others airlifted food into Wounded Knee. Facing constant gunfire from the U.S. side, the poorly armed occupation forces practiced what Means calls "the fine art of deception." For example, an Indian woman he calls "Wounded Knee Winona" (278) used a bullhorn to communicate with the enemy and convince them to give up the fight. Exploiting the charge that the organization was a Communist front group, AIM members displayed a stovepipe in order to convince federal forces that they had acquired a Soviet bazooka. Similarly, on another occasion, according to Crow Dog, "some of our guys made a big show of burying a number of large, empty film containers left behind by a TV crew. Immediately you could hear the alarm spreading on the feds' shortwave: 'Those Indians are planting Teller mines!' All the APCs took off in a hurry and we had scored another coup" (135).

The preceding discussion suggests that far from being a civilian police action, the attack on AIM at Wounded Knee was a decidedly military operation. In fact, the military response to the occupation violated U.S. law. The military response to Wounded Knee contravened the Posse Comitatus Act of 1879, which made it a felony to employ military personnel in domestic police actions except when authorized by the Constitution or an act of Congress. The aim of the act was to ensure due process for U.S. citizens and protect them from the arbitrary use of power that characterizes the rules of war. And while the presence of Pentagon advisers at Wounded Knee violated the letter of the law, the use of military hardware and tactics violated its spirit. The charge that the occupation was a criminal act served to camouflage the state's own criminality. Or, in the words of Leonard Peltier, the U.S. government

> hid behind their usual cloak of "national security" to do their dirty work. Their first tactic: forget the law, the law's for suckers, subvert the law at will to get your man, however innocent he may be; suborn the whole legal and judicial system; lie whenever and wherever you have to to keep the focus of inquiry on your victims, not on your own crimes. I have to admit, they succeeded brilliantly. In the name of Law, they violated every law on the books, and, in their deliberate strategy of putting me—and how many other innocents?—away in a cell or a grave, they turned the Constitution of the United States into pulp fiction.[54]

Echoing Peltier, Russell Means concludes "Wounded Knee was never about criminal activities. It was, from the first, a political matter. Did the Fort Laramie Treaty mean what it said? Did the U.S. Constitution mean anything?" (299). What is more, the tendentious, ideological argument that the U.S. response to Wounded Knee was a civilian police action ultimately served to delegitimate Indian sovereignty. For the state to concede that its actions against AIM were a military operation would be tantamount to admitting that Indian peoples constituted sovereign nations. By defining Wounded Knee in civilian terms, in other words, the state maintained the powerful legal fiction that, as "domestic dependents," Indian nations had no rights of self-determination or treaty making. In practice, such a position rendered moot the Fort Laramie Treaty and undermined Lakota rights to the uranium-rich Black Hills.

Flash-forward to 1982, when the Reagan Department of Defense successfully argued for a relaxation of the Posse Comitatus Act so that the military could join in drug enforcement. As a result, the war on drugs was increasingly governed by "low-intensity conflict doctrine," a set of ideas that were first tried out in Vietnam and subsequently perfected at Wounded Knee. Similarly, starting in the 1980s, the drug war increasingly mobilized some of the same military hardware that was utilized at Pine Ridge, including helicopters, APCs, automatic weapons, and infrared goggles. Added to this arsenal were reconnaissance planes, advanced radar systems, communications technology, motion-detection sensors, and the automated "drones" described at the start of this chapter. If the siege at Wounded Knee was a rerun of Vietnam, in other words, the war on drugs partly replayed the events at Pine Ridge.

Similarly, in *Almanac of the Dead* Silko suggests that the war on drugs echoes imperial wars such as Vietnam and Wounded Knee. She further indicates that the U.S. war on drugs of the 1980s was a specific moment in a longer series of hemispheric Indian struggles against different state military police powers and the invading legal systems that they enforced. In order to substantiate these claims, I will now turn to Silko's remarkable novel.

"At War with the U.S. Government": The War on Drugs and the Limits of State Power

Silko's character Sterling, a Laguna Pueblo Indian living in Tucson, is fascinated with Indian "outlaws" who defy state authority. Sterling has been exiled from Laguna in part because, while supervising a group of Hollywood filmmakers, he could not prevent them from trespassing onto Pueblo land. While aboard a bus to Tucson, Sterling dreams of that unhappy day: "The Chevy Blazer is racing toward the restricted area of the tribe's huge open-pit uranium mine." When he wakes up from his bad dream, Sterling catches a glimpse of a local newspaper with a headline concerning war in the Middle East and the narrator explains that "Sterling doesn't understand international killing. But he has made it his hobby to learn and keep up with the history of outlaws and famous criminals." As he looks out the window of the bus, Sterling sees a "white Arizona Highway Patrol car" and then reflects that since being exiled, he "couldn't help thinking about the law, and what the law means. About people who get away with murder because of who they are, and whom they know. Then there were people like him, Sterling, people who got punished for acts they had no part in" (26).

Sterling first became interested in the law while at Indian boarding school, "[b]ecause everything the white teachers had said and done to Indian children had been 'required by law.'" He is also an avid reader of magazines such as the *Police Gazette* and *True Detective*. Scanning stories about Pretty Boy Floyd, Ma Barker, Billy Frenchette ("John Dillinger's girlfriend"), and the nineteenth-century Apache leader Geronimo makes Sterling think that "injustice had been going on for a long time." Sterling's crime magazines feature stories on all of these "outlaws," and he reflects that the Depression-era public enemies were all part Indian. When he gets off the bus, Sterling walks around the downtown park, where he sees a Tucson police cruiser. "The cop looked sleepy, but Sterling was careful to avoid the cop's eyes. Even if he was well dressed in his black-and-white-checkered slacks and blue short-sleeve shirt, Sterling knew some cops didn't need any excuse to go after Indians." After visiting the park, he walks to the Congress Hotel—"Where else could he have a cold beer at the same place Dillinger and his gang had been drinking beer in 1934?" (29).

There he meets one of his future employers, Ferro, part of a family of Yaqui cocaine traffickers who employ Sterling as their gardener. The operation is run by Ferro's Aunt Zeta, a powerful member of the Yaqui diaspora in Tucson. When the novel starts they are joined by Zeta's twin sister, Lecha, a former psychic on TV and for the police, and her nurse, Seese, a young white woman whose child was kidnapped by drug lords and who hopes that Lecha can help find him. Zeta is well armed and her compound is protected by a remote-control security gate, a video surveillance system, and roving guard dogs. With imposing names such as Cy(anide), Nitro(glycerine), Mag(num), and Stray Bullet, the dog patrol is outfitted with radio transmitters and video cameras in their collars.

At one point Lecha sends Sterling and Seese to Tucson on several errands, including a trip to a Yaqui drug smuggler named Calabazas for some "medicine." On the way they ride by the bungalow where the police captured Dillinger and Billy Frenchette and extradited them to Indiana. In the stories he tells Seese, Sterling seemingly rereads those events in light of the illegal and violent forms of counterinsurgency the United States practiced against AIM. Revising accounts from his crime magazines, Sterling's retelling emphasizes that the police illegally extradited Dillinger across state lines and that it was the FBI who ultimately shot the gangster outside a Chicago movie theater. Parked in front of Dillinger's bungalow, however, Sterling once again reflects on his status as an Indian in the heavily policed space of southern Arizona: "Right then Sterling had noticed a man across the street suspiciously eyeing them. . . . He and the blond woman were making a spectacle of themselves, which was exactly what Dillinger's gang had done, and look how they had ended up. . . . If they got questioned by the police, Sterling knew that would be the end of both their jobs" (77). Continuing the "true crime" tour of Tucson, Sterling then drives to the next stop, a nearby house where Geronimo "sign[ed] the papers declaring he and his warriors had surrendered." There Sterling narrates how Geronimo was "trick[ed]" into surrendering with the promise that he and other

Apaches could return to their homelands. "None of the promises were ever kept" (79). Instead, Sterling reflects, local white settlers made money from the ongoing Indian wars of the nineteenth century. "So this might be the first time Sterling had ever lived anywhere near a place founded mostly by criminals." Sterling concludes that "the fences and gates and even the guard dogs might be a wise precaution around people who had got rich off the suffering of Geronimo and his people" (81).

Throughout these early scenes from *Almanac,* Sterling's peripheral vision, as it were, is often focused on the relative risks of running into the police. He is interested in crime and punishment in part because they saturate the social spaces that Indian people must negotiate. Sterling's anxious observation of the police suggests the extent to which dominant powers interpellate Indians as criminals. The presumption of Indian criminality that Sterling registers thus recalls Peltier's claim that he was always already constructed as a criminal. Or, as Sterling suggests, the law constitutes legal subjects differently such that Indians are punished and non-Indians get away with murder. Further, Sterling's moment-to-moment monitoring of his own vulnerability to police hailing is informed by longer histories of confrontation between Indians and U.S. military and police power. Through his tour of Tucson Sterling constructs a historical genealogy of Indian "outlaws" that stretches from Geronimo, to Dillinger and Frenchette, and finally to the Yaqui drug smugglers—figures who all live in similar geographic and historical neighborhoods. Sterling in this way posits continuities between the nineteenth-century Indian wars and the subsequent criminalization of Indians. From this perspective, the subordination of Indian peoples within a U.S. criminal justice system constitutes a war on Indians by other means.

Which is to say that Sterling's list of Indian outlaws are figures engaged in battles over the limits of U.S. law in the face of tribal sovereignties. Historically the imposition of U.S. legal systems onto Indian peoples and lands has been a central means of imperial domination. As Vine Deloria Jr. and David E. Wilkins note, Native peoples had their earliest encounters with the United States in the form of treaties.[55] In the eighteenth and early nineteenth centuries, the United States was often compelled to make treaties to forestall Indian alliances with imperial rivals such as the English and the French, or in order to negotiate an end to costly wars. Superior Sioux forces, for example, forced the United States to sign the Fort Laramie Treaty of 1868. In 1871, however, the United States passed a law against all future treaties. And while this law expressly exempted prior treaties, it was subsequently used to retroactively void all of them, including the Fort Laramie Treaty.

The United States has further supplemented its practice of violating treaties by imposing alien legal systems onto Native peoples. One result of U.S. military domination was the uneven but aggressive extension of state legal authority over Indians, power enforced in the last instance by military and police forces. Just as treaty violations disregard Indian sovereignty and assert U.S. dominion, the extension of the U.S. legal system subordinates Indian social and political institutions to state authority. Historically, the imposition of property laws served to displace competing Indian land practices and to dispossess Indian lands. Similarly, laws aimed at "civilizing" Indians severely restricted the practice of Indian religions. The same civilizing mission also led the state to support boarding schools for Indian children that took them away from their people and distanced them from indigenous educational systems. Although all of these forms of law have been important in the history of U.S. imperialism in North America, in what follows I focus on the criminal justice system that the United States has attempted to impose on Indian peoples.

The Supreme Court case *Ex parte Crow Dog* provides an influential example of the conflict between U.S. criminal justice and Indian practices. The 1883 case involved a Brule Sioux named Crow Dog who was an ancestor of Leonard Crow Dog, the medicine man who helped occupy Wounded Knee ninety years later. The nineteenth-century Crow Dog appealed to the Supreme Court to overturn his conviction for murder by a territorial court. After he had killed tribal chief Spotted Tail, Crow Dog's family followed long-standing Sioux practice and compensated Spotted Tail's relatives. The territorial court overrode the Sioux settlement by convicting Crow Dog of murder and seeking to imprison him. The Supreme Court sided with Crow Dog, arguing that under existing treaties the United States did not have jurisdiction over crimes between Indians on reservations. Members of the public, the BIA, and Christian reformers reacted by pressing Congress to pass the Seven Major Crimes Act of 1885, which effectively extended federal jurisdiction for many crimes to the reservations.[56] With this law the federal government asserted legal authority over Indians by criminalizing competing forms of Indian authority.

The United States further strengthened its legal authority over Indians by establishing tribal criminal courts responsible for enforcing non-felony laws. Although government officials argued that Indian judges should preside over such courts in order to ensure Indian compliance, they also stressed the need to choose jurists who supported the law's civilizing mission.[57] As Commissioner of Indian Affairs Thomas J. Morgan wrote in 1892, only "Indians who read and write English readily, wear citizens' dress, and engage in civilized pursuits" should become judges.[58] Such courts were first instituted in 1883 by Secretary of the Interior Henry M. Teller, who said that they were a necessary step toward civilization: "Many of the agencies are without law of any kind, and the necessity for some rule of government on the reservations grows more and more apparent each day. If it is the purpose of the Government to civilize the Indians, they must be compelled to desist from the savage and barbarous practices that are calculated to continue them in savagery, no matter what exterior influences are brought to bear on them." Tribal courts were thus charged with imposing "civilized" legal norms and thereby criminalizing Indian norms. The courts banned Indian religious practices such as the Sun Dance; outlawed the destruction of property in Indian mourning rituals; imposed the heterosexual marriage contract against Indian practices of serial monogamy or plural marriage; and, perhaps most important for the present context, criminalized tribal medicine men.

From at least the late nineteenth century and extending to the late twentieth century and beyond, recurring conflicts between state doctors and Indian medicine men represented struggles over the extension of a U.S. legal system that tended to prescribe Western medicine and punish Indian alternatives. Starting in the 1890s, U.S.-sponsored tribal courts were charged, for example, with enforcing the following law:

> Any Indian who shall engage in the practices of so-called medicine men, or who shall resort to any artifact or device to keep the Indians of the reservation from adopting and following civilized habits and pursuits, or shall adopt any means to prevent the attendance of children at school, or shall use any arts of a conjurer to prevent Indians from abandoning their barbarous rites and customs, shall be deemed guilty of an offense, and upon conviction thereof, for the first offense shall be imprisoned for not less than ten nor more than thirty days.[59]

Similarly, the original architect of the tribal court system, Teller, argued that the medicine men should be replaced with government physicians: "While they profess to cure diseases by the administering of a few simple remedies, still they rely mainly on their art of conjuring. Their services are not required even for the administration of the few simple remedies they are competent to recommend, for the Government supplies the several agencies with skillful physicians, who practice among the Indians without charge to them."[60] In these ways, U.S. officials criminalized medicine men for sustaining Indian practices that potentially blocked the imposition of "civilized habits." Such criminalization prepared the way for the situation that Mary Crow Dog described, in which prison officials confiscated the pipe and tobacco pouch of Leonard Crow Dog and supplied him instead with a prison-psychiatrist. These struggles between the U.S. state and Indian peoples over different kinds of "medicines"—peyote or prison-prescribed "meds," for instance—represent an important precondition for the U.S. war on drugs that was initiated in the 1980s.

Returning to *Almanac,* Silko suggests that the war on drugs is consistent with a longer history of conflict between state legal systems and Indian "outlaws." A good example is Sterling's boss, Zeta, the Yaqui cocaine and weapons smuggler. Zeta recalls not only Ma Barker but also the "pistol-packing mamas" at Wounded Knee that Mary Crow Dog describes. In order to evade the infrared goggles used by the military as part of the war on drugs (and before that, at Wounded Knee), Zeta begins the novel by dying all her clothes dark brown—"I don't want to be visible at night" (20). And like the members of AIM, who responded to military attacks and clandestine operations with their own forms of militarization and subterfuge, Zeta counters the militarization of the war on drugs with a private arsenal and a high-tech compound. Moreover, Zeta is part of a larger diaspora in and around Tucson that partly originated in nineteenth- and early-twentieth-century struggles between Yaquis and the Mexican state.

After independence from Spain and the formation of the new republic, Mexican officials attempted to extend their authority over Yaqui and other Indian lands and laborers in the north by incorporating Indians as citizens. Many Yaquis resisted citizenship because it constituted submission to a Mexican legal system that violated Yaqui views of land, law, and government. Yaquis opposed citizenship in part because it entailed models of individual property rights that conflicted with conceptions of communal ownership. In practice, the extension of Mexican citizenship became a wedge that opened Yaqui lands to dispossession and colonization. In the second half of the nineteenth century, the predication of citizenship on individual property rights led the Mexican state to allot prescribed amounts of land to individual Indians and to confiscate and sell the "surplus." Moreover, under Mexican state rule, Indian-owned land could be taxed, and Indians therefore lost land to markets and settlers when they could not or would not pay. The imposition of Mexican citizenship had the further effect of promoting the formation of both haciendas and the Indian labor pools that they exploited. The fact that newly landless Yaquis increasingly took work on the haciendas indicates that Mexican citizenship and land law made both Indian land and ultimately Indian labor available for Mexican elites.[61]

During the second half of the nineteenth century, many Indians attempted to counter the state through guerrilla warfare. Groups of Yaquis—with bows and arrows and increasingly with guns and similar weapons—attacked Mexican haciendas and settlements throughout these years. Combined with Apache warfare near the U.S. border, Yaqui resistance in northwest Mexico constituted a serious limit to state authority in the region. Around the turn of the century, Mexico launched an aggressive program in which the Federal Rural Police arrested thousands of Yaquis and deported them to work as veritable slaves on plantations in Oaxaca and Yucatán. Fleeing the federal police, more than a thousand Yaqui came to the United States from 1900 to 1910 during the Díaz dictatorship's deportation campaign, with a second wave following in 1916–17, during Obregón's revolutionary removal policies. By 1922 there were two Yaqui communities of 250 each in Tucson. But the economic survival of the Yaqui diaspora was precarious, in part because they were "squatters" without a stable land base. Although by the 1970s the Yaquis of New Pascua in southern Arizona communally owned land through their nonprofit organization, the majority of Yaquis in the region maintained only a precarious legal claim to land.[62]

With Zeta, Silko constructs a character that condenses many elements of this brief history of the Yaqui diaspora. Historically, the Yaqui have participated in fairly wide-ranging circuits of trade between northern Mexico and the United States. Zeta recalls these long histories of transborder traffic and travel. She began her career in smuggling, for example, by first working for "Mexico Tours," a Tucson company that used tour buses to clandestinely transport Indian artifacts between Mexico and the United States. Eventually she joins another Yaqui, her "clan brother" Calabazas, who traffics in marijuana. Calabazas sees his smuggling as part of what he calls "the war that had never ended" (178), the battle for the return of Indian land. Ultimately, however, Zeta and Calabazas go their separate ways:

> Calabazas had wanted to stay strictly with dope. Because with guns there was politics, right off the bat. Zeta had argued with Calabazas for years. They had always been at war with the invaders. For five hundred years, the resistance had fought. Calabazas might avoid it for another five years, at most ten. But sooner or later politics would come knocking at his door; because dope was good as gold; and politics always went where the gold was. (178–79)

Drugs are "as good as gold," in this account, because they generate huge profits that in turn purchase weapons used to leverage even more wealth. Zeta here articulates one of the larger claims of this chapter and the book as a whole—that modern drug traffics fuel imperialism.

Zeta's commitment to the combination of drug and gun running places her within a history of Yaqui rebellion. Her precursors in the late nineteenth and early twentieth centuries often supported resistance to the Mexican state by engaging in the clandestine trade of weapons and other contraband. From bases in Arizona, Yaquis opposed the extension of Mexican state power by running weapons and organizing opposition to the Díaz regime, sometimes in conjunction with revolutionary movements such as the Magón brothers' Partido Liberal Mexicano. Further, responding to renewed state efforts in 1918 to deport them into slavery in Yucatán, Yaquis in Tucson smuggled guns and ammunition to fighters in northwest Mexico.[63] At about the same time, Yaqui gunrunning out of Tucson helped to provoke a crisis over U.S. national sovereignty and Yaqui insubordination. In January 1918 soldiers from Fort Huachuca— the same institution that in the 1980s and 1990s would become one center of the war on drugs in Arizona—stumbled upon a group of nine armed Yaquis on their way to Mexico to "defend the Yaqui country." Like the Magóns, the Yaquis were imprisoned and tried before a federal judge in Tucson on charges of violating U.S. neutrality laws. The charges were ultimately dismissed when the accused agreed not to reorganize their band. Nonetheless, the case helped motivate official plans to control Yaqui migration and gun running by containing Indians in one community. The result was the founding of Pascua Village, a forty-acre Yaqui settlement six miles north of Tucson. The plan, devised by U.S. district attorney Kirke Moore, divided the land into individual plots that Yaqui households could buy on installment. Twenty families accepted the invitation, but the majority of Yaquis in the area declined it. Faced with a militant transnational people who challenged U.S. territorial sovereignty, the United States responded with a proposal that reproduced, in miniature, the very systems of land allotment and individual property ownership that the Yaquis had resisted in Mexico.[64]

Zeta's life as a smuggler, I would argue, should be read in light of these complex battles between Yaquis and different states. Through the character of Zeta, Silko questions efforts to subordinate Yaqui sovereignty to state sovereignty in a number of ways. First, she foregrounds Yaqui insubordination to the Mexican state. Zeta memorializes past struggles through her relationship with her grandmother, Yoeme. Yoeme was a gunrunner and rebel who lived through the period of Mexican deportation and enslavement policies, and her stories inform the rebellious acts of her granddaughter. Second, Silko recontextualizes Zeta's smuggling operation as a response to the experience of the Yaqui diaspora in Tucson. Zeta's private arsenal and high-tech compound, in other words, serve to counter and defend against an immediate local history in which U.S. state officials had attempted to tie Yaquis to land allotments through debt and contain them in planned villages. Or, to revise Sterling's idea, the fences and gates and even the guard dogs might be a wise precaution around states such as Mexico and the United States. And finally, with her focus on Zeta's transborder traffic, Silko challenges the ways in which the war on drugs and the militarization of the border enforces U.S. state sovereignty over Indian peoples.

In a discussion with Calabazas, Zeta defends her smuggling operations as part of a long history of defiance of imperial law:

> The people had been free to go traveling north and south for a thousand years, traveling as they pleased, then suddenly white priests had announced smuggling as a mortal sin because smuggling was stealing from the government. . . . How could one steal if the government itself was the worst thief? There was not, and there never had been, a legal government by Europeans anywhere in the Americas. Not by any definition, not even by the Europeans' own definitions and laws. Because no legal government could be established on stolen land. Because stolen

land never had clear title. . . . Every waking hour Zeta spent scheming and planning to break as many of their laws as she could. War had been declared the first day the Spaniards set foot on Native American soil, and the same war had been going on ever since: the war was for the continents called the Americas. (133)

Zeta here asserts an Indian right of free travel in defiance of (il)legal governments that were founded on theft. Her assertion of an alternative conception of land and law parallels conflicts between nineteenth-century "Yaqui law" and Mexican antagonists. In the second half of the century, the state justified policies of deportation and enslavement by arguing that the Yaquis were "inherently warlike, lawless, barbarically cruel, and uncivilizable except through force."[65] From a contemporary Yaqui perspective, however, this image appears more like a displaced representation of the Mexicans themselves, particularly in their ongoing Indian campaigns. According to Spicer, Yaquis saw Mexicans as

inherently warlike, fighting constantly among themselves as well as with peaceful people in their region. They were also basically lawless in their behavior. There was much experience to back this up; they ignored long-established territorial boundaries, invaded without warning, then backed up what they had stolen with military force. . . . They killed individuals indiscriminately, for such causes as protesting the appropriation of land which a family had farmed from time immemorial. They always sent soldiers in if Yaquis tried to defend themselves. . . . They were wholly ignorant of how normal, peaceful, governing institutions worked. They had no concept of where authority really lay. They forever sought to negotiate for peace with a military commander, ignoring the constituted and duly elected governors. They gave their own military commanders full authority to negotiate peace. . . . The way in which they behaved in connection with peaceful dealings showed how their own way of life rested on fighting forces and military power. Leadership for them was military leadership. . . . This weakness of Mexicans—their lack of understanding of human government and basis of its authority—lay at the root of their great capacity for creating evil relations among men.[66]

The Yaqui conception of human government facilitated by elected governors brings into critical relief the weakness of a Mexican system governed by military aggression and greed. Whereas the state pursued its

Indian policies in the name of the law, the Yaquis viewed it as in fact lawless. In the above account, for instance, the state violates laws governing murder and property—some of the very laws it purported to enforce when it attempted to extend its authority over the Yaqui. Through the character of Zeta, Silko in effect transfers this Yaqui critique of Mexican state ideology to the U.S. context. According to Zeta, because all European governments in the hemisphere, including the United States, are founded on stolen land, none are legitimate, "even by the Europeans' own definitions and laws."

As *Almanac* unfolds, Zeta uses money from cocaine smuggling to buy weapons, until she finds herself in a web of international drug deals and state-sponsored terror. Her arms dealer, for example, is a Tucson gunrunner with CIA connections named Greenlee. Greenlee is part of a hemispheric network of military and police power, supplying weapons and other hardware to U.S. proxies in Mexico, Guatemala, and throughout Latin America. One of his best customers is "Universal Insurance," a company that employs a private army in order to protect wealthy property owners in southern Mexico from Indian rebellions (264–66). This army is led by the Mexican "General J.," who "has friends at the U.S. CIA" (291). The general sees his work with the company as part of a war against "Indian bandits and criminals" (293) along Mexico's southern border, including a group of Mayan revolutionaries. Over the course of the novel, Universal Insurance increasingly receives "emergency calls from clients in Guatemala, San Salvador, and Honduras—day and night—with claims for warehouses and property gutted by fires set by Indian guerrilla units" (482). Weapons for anti-Indian counterinsurgency come not only from Greenlee but also from the United States. The state, for example, supplies aircraft and helicopters to patrol in Mexico for refugees from U.S.-sponsored wars in Guatemala and El Salvador. Arguing that "'disappearances' and death squads were superior to Hitler's death factories," General J. opposes the idea of refugee camps and instead uses U.S. military support to kill Indians: "Indians were a waste of time and money. No refuge for them—the best policy was quick annihilation on the spot, far, far from satellite TV cameras" (495). Zeta ultimately discovers that her dealings with Greenlee make her an unwitting accomplice in another set of Indian wars—the U.S.-sponsored wars in Central America. Just as Wounded Knee activists such as Mary Crow Dog and Russell Means discovered that drug taking and dealing indirectly contributed to the subordination of Indians in

North America, Zeta soon learns that because the United States "supports covert forces and supplies them with weapons got by trading cocaine through Tucson" (318), her participation in the cocaine trade indirectly supports the repression of Indians in Central America.

Ultimately a "message from the South" (703) convinces Zeta to kill Greenlee. The message presumably comes from a group of Mayan rebels in Chiapas, who, under the prophetic leadership of twin brothers and a militant woman named "La Escapia," have been marching north toward ancestral lands in the U.S. Southwest, called "Aztlán" by many Indians and Chicanos. As the novel comes to a close, Zeta seems prepared to join in armed rebellion for Native lands. By thus placing the contemporary war on drugs in the larger historical context of struggles over land, law, and sovereignty, Silko deconstructs the ideological opposition between military and police power that has served to support the domination of indigenous peoples in the United States. Recall how the state maintained that the response to the Wounded Knee occupation was a domestic police action even though it was pursued with military tactics and weapons. This assertion of domestic police authority over AIM was consistent with a long legal history that denied Indian sovereignty by making Indians "domestic dependents" of the state. Silko undermines this logic by focusing on the consequences for Native peoples of the militarization of border enforcement, suggesting that as a new kind of Indian war, the war on drugs contradicts the claim that Indians have been subsumed within domestic legal authority.

By indicating that the war on drugs is also an Indian war, Silko makes visible a crisis in the world system and the place of the United States in it. In an essay titled "America and the World: Today, Yesterday, and Tomorrow," first published in 1992, one year after the publication of *Almanac,* Immanuel Wallerstein projected the following "vision of the coming fifty years" in the Americas:

[O]n the one side, an increasingly wealthy North, a relatively internally egalitarian North (for its citizens), and a United States no longer in the lead economically or even geopolitically but in the lead in terms of social equality; on the other side, an increasingly disadvantaged South, ready to use its military power, which shall increase to disrupt the world-system, often turning against all the values the West has cherished, with a large part of its population trying the route of individual migration to the North, and creating thereby the South within the North.[67]

Although one could elaborate or amend this projection, for now I want to focus on the last part, where Wallerstein emphasizes the continued movement of the South to the North. He concludes that massive migration could provoke several extreme U.S. responses. In an attempt to "isolate itself from the hopelessness and costs of Third World wars," it might protect its wealth by becoming "fortress America." Or, failing to control migration, "it might turn toward creating a dike between the entitlements of citizens and those of noncitizens. Within no time, the United States could find itself in a position where the bottom thirty percent, even fifty percent, of its wage-labor was noncitizens, with no suffrage and limited access to social welfare."[68] It would seem that Wallerstein's prediction about fortress America was in the process of becoming true when he wrote his essay, as my discussion of the drug war and the militarization of the border suggests. Yet by posing them as alternative futures, Wallerstein obscures the fact that in recent history the building of fortress America has often coincided with the erection of a fire wall between "the entitlements of citizens and those of noncitizens." In the 1980s and 1990s, a series of political measures were aimed precisely at depriving noncitizens and their children of government services. And although there was some talk of "stemming the tide of migration," the emphasis on entitlements suggests that such measures were more concerned with managing workers than excluding them from the United States completely. This shifting and uneven combination of border policing and entitlement enforcement ultimately constitutes a set of makeshift efforts to manage the crisis of the South in the North.

Like Wallerstein's essay, *Almanac* is a prescient piece of speculative fiction about the possible political economies of the near future. But Silko reminds us that the "South" is largely made up of Indians from Mexico, Central America, and elsewhere. One sign of this unprecedented demographic shift is data from the 2000 census indicating that the border state of California now has the largest Indian population in the United States. In an essay called "The Border Patrol State," Silko in effect asks how the United States will respond to the unstoppable movement of Indians north. She begins by recounting her own experiences with the newly militarized war on drugs after a book-signing event for *Almanac*. According to José David Saldívar, in this essay Silko argues that "immigration and drug enforcement laws single out for punishment racialized border-crossers from the South while they simultaneously target 'people of color' from the North by restricting their free movement within the nation's borders."[69] "The Border Patrol State" is also an apt gloss on the title of this chapter, "Drug Wars Are Indian Wars." As she tells it, on the way back to Tucson, with a "small amount of medicinal marijuana" in her purse, Silko was pulled over by the Border Patrol.

> I will never forget that night beside the highway. There was an awful feeling of menace and violence straining to break loose.... The night was very dark, and no other traffic had come down the road since we had been stopped. All I could think about was a book I had read— *Nunca Más*—the official report of a human rights commission that investigated and certified more than twelve thousand "disappearances" during Argentina's "dirty war" in the late 1970s.... I thought how easy it would be for the Border Patrol to shoot us and leave our bodies and car beside the highway, like so many bodies found in these parts and ascribed to drug runners.[70]

Although the Border Patrol did not find her marijuana and ultimately released her, the incident leads Silko to reflect upon the consequences of the war on drugs for Indians and mestizos:

> Deep down the issue is simple: the so-called Indian Wars from the days of Sitting Bull and Red Cloud have never really ended in the Americas. The Indian people of southern Mexico, of Guatemala, and those left in El Salvador, too, are still fighting for their lives and for their land against the cavalry patrols sent out by the governments of those lands. The Americas are Indian country, and the "Indian problem" is not about to go away.[71]

She ends her essay by considering the "dark young men, Indian and mestizo," who she sees riding on boxcars headed for Tucson in defiance of the border patrol state. "I was reminded of the ancient story of Aztlán, told by the Aztecs but known in other Uto-Aztecan communities as well. Aztlán is the beautiful land to the north, the origin place of the Aztec people. I don't remember how or why the people left Aztlán to journey farther south, but the old story says that one day, they will return."[72]

How will the United States greet this return? Will it take, as Wallerstein thinks possible, "the upright path of violent social conflict, in which the restive underclass are held down forcefully with brutality and prejudice—a sort of neofascist path?" Or will it take "the path of national solidarity, a communal reaction to a shared social stress"? Or will the United States come to the conclusion "that there is no salvation that is not salvation of all humankind"?[73] In *Almanac of the Dead,* the world now runs on Indian time, and the question it raises is "what will the state do?"

Notes

INTRODUCTION

1. John J. O'Connor, "Role for Nancy Reagan," *New York Times*, 18 March 1983, C26.

2. Alexander Cockburn and Jeffrey St. Clair, *Whiteout: The CIA, Drugs and the Press* (New York: Verso, 1998), 73, 238–40. See also Alfred McCoy, with Catherine Read and Leonard Adams II, *The Politics of Heroin in Southeast Asia* (New York: Harper and Row, 1972) and Alfred McCoy, *The Politics of Heroin: The Complicity of the CIA in the Global Drug Trade* (New York: Lawrence Hill and Co., 2003).

3. Ibid., 167–87, 277–315.

4. For an example of a conservative critique of drug-war spending, see "Colombia's Drug Business: The Wages of Prohibition," *Economist*, 24 December 1994–26 January 1995, 21–24. For spending figures, see Eric Blumenson and Eva Nilson, "Policing for Profit: The Drug War's Hidden Economic Agenda," *University of Chicago Law Review* (winter 1998): 35; and Ira Glasser, "American Drug Laws: The New Jim Crow," *Albany Law Review* (2000): 720. According to Glasser, since 1982, the federal money spent on drug enforcement increased from $1.65 billion to $18 billion—and this was in addition to the billions spent at the state and local level.

5. See Hawkeye K. Gross, *Reefer Warrior: How My Friends and I Found Adventure, Wealth, and Romance Smuggling Marijuana—Until We All Went to Jail* (Boulder, Colo.: Paladin Press, 1998); Terrence E. Poppa, *Drug Lord: The Life and Death of a Mexican Kingpin* (New York: Pharos Books, 1990); Bruce Porter, *Blow: How a Smalltown Boy Made $100,000 with the Medellín Cocaine Cartel and Lost It All* (New York: HarperCollins, 1993); Berkeley Rice, *Trafficking: The Boom and Bust of the Air America Cocaine Ring* (New York: Scribners,

1989); Robert Sabbag, *Loaded: A Misadventure on the Marijuana Trail* (Boston: Little, Brown, 2002); Richard Smitten, Max Mermelstein, and Robin Moore, *Inside the Cocaine Cartel: The Riveting Eyewitness Account of Life Inside the Colombian Cartel* (New York: Spi Books, 1993); Kay Wolf with Sybil Taylor, *The Last Run: An American Woman's Years Inside a Colombian Drug Family— And Her Dramatic Escape* (New York: Viking, 1989).

6. Pola Reyburd, "Who Are the Bad Guys? Literary Images of Narco-traffickers," in *Drug Trafficking in the Americas,* ed. Bruce M. Bagley and William O. Walker III (New Brunswick, Fla.: North-South Center, University of Miami, Transaction Publishers, 1995), 535–47.

7. Jimmie Lynn Reeves and Richard Campbell, *Cracked Coverage: Television News, the Anti-Cocaine Crusade, and the Reagan Legacy* (Durham, N.C.: Duke University Press, 1994).

8. *Scarface* (1983), *Cocaine Wars* (1986), *Lethal Weapon* (1987), *Robocop* (1987), *Crocodile Dundee* (1987), *Covert Action* (1988), *Above the Law* (1988), *Colors* (1988), *K-9* (1989), *L.A. Heat* (1989), *License to Kill* (1989), *Tropical Snow* (1989), *White Hot* (1989), *Clear and Present Danger* (1990), *Air America* (1990), *Die Hard 2* (1990), *Last of the Finest* (1990), *Carlito's Way* (1990), *Cartel* (1990), *Delta Force 2* (1990), *Predator 2* (1990), *New Jack City* (1991), *American Me* (1992), *Deep Cover* (1992), *El Mariachi* (1992), *Bad Boys* (1995), *Traffic* (2000), *Blow* (2001), and *Training Day* (2001). All of these films focus on some aspect of drug traffic and enforcement set in the United States, Latin America, or some combination of the two.

9. Michael Tonry, *Malign Neglect: Race, Crime, and Punishment in America* (New York: Oxford University Press, 1995).

10. Blumenson and Nilson, "Policing for Profit," 38, 47–48, 63–64.

11. Ibid., 82.

12. Donald J. Mabry, "The U.S. Military and the War on Drugs," and William O. Walker, "The Bush Administration's Andean Drug Strategy in Historical Perspective," in Bagley and Walker, *Drug Trafficking in the Americas,* 54, 12.

13. Noam Chomsky, *Rogue States: The Rule of Force in World Affairs* (Cambridge, Mass.: South End Press, 2000), 77, 154.

14. J. Patrick LaRue, "The 'ILL-LICIT' Effects of NAFTA: Increased Drug Trafficking into the United States through the Southwest Border," *Currents: International Trade Law Journal* (summer 2000): 42–43.

15. See Miguel Ruiz-Cabañas, "Mexico's Changing Illicit Drug Supply Role," in *The Drug Connection in U.S.–Mexican Relations,* ed. Guadalupe Gonzalez and Marta Tienda (San Diego: Center for U.S.-Mexican Studies, UC San Diego, 1989), 58–61. See also Robert E. Powis, *The Money Launderers: Lessons from the Drug Wars—How Billions of Illegal Dollars Are Washed through Banks and Businesses* (Chicago: Probus Publishing, 1992).

16. In the mid-1980s, the federal government sought to enforce antilaundering laws, but such efforts merely prompted traffickers and capitalists to instead hide drug profits through the black market in pesos. Colombian drug

traffickers sell their product in the United States and then exchange their dollars for pesos through a broker. The broker in turn sells the dollars to Colombian importers who use the money to buy U.S. consumer goods that they then sell in Colombia. See Lowell Bergman, "U.S. Companies Tangled in Web of Drug Dollars," *New York Times*, 10 October 2000, sec. A, 1, and *How U.S. Companies Are Used to Launder Money: Hearings before the Senate Caucus on International Narcotics Control*, 106th Congress, 1st session, 21 June 1999 (Washington, D.C.: U.S. Government Printing Office, 1999).

17. Bergman, "U.S. Companies Tangled in Web of Drug Dollars."

18. LaRue, "'ILL-LICIT' Effects," 43. See also Cockburn and St. Clair, *Whiteout*, 347–84.

19. Arnold Chien, Margaret Conners, and Kenneth Fox, "The Drug War in Perspective," in *Dying for Growth*, ed. J. Y. Kim, J. Millen, A. Irwin, and J. Gershman (Cambridge, Mass.: Common Courage, 2000), quoted by Chomsky, *Rogue States*, 81.

20. See John Beverley, *Subalternity and Representation: Arguments in Cultural Theory* (Durham, N.C.: Duke University Press, 1999). For a relevant discussion of "the poor," see Michael Hardt and Antonio Negri, *Empire* (Cambridge: Harvard University Press, 2000), 156–59.

21. Chomsky, *Rogue States*, 7.

22. See chapter 7.

23. Ricardo Vargas Meza, *The Revolutionary Armed Forces of Colombia (FARC) and the Illicit Drug Trade*, Acción Andina (Bolivia), TNI (Netherlands), WOLA (Washington, D.C.), June 1999, quoted by Chomsky, *Rogue States*, 74.

24. Amnesty International, *Amnesty Action: The Colombia Papers* (winter 1997), quoted by Chomsky, *Rogue States*, 151.

25. Mabry, "U.S. Military," 51.

26. Quoted by Cockburn and St. Clair, *Whiteout*, 380–81.

27. See LaRue, "'ILL-LICIT' Effects," 38–48.

28. The preceding two figures are from Glasser, "American Drug Laws," 718.

29. Reeves and Campbell, *Cracked Coverage*, 211–12. See also Loren Siegel, "The Pregnancy Police Fight the War on Drugs," in *Crack in America: Demon Drugs and Social Justice*, ed. Craig Reinarman and Harry G. Levine (Berkeley: University of California Press, 1997), 249–58.

30. Glasser, "American Drug Laws," 719.

31. Ibid., 721.

32. Ibid., 715, 723.

33. Although Fredric Jameson has developed the concepts of "cognitive mapping" and "totality" in a number of places, I have been particularly influenced by his discussion in *The Geopolitical Aesthetic: Cinema and Space in the World System* (Bloomington: Indiana University Press, 1992).

34. The drug lord in *New Jack City*, for example, obsessively watches the film in his private screening room, whereas one of the drug dealers in *Deep*

Cover mimics Montana's distinctive accent. And as we shall see, a number of other films more indirectly use *Scarface* as a model. In rap music, the film and its hero are common sources of inspiration. Rappers such as Ice-T from the West Coast ("High Rollers," *Power,* Sire Records, 1988), Eric B. and Rakim from the East Coast ("Untouchables," *Let the Rhythm Hit 'Em,* MCA Records, 1990), and the Geto Boys ("Scarface," *Grip It on That Other Level,* Rap-A-Lot Records, 1989) all reference *Scarface.* This last album, in fact, contains repeated samples of Al Pacino's dialogue from the film. One of the Geto Boys has even assumed the stage name "Scarface."

35. See Vincent Canby, "Al Pacino Stars in Scarface," *New York Times,* 9 December 1983, C18, and "How Should We React to Violence," *New York Times,* 11 December, sec. 2, 23; Bob Thomas, *"Scarface,"* Associated Press, 12 December 1983, Lexis-Nexis Academic Universe. Concerns over the film's violence even spilled over onto the editorial page. See, for example, George F. Will's "Doing Violence to Art," *Washington Post,* 15 December 1983, A19.

36. Timothy Dunn, *The Militarization of the U.S.–Mexican Border, 1978– 1992: Low-Intensity Conflict Doctrine Comes Home* (Austin, Tex.: CMAS Books, 1996), 28, 108, 110, 114.

37. Richard Slotkin, *Gunfighter Nation: The Myth of the Frontier in Twentieth-Century America* (Norman: University of Oklahoma Press, 1998).

38. *Scarface's* novel use of automatic weapons and other military hardware was also echoed by the action-film franchises of the 1980s and 1990s such as the *Rambo, Terminator,* and *Die Hard* films. See Susan Jeffords, *Hard Bodies: Hollywood Masculinity in the Reagan Era* (New Brunswick, N.J.: Rutgers University Press, 1994).

39. Geto Boys, "Trigga Happy Nigga," *Grip It On That Other Level.*

40. Mike Davis, *City of Quartz: Excavating the Future in Los Angeles* (New York: Vintage Press, 1990), 251–52.

41. Ibid., 265–322; Robin D. G. Kelley, "Kickin' Reality, Kickin' Ballistics: 'Gangsta Rap' and Postindustrial Los Angeles," in *Race Rebels: Culture, Politics, and the Black Working Class* (New York: Free Press, 1994), 193.

42. Quoted in Cockburn and St. Clair, *Whiteout,* 65.

43. In *narcocorrido* slang, AK-47s are called *cuernos de chivos* or "goat horns" because of the weapon's curved grip. See Elijah Wald, *Narcocorrido: A Journey into the Music of Drugs, Guns, and Guerrillas* (New York: Harper-Collins, 2001), 114. For examples of *narcocorrido* album art and film posters featuring automatic weapons, see the photos between pages 208 and 209; Sam Quinones, "The Ballad of Chalino Sánchez," *True Tales from Another Mexico* (Albuquerque: University of New Mexico Press, 2001), 11, 20–21, 26–27; Sam Dillon, "Mexico's Troubadours Turn from Amor to Drugs," *New York Times,* 19 February 1999; Richard Grant, "Cocaine Cowboys," *Details* (November 1998): 134–48; and Tony Ortega, "Viva los Outlaws," *New Times L.A.,* 10 January 2002.

44. See Wald, *Narcocorrido,* 86, 208–9.

45. Ibid., 78–79.

46. As Quinones notes, the famous *narcocorridista* Chalino Sánchez established his musical career after settling in Inglewood. In the late 1990s, a working-class Mexican youth subculture emerged in Los Angeles that combined elements of gangsta rap with *narcocorridos* (Quinones, "The Ballad of Chalino Sanchez," 14, 11, 27).

47. David R. Maciel, "The Celluloid Frontier: The U.S.–Mexico Border in Contemporary Cinema, 1970–1988," *Renato Rosaldo Lecture Series Monograph* 5, series 1987–88 (Tucson, Ariz.: Mexican American Studies and Research Center, 1989), 17–18; Carl J. Mora, *Mexican Cinema: Reflections of a Society, 1896–1988*, rev. ed. (Berkeley: University of California Press, 1989), 159–60.

48. Brian De Palma, *The Making of Scarface* (1996), documentary included on the *Scarface* DVD, Universal. See also Thomas McKevey Cleaver's article "Scarface," in which he interviews the film's cinematographer, John Alonzo (*American Cinematographer* 64, no. 12 [December 1983]: 58–61).

49. John Alonzo, quoted by Cleaver, "Scarface," 60–61.

50. Dunn, *Militarization of the U.S.–Mexican Border*, 29.

51. See De Palma, *The Making of Scarface*. Compare Jacqui Jones's reading of *New Jack City*, where she concludes that it encouraged audience identification with the police and promotes vigilantism ("Crime and Punishment," *Black Film Review* 6:4 [summer 1991]: 10–11, 19).

52. De Palma, *The Making of Scarface*.

53. Internet Movie Data Base (imdb.com), "Trivia for *Clear and Present Danger*."

54. Quoted by Chris Hodenfield, "Is Hollywood Dying the Death of a Thousand Cuts?" *Premiere* (July 2002): 45.

55. See Christopher Kelly, "Intelligence Overcomes 'Spy Game' Failings," *Chattanooga Times/Chattanooga Free Press*, 30 November 2001, H23; Michael Rechtshaffen, "City Hall," *Hollywood Reporter*, reprinted by BPI Entertainment News Wire, 8 February 1996, Lexus-Nexus Academic Universe, Entertainment News; Steve Persall, "Stone Makes a U-Turn," *St. Petersburg Times*, 3 October 1997, Weekend Section, 3; Andy Seiler, "'The Art of War' Tries to Woo and Fails," *USA Today*, 28 August 2000, 4D.

56. *Variety*'s Todd McCarthy, for example, likened Michael Bay's editing style to "a machine gun stuck in the firing position for two and a half hours" (quoted by John Burlingame, "'Armageddon' Draws Cutting Commentary; Rapid-Fire Editing in the Fast-Paced Asteroid Film Elicits Strong Criticism from Some Reviewers and Reignites the Debate of Imagery versus Storytelling," 7 July 1998, Calendar, Part F, 1). See also Eric Mink, "'Tribeca': Unique, Welcome Addition," *St. Louis Post-Dispatch*, 22 March 1993, *Everyday Magazine*, 5D; and Lewis Beale, "A Critic Critiques the Trailers," *New York Daily News*, reprinted in the *Dayton Daily News*, 24 August 1994, no page numbers, Lexus-Nexus Academic Universe, Entertainment News.

57. Robert Rodriguez, *Rebel without a Crew, or How a 23-Year-Old Film-maker with $7,000 Became a Hollywood Player* (New York: Plume, 1996), 32, 39–40, 42.

58. Robert Rodriguez, director's commentary, *El Mariachi* DVD, Columbia Pictures, 1998.

59. "Interview with Garrett Brown, Inventor of the Steadicam," *Film-crew*, issue 16 (1997).

60. *San Francisco Chronicle*, 27 September 2001.

61. Rodriguez, *Rebel*, 142 and 143.

62. Ibid., 24.

63. Rodolfo F. Acuña, *Anything but Mexican: Chicanos in Contemporary Los Angeles* (New York: Verso Press, 1996), 118–21.

64. Jameson, *Geopolitical Aesthetic*, 11.

65. Grupo Exterminador, *Narco Corridos 2*, Fonovisa, 1997. For a similar rap graphic, see Eric B. and Rakim's *Paid in Full*, MCA Records, 1987.

66. "New Jack Hustler (Nino's Theme)," *New Jack City*, Giant Records, 1991.

67. Geto Boys, "Mind Playing Tricks on Me," *We Can't Be Stopped*, Rap-A-Lot Records, 1991.

68. Jacqui Jones, "Undercover of Blackness," *Black Film Review* 7:4 (fall 1992): 33.

69. See Quinones, "Ballad," 14. Similarly, the members of Los Tucanes de Tijuana started as factory workers, and the famous Rivera family grew up in the working-class barrios of Long Beach, California.

70. For class and poverty among rap performers and audiences, see Kelly, "Kickin' Reality"; and Tricia Rose, *Black Noise: Rap and Black Culture in Contemporary America* (Hanover, N.H.: University Press of New England, 1994). For musicians' self-conscious address to other poor people, see Wald, *Narcorrido*, 93.

71. See Ortega, "Viva los Outlaws."

72. Quoted in ibid. See also the entry for Jenni Rivera on the Web site for her label, Cintas Acuario.

73. Quoted by Wald, *Narcocorrido*, 142.

74. *Scarface* producer Martin Bergman, *The Making of Scarface*.

75. "Art Imitates Politics," *The Record*, 25 July 1990, A02.

76. Ibid.

77. Melanie McAlister, *Epic Encounters: Culture, Media, and U.S. Interests in the Middle East, 1945–2000* (Berkeley: University of California Press, 2001), 186–87, 197, 238.

78. Quoted by Michael Isikoff, "Reagan Signs Sweeping Anti-Drug Bill," *Washington Post*, 19 November 1988, first section, A3.

79. *Washington Post*, 13 October 1983, D9.

80. *Washington Post*, 23 July 1987, C10; *Los Angeles Times*, 14 August 1986, part 6, 11.

81. "Drug War Propaganda," *Propaganda Review* 6 (winter 1990): 6–8, 43–44.

82. Daniel Forbes, "Prime-Time Propaganda," Salon.com, 13 January 2000.

83. Jonathan M. Moses, "Advertisers Plug Products with Antidrug Message; Marketing Experts Say They Have Cachet, Crosses All Cultural, Economic Classes," *Washington Post*, 2 September 1988, financial section, 3; *Los Angeles Times*, 1 September 1988, part 1, p 1; *New York Times*, 27 August 1987, D19.

84. Moses, "Advertisers," 3. As a result, the Doritos Company invested $2 million in order to print "Just Say No" on 120 million bags of corn chips. Other companies that have used the antidrug message to sell products include MasterCard and McDonald's (ibid.).

85. For quotes and information concerning the National Youth Anti-Drug Media Campaign's "Multicultural Outreach," see its official Web site, www.mediacampaign.org.

86. "Entertainment Outreach," National Youth Anti-Drug Media Campaign Web site, www.mediacampaign.org.

87. Ice Cube, *Death Certificate* (Priority, 1991), cited by Kelley, "Kickin' Reality," 195.

88. Kelley, "Kickin' Reality," 202.

89. Wald, *Narcocorrido*, 41–42.

90. "Antes de certificar, primero limpien sus campos." Quoted and translated in ibid., 41.

91. Wald, *Narcocorrido*, 295.

92. Quinones, "Ballad," 14–19.

93. Mora, *Mexican Cinema*.

1. The Globe in an Opium Bowl

1. Sing-wu Wang, *The Organization of Chinese Emigration, 1848–1888* (San Francisco: Chinese Materials Center, 1978), 244.

2. Ibid., 231.

3. Intertitle, *Broken Blossoms* DVD, Kino International, 2001. For a survey of criticism on the film and an influential analysis of its central portion, see Gina Marchetti, "The Rape Fantasy: *The Cheat* and *Broken Blossoms*," in *Romance and the "Yellow Peril": Race, Sex, and Discursive Strategies in Hollywood Fiction* (Berkeley: University of California Press, 1993), 10–45.

4. For a description of the effect and its implied setting, see the interview with Lillian Gish on the *Broken Blossoms* DVD.

5. John Haddad, "The Laundry Man's Got a Knife!: Chinese and Chinese America in Early United States Cinema," in *Chinese America: History and Perspectives* (San Francisco: Chinese Historical Society of America, 2001), 34–35. Thanks to Judy Yung for bringing this source to my attention.

6. For the influence of the Boxer Rebellion on U.S. silent films, see ibid., 37–41.

7. James S. Moy, *Marginal Sights: Staging the Chinese in America* (Iowa City: University of Iowa Press, 1993), 64–81; and Nayan Shah, *Contagious Divides: Epidemics and Race in San Francisco's Chinatown* (Berkeley: University of California Press, 2001), 92–93.

8. Haddad, "The Laundry Man's Got a Knife!" 34–35.

9. See Virginia Berridge and Griffith Edwards, *Opium and the People: Opiate Use in Nineteenth-Century England* (New York: St. Martin's Press, 1982); Brian Inglis, *The Forbidden Game: A Social History of Drugs* (New York: Scribners, 1975); Barry Milligan, *Pleasures and Pains: Opium and the Orient in Nineteenth-Century British Culture* (Charlottesville: University Press of Virginia, 1995).

10. At its high point in 1881, the Chinese residing in England numbered only 665, with 109 concentrated in London (Ng Kwee Choo, *The Chinese in London* [London: Oxford University Press, 1968], 5–6). See also J. P. May, "The Chinese in Britain, 1860–1914," in *Immigrants and Minorities in British Society*, ed. Colin Holms (London: George Allen and Unwin, 1978); Alan Palmer, *The East End: Four Centuries of London Life* (London: John Murray Publishers, 1989), 108–9; and Rozina Visram, *Ayahs, Lascars and Princes: Indians in Britain, 1700–1947* (Dover, N.H.: Pluto Press, 1986).

11. Virginia Berridge, "East End Opium Dens and Narcotic Use in Britain," *London Journal* 4:1 (1978): 3–28. In 1877, the *Friend of China*, a London-based anti-opium journal, reported that there were five opium dens in London (September 1877, 19). A decade later the same publication reported an increase of only two (October 1887, 172). For examples of sporadic English opposition to Chinese labor, see May, "Chinese in Britain," 111, 116–18.

12. This figure reflects movements from 1848 to 1888 (Wang, *Organization of Chinese Emigration*, xi).

13. See ibid., 324 and passim for immigration figures for each destination. For histories of the Chinese in Australia, see Persia Crawford Campbell, *Chinese Coolie Emigration to Countries within the British Empire* (London: P. S. King and Son, 1923); C. Y. Choi, *Chinese Migration and Settlement in Australia* (Sydney: Sydney University Press, 1975); and Kathryn Cronin, *Colonial Casualties: Chinese in Early Victoria* (Carlton, Victoria: Melbourne University Press, 1982). For British Guiana, see Campbell, *Chinese Coolie Emigration*, 159. Chinese immigration to the British West Indies began in 1853, lapsed, and then began again in 1859 before greatly diminishing around 1866. See Walton Look Lai, *Indentured Labor, Caribbean Sugar: Chinese and Indian Migrants to the British West Indies, 1839–1918* (Baltimore: Johns Hopkins University Press, 1993), 177, 18. For Canada and Malaysia, see Campbell, *Chinese Coolie Emigration*, 37, 51, 20.

14. Carl A Trocki, "Drugs, Taxes, and Chinese Capitalism in Southeast Asia," in *Opium Regimes: China, Britain, and Japan, 1839–1952*, ed. Timothy

Brook and Bob Tadashi Wakabayashi (Berkeley: University of California Press, 2000), 99.

15. Toni Morrison, *Playing in the Dark: Whiteness and the Literary Imagination* (New York: Random House, 1992), 46–47, 6–8, 11–12.

16. The following account of the opium trade and the two Anglo-Chinese Opium Wars draws upon a number of other sources, including Brook and Wakabayashi, *Opium Regimes;* Dilip K. Basu, "The Peripheralization of China: Notes on the Opium Connection," in *The World-System of Capitalism: Past and Present,* ed. Walter L. Goldfrank (Beverly Hills, Calif.: Sage Publications, 1979); Jack Beeching, *The Chinese Opium Wars* (London: Hutchinson and Co., 1975); Tan Chung, *China and the Brave New World: A Study of the Origins of the Opium War, 1840–42* (Durham, N.C.: Carolina Academic Press, 1979); Peter Ward Fay, *The Opium War, 1840–1842* (Chapel Hill: University of North Carolina Press, 1975); J. Spenser Hill, *The Indo-Chinese Opium Trade* (London: Henry Frowde, 1884); Immanuel C. Y. Hsu, *The Rise of Modern China,* 5th ed. (New York: Oxford University Press, 1995), 168–95; P. C. Kuo, *A Critical Study of the First Anglo-Chinese War* (1935; Westport, Conn.: Hyperion Press, 1975); David Owen, *British Opium Policy in China and India* (New Haven: Yale University Press, 1934); Jonathan Spence, "Opium Smoking in Ch'ing China," in *Conflict and Control in Late Imperial China,* ed. Frederic Wakeman Jr. and Carolyn Grant (Berkeley: University of California Press, 1975), 143–73; Joshua Rowntree, *The Imperial Drug Trade* (London: Methuen, 1905); J. F. B. Tinling, *The Poppy-Plague and England's Crime* (London: Elliot Stock, 1876); Arthur Waley, *The Opium War through Chinese Eyes* (London: Allen and Unwin, 1958); Wen-Tsao Wu, *The Chinese Opium Question in British Opinion and Action* (New York: Academy Press, 1928).

17. For opium profits, see Brian Inglis, *The Opium War* (London: Hodder and Stroughton, 1976), 47, 183. For the role of opium revenue in funding British military campaigns and colonial administrations, see Gregory Blue, "Opium for China"; Trocki, "Drugs, Taxes, and Chinese Capitalism in Southeast Asia"; and Christopher Munn, "The Hong Kong Opium Revenue, 1845–1885," all in Brook and Wakabayashi, *Opium Regimes,* 33–34, 79–104, 105–26.

18. For Chinese efforts to ban opium importation, see Beeching, *Chinese Opium Wars,* 25–27, 35–36; and Spence, "Opium Smoking in Ch'ing China," 154–61.

19. For information on Lin, see Beeching, *Chinese Opium Wars,* 73–93; Whaley, *Opium War through Chinese Eyes;* Wu, *Chinese Opium Question,* 33–37; and Hsin-pao Chang, *Commissioner Lin and the Opium War* (Cambridge: Harvard University Press, 1964); the Basu quotation is on page 178.

20. Fay, *Opium War, 1840–1842,* 345.

21. Kuo, *Critical Study of the First Anglo-Chinese War,* 145, 149–50, 153, 157–60.

22. Fay, *Opium War, 1840–1842,* 224–25, 315, 318.

23. Ibid., 300.

24. *London Times,* 22 November 1842, quoted in ibid., 367.

25. For the Treaty of Nanking, see Beeching, *Chinese Opium Wars,* 153–55; Wu, *Chinese Opium Question,* 47–48; and Hsu, *Rise of Modern China,* 189–93; the quotation from Hsu in on page 192.

26. In addition to Marx's account of the incident that precipitated the war, see Beeching, *Chinese Opium Wars,* 213–18, 225–32; and Hsu, *Rise of Modern China,* 205–11.

27. Quoted by Beeching, *Chinese Opium Wars,* 305.

28. See ibid., 315–25.

29. *Oxford English Dictionary.*

30. Beeching, *Chinese Opium Wars,* 331.

31. C. F. Gordon Cumming, "Rambles in Canton," *Belgravia,* November 1885, 55.

32. For information on these treaties, see Beeching, *Chinese Opium Wars,* 260–62, 264–65, 267, 277–78; and Wu, *Chinese Opium Question,* 23–62. The "one-seventh" figure is a commonplace in both nineteenth-century and subsequent accounts of the trade.

33. E. J. Hobsbawm, "Britain in the World Economy," in *Industry and Empire: An Economic History of Britain since 1750* (London: Weidenfeld and Nicolson, 1968), 123.

34. Bruce D. Johnson, "Righteousness before Revenue: The Forgotten Moral Crusade against the Indo-Chinese Opium Trade," *Journal of Drug Issues* 5:4 (fall 1975): 305–26; Wu, *Chinese Opium Question,* 155–88.

35. Karl Marx, "Revolution in China and in Europe," in *Karl Marx, Frederick Engels: Collected Works* (New York: International Publishers, 1975), 15: 94–95.

36. On the concepts of core and periphery, see Immanuel Wallerstein, "The Commodification of Everything: Production of Capital," in *Historical Capitalism with Capitalist Civilization* (New York: Verso, 1995), 11–43; and "Rise and Future Demise of the Capitalist System," *The Capitalist World-Economy* (Cambridge: Cambridge University Press, 1979), 1–36. For a discussion of these concepts in the context of Anglo-Chinese relationships, see Basu, "Peripheralization of China."

37. Marx refers, for example, to British aggressions during the Second Opium War as the "Canton massacres" and the "Chinese massacres" ("Parliamentary Debates on the Chinese Hostilities," in *Collected Works,* 15:208; "Defeat of the Palmerston Ministry," in *Collected Works,* 15:214). Also see "The New Chinese War," in *Collected Works,* 16:508, 517; and "English Atrocities in China," in *Collected Works,* 15:234.

38. Karl Marx, "The Indian Revolt," in *Collected Works,* 15: 353–54.

39. Ibid., 353. Also, see Karl Marx, "Investigation of Tortures in India," in *Collected Works,* 15:336, 338.

40. See Inglis, *Opium War,* 25–27, 33, 39, 47–48; and Rowntree, *Imperial Drug Trade,* 193–95.

41. Marx, "English Atrocities in China," in *Collected Works,* 15:234.

42. Choi, *Chinese Migration and Settlement in Australia,* 15; Cronin, *Colonial Casualties,* 8; Wang, *Organization of Chinese Emigration,* 7, 12–13, 25.

43. V. G. Kiernan, "The British in Malaya," in *The Lords of Humankind: Black Man, Yellow Man, and White Man in an Age of Empire* (Boston: Little, Brown and Company, 1969), 82–87.

44. Jan Ryan, *Ancestors: Chinese in Colonial Australia* (South Fremantle, Western Australia: Fremantle Arts Centre Press, 1995), 16–23; Wang, *Organization of Chinese Emigration,* 144–47; Campbell, *Chinese Coolie Emigration,* 9. According to Ryan, Chinese signed contracts in Singapore for work in the Federated and Native Malay States, British North Borneo, Western Australia, Queensland, Thursday Island, Siamese Territories, German New Guinea, East Africa, and a number of Dutch colonies, especially Indonesia (22–23). British imperial governments subsidized emigration either directly, by partially defraying the cost of transportation to the colonies such as Western Australia and Guiana (Ryan, *Ancestors,* 26; Lai, *Indentured Labor, Caribbean Sugar,* 45, 51–52), or indirectly, by administering recruitment at points of departure such as Hong Kong and Singapore.

45. Trocki, "Drugs, Taxes, and Chinese Capitalism in Southeast Asia," 80, 100. The phrase "opium regime" also comes from this volume, *Opium Regimes,* where the editors, Brook and Wakabayashi, use it to describe "a system in which an authority declares its right to control certain practices, and develops policies and mechanisms to exercise that right within its presumed domain. . . . What characterizes a regime more generally is its ability to impose conformity to policies that are profitable to it in the public realm" (4).

46. Choi, *Chinese Migration and Settlement in Australia,* 4; Cronin, *Colonial Casualties,* 17–18; Wang, *Organization of Chinese Emigration,* 12; Lai, *Indentured Labor, Caribbean Sugar,* 38–40. While all of these sources note that a variety of forces informed nineteenth-century Chinese immigration, they agree that British imperialism was a key factor. For an apt summary, see June Mei, "Socioeconomic Origins of Emigration: Guangdong to California, 1850 to 1882," in *Labor Immigration under Capitalism: Asian Workers in the United States before World War II,* ed. Lucie Cheng and Edna Bonacich (Berkeley: University of California Press, 1984), 224.

47. Marlon K. Hom, *Songs of Gold Mountain: Cantonese Rhymes from San Francisco's Chinatown* (Berkeley: University of California Press), songs 201–2, 204 (pages 300–301, 303); Ryan, *Ancestors,* 107, 177, Cronin, *Colonial Casualties,* 130; Lai, *Indentured Labor, Caribbean Sugar,* 177.

48. Munn, "Hong Kong Opium Revenue," 111; Trocki, "Drugs, Taxes, and Chinese Capitalism in Southeast Asia," 82.

49. Trocki, "Drugs, Taxes, and Chinese Capitalism in Southeast Asia,"

88, 90; I. L. Bishop, "Sketches in the Malay Peninsula," *Leisure Hour,* January 1883, 17–23.

50. The two opium merchants were Dent & Co. and Jardine, Matheson, & Co. See Wang, *Organization of Chinese Emigration,* 355–60.

51. Munn, "Hong Kong Opium Revenue," 110.

52. Ryan, *Ancestors,* 35; Wang, *Organization of Chinese Emigration,* 203.

53. See Syed Hussein Alatas, *The Myth of the Lazy Native: A Study of the Image of the Malays, Filipinos and Javanese from the 16th to the 20th Century and Its Function in the Ideology of Colonial Capitalism* (London: Frank Cass, 1977), 91–92.

54. Trocki, "Drugs, Taxes, and Chinese Capitalism in Southeast Asia," 87–88.

55. Ibid., 89–90.

56. Wang, *Organization of Chinese Emigration,* 62–64; and Campbell, *Chinese Coolie Emigration,* 117–18.

57. For Hong Kong, see Campbell, *Chinese Coolie Emigration,* 150–60; Wang, *Organization of Chinese Emigration,* 17, 124–30; and Lai, *Indentured Labor, Caribbean Sugar,* 72–73. For Singapore, see Ryan, *Ancestors,* 27–28, 167.

58. For ship conditions and mortality rates, see Campbell, *Chinese Coolie Emigration,* 97; Wang, *Organization of Chinese Emigration,* 180, 182–83, 209, 231, 245; and Cronin, *Colonial Casualties,* 11. The British consul at Canton concluded that more than 13 percent of Chinese immigrants—more than eleven thousand—died on English and French ships between 1847 and 1866. English ships carrying Chinese to Cuba had a 14 percent mortality rate, with more deaths than ships of any other national origin (Wang, *Organization of Chinese Emigration,* 209–12, 231).

59. On emigrant depots and job-related deaths, see Ryan, *Ancestors,* 33, 137, 138, 147. Conditions in British Guiana were particularly hard. See Lai, *Indentured Labor, Caribbean Sugar,* 62, 65–66, Campbell, *Chinese Coolie Emigration,* 132–32, and Alan H. Adamson, "The Impact of Indentured Immigration on the Political Economy of British Guiana," in *Indentured Labour in the British Empire 1834–1920,* ed. Jay Saunders (London: Croom Helm, 1984), 42–56. For a contemporary account of plantation working conditions in the British West Indies, see Edward Jenkins, *The Coolie: His Rights and Wrongs* (New York: George Routledge and Sons, 1871); and Henry Kirke, *Twenty-Five Years in British Guiana* (Westport, Conn.: Negro Universities Press, 1979 [1898]).

60. British troops were called in and several lives were lost (Lai, *Indentured Labor, Caribbean Sugar,* 89).

61. Ibid., 101–2. For threats of rebellion in British Guiana, see Jenkins, *Coolie.*

62. For a contemporary account, see W. A. Pickering, "The Chinese in the Straits of Malacca," *Fraser's Magazine,* October 1876, 438–45. Pickering was an official government translator in the region.

63. Ibid., 438.

64. This account of English periodicals has been informed by Deborah Wynne, *The Sensation Novel and the Victorian Family Magazine* (New York: Palgrave Press, 2001), 14–22; Kate Jackson, "George Newnes and the 'Loyal Tit-Bits': Editorial Identity and Textual Interaction in *Tit-Bits*," in *Nineteenth-Century Media and the Construction of Identities,* ed. Laurel Brake, Bill Bell, and David Finkelstein (New York: Palgrave Press, 2000), 11–26; Margaret Beetham, "Towards a Theory of the Periodical as a Publishing Genre," in *Investigating Victorian Journalism,* ed. Laurel Brake, Aled Jones, and Lionel Madden (London: MacMillan Press, 1990), 19–32. For a particularly cogent discussion of twentieth-century mass-media antecedents in the study of Victorian periodicals, see Lyn Pykett, "Reading the Periodical Press: Text and Context," in Brake, Jones, and Madden, *Investigating Victorian Journalism,* 3–18.

65. For Jameson's notion of "cognitive mapping," see the Introduction and the discussion in the next section.

66. See Wynne, *Sensation Novel,* 21. Similarly, see Beetham, who analyzes the heterogeneous, "open-ended" practice of reading Victorian periodicals ("Towards a Theory of the Periodical," 24–27).

67. Wynne, *Sensation Novel,* 22. The figures are for 1859–65.

68. See the following *All the Year Round* stories: "A Chinese Fairy Tale," 11 November 1871, 567–69; "Married Life in China," 8 November 1873, 42–45; "Funeral Rites in China," 14 June 1873, 162–64; "Chinese Festivals," 12 July 1873, 256–58; "Chinese Fortune-Tellers," 16 August 1873, 366–69; "Chinese Proper Names," 5 December 1874, 187–89; "Chinese Street Life," 21 March 1874, 498–502; "Chinese Superstitions," 2 May 1874, 64–67; "Chinese Shops and Shop-Signs," 13 June 1874, 196–99; "Chinese Folk-Lore," 24 January 1880, 204–10; "Chinese Officials," 29 May 1880, 54–59; "Chinese Police," 21 May 1881, 173–78; "Some Orient Pearls," 15 July 1882, 514–17; "Flowers in the Flowery Land," 27 September 1884, 509–14; "Bits of China," 31 October 1885, 204–8; "Chinese Superstitions," 28 May 1887, 437–42; "Telegraphy in China," 6 April 1889, 317–22. Also see similar essays in other miscellanies: *Leisure Hour:* "Chinese Gratitude," 27 September 1879, 623; "Chinese Superstitions," 9 October 1880, 645–47; "Chinese Population," 1890; "Chinese Ideas of the Status of Woman," 1890, 789–90; "Chinese Ladies Feet," December 1893, 134–35; "The Emperor of China," June 1898, 537–38; "Chinese Sailors," June 1898, 543; as well as "The Chinese"; *Bow Bells:* 7 January 1873, 592; F. Thorson Dickson, "Some Aspects of the Chinaman," *Belgravia,* September 1897, 87–91, and March 1898, 358–63. English writers further discussed the Chinese "labor question" in a variety of contexts, including California, British Columbia, Australia, and Malaysia. See Emily Faithfull, *Three Visits to America* (Edinburgh: David Douglas, 1884), 231–32; Emily A. Acland, "A Lady's 'American Notes,'" *Nineteenth Century,* March 1888, 407; "John Chinaman in America," *All the Year Round,* 10 December 1881, 321–25; J. W. Fortescue, "The Seamy Side of

Australia" and Howard Willoughby, "'The Seamy Side of Australia': A Reply from the Colonies," *Nineteenth Century,* August 1891, 300; J. W. Fortescue, "Guileless Australia: A Rejoinder," *Nineteenth Century,* September 1891, 439; Edmund Mitchell, "The Chinaman Abroad," *Nineteenth Century,* October 1894, 612–13; F. Thorold Dickson, "Some Aspects of a Chinaman," 87, 89; Pickering, "The Chinese in the Straits of Malacca"; G. R. Cole, "John Chinaman Abroad," *Fraser's Magazine,* October 1878.

    69. "Across China," *All the Year Round,* 5 July 1879, 59–62; C. F. Gordon Cumming, "New Year's Day in Canton," *Leisure Hour,* 3 January 1880, 8–13, and "Rambles in Canton," *Belgravia,* November 1885, 54–70; "A Street Scene in Foochow," *All the Year Round,* 15 October 1881, 129–33; "A Brush with Chinese Pirates," *All the Year Round,* 26 February 1887, 137–39; "The Child of the Ocean: The Yangtse-Kiang," *All the Year Round,* 26 October 1889, 391–95; *All the Year Round,* 5 October 1889, 324–29, 12 October 1889, 345–49; "Shanghai, from a Bedroom Window," *All the Year Round,* 19 January 1889, 54–58; Lise Boehm, "Up the Yangtsze," *Belgravia,* January 1895, 272–88; L. A. L., "Reminiscences of a Visit to India and China," in three parts, *London Society,* June 1895, 584–99, August 1895, 133–48, and September 1895, 247–63; A. Clarke White, "Chat about China," *London Society,* March 1898, 305–12; "Over-Sea Notes: Eastern China," *Leisure Hour,* May 1898, 470; "The New Open Port in North China" *Leisure Hour,* January 1900, 280–82.

    70. See, for example, A. A. Hayes, "A Passenger from Shanghai," *Belgravia,* June 1885, 461–70. Similarly, throughout 1880, *Leisure Hour* serialized a translation of *The Troubles of a Chinaman* by Jules Verne. For Hong Kong, see L. A. L., "Reminiscences of a Visit to India and China," part 3, 247–50.

    71. John Pope Hennessy, "The Chinese in Australia," *Nineteenth Century,* April 1888, 617–19; "Chinese in Australia," *Leisure Hour,* vol. 48, 1891; J. W. Fortescue, "The Seamy Side of Australia," *Nineteenth Century,* April 1891, 523–37.

    72. See Halbro Denham, "Yan," *London Society,* March 1898, 245–58; Ethel Mills, "The Chee Child: A Story for Children," *Pall Mall Magazine* vol. 36, no. 151, 646–49.

    73. I. L. Bishop, "Sketches in the Malay Peninsula," *Leisure Hour,* January 1883, 17. See also F. Thorold Dickson, "Some Aspects of the Chinaman," *Belgravia,* March 1898, 358–63 and September 1887, 87–91; "Mengamok," *All the Year Round,* 28 May 1892, 514–16; and Pickering, "Chinese in the Straits of Malacca," 438–45.

    74. See "Chinese Labor Acts," *Leisure Hour,* July 1883, 448; and Acland, "A Lady's 'American Notes,'" 407.

    75. Albert Dorrington, "The Face of Typhoo Shang," *Pall Mall Magazine,* vol. 46, no. 209, 490–93; "The Chinese Returning to America," *Leisure Hour,* January 1898, 199; "Americans and the Chinese," *Leisure Hour,* January 1900, 280–82; "Immigration Limitation," *Leisure Hour,* April 1897, 404; "San Francisco," *Leisure Hour,* October 1883, 635; "Chinese in the United States,"

Leisure Hour, July 1884, 444; "John Chinaman in America," *All the Year Round,* December 10, 1881, 321–25; Jack London, "Yellow Handkerchief," *Pall Mall Magazine,* vol. 36, no. 149, 333–39.

76. In addition to the titles already cited, see F. Thorold Dickson, "Broken China," *Belgravia,* September 1898, 198–200; Mayne Lindsay, "The Missionary," *Pall Mall Magazine,* vol. 34, no. 137, 66–72; Charles C. Rothwell, "The Chinaman's Spider," *Belgravia,* November 1887, 178–87; J. Arbuthnot Wilson, "The Chinese Play at the Haymarket," *Belgravia,* Christmas Annual, 1880, 90–100; V. D., "Lao Ren, a Chinese Story," *Argosy,* April 1900, 470–75. Fiction about Chinese workers includes Dorrington, "The Face of Typhoo Shang"; "Qwee," *Pall Mall Magazine,* May 1895, 134–51, June 1895, 243–56; Denham, "Yan."

77. C. E. Meetkerke, "The Opium Poppy," *Argosy,* September 1882, 229. See also W. J. Gordon, "The Ports of London," part 2, December 1898, 93; "Under the Hammer: Foreign and Colonial Produce," *All the Year Round,* 11 September 1875, 564–69; and Rudyard Kipling, "In an Opium Factory," in *The Writings in Prose and Verse of Rudyard Kipling* (New York: Charles Scribner's and Sons, 1899), 433–41.

78. Captain Lindsay Anderson, *A Cruise in an Opium Clipper* (London: George Allen and Unwin, 1891), reprinted 1935; and *Among Typhoons and Pirate Craft* (London: Chapman and Hall, 1892), 60–62, 129–30.

79. Albert Dorrington, "The Opium Dealers: Stories of a South Sea Buccaneer," *Pall Mall Magazine,* vol. 42, no. 185, 332–41.

80. The *Nineteenth Century* published a series of influential essays on the history and morality of the trade, including Rutherford Alcock, "Opium and Common Sense" (December 1881, 855–68); Alexander J. Arbuthnot, "The Opium Controversy" (March 1882, 403–13); James Fitzjames Stephen, "The Opium 'Resolution'" (June 1891, 851–56); Storrs Turner, "Opium and England's Duty," (February 1882, 242–53); and James Fitzjames Stephen, "The Opium 'Resolution,'" (June 1891, 851–56). Also of note are several accounts in the *London Times* such as "The China Opium Trade" by "N. C.," a Chinese, Resident at present in London" (6 July 1874, 4); George Birdwood, "The Morality of Opium (6 December 1881, 9) and "The Opium Question (20 January 1882, 3); J. Llewelyn Davis (20 January 1882, 3); John Attfield, "The Opium Question" (3 February 1882, 411); as well as two essays in *Leisure Hour,* "Opium in China" (vol. 39, 1890, 211–12) and "Opium as a Medium of Exchange" (vol. 48, 1891, 789). Late-nineteenth- and early-twentieth-century books on the subject include Hill, *Indo-Chinese Opium Trade* (1884); Rowntree, *Imperial Drug Trade* (1905); Turner, "Opium and England's Duty" (1876); and Tinling, *Poppy-Plague and England's Crime* (1876).

81. Anderson, *Indo-Chinese Opium Trade,* 44–45; Bishop, "Sketches in the Malay Peninsula," 22, 98, 100; "Opium Public-Houses in London and Shanghai," *Friend of China,* November 1884, 219–21; J. D. Vaughan, *The Manners and Customs of the Chinese of the Straits Settlements* (1879; New York: Oxford

University Press, 1971), 61–63. English writers produced numerous records of their trips to opium dens in San Francisco: Faithfull, *Three Visits to America,* 209; Acland, "A Lady's 'American Notes,'" 407; W. H. Gleandell, "Night Scenes in Chinatown, San Francisco," *Gentleman's Magazine,* June 1895, 576–84; Iza Duffus Hardy, "In China Town," *Belgravia,* November 1880, 217–26; Baron Henry Hussey Vivian Swansea, *Notes of a Tour in America* (London: Edward Standford, 1878), 133–51; H. H. Kane, "American Opium-Smokers," *Harpers,* reprinted in *Friend of China,* December 1881, 440–44; "Opium Smoking," *Bow Bells,* vol. 28, no. 705, 1878, 114. The *Friend of China* reprinted numerous stories from other publications about opium smoking in British colonies such as Hong Kong, Australia, and British Columbia. For some examples see *Friend of China,* May 1875, 99 and January 1885, 14; and J. Thompson, "Vice in Hong Kong," in *The Straits of Malacca, Indo-China, and China,* excerpted in *Friend of China,* February 1876, 311; Rev. G. Smith, *Illustrated Missionary News,* reprinted in *Friend of China,* April 1875, 51.

    82. Johnson, "Righteousness before Revenue," 309, 310–11. For other accounts of the SSOT, see Berridge and Edwards, *Opium and the People,* 173–94; and Geoffrey Harding, "The Anti-Opium Crusade," in *Opium Addiction, Morality and Medicine: From Moral Illness to Pathological Disease* (New York: St. Martin's Press, 1988), 31–37.

    83. *Friend of China,* July 1890, 281; August 1876, 60–61.

    84. See the translation of a Chinese anti-opium tract sold in Canton, "New Selection of Pearl River Letters," *Friend of China,* February 1876, 310; and "Opium Balled," translated by Rev. J. Sadler, London Missionary Society, Amoy: "The foreign fellows are exceedingly dangerous / They introduce opium—it is a fact! / The schemes of these foreigners are marvelous / To hurt us Chinamen, by means of the opium" (*Friend of China,* December 1875, 262–63). See also "Chinese Anti-Opium Action," *Friend of China,* December 1883, 299.

    85. In 1883, issues of the *Regions Beyond* printed illustrations of Indian opium production and large passages from an anti-opium speech in London by Mr. Tong King-sing (*Friend of China,* December 1883, 299). See also "New Selection of Pearl River Letters," reprinted in *Friend of China,* February 1876, 310.

    86. F. S. Turner, *British Opium Policy and Its Results to India and China* (London: Sampson Low, Marston, Searle, & Rivington, 1876), 279–83, 123–27.

    87. *Friend of China,* February 1881, 235; December 1883, 298–99. The engravings appear in the 20 October issue of the *Graphic.*

    88. *Friend of China,* August 1876, 60.

    89. *Friend of China,* August 1879, 374.

    90. Blue, "Opium for China," 45.

    91. See Stephen, "The Opium 'Resolution,'" 855, and Birdwood, "The Morality of Opium," 9.

    92. Such scenes were common in *Friend of China.*

93. *London Times,* July 6, 1875, 4.

94. "Opium Traffic," *Leisure Hour,* October 1881, 639–40. The story seems to refer to a similar statement made by the Chinese government's director of foreign relations, Li Hongzhang, quoted by Brook and Wakabayashi, *Opium Regimes,* 10. Brook and Wakabayashi conclude that "Li's appeal to the foreigners was phrased as morality, but his chief concern was to stop the drain of silver" (10–11).

95. Marx, "History of the Opium Trade," 19.

96. See Hardy, "In China Town," 218; Gleandell, "Night Scenes in Chinatown," 576; Samuel A. Barnett, "Man, East and West," *Nineteenth Century,* January 1892, 129; *Leisure Hour,* 27 September 1879, 623; L. A. L., *London Society,* September 1895, 261; Dickson, "Some Aspects of the Chinaman," *Belgravia,* March 1898, 362; and "Two Days in Canton," *All Year Round,* 5 October 1889, 325. For complementary pieces of fiction, see Boehm, "Up the Yangtsze," 272–88; Rothwell, "The Chinaman's Spider," 179–87; Denham, "Yan," 245–58; Mills, "The Chee Child," 646–49; V. D., "Lao Ren: A Chinese Story," 471–75.

97. "The Biography of a Chinaman: Lee Chew," *Independent,* 19 February 1903, reprinted in *Plain Folk: The Life Stories of Undistinguished Americans,* ed. David M. Katzman and William M. Tuttle Jr. (Urbana: University of Illinois Press, 1982), 167–68, 172.

98. W. E. B. Du Bois, *The Souls of Black Folk* (Boston: Bedford Books, 1997), 37.

99. "The Foreign Relations of China," *Fraser's Magazine,* March 1877, 359–73.

100. Editorial from *Shen Pao,* a Chinese-language paper published at Shanghai, reprinted as "A Chinese View of the Opium Question," *Friend of China,* August 1879, 374–76.

101. "What the Chinese Really Think of Europeans," *Fraser's Magazine,* March 1871, 399; "The Opium-Smokers," *Illustrated London News,* 1 August 1874, 99.

102. *London Times,* 6 July 1875, 4.

103. Turner, "Opium and England's Duty," *Nineteenth Century,* February 1882, 242–53. See also Turner's *British Opium Policy and Its Results to India and China,* 83–84, 87; Tinling, *Poppy-Plague and England's Crime,* 80; and Sir George Campbell's 1881 letter to the *London Times,* quoted by Wu, *The Chinese Opium Question,* 60; and the *Illustrated Missionary News,* quoted in *Friend of China,* December 1875, 264.

104. See "Under the Hammer: Foreign and Colonial Produce," *All the Year Round,* 11 September 1875, 565; "Opium Traffic with China," *Leisure Hour,* 10 May 1879, 304; and Davis, in his letter to the *London Times,* 3.

105. Fredric Jameson, "Modernism and Imperialism," in Terry Eagleton, Fredric Jameson, and Edward W. Said, *Nationalism, Colonialism, and Literature* (Minneapolis: University of Minnesota Press, 1990), 50–51.

106. Charles W. Wood, "In the Night-Watches," *Argosy,* February 1898, 198.

107. "Opium-Smoking in London," *London City Mission Magazine,* reprinted in *Friend of China,* September 1877, 20.

108. "The Opium-Smokers," *Illustrated London News,* 1 August 1874, 99.

109. James Platt, "Chinese London and Its Opium Dens," *Gentleman's Magazine,* September 1895, 273; Conan Doyle, "The Man with the Twisted Lip," in *The Annotated Sherlock Holmes,* vol. 1, ed. William S. Baring-Gould (New York: Clarkson N. Potter, 1967), 369. Similarly, see "London Opium Dens by a Social Explorer," *Good Works* 26 (1885): 190.

110. *All the Year Round,* 12 May 1866, 422–23. This story, which appeared while Dickens was the editor of *All the Year Round,* probably influenced the more famous *Mystery of Edwin Drood.*

111. For the etymology of the word *Lascar,* see Visram, *Ayahs, Lascars and Princes,* 231. For the stories of Lascars and Chinese sailors, see Charles Dickens, *The Mystery of Edwin Drood* (London: Oxford University Press, 1989); Gustave Dore and Blanchard Jerrold, *London: A Pilgrimage* (1872; New York: Benjamin Blom, 1968), 146–50; Rev. George Piercy, "Opium Smoking in London," *Methodist Recorder,* reprinted in *Friend of China,* September 1883, 239–42; J. Randal, "A Chinese Opium Den in East London," *London Society,* May 1884, 543–44; Wood, "In the Night-Watches," 191–223; Thomas Archer, *The Pauper, the Thief and the Convict* (New York: Garland Publishing, 1985), 131–34.

112. See Bishop, "Sketches in the Malay Peninsula," 17–23; "Mengamok," 514–17. See also Alatas, *Myth of the Lazy Native,* 43–51; and Kiernan, "British in Malaya," 83.

113. *Morning Advertiser,* reprinted in *Friend of China,* November 1884, 219; "Opium-Smoking in London," *London City Mission Magazine,* reprinted in *Friend of China,* September 1877, 19–20. See also A. C. W., "Opium-Smoking in Bluegate Fields," *Chemist and Druggist,* 15 September 1870, 259–61.

114. Pearl Fisher, "Opium Smoking in London," *Word and Work,* 9 December 1887, reprinted in *Friend of China,* January 1888, 1922; "A Night in an Opium Den," *Strand* 1 (1891): 624–27. Similarly, an intertitle tells us that the opium den in *Broken Blossoms* is populated by "Chinese, Malays, Lascars, where the orient squats at the portal of the West."

115. The common bed or mattress is a staple of opium den literature. The most famous examples include the dens in *Edwin Drood* and *Dorian Gray.*

116. The use of mixed-race characters similarly signifies the intimacy of imperial relations. Fisher claims that the dens in London are filled with "Chinese and Chino-Malayans" ("Opium Smoking in London," 19–22), while Wilde's opium den is presided over by a "half-caste" bartender "in a ragged turban and a shabby ulster" (*The Picture of Dorian Gray,* ed. Peter Ackroyd [New York: Penguin Books, 1985], 224). In Dore and Jerrold's *London: A Pilgrimage,* the Frenchmen accompany a policeman to an East End opium den populated by someone they call a "Lascar" but represent in the accompanying engraving as if he were Chinese (147–50).

117. There are a few exceptions, mostly among texts written expressly to denounce the trade, such as Fisher's "Opium Smoking in London," where one Chinese opium den patron tells the author that the drug is grown in China, "but you taught us to smoke; you brought it to us; you tempted us; now we love it, and grow it for ourselves" (193).

118. Chatter: Albert Woolf, "In an Opium Den," *Ragged School Union Magazine,* February 1868, 199; Walter Besant, *East London* (London: Chatto and Windus, 1903), 205. Compare Wilde's Malays, who also "chattered" (*Picture of Dorian Gray,* 223). For uses of the "jabber," see "A Scene at an Opium Den," *Daily Chronicle,* October 17, reprinted in *Friend of China,* January 1882, 28; and "Lazarus, Lotus-Eating," 425. For the opium den pidgin quoted, see "Travels in the East," part 7, *All the Year Round,* 12 April 1884, 493–94.

119. Platt, "Chinese London and Its Opium Dens," 272; L. A. L., "Reminiscences of a Visit to India and China," part 3, 249–50.

120. Wood, "In the Night-Watches," 208. For a similar scene and dialogue, see "London Opium Dens: Notes of a Visit to the Chinaman's East-End Haunts, by a Social Explorer," *Good Words,* vol. 26, 1885, 119–20.

121. I have found only three narratives in which English visitors admit to smoking opium when it was offered, A. C. W.'s, "Opium Smoking in Bluegate Fields"; Henry Hussey Vivian's *Notes of a Tour in America* (1878), 133–51; and the anonymous "A Night in an Opium Den" (1891).

122. "The Opium-Smokers," *Illustrated London News,* 1 August 1874, 99; *Bow Bells,* vol. 28, no. 705, 1878, 114; Hardy, "In China Town," 217–26; "London Opium Dens: Notes of a Visit to the Chinaman's East-End Haunts by a Social Explorer," 188–92; Platt, "Chinese London and Its Opium Dens," 272–82; Wood, "In the Night-Watches," 203–7. Four more articles about London dens appeared or reappeared in the *Friend of China:* "An Opium-Smoking Chinaman Drowned," January 1877, 110; "A Scene at an Opium Den," January 1882, 28; "Opium-Smoking in London," September 1877, 19–20; and "Smoking at the East End," October 1887, 172–74.

123. See "Travels in the East," 492–97; "Opium Smoking in London," *Friend of China,* February 1888, 51; A. C. W., "Opium Smoking in Bluegate Fields," 259–61; "A Chinese Opium Den in East London," *London Society,* May 1884, 543–44; "Lazarus, Lotus-Eating," 421–25; Vivian, *Notes of a Tour,* 133–51; Woolf, "In an Opium Den," 198–201; Fisher, "Opium Smoking in London," 192–94; Archer, *Pauper, the Thief, and the Convict,* 128–34; "East London Opium Smokers," *London Society,* vol. 14, 1868, 68–72; "A Night in an Opium Den," *Strand* 1 (1891); Dore and Jerrold, *London: A Pilgrimage,* 145–50; "Consumption of Opium in England," *Friend of China,* July 1879, 361–63; Piercy, "Opium Smoking in London"; "Opium Public Houses in London and Shanghai," *Morning Advertiser,* reprinted in *Friend of China,* November 1884, 219–21; "Opium Smoking in America and China," *Friend of China,* April 1882, 121 and May 1882, 157–60; H. H. Kane, "American Opium-Smokers," *Harper's Weekly,* reprinted in *Friend of China,* December 1881, 440–44; Wilde, *Picture*

of Dorian Gray; Conan Doyle, "The Man with the Twisted Lip"; Dickens, *Mystery of Edwin Drood.*

124. See Woolf, "In an Opium Den," 199.

125. Conan Doyle, "Man with the Twisted Lip," 368, 370.

126. In 1888, Fisher visited seven London opium dens and discovered that five of the den keepers lived with English women ("Opium Smoking in London," 194).

127. Ibid., 193–94.

128. Archer, *Pauper, the Thief, and the Convict,* 132. Compare the descriptions of the English women called "Mother Abdallah," "Cheeny (China) Emma," and "Lascar Sal" in "Lazarus Lotus-Eating" (423), as well as the prostitute in *Dorian Gray,* who has "a crooked smile, like a Malay crease" (225).

129. The same dynamics are at work in writings about the Chinese throughout the British Empire. See Lai, *Indentured Labor, Caribbean Sugar,* 100; Campbell, *Chinese Coolie Emigration,* 42–43; *Weekly Echo,* quoted in *Friend of China,* January 1885, 14; Cronin, *Colonial Casualties,* 64–65, 68–69, 78, 129–30; Ryan, *Ancestors,* 54; Cole, "John Chinaman Abroad," 448; and *Overland China Mail,* quoted in *Friend of China,* May 1875, 99.

130. See "The Opium Smokers," *Illustrated London News.*

131. James Fields, in *Dickens: Interviews and Recollections,* vol. 2, ed. Philip Collins (Totowa, N.J.: Barnes and Noble Books, 1981), 306–7.

132. My reading of the novel has been influenced by Eve Kosofsky Sedgwick's in *Between Men: English Literature and Male Homosocial Desire* (New York: Columbia University Press, 1985), 180–200.

133. Sigmund Freud, *An Outline of Psycho-Analysis,* quoted in J. Laplanche and J. B. Pontalis, *The Language of Psychoanalysis,* trans. Donald Nicholson-Smith (London: Hogarth Press, 1973), 119. See also Sigmund Freud, "Fetishism" and "Splitting of the Ego in the Defensive Process," in *Sexuality and the Psychology of Love,* ed. Philip Rieff (New York: Collier Books, 1963), 214–19, 220–23.

134. Mary Gertrude Mason, *Western Concepts of China and the Chinese, 1840–1876* (1939; Westport, Conn.: Hyperion Press, 1973), 114.

2. STRANGE BEDFELLOWS

1. Oscar Wilde, *The Complete Works of Oscar Wilde* (New York: Harper and Row, 1966), 139–40. Subsequent references are given in the text.

2. My analysis of opium and sexuality has been influenced by Eve Kosofsky Sedgwick, *Epistemology of the Closet* (Berkeley: University of California Press, 1990), 175, and *Between Men: English Literature and Male Homosocial Desire* (New York: Columbia University Press, 1985), 180–200.

3. On conflicts between the British imperial state, which favored continued Chinese immigration, and Australia, which was in favor of restrictions, see Persia Crawford Campbell, *Chinese Coolie Emigration to Countries within the British Empire* (London: P. S. King and Son, 1923), 57, 66, 129–30. See also

Jan Ryan, *Ancestors: Chinese in Colonial Australia* (South Fremantle, Western Australia: Fremantle Arts Centre Press, 1995), 54–55.

4. Peter Brooker and Peter Widdowson, "A Literature for England," in *Englishness: Politics and Culture,* ed. Robert Colls and Phillip Dodd (London: Croom Helm, 1986), 117, 122.

5. In terms of queer theory, see Sedgwick on Wilde, cited in note 2. As for postcolonial theory see Edward Said, *Orientalism* (New York: Pantheon Books, 1978), *Culture and Imperialism* (New York: Knopf, 1993), and his essay on Kipling ("Introduction," in *Kim* [New York: Penguin Books, 1989], 7–46).

6. Thomas F. Plowman, *Pall Mall Magazine,* January 1885, 39.

7. Kevin O'Brien, *Oscar Wilde in Canada* (Toronto: Personal Library, 1982), 158, 168–69, 170–73.

8. This review originally appeared in *Woman's World,* November 1888, but it is reprinted in Oscar Wilde, *Reviews by Oscar Wilde* (London: Methuen and Co., 1908), 327.

9. Wilde makes these claims in a typescript for "The English Renaissance" at the William Andrews Clark Memorial Library, UCLA.

10. For a discussion of the notion of an Aesthetic Empire see Curtis Marez, "The Other Addict: Oscar Wilde's Opium Smokescreen," *English Literary History* 64 (1997).

11. Frantz Fanon, *Black Skin, White Masks,* trans. Charles Lam Markham (New York: Grove Weidenfeld Press, 1967), 212. See also Fanon's "Racism and Culture," in *Toward the African Revolution* (New York: Grove Weidenfeld Press, 1967), 33–35.

12. *Leisure Hour,* 5 April 1880, 213–16.

13. Quoted by Walton Look Lai, *Indentured Labor, Caribbean Sugar: Chinese and Indian Migrants to the British West Indies, 1839–1918* (Baltimore: Johns Hopkins University Press, 1993), 213.

14. Anonymous, "A Day with an East-End Photographer," *Strand* (1891), 461.

15. W. J. Gordon, "The Ports of London I," *Leisure Hour,* 26.

16. G. R. Cole, "John Chinaman Abroad," *Fraser's Magazine,* October 1878, 450. Similarly, see F. Thorold Dickson, "Some Aspects of a Chinaman," *Belgravia,* March 1898, 89.

17. Kathryn Cronin, *Colonial Casualties: Chinese in Early Victoria* (Carleton, Victoria: Melbourne University Press, 1982), 128.

18. Alexander Saxton, *The Indispensable Enemy: Labor and the Anti-Chinese Movement in California* (Berkeley: University of California Press, 1995), 73–74, 168–69, 181–84, 213–18; Nayan Shah, *Contagious Divides: Epidemics and Race in San Francisco's Chinatown* (Berkeley: University of California Press, 2001), 158–78.

19. Cronin, *Colonial Casualties,* 128.

20. Lisa Lowe, *Immigrant Acts: On Asian American Cultural Politics* (Durham, N.C.: Duke University Press, 1996), 28.

21. Karl Marx, *Capital*, vol. 1, ed. Frederick Engels (New York: International Publishers, 1987), 77, 78–79.

22. Lary May, "The Chinese in Britain, 1860–1914," in *Immigrants and Minorities in British Society*, ed. Colin Holms (London: George Allen and Unwin, 1978), 115–16; Colin Holms, *John Bull's Island Immigration and British Society, 1871–1971* (Basingstoke, UK: MacMillan, 1988), 78–79.

23. *Fortnightly Review*, quoted by Cole, "John Chinaman Abroad," 450. See also May, "The Chinese in Britain, 1860–1914," 112–13.

24. Cole, "John Chinaman Abroad," 450, 457.

25. *All the Year Round*, 24 January 1880, 210.

26. Edmund Mitchell, "The Chinaman Abroad," *Nineteenth Century*, October 1894, 612–13, 617, 620.

27. Cole, "John Chinaman Abroad," 448, 457. The *London Times* made similar claims. See May, "The Chinese in Britain, 1860–1914," 112–13.

28. Dickson, "Some Aspects of a Chinaman," 88–89.

29. Quoted by O'Brien, *Oscar Wilde in Canada*, 62–63.

30. Clipping, no page number, William Andrews Clark Memorial Library, UCLA.

31. The William Andrews Clark Memorial Library, UCLA, holds the original drawing.

32. See, for example, the Beerbohm and Hodges drawings in Ellmann, 492–93.

33. E. H. Mikhail, *Oscar Wilde: Interviews and Recollections* (London: Macmillan, 1979), 2:299.

34. Captain Lindsay Anderson, *A Cruise in an Opium Clipper* (London: George Allen and Unwin, 1891), 177–79, 219. Similarly, in the wake of the Indian rebellions, English sailors continued to exact vengeance on the bodies of their Lascar colleagues by flogging them or forcing them to eat pork (Rozina Visram, *Ayahs, Lascars and Princes: Indians in Britain, 1700–1947* [Dover, N.H.: Pluto Press, 1986], 35).

35. A. C. W., "Opium-Smoking in Bluegate Fields," *Chemist and Druggist*, 15 September 1870, 260.

36. V. G. Kiernan, "The British in Malaya," in *The Lords of Humankind: Black Man, Yellow Man, and White Man in an Age of Empire* (Boston: Little, Brown and Company, 1969), 76–97, 122–31.

37. Dickson, "Some Aspects of the Chinaman," 361.

38. Cronin, *Colonial Casualties*, 75, 122, 128.

39. Quoted in ibid., 50.

40. Quoted by Campbell, *Chinese Coolie Emigration*, 110.

41. Ibid., 211.

42. Ronald Hyam, *Empire and Sexuality: The British Experience* (Manchester: Manchester University Press, 1990), 99–100; and *Elgin and Churchill at the Colonial Office, 1905–1908* (London: St. Martin's Press, 1968), 88.

43. Campbell, *Chinese Coolie Emigration,* 206. Campbell describes a subsequent panic concerning the Chinese in British Malaysia (24).

44. Rudyard Kipling, "The Gate of the Hundred Sorrows," *Civil and Military Gazette,* 26 September 1884, subsequently collected in *Plain Tales from the Hills* (New York: R. F. Fenno, 1899). Kipling's Calcutta sketches appeared in the *Pioneer* during the summer of 1888. They were subsequently collected in *The City of Dreadful Night* (not to be confused with an essay of the same name about Lahore) (New York: A. Gross and Company, 1899). "In An Opium Factory," *Pioneer* and *Pioneer Mail,* 16 and 17 April 1888, is collected in *The City of Dreadful Night.* Kipling's letter about San Francisco's Chinatown first appeared in the *Pioneer,* 6 and 7 December and the *Pioneer Mail,* 11 December 1889, collected in *From Sea to Sea: Letters of Travel* (New York: Charles Scribner's Sons, 1899). For further bibliographical information, see James McG. Stewart, *Rudyard Kipling: A Bibliographical Catalogue,* ed. A. W. Yeates (Toronto: University of Toronto Press, 1959).

45. According to Louis L. Cornell, Kipling supported government opium policy (*Kipling in India* [London: MacMillan Press, 1966], 93). See also Kipling's column for the *Civil and Military Gazette,* 15 April 1886, reproduced in *Kipling's India: Uncollected Sketches, 1884–88,* ed. Thomas Pinney (London: MacMillan Press, 1986), 158–60.

46. Rudyard Kipling, *Something of Myself and Other Autobiographical Writings,* ed. Thomas Pinney (New York: Cambridge University Press), 33.

47. Charles Carrington, *Rudyard Kipling: His Life and Work* (London: MacMillan, 1955,) 124.

48. Kiernan, "The British in Burma," 78–82.

49. Kipling, *From Sea to Sea,* Part I, *The Writings in Prose and Verse of Rudyard Kipling,* 243, 239, 268, 252–55, 280, 289, 326, 343.

50. Ibid., 326, 272–73, 274, 283–84, 343, 341.

51. Ibid., 277, 338, 339. See also 272–73.

52. Ibid., 343.

53. Ibid., 273, 337, 338.

54. Ibid., 339–40.

55. John A. McClure, *Kipling and Conrad: The Colonial Fiction* (Cambridge: Harvard University Press, 1981), 79; Said, *Culture and Imperialism,* 146–48; Carrington, *Rudyard Kipling,* 114; and Cornell, *Kipling in India,* 152.

56. Paul B. Rich, *Race and Empire in British Politics* (Cambridge: Cambridge University Press, 1990), 13, 17.

57. Sucheta Mazumdar, "Asian American Studies and Asian Studies: Rethinking Roots," in *Asian Americans: Comparative and Global Perspectives,* ed. Shirley Hune, Hyung-Chan Kim, Stephen S. Fugita, and Amy Ling (Pullman: Washington State University Press, 1991), 34.

58. Reginald Horsman, *Race and Manifest Destiny: The Origins of Racial Anglo-Saxonism* (Cambridge: Harvard University Press, 1981), 227, 292.

59. Dilip K. Basu, "Peripheralization of China," in *The World-System of Capitalism: Past and Present*, ed. Walter L. Goldfrank (Beverly Hills, Calif.: Sage Publications, 1979), 176–77, 182–85. Basu notes that the fortunes of the American traders John M. Cushing and John M. Forbes were made through partnerships with Chinese Hong merchants.

60. See chapter 10 of Henry Hussey Vivian Swansea's *Notes on a Tour of America* (London: Edward Standford, 1878). The quotation appears on 146.

61. Iza Duffus Hardy, "In China Town," *Belgravia*, November 1880, 217.

62. Captain Willard Glazier, *Peculiarities of American Cities* (Philadelphia: Hubbard Brothers Publishers, 1886), 464–65.

63. Hardy, "In China Town," 223.

64. Ibid., 223.

65. H. H. Kane, "American Opium-Smokers," *Harper's Weekly*, reprinted in *Friend of China*, December 1881.

66. Kipling, *From Sea to Sea*, Part II, 34.

67. Ibid., 35–36.

68. All quotes concerning Kipling's visit to Chinatown occur in chapter 24 of ibid., 51–55.

69. Similarly, the opium den proprietor in "The Gate of the Hundred Sorrows," Fung-Tching, is described as "a one-eyed little chap, not much more than five feet high, and both his middle fingers were gone" (298).

70. Just as Kipling places his opium den narrative in the service of white supremacy, in *Kim* he deploys opium as a means for reproducing the Indian empire. Kim's father was an opium addict, and the drug apparently contributed to his early death (4). Initially an emblem of the orphaned Kim's vulnerability in the world, opium eventually becomes an important tool in his imperial duties. In order to go undercover, at one point Kim must darken his skin. This is accomplished through a strange ritual in which a blind witch, Huneefa, stupefies him with opium smoke and then dyes his skin (214–16). Kim in turn uses opium to both fortify and disguise a fellow agent (244–45).

71. Kipling, *From Sea to Sea*, Part I, 272.

72. Ibid., 305.

73. Ibid., 341.

3. Anarchy in the USA

1. See Daniel Nugent, "Introduction," in *Rural Revolt in Mexico: U.S. Intervention and the Domain of Subaltern Politics*, ed. Daniel Nugent (Durham, N.C.: Duke University Press, 1998), 1–22.

2. John H. Coatsworth, "Measuring Influence: The United States and the Mexican Peasantry," in Nugent, *Rural Revolt*, 64–71. The quotation is from 70.

3. John Mason Hart, "Social Unrest, Nationalism, and American Capital in the Mexican Countryside, 1876–1920," in Nugent, *Rural Revolt*, 72–88.

4. Rubén Osorio, "Villismo: Nationalism and Popular Mobilization in Northern Mexico," in Nugent, *Rural Revolt,* 89–103.

5. Helen Delpar, *The Enormous Vogue of Things Mexican: Cultural Relations between the United States and Mexico, 1920–1935* (Tuscaloosa: University of Alabama Press, 1992).

6. I borrow the concept of the "image repertoire" from Roland Barthes, *Mythologies* (New York: Hill and Wang, 1972).

7. See Curtis Marez, "Signifying Spain, Becoming Comanche, Making Mexicans: Indian Captivity and the History of Chicana/o Popular Performance," *American Quarterly* 53:2 (June 2001).

8. For a brief discussion of Mexican marijuana production, traffic, and uses, see Richard J. Bonnie and Charles H. Whitebread, *The Marihuana Conviction: A History of Marihuana Prohibition in the United States* (Charlottesville: University of Virginia Press, 1974), 33. For the drug traffic through border towns in this period, see F. Arturo Rosales, *Pobre Raza: Violence, Justice, and Mobilization among Mexico Lindo Immigrants, 1900–1936* (Austin: University of Texas Press, 1999), 71–74; and Douglas W. Richmond, "Mexican Immigration and Border Strategy during the Revolution, 1910–1920," *New Mexico Historical Review* 57:3 (July 1982): 280.

9. Rosales, *Pobre Raza,* 71.

10. Cited in ibid., 72.

11. Manuel Gamio, *The Life Story of the Mexican Immigrant* (New York: Dover Publications, 1971 [1929]), 71–75.

12. See Hart, "Social Unrest," 74; Friedrich Katz, *The Secret War in Mexico: Europe, the United States and the Mexican Revolution* (Chicago: University of Chicago Press), 7–18.

13. More precisely, Fierro's mother was a "Magonista," a group I discuss later in this chapter. For more on Fierro, see chapter 5.

14. Interview with Josefina Fierro, 11 January 1995, VHS tape 1, Special Collections, Green Library, Stanford University. The interview was conducted by Albert Camarillo, Department of History, Stanford University. It is part of a biography of Josefina Fierro to be published by Camarillo.

15. See Rosales, *Pobre Raza,* 72, 97–98.

16. Ibid., 66–67, 72–73.

17. Ibid., 71, 87.

18. On my use of the concept of fetishism, see the conclusion of chapter 1.

19. See Richard Rudisill, ed., *Santa Fe Trails: The Postcard Archive Series* (Santa Fe: Museum of New Mexico Press, 1995); *The Burro,* compiled by Rudisill and Marcus Zaforano (Santa Fe: Museum of New Mexico Press, 1979); the collections at the New Mexico State Records Center and Archives (hereafter NMSRCA), indexed under the headings "Animals—Burros" and "Transportation"; the collection of picture postcards in the Historical Society of New Mexico Collection (hereafter HSNMC), NMSRCA, box 91-A, file no. 1, numbers 55045, 55227, 55170–55188.

20. For the history of the artist colonies, see Chris Wilson, *The Myth of Santa Fe: Creating a Modern Regional Tradition* (Albuquerque: University of New Mexico Press, 1997); Charles C. Eldredge, Julie Schimmel, and William H. Truettner, eds., *Art in New Mexico, 1900–1945: Paths to Taos and Santa Fe* (New York: Abbeville Press, 1986); Sylvia Rodriguez, "Art, Tourism, and Race Relations in Taos: Toward a Sociology of the Art Colony," *Journal of Anthropological Research* 45:1 (September 1989): 77–99; and Marta Weigle and Kyle Fiore, *Santa Fe and Taos: The Writer's Era, 1916–1941* (Santa Fe, N.Mex.: Ancient City Press, 1982).

21. See T. M. Pearce, ed., *Literary America, 1903–1934: The Mary Austin Letters* (Westport, Conn.: Greenwood Press, 1979), 203–4.

22. Willa Cather, *Death Comes for the Archbishop* (New York: Vintage Books, 1971), 59–64.

23. Frank G. Applegate, "Burros," "Old Juan Mora's Burro," and "Tomacito and the Burro," in *Native Tales of New Mexico* (Philadelphia: J. B. Lippincott, 1932), 59–62, 65–76, 153–58; Mary Austin, *The Land of Journeys' Ending* (London: George Allen and Unwin, 1924), frontispiece; Peggy Pond Church, *The Burro of Angelitos,* illustrated by Gigi Shaulf Johnson (New York: Suttonhouse, 1936).

24. Alice Corbin Henderson, *Red Earth: Poems of New Mexico* (Chicago: Ralph Fletcher Seymour, 1921), 43.

25. See Henry Herbert Knibbs's "Burro"; Lynn Riggs, "Morning Walk—Santa Fe"; Whitter Bynner, "New Mexican Desert"; and William Haskell Simpson, "Don Feliciano Garcia: Wood-Hauler," in *Turquoise Trail: An Anthology of New Mexico Poetry,* ed. Alice Corbin Henderson (Boston: Houghton Mifflin, 1928).

26. Weigle and Fiore, *Santa Fe and Taos,* 37–38. The film is housed at the NMSRCA.

27. See Rodriguez, "Art, Tourism, and Race Relations in Taos," 84–86; and Julie Schimmel, "The Hispanic Southwest," in Eldredge, Schimmel, and Truetter, *Art in New Mexico, 1900–1945,* 43–145.

28. For reproductions of these paintings, see Schimmel, "The Hispanic Southwest," 118, 120, 121, 137. My own reading has been influenced by her analysis on 116.

29. Mary Austin, "The Politeness of Cuesta La Plata" and "Business at Cuesta La Plata," in *One-Smoke Stories* (New York: Houghton Mifflin Company, 1934), 160–68, 200–210; Corbin Henderson, "Juan Quintana," in *Turquoise Trail,* 25–27.

30. Mary Austin and Frank G. Applegate, "Spanish Colonial Arts" (1934), unpublished manuscript, Austin Papers, Huntington Library, San Marino, California. See also Marta Weigle, "The First Twenty-Five Years of the Spanish Colonial Arts Society," in *Hispanic Arts and Ethnohistory in the Southwest: New Papers Inspired by the Work of E. Boyd,* ed. Marta Weigle, Claudia Larcombe, and Samual Larcombe (Santa Fe, N.Mex.: Ancient City Press, 1983),

194–96. Schimmel reproduces the paintings by Blumenschein (121), and Phillips (122).

31. Cather, *Death Comes for the Archbishop*, 28.

32. Weigle, "The First Twenty-Five Years," 181–203.

33. On state efforts to "revive" Mexican crafts and the resulting split labor market, see Sarah Deutsch, *No Separate Refuge: Culture, Class, and Gender on an Anglo-Hispanic Frontier in the American Southwest* (New York: Oxford University Press, 1994), 190–99.

34. Corbin Henderson, *Red Earth*, 43.

35. Mary Austin, "Mexicans and New Mexico," in *America in the Southwest: A Regional Anthology*, ed. T. M. Pearce and Telfair Hendon (Albuquerque: University of New Mexico Press, 1933), 35–36.

36. David R. Roediger, *Towards the Abolition of Whiteness* (New York: Verso Press, 1994), 64.

37. See "Sharecropping with Sheep," in *Tewa Basin Study*, vol. 3 (1935), reprinted in *Hispanic Villages of Northern New Mexico: A Reprint of Volume Two of the 1935 Tewa Basin Study*, ed. Marta Weigle (Santa Fe, N.Mex.: Lightning Tree, 1975), 213–22; and Deutsch, *No Separate Refuge*, 22–23.

38. Austin, "Mexicans and New Mexico," 39.

39. Two good examples are Blumenschein's "Plasterer," modeled on his handyman, Epimineo Tenorio, and Phillips's "Our Washerwoman's Family" (Schimmel, "The Hispanic Southwest," 121, 124; Rodriguez, "Art, Tourism, and Race Relations in Taos," 81–84).

40. See Corbin Henderson's poem "Juan Quitana" (*Red Earth*, 52, 43), as well as Cather's description of Juan Tellamantez in *The Song of the Lark*, ed. Sherrill Harbison (New York: Penguin Books, 1999 [1915]), 41.

41. Applegate, "Burros," 61.

42. T. M. Pearce, "Ina Sizer Cassidy: A Tribute," in *Presentation of the Gerald Cassidy Memorial Art Library*, Gallery of the College of Fine Arts, University of New Mexico, 25 January 1945 (Cassidy Family Portraits [CFP], arts and crafts folder 1, carton 13).

43. See the pamphlet *Over the Turquoise Trail*, vol. 1, no. 1 (1937), 28; and another of the same name, vol. 1, no. 1 (autumn 1938), by the New Mexico Writer's Guild (not an FWP publication, but edited by Cassidy), CFP, WPA file, box 8.

44. See photo 31, Santa Fe, 1923, CFP, Bancroft Library.

45. For the letter from the DAR secretary, see Tingley Papers, "Dispersal of 'Sit Down' Strikers from Governor's Office," file no. 272, NMSRCA.

46. "DAR Conclave Here Opposes World Union," *Santa Fe New Mexican*, 25 October 1950, no page, carton 14, Ina Sizer Cassidy clippings, file no. 2, CFP.

47. *New Mexico: A Guide to the Colorful State* (New York: Hastings House, 1940), photo facing page 269. Subsequent references are given in the text.

48. See *New Mexico: A Guide to the Colorful State,* revised by Joseph Miller (New York: Hastings House, 1962).

49. See Ina Sizer Cassidy, "The Smoke of a Thousand Dreams" file (no page numbers), carton 2, CFP. Courtesy of the Bancroft Library, University of California, Berkeley.

50. See the uncataloged state penitentiary records for the 1920s, NMSRCA.

51. Ibid. See also the state penitentiary's annual reports, NMSRCA.

52. Edmundo Delgado, "New Mexico's First Prison: The Largest Brick Plant in the West," *Round the Roundhouse,* 28 May–25 June 1993, 10.

53. See William E. Tydeman, "A New Deal for Tourists: Route 66 and the Promotion of New Mexico," *New Mexico Historical Review* 66:2 (April 1991): 211, 213, 15; and Rodriguez, "Art, Tourism, and Race Relations in Taos," 90.

54. Marta Weigle, "Finding the 'True America': Ethnic Tourism in New Mexico during the New Deal," in *Folklife Annual 1988–89,* ed. James Hardin and Alan Jabbour (Washington, D.C.: Smithsonian Institute, 1989), 63.

55. See Tydeman, "A New Deal for Tourists," 206, 211–13; and the Tingley Papers, State Publicity Program, file no. 237, NMSRCA.

56. Tydeman, "A New Deal for Tourists," 212–13.

57. "Memorandum for Publicity Bureau," Tingley Papers, State Publicity Program, file no. 236, NMSRCA.

58. Weigle, "Finding the 'True America,'" 61–66.

59. Richard Melzer, *Madrid Revisited: Life and Labor in a New Mexican Mining Camp in the Years of the Great Depression* (Santa Fe: Lightning Tree— Jene Lyon, 1976), 6.

60. See "Lights over Madrid, New Mexico" (1935), unpublished photo essay, Margaret McKittrick Papers, NMSRCA.

61. Melzer, *Madrid Revisited,* 16.

62. Ibid., 18–19.

63. For further information on the Madrid strike, see ibid., 22–37; and Tingley Papers, "Madrid," file no. 260, NMSRCA.

64. See Harry R. Rubenstein, "The Great Gallup Coal Strike of 1933," *New Mexico Historical Review* (July 1977): 173–91; Tingley Papers, "Gallup Coal Strike," file nos. 253–68, NMSRCA; Melzer, *Madrid Revisited,* 6. For other actions, see Tingley Papers, "Madrid," file no. 260, and "El Paso Electric Co. Strikes," file no. 258. In addition, under Tingley's administration strikes also occurred in the mines of Dawson, near Raton in northeast New Mexico (Richard Melzer, "A Death in Dawson: The Demise of a Southwestern Company Town," *New Mexico Historical Review* [October 1980]: 309–30; and Carlos J. Craig "The Unionization of the Mines in Dawson, New Mexico," masters' thesis, New Mexico Highlands University, 1970).

65. Deutsch, *No Separate Refuge,* 166, 173. Researchers for the Tewa Basin Study, vol. 2 (reprinted as *Hispanic Villages of Northern New Mexico,* ed. Marta Weigle) noted in 1935 that many villages in the region, including those

whose men worked as miners, had active chapters of La Liga (41, 44, 51, 61, 78, 85, 196, 104, 110).

66. See Rubenstein, "The Great Gallup Coal Strike of 1933," 177, 181, 188; and Melzer, *Madrid Revisited,* 22, 36.

67. In Gallup in 1935, one policeman and two miners were killed when state police teargassed a group of protesters and fired into the crowd (see the Tingley Papers, Gallup Strike files).

68. See the letters of protest from Liga members to Governor Tingley protesting the use of the state militia ("Madrid," file no. 260, Tingley Papers, NMSRCA).

69. Both a copy of the strikers' demands and the mass-meeting flyer are in the Tingley Papers, "Dispersal of 'Sit Down' Strikers from Governor's Office," file no. 272.

70. Ibid.

71. See Gallup Defense Committee pamphlet, Tingley Papers, *Gallup Coal Strike,* file no. 266; and *Albuquerque Journal,* 8 April 1937, 1. This last story concerns a group called the "Anti-Communist Association of New Mexico." For the use of private security forces, see the telegram from Nicholas Fontecchio concerning the Madrid strike (Tingley Papers, "Madrid," file no. 260), as well as Melzer, *Madrid Revisited,* 24, 33–35.

72. F. O. Matthiessen, "The New Mexican Workers' Case," *New Republic,* 8 May 1935, 363.

73. Quoted by Rosales, *Pobre Raza,* 19. See also Neil Foley, *The White Scourge: Mexicans, Blacks, and Poor Whites in Texas Cotton Culture* (Berkeley: University of California Press, 1997), 56.

74. Alan Knight, "The United States and the Mexican Peasantry, circa 1880–1940," in Nugent, *Rural Revolt,* 25–63.

75. Albert B. Fall, "The Crisis in Mexico and Its Cause," *Leslie's Illustrated Weekly Newspaper,* 14 August 1913, 151, 160.

76. See John R. Chávez, *The Lost Land: The Chicano Image of the Southwest* (Albuquerque: University of New Mexico Press), 74–76.

77. Ibid., 76–77.

78. For the influence of anarchism in revolutionary Mexico City, see John M. Hart, "The Urban Working Class and the Mexican Revolution: The Case of the Casa del Obrero Mundial," *Hispanic American Historical Review* 58:1 (1978): 1–20.

79. Tom Bottomore, ed., with Lawrence Harris, V. G. Kiernan, and Ralph Miliband, *A Dictionary of Marxist Thought* (Cambridge: Harvard University Press, 1983), 18–19, 476.

80. Emilio Zamora, *The World of the Mexican Worker in Texas* (College Station: Texas A&M University Press, 1993), 84.

81. For information on the Plan de San Diego and its consequences, see Chávez, *Lost Land,* 79–82; David Montejano, *Anglos and Mexicans in the Making of Texas, 1836–1986* (Austin: University of Texas Press, 1987), 117–25;

Robert J. Rosenbaum, *Mexicano Resistance in the Southwest* (Dallas: Southern Methodist University Press, 1981), 50–52; and Zamora, *World of the Mexican Worker,* 81–84.

82. Rosales, *Pobre Raza,* 15–16.

83. Reproduced in Paul J. Vanderwood and Frank N. Samponaro, *Border Fury: A Picture Postcard Record of Mexico's Revolution and U.S. War Preparedness, 1910–1917* (Albuquerque: University of New Mexico Press, 1988), 98.

84. See interviews with Columbus residents, 1936–37, WPA file no. 102, NMSRCA.

85. Hart, "Social Unrest," 79–80; and Knight, "The Working Class and the Mexican Revolution, c. 1900–1920," *Journal of Latin American Studies* 16: 65–68.

86. See Foley, *White Scourge,* 57; Zamora, *World of the Mexican Worker,* 91; and Douglas Monroy, *Rebirth: Mexican Los Angeles from the Great Migration to the Great Depression* (Berkeley: University of California Press, 1999), 221–22.

87. For Pallares and the UMW, see Philip Stevenson, "Deporting Jesus," *Nation,* 18 July 1936; Melzer, *Madrid Revisited,* 23, 34; and Harry R. Rubenstein, "Political Repression in New Mexico: The Destruction of the National Miners' Union in Gallup," in *Labor in New Mexico: Unions, Strikes, and Social History since 1881,* ed. Robert Kern (Albuquerque: University of New Mexico Press), 116, 120. For a general study of similar actions in the Southwest, see D. H. Dinwoodie, "Deportation: The Immigration Service and the Chicano Labor Movement in the 1930s," *New Mexico Historical Review* 52:3 (July 1977): 193–206.

88. See Bonnie and Whitebread, *The Marihuana Conviction,* 32–52.

89. See ibid. and "The Forbidden Fruit and the Tree of Knowledge: An Inquiry into the Legal History of American Marijuana Prohibition," *Virginia Law Review* 56:6 (October 1970): 1048–63; Lester Grinspoon, *Marihuana Reconsidered,* 2d ed. (Cambridge: Harvard University Press, 1977), 10–29; John Helmer, "Mexicans and Marijuana," *Drugs and Minority Oppression* (New York: Seabury Press, 1975), 54–79; Jerome L. Himmelstein, *The Strange Career of Marihuana: Politics and Ideology of Drug Control in America* (Westport, Conn.: Greenwood Press, 1983), 49–75; Patricia A. Morgan, "The Making of a Public Problem: Mexican Labor in California and the Marijuana Law of 1937," in *Drugs in Hispanic Communities,* ed. Ronald Glick and Joan Moore (New Brunswick, N.J.: Rutgers University Press, 1990), 233–51; David F. Musto, *The American Disease: Origins of Narcotic Control* (New Haven: Yale University Press, 1973), 210–29; and Henry O. Whiteside, *Menace in the West: Colorado and the American Experience with Drugs, 1873–1963,* (Denver: Colorado Historical Society, 1997), 47–48, 52–54, 63–66, 82.

90. *Taxation of Marihuana: Hearings before the Committee on Ways and Means, House of Representatives, H.R. 6385,* 27 April–4 May 1937, 90 (here-

after cited as *TM Hearings*). For similar claims, see 18 and 37. The *Oxford English Dictionary* indicates, moreover, that in the 1920s the word *marijuana* was defined as a distinctly Mexican drug (*OED*, entry for "muggle," slang for marijuana).

91. For testimony that bears out these sensational generalizations, see *TM Hearings*, 45, 32, 38, 33, 123–24.

92. Quoted by Grinspoon, *Marihuana Reconsidered*, 17.

93. See Francisco E. Balderrama and Raymond Rodriguez, *Decade of Betrayal: Mexican Repatriation in the 1930s* (Albuquerque: University of New Mexico Press, 1995), 18–19, 139; and Mark Reisler, "Always the Laborer, Never the Citizen: Anglo Perceptions of the Mexican Immigrant during the 1920s," in *Between Two Worlds: Mexican Immigrants in the United States*, ed. David G. Gutierrez (Wilmington, Del.: A Scholarly Resources Inc. Imprint, 1996), 45–85.

94. *TM Hearings*, 33.

95. Michel Foucault, *The History of Sexuality*, vol. 1, *An Introduction* (New York: Vintage Books, 1990), 139–41.

96. Aihwa Ong, "The Gender and Labor Politics of Postmodernity," in *The Politics of Culture in the Shadow of Capital*, ed. Lisa Lowe and David Lloyd (Durham, N.C.: Duke University Press, 1997), 71–72.

97. "The Narcotic Invasion of America," *Washington Herald*, 10 April 1937, quoted in *TM Hearings*, 88.

98. "Handling of a Cash Crop," Regional Bulletin no. 46, Conservation Economics Series no. 19 (July 1937), U.S. Department of Agriculture, reprinted in Weigle, *Hispanic Villages of Northern New Mexico*, 223–34.

99. Tey Diana Rebolledo, ed., *Nuestras Mujeres: Hispanas of New Mexico, Their Images and Their Lives, 1582–1992* (Albuquerque: El Norte Publications, 1992).

100. Rosaura Sánchez, *Telling Identities: The Californio Testimonios* (Minneapolis: University of Minnesota Press, 1995), 194–96.

101. Deutsch, *No Separate Refuge*, 185–86.

102. Ibid, 182–83.

103. See also Camille Guerin-Gonzales, *Mexican Workers and American Dreams: Immigration, Repatriation, and California Farm Labor, 1900–1939* (New Brunswick, N.J.: Rutgers University Press, 1994), 79.

104. Out of a total of 53 prisoners, 4 are listed as "American," 1 as an "Amerc. Negro" *[sic]*. Of the remaining 48, 45 are marked as "Mexican," with 8 born in Mexico and the rest born in New Mexico or some other U.S. state. During this same period, only one woman charged with marijuana possession appears on penitentiary rap sheets and her nationality is listed as "American." See the uncataloged state penitentiary records, 1930–39, NMSRCA.

105. About half of the prisoners were arrested between 1935 and 1938 during peak years of La Liga activities throughout northern New Mexico and Colorado, and strikes in the mines of Madrid, Terrero, and Dawson. And arrests

were concentrated in labor activist counties with 14 in Bernalillo, 4 in Santa Fe, 6 in Colfax, and 3 in Rio Arriba.

106. Four miners were imprisoned between 1933 and 1936. Two of them received sentences of one to two years. The longer sentences are unique among cases involving mere possession, and were usually reserved for those convicted of selling the drug.

107. Montejano, *Anglos and Mexicans*, 205.

108. See the annual *New Mexico State Penitentiary, Santa Fe, Report of Board of Commissioners and Superintendent to the Governor of New Mexico*, which includes a prisoner "Occupation Report"; and the U.S. Prison Industries Reorganization Administration, *The Prison Labor Problem in New Mexico* (Washington, D.C.: U.S. Government Printing Office, 1938).

109. U.S. Prison Industries Reorganization Administration, *The Prison Labor Problem in New Mexico*, 6.

110. Governor's press release, 31 August 1998 (http://www.governor.state. nm.us/hotissues/news/8-31-98PrisonClosing.htm).

111. *Who Is in New Mexico's Prisons?*, Working Paper 15, Institute for Social Research, University of New Mexico, July 1996; and "Statistical Information: Ten Most Common Offenses among Incarcerated Males and Females FY99," *Corrections Department Annual Report*, 1998–99. (http://www.state. nm.us/corrections/anrpt68.html).

112. See *Who Is in New Mexico's Prisons?*

113. "Corrections Industries," *Corrections Department Annual Report*, 1998–99.

114. Ibid.

115. Ibid.

116. See petitions from League chapters in Bernalillo County and Albuquerque, Tingley Papers, "Gallup Strike, May 1935," file no. 255, and "Strike against El Paso Electric Co., May 1935," file no. 253.

117. Stevenson, "Deporting Jesus," 68–69.

118. Tingley Papers, "Gallup Strike, May 1935," file no. 255.

119. Tingley Papers, "Dispersal of 'Sit Down' Strikers from Governor's Office," file no. 272.

120. This sentence is indebted to Ong, "Gender and Labor Politics of Postmodernity," 82.

121. Tingley Papers, "Dispersal of 'Sit Down' Strikers from Governor's Office," file no. 272.

122. Américo Paredes, *A Texas-Mexican Cancionero: Folksongs of the Lower Border* (Austin: University of Texas Press, 1995), 43.

123. María Herrera-Sobek, "The Theme of Drug Smuggling in the Mexican Corrido," *Revista Chicano-Riquena* 7:4 (1979): 49–61.

124. Aurora Lucero-White, "The Corrido and Other Poetic Compositions of New Mexico," unpublished manuscript, WPA files, Fray Angélico Chávez History Library, Palace of Governors, Santa Fe, New Mexico.

125. "Marijuana, La Soldadera," recorded in Los Angeles by Hermanos Banuelos (1929), *The Mexican Revolution: Corridos about the Heroes and Events 1910–1920 and Beyond*, Arhoolie Folklyric Records.

126. "La Marihuana," recorded by Trio Garnica-Ascencio, *Los Primeros Duetos Feminas, 1930–1955*, Arhoolie Folklyric Records.

127. Paredes, *Texas-Mexican Cancionero*, 43.

128. Ibid., 89–91. For variants, see "The Francisco Villa Cycle," CD 2, *The Mexican Revolution*, Arhoolie Folkloric Records.

129. Ong, "Gender and Labor Politics of Postmodernity," 62.

130. David Lloyd and Lisa Lowe, "Introduction," in Lowe and Lloyd, *Politics of Culture in the Shadow of Capital*, 23.

4. LAPD, THE MOVIE

1. Anthony Quinn, *The Original Sin: A Self-Portrait* (Boston: Little, Brown and Company, 1972).

2. Ibid., 9–11.

3. Quoted by the *Los Angeles Times*, 4 June 2001, sec. 1, 1.

4. *The Plainsman* was not Quinn's first film, but it did give him his largest role to date. See *Original Sin*, as well as Quinn's second autobiography, with Daniel Paisner, *One Man Tango* (New York: HarperCollins, 1995), 9–11.

5. Quinn, *Original Sin*, 23–24.

6. Quinn, *One Man Tango*, 13.

7. Ibid., 16–17.

8. Ibid., 188. For the criminalization of *pachucos* as marijuana addicts, recall not only Quinn's remarks to his doctor but see also the news clippings collected by Carey McWilliams, 1930–40, UCLA Research Library, Microfilm HV6439.U5 L89m.

9. Jon Lewis, "'We Do Not Ask You to Condone This': How the Blacklist Saved Hollywood," *Cinema Journal* 39:2 (2000): 3–30.

10. Quoted by Lewis, "'We Do Not Ask You to Condone This,'" 14. See also 8 and note 16. "I used to pass long hours discussing Marxist theories [with Lawson] and I was often swayed by his arguments" (Quinn, *One Man Tango*, 188).

11. Quoted in Quinn, *One Man Tango*, 155.

12. Ibid., 182.

13. Here I quote from the MPA's mission statement, included in a 1944 pamphlet. See Thomas Schatz, *Boom and Bust: American Cinema in the 1940s* (Berkeley: University of California Press, 1996), 165.

14. Jeffrey Meyers, *Gary Cooper, American Hero* (New York: William Morrow, 1998), 207–13. Cooper was a friendly witness, but remained rather vague about the existence of communism in the industry, and did not name names, though several of his fellow MPA members did.

15. James J. Lorence, *The Suppression of Salt of the Earth: How Holly-*

wood, Big Labor, and Politicians Blacklisted a Movie in Cold War America (Albuquerque: University of New Mexico Press, 1999), 2–4, 88–90.

16. See Meyers, *Gary Cooper.* For Cooper and Del Rio, see Alicia I. Rodríquez-Estrada, "Dolores Del Rio and Lupe Velez: Images on and off the Screen, 1925–1944," in *Writing the Range: Race, Class, and Culture in the Women's West,* ed. Elizabeth Jameson and Susan Armitage (Norman: University of Oklahoma Press, 1997), 475–92.

17. Gerald Horne, *Class Struggle in Hollywood, 1930–1950: Moguls, Mobsters, Stars, Reds, and Trade Unions* (Austin: University of Texas Press, 2001), 115.

18. All quotations in this paragraph are from Carey McWilliams, "Hollywood Plays with Fascism," *Nation,* 29 May 1934, 323–24.

19. Ibid.

20. As McWilliams notes, the Hussars were one of three similar groups. For more information on these groups and on the appeal of fascism in 1930s Hollywood, see Anthony Slide, "Hollywood's Fascist Follies," *Film Comment* 27:4 (July–August 1991): 62–67.

21. Carey McWilliams, *It Can Happen Here: Active Anti-Semitism in Los Angeles* (Los Angeles: American League Against War and Fascism and the Jewish Anti-Nazi League of Southern California, 1934), from the Radical Pamphlets Collection, Northern Illinois University, Dekalb, Illinois, HX R355X no. 245.

22. Edward J. Escobar, *Race, Police, and the Making of a Political Identity: Mexican Americans and the Los Angeles Police Department, 1900–1945* (Berkeley: University of California Press, 1999), 226, 282.

23. Fricke's associate, W. J. Herwig, spoke on the need for tough drug enforcement before the Federated Church Brotherhoods of California on 10 June 1928 (*Los Angeles Times,* 11 June 1928, sec. 2, 10). See a story about publicity events staged by the International Narcotics Education Association during "Narcotics Education Week" (21 February 1933, sec. 2, 16), and another story on "Narcotics Week" in 1934 (20 February 1934, sec. 1, 10).

24. "Narcotic Peril Stressed," *Los Angeles Times,* 29 May 1929, sec. 2, 1–2.

25. Fricke, *American Citizenship and Law,* no publication information, 112–13, 117, 121, 128.

26. Mike Davis, *City of Quartz: Excavating the Future in Los Angeles* (New York: Verso Press, 1990), 144–20, 101. See also Robert Gottlieb and Irene Wolt, *Thinking Big: The Story of the Los Angeles Times, Its Publishers and Their Influence on Southern California* (New York: G. P. Putnam's Sons), 1977; and Carey McWilliams, *Southern California Country: An Island on the Land* (1946; Salt Lake City: Peregrine Smith Books, 1995).

27. Michael Rogin, *Blackface, White Noise: Jewish Immigration in the Hollywood Melting Pot* (Berkeley: University of California Press, 1996); Slide, "Hollywood's Fascist Follies," 62–67; and Horne, *Class Struggle in Hollywood,* especially 120–49.

28. Lary May, *Screening Out the Past: The Birth of Mass Culture and the Motion Picture Industry* (Chicago: University of Chicago Press, 1980), 182.

29. Davis, *City of Quartz,* 114.

30. *Mexicans in California,* report of Governor C. C. Young's Mexican Fact-Finding Committee (Sacramento: California State Printing Office, 1930), 90, 78–79.

31. Ibid., 87, 91.

32. Quoted by George J. Sánchez, *Becoming Mexican American: Ethnicity, Culture and Identity in Chicano Los Angeles, 1900–1945* (New York: Oxford University Press, 1993), 188.

33. The criminalization of Mexicans in California goes back to the mid-nineteenth century. See Shelley Streeby, "Joaquín Murrieta and the American 1848," in *Post-Nationalist American Studies,* ed. John Carlos Rowe (Berkeley: University of California Press, 2000), 160–96.

34. Escobar, *Race, Police, and the Making of a Political Identity,* 27.

35. This is one of the arguments McWilliams develops in "The Politics of Utopia," in *Southern California Country,* 273–94.

36. For evidence of arrest disproportions see table 30, covering the period from 1 July 1927 to 30 June 1929, in *Mexicans in California,* 202. On the following page see also table 32, "Total Arrests and Number of Mexicans Arrested by Los Angeles City Police, by Classification of Offenses, with Percentage Which Mexicans Represent of the Total, 1927–28" (from annual LAPD report).

37. Carey McWilliams, "California Labor: Total Engagement," and "California's Peculiar Institution," in *California: The Great Exception* (Westport, Conn.: Greenwood Press, 1949), 127–49, 150–70.

38. Escobar, *Race, Police, and the Making of a Political Identity,* 37–42, 49–51, 90–101.

39. See Davis, *City of Quartz,* 25–35; Escobar, *Race, Police, and the Making of a Political Identity,* 27, 31, 42–49, 69–70.

40. Escobar, *Race, Police, and the Making of a Political Identity,* 69–70.

41. For information on the Red Squad and antiradicalism in Los Angeles, see Gottlieb and Wolt, *Thinking Big,* 185–201; Horne, *Class Struggle in Hollywood,* 42–43; and McWilliams, *Southern California Country,* 289–94.

42. Horne, *Class Struggle in Hollywood,* 42–43.

43. Escobar, *Race, Police, and the Making of a Political Identity,* 87–88, 95–101.

44. For discussion of the American Legion's red-baiting role, see Gottlieb and Wolt, *Thinking Big.* For evidence of Klan activity against radicals, see "Cárcel para 15 Miembros del Ku-Klux-Klan," *La Opinión,* 12 December 1933, 1. The news report concerns Klan plans to launch an anticommunist raid in Long Beach.

45. Los Angeles reporter Harold Story, quoted by Gottlieb and Wolt, *Thinking Big,* 199.

46. "Marijuana Haul Made in Drug Raid," *Los Angeles Times*, 27 November 1927, sec. 2, 3.

47. *The Trend of Drug Addiction in California*, report to the California State Legislature (Sacramento: California State Printing Office, 1931), 23–24; *Report on Drug Addiction in California* (Sacramento: California State Printing Office, 1926), 20; *Report of the State Narcotic Committee*, 1 January 1929 (Sacramento: California State Printing Office, 1929), 9; and California State Senate Interim Narcotic Committee, *Report on Drug Addiction in California* (Sacramento: California State Printing Office, 1936), 30.

48. Report of the State Narcotic Committee to the California State Legislature, *Survey of Drug Addiction in California* (Sacramento: California State Printing Office, 1932), 31. Committee reports from previous years make similar claims. See *The Trend of Drug Addiction in California*, 1931, 14; and *Report on Drug Addiction in California*, 1926, 13–14.

49. Between 1927 and 1928, 41.3 percent of all those arrested for narcotics were Mexicans, or 99 out of a total of 240 (*Mexicans in California*, 203). According to police statistics reproduced in State Narcotic Committee report, *The Trend of Drug Addiction in California* (1931), for varying periods of time between 1925 and 1930, Mexicans made up more than 40 percent of all narcotics arrests in Los Angeles—more than any other group (15). Another survey by the committee reported that between 1 July 1931 and 30 June 1932, more than half of those arrested by the Los Angeles Narcotics Squad were Mexicans, or 315 out of a total of 579. Moreover, 60 percent of these arrests were for marijuana (*Survey of Drug Addiction in California*, 31, 26). The committee's report the following year noted that between 1931 and 1932, more than half of all Narcotics Squad arrests fell under the heading of "Foreign (largely Mexican)." See *Los Angeles Times*, 4 February 1930, sec. 1, 4. It is important to keep in mind, as Escobar *(Race, Police, and the Making of a Political Identity)* notes, that arrest rates do not reveal how many Mexicans were convicted of narcotics crimes, let alone how many actually used or trafficked in drugs. Moreover, given the history of LAPD corruption in Mexican neighborhoods documented by Escobar, we have reason to be skeptical concerning arrest rates. What these statistics *do* tell us, however, is how police power was mobilized.

50. Escobar, *Race, Police, and the Making of a Political Identity*, 28, 162–66; Gottlieb and Wolt, *Thinking Big*, 193–96, 219–25; Horne, *Class Struggle in Hollywood*, 23; and Joseph G. Woods, "The Legacy of August Vollmer," in *Law Enforcement in Los Angeles* (New York: Arno Press, 1974), ii.

51. "Police Show Jiu-Jitsu Tactics, Demonstrations Will Be Given at Coliseum," *Los Angeles Times*, 23 May 1933, sec. 2, 1. See also Jay Rand, "Hitlerites in Hollywood," *New Masses*, 23 July 1935, 29–30.

52. "Beach Policemen Don Prison Garb, Stage Costume of Stripes for Cops' Chorus of Santa Monica," *Los Angeles Times*, 4 February 1928, sec. 1, 6.

53. *Los Angeles Times*, 4 February 1930, sec. 2, 4; 13 February 1930, sec. 1,

6; 19 January 1931, sec. 2, 2; 4 February 1932, sec. 2, 2; 16 March 1934, sec.2, 2; and 29 April 1934, sec. 1, 17.

54. "Couple Held on Drug Charges," *Los Angeles Times*, 2 November 1928, sec. 2, 2.

55. See, for example, *Los Angeles Times*, 5 February 1929, sec. 2, 6; 10 December 1931, sec. 1, 13; and 14 September 1932, sec. 1, 9.

56. *Los Angeles Times*, 20 July 1931, sec. 2, 16. For similar *Times* reports, see "Official Eye on Hemp Growers," 30 November 1927, sec. 2, 10; and "Drug Traffic Struck Blow," 13 February 1930, sec. 1, 6.

57. *Los Angeles Times*, 6 March 1930, sec. 2, 7; 27 November 1927, sec. 2, 4; 4 February 1930, sec. 2, 4; 13 February 1939, sec. 1, 6.

58. In addition to the *Los Angeles Times* stories cited in the preceding paragraph, see "Six Arrested and Marihuana Ranch Found," 14 September 1932, sec. 1, 9; and "Officers Report Marihuana Find," 10 December 1931, sec. 1, 13.

59. "F. G. White, Former Venice Churchman, Trapped in Asserted Dope-Smuggling Ring," *Los Angeles Times*, 4 February 1932, sec. 2, 2.

60. Myra Nye, "County Federation of Women's Clubs Enlisted in Battle against Narcotic Evil." *Los Angeles Times*, 11 September 1934, sec. 2, 7.

61. "Marihuana Haul Made in Drug Raid," *Los Angeles Times*, 27 November, sec. 2, 3.

62. See *Mexicans in California*, 201–2. The report assumes that Mexicans make up 10 percent of the L.A. population but concludes that Mexican women made up 12.7 percent of prostitution arrests (for a total of 215) and 20.8 percent of "sex crimes" arrests (for a total of 5).

63. "A recurrent pattern emerges: the 'top' attempts to reject and eliminate the 'bottom' for reasons of prestige and status, only to discover, not only that it is in some way frequently dependent upon the low-Other... but also that the top *includes* that low symbolically, as a primary eroticized constituent of its own fantasy life. The result is a mobile, conflictual fusion of power, fear, and desire in the construction of subjectivity: a psychological dependence upon precisely those others which are being rigorously opposed and excluded at the social level. It is for this reason that what is socially peripheral is so frequently *symbolically* central" (Peter Stallybrass and Allon White, quoted in Stuart Hall, "What Is This 'Black' in Black Popular Culture?" in *Black Popular Culture*, ed. Gina Dent [Seattle: Bay Press, 1992], 33).

64. "Six Arrested and Marihuana Ranch Found," *Los Angeles Times*, 14 September 1932, sec. 1, 9.

65. See *Los Angeles Times*, 19 January 1931, sec. 2, 2; and 29 April 1934, sec. 1, 17.

66. All quotations and information from the story are in the *Los Angeles Times*, 4 February 1932, sec. 2, 2 (see note 59 above).

67. Ella Shohat, "Ethnicities-in-Relation: Toward a Multicultural Reading of American Cinema," in *Unspeakable Images: Ethnicity and the American*

Cinema, ed. Lester D. Friedman (Urbana and Chicago: University of Illinois Press, 1991), 234–35.

68. Nick Browne, "Race: The Political Unconscious in American Film," *East-West Film Journal* 6:1 (January 1992): 8. See also Miriam Hansen, *Babel and Babylon: Spectatorship in American Silent Film* (Cambridge: Harvard University Press, 1991), 255–56.

69. See Ana M. López, "Are All Latins from Manhattan?: Hollywood, Ethnography, and Cultural Colonialism," in Friedman, *Unspeakable Images,* 410.

70. See Adrienne L. McLean, "'I'm a Cansino': Transformation, Ethnicity, and Authenticity in the Construction of Rita Hayworth, American Love Goddess," *Journal of Film and Video* 44:3–4 (fall–winter 1992–93): 8–26; and Shari Roberts, "'The Lady in the Tutti-Frutti Hat': Carmen Miranda, a Spectacle of Ethnicity," *Cinema Journal* 32:3 (spring 1993): 3–25.

71. See Alfred Charles Richard Jr., *The Hispanic Image on the Silver Screen: An Interpretive Filmography from Silents into Sound, 1898–1935* (New York: Greenwood Press, 1992), 100, 234.

72. López, "Are All Latins from Manhattan?" 408.

73. For a good example, see *Broken Wing* (Paramount, 1932), which focuses on the beautiful Lolita (Lupe Vélez), who resists the advances of a local petty dictator named Captain Innocencio (Carrillo).

74. Richard, *Hispanic Image on the Silver Screen,* 178.

75. *Border Café* (RKO, 1937), research copy, Film and Television Library, UCLA.

76. Information on the film is from the *American Film Institute Catalogue,* http://afi.chadwyck.com. For a similar story, see the plot summary in the same source for *Border Law* (Columbia, 1931). The classic text on the Texas Rangers and Mexican reactions to them is Américo Paredes's *With His Pistol in His Hand: A Border Ballad and Its Hero* (Austin: University of Texas Press, 1970).

77. *American Film Institute Catalog.*

78. Douglas Monroy, *Rebirth: Mexican Los Angeles from the Great Migration to the Great Depression* (Berkeley: University of California Press), 120–21, 123; Vicki Ruiz, *Cannery Women/Cannery Lives: Mexican Women, Unionization, and the California Food Processing Industry, 1930–1950* (Albuquerque: University of New Mexico Press, 1987); Sánchez, *Becoming Mexican American,* 100, 201–3.

79. S. H. Bowman, "A Brief Study of Arrests of Mexicans in Los Angeles for a Twelve-Month Period," in *Mexicans in California,* 149.

80. Although it is estimated that Mexicans made up less than 10 percent of the total Los Angeles population in the late 1920s, between 1927 and 1928 Mexican women accounted for 20.3 percent of all women arrested for assault and battery (or 15 cases out of a total of 74) and 15 percent of those arrested for vagrancy (or 24 cases out of a total of 160) (see *Mexicans in California,* 201–2). Mexican women accounted for almost 14 percent of all women arrested for violating prohibition, more than 23 percent of those arrested for bootlegging,

almost 13 percent of those charged with prostitution, and more than 20 percent of those detained for other sex crimes (ibid.).

81. Contrast Virginia Wright Wexman, who asserts that in silent westerns the cantina girl represents the "new cash economy" ("The Family on the Land: Race and Nationhood in Silent Westerns," in Daniel Bernardi, ed., *The Birth of Whiteness: Race and the Emergence of U.S. Cinema* [New Brunswick, N.J.: Rutgers University Press, 1996], 158). Although suggestive, the claim obscures the cash economy's dependence on labor.

82. Juan Gómez-Quiñones, *Sembradores: Ricardo Flores Magón y El Partido Liberal Mexicano: A Eulogy and Critique* (Los Angeles: Aztlán Publications, Chicano Studies Center, University of California, Los Angeles, monograph no. 5, 1973), 26–27. See also Monroy, *Rebirth*, 219–21. For a primary text concerning women and the PLM, see Ricardo Flores Magón, *A la Mujer* (Oakland: Prensa Sembradora, 1974). For a critical assessment of this last document, see Emma A. Pérez, "'A la Mujer': A Critique of the Partido Liberal Mexicano's Gender Policy on Women," in *Between Borders: Essays on Mexicana/Chicana History*, ed. Adelaida R. Del Castillo (Encino, Calif.: Floricanto Press, 1990).

83. Manuel Gamio, *The Life Story of the Mexican Immigrant* (New York: Dover Publications, 1971 [1929]). I am indebted here to Sánchez's discussion of the interviews conducted for Gamio's work (*Becoming Mexican American*, 137–38).

84. For a discussion of "queer intimacy," see chapter 2.

85. "Isobel Sandoval" (Gloria Navas), quoted in Manuel Gamio, *Notes Gathered for His Book Mexican Immigration to the United States and Related Material, 1926–1928*, microfilm reel 2, interview 56, 5–6, Bancroft Library, University of California, Berkeley.

86. Carla Freccero, *Popular Culture: An Introduction* (New York: New York University Press, 1999).

87. Compare "Isobel Sandoval" in Gamio's *Life Story of the Mexican Immigrant* to the interview with Gloria Navas on which it is based. See Gamio, *Notes Gathered for His Book Mexican Immigration to the United States.*

88. Table 30, "Total Number of Prisoners Booked in Los Angeles County Jail, by Causes of Arrest, July 1, 1927, to June 30, 1928, Number of Mexican Prisoners, and Percentage Which Mexicans Represent of Total," in *Mexicans in California,* 201–2. Mexicans represent 23 percent of those booked for rape (or 55 of 237), 47.8 percent of those charged with prostitution (11 of 23), 12.5 percent of those charged with violating the Mann Act (3 of 24), and 10.6 percent of miscellaneous sex crimes. It should be recalled that Mexican men were also subject to arrest for violating the lodging ordinance if they lived with a woman out of wedlock.

89. "Official Eye on Hemp Growers," *Los Angeles Times,* 30 November 1927, sec. 2, 10.

90. Nye, "County Federation of Women's Clubs Enlisted in Battle against Narcotic Evil."

91. *Marihuana: Weed with Roots in Hell,* dir. Dwain Esper, Roadshow Attractions Co., 1936; released on video by Something Weird Video, Seattle, 1994. For histories of exploitation films in the United States, see Randall Clark, *At a Theater or Drive-in Near You: The History, Culture, and Politics of the American Exploitation Film* (New York: Garland Publishing, 1995); and Eric Schaefer, *"Bold! Daring! Shocking! True!": A History of Exploitation Films, 1919–1939* (Durham, N.C.: Duke University Press, 1999). For drug films in particular, see Schaefer, 228–42.

92. The "Latinnesss" of the characters of Nick and Tony is marked by their contrast with the blond young people that they prey on, but the drug dealers remain indeterminate in terms of race and ethnicity, perhaps combining stereotypical elements of the Italian gangster and the Mexican marijuana dealer.

93. Bret Wood, *Marihuana, Motherhood, and Madness: Three Screenplays from the Exploitation Cinema of Dwain Esper* (Lanham, Md.: Scarecrow Press, 1998), 321.

94. Examples include *Martyrs of the Alamo* (1915), *The Drug Terror* (1914), *Dope* (1914), *The Border Runner* (1915), *On the Border* (1915), *The Perilous Leap* (1917), *Border Raiders* (1917), and *The Drug Traffic* (ca. 1920). Most of these films have been lost, but their plots have been reconstructed on the basis of reviews in newspapers and trade magazines. See Richard, *Hispanic Image on the Silver Screen,* 117, 118–19, 140–41, 157, 203, 208, 272. For a brief discussion of the first film in the list, see Rosa Linda Fregoso, "Reproduction and Miscegenation on the Borderlands: Mapping the Maternal Body of Tejanas," in *Chicana Feminisms,* ed. Gabriela F. Arredondo, Aída Hurtado, Norma Klahn, Olga Nájera-Ramírez, and Patricia Zavella (Durham, N.C.: Duke University Press, 2003).

95. William Troy, "The Marquis de Villa," *Nation,* 2 May 1934, 316, 318.

96. Eve Kosofsky Sedgwick, *Between Men: English Literature and Male Homosexual Desire* (New York: Columbia University Press, 1993).

97. Hawks was initially assigned to direct *Viva Villa* and he in fact spent ten weeks filming in Mexico before he was replaced by Jack Conway. See Howard Hawks, in interview with Joseph McBride, *Hawks on Hawks* (Berkeley: University of California Press, 1982), 62–63.

98. Ibid., 62.

99. Ibid.

100. Ibid.

101. C. L. R. James, *American Civilization* (Cambridge, Mass.: Blackwell, 1983 [ca. 1950]), 123–24.

102. Ibid, 127.

103. This reading is indebted to Shelley Streeby's "Joaquín Murrieta and Popular Culture," in *American Sensations: Class, Empire, and the Production of Popular Culture* (Berkeley: University of California Press, 2002), 251–90.

104. *Motion Picture Daily,* 27 March 1934 (no page numbers), clipping, Margaret Herrick Library.

105. Slide, "Hollywood's Fascist Follies," 63.

106. Carl Gutiérrez-Jones, *Rethinking the Borderlands: Between Chicano Culture and Legal Discourse* (Berkeley: University of California Press, 1995).

107. In chapter 5 I analyze in greater detail the "diegetic illusion" in the context of Mexican Los Angeles.

108. *Los Angeles Times*, 19 January 1931, sec. 2, 1.

109. *Los Angeles Times*, 13 February 1930, sec. 2, 2; emphasis added.

110. *Los Angeles Times*, 30 November 1927, sec. 2, 10.

111. *Los Angeles Times*, 20 May 1932, sec. 1, 6.

5. LA CUCARACHA IN BABYLON

1. See Nick Browne, "Race: The Political Unconscious in American Film," *East-West Film Journal* 6:1 (January 1992): 5–6; Jane Gaines, *Fire and Desire: Mixed-Race Movies in the Silent Era* (Chicago: University of Chicago Press, 2001), 1–2, 6–8; and Ella Shohat, "Ethnicities-in-Relation: Toward a Multicultural Reading of American Cinema," in *Unspeakable Images: Ethnicity and the American Cinema*, ed. Lester D. Friedman (Urbana and Chicago: University of Illinois Press, 1991), 215. For an excellent collection that addresses this topic, see Daniel Bernardi, ed., *The Birth of Whiteness: Race and the Emergence of U.S. Cinema* (New Brunswick, N.J.: Rutgers University Press, 1996).

2. For excellent studies of the representation of Mexicans in silent and early sound films, see Chon A. Noriega's "Birth of the Southwest: Social Protest, Tourism, and D. W. Griffith's *Ramona*," in Bernardi, *Birth of Whiteness*, 203–26; and "Citizen Chicano: The Trials and Titillations of Ethnicity in the American Cinema, 1935–1962," *Social Research* 58:2 (summer 1991): 413–38. For Hollywood's influence on Mexicans in Los Angeles, see Douglas Monroy, *Rebirth: Mexican Los Angeles from the Great Migration to the Great Depression* (Berkeley: University of California Press, 1999), 165–207; and Vicki L. Ruiz, "'Star Struck': Acculturation, Adolescence, and the Mexican American Woman, 1920–1950," in *Building with Our Hands: New Directions in Chicana Studies*, ed. Adela de la Torre and Beatríz Pesquera (Berkeley: University of California Press, 1993), 109–29. The absence of a sustained study of the silent "greaser film" is particularly noteworthy (Bernardi, "Introduction," in *Birth of Whiteness*, 9). For an important exception, see Blain P. Lamb, "The Convenient Villain: The Early Cinema Views the Mexican American," *Journal of the West* 14 (October 1975): 75–89. Although in this chapter I focus on silent and early sound films, sustained considerations of what I am calling the "Mexican question" are also missing from studies of subsequent periods.

3. *Los Angeles Times*, 3 June 1916, sec. 2, 3.

4. Colin M. MacLachlan, *Anarchism and the Mexican Revolution: The Political Trials of Ricardo Flores Magón in the United States* (Berkeley: University of California Press, 1991), 60, 80, 81. The brothers were also convicted of indecency in a second Los Angeles trial in 1918. See also Edward J. Escobar, *Race, Police, and the Making of a Political Identity: Mexican Americans and the Los*

Angeles Police Department, 1900–1945 (Berkeley: University of California Press, 1999), 54–61.

5. For brief discussions of the commune and its inhabitants' critique of marriage, see Juan Gomez-Quiñones, *Sembradores: Ricardo Flores Magón y El Partido Liberal Mexicano: A Eulogy and Critique* (Los Angeles: Aztlán Publications, Chicano Studies Center, University of California, Los Angeles, 1973), 219–20.

6. See the *Los Angeles Times* story about the brothers' conviction in 1912 for violating the Neutrality Act because they supposedly published in the United States calls for volunteers to join in the revolution. The headline reads "Howling Mob Threatens When Magons Convicted" (23 June 1912, sec. 2, 1). The paper recalled this "mob" a few years later in its coverage of the Magóns' trial in 1916 ("One-time Mob Leader Rejects Questions, Stamps Feet," 2 June 1916, sec. 2, 2). At the time of their arrest the *Times* reported that the police were rushed by a dozen Mexican women who waved their arms "threateningly" and assailed the officers with "foul language" (19 February 1916, sec. 2, 1).

7. El Congreso de Pueblos de Hablan Español was organized in 1939 by Fierro, Luisa Moreno, and others. Most discussions of Fierro's life are based on Mario T. Garcia's *Mexican Americans: Leadership, Ideology, and Identity, 1930–1960* (New Haven: Yale University Press, 1989), 145–59. See, for example, brief discussions of Fierro and El Congreso in Escobar, *Race, Police, and the Making of a Political Identity,* 150–54; Monroy, *Rebirth,* 258–59; and George J. Sánchez, *Becoming Mexican American: Ethnicity, Culture and Identity in Chicano Los Angeles* (New York: Oxford University Press, 1993), 246–47. Like Vicki L. Ruíz's account (*From Out of the Shadows: Mexican Women in Twentieth-Century America* [New York: Oxford University Press, 1998], 94–98), however, my discussion is based on a videotaped interview with Fierro, conducted by Albert Camarillo of the history department at Stanford, housed at the Green Library, Stanford University. It is part of a biography of Josefina Fierro to be published by Camarillo.

8. See Ethel Duffy Turner, *Revolution in Baja California: Ricardo Flores Magón's High Noon* (Detroit: Blaine Ethridge Books, 1981).

9. See the publicity photograph of Paul Fierro with Mae West in the Fierro photograph collection, Green Library, Stanford University.

10. Luisa Moreno, according to Fierro, also married a screenwriter. See the Camarillo interview.

11. Fierro, Camarillo interview.

12. "Three Burbank Men Arrested in Race Quarrel," *Los Angeles Times,* 30 November 1927, sec. 1, 16.

13. Camille Guerin-Gonzales, *Mexican Workers and American Dreams: Immigration, Repatriation, and California Farm Labor, 1900–1939* (New Brunswick, N.J.: Rutgers University Press, 1994), 77–94. See also Francisco E. Balderrama and Raymond Rodríguez, *Decade of Betrayal: Mexican Repatriation in the* 1930*s* (Albuquerque: University of New Mexico Press, 1995); and Abra-

ham Hoffman, *Unwanted Mexicans in the Great Depression: Repatriation Pressures, 1929–1939* (Tucson: University of Arizona Press, 1974).

14. Manuel Gamio, *Mexican Immigration to the United States* (New York: Dover Publications, 1971). According to Sánchez, a U.S. Department of Labor study for the years 1934–36 found that even during the Depression, more than a third of Mexican families in Los Angeles owned radios (*Becoming Mexican American*, 172).

15. John Beverley, *Subalternity and Representation: Arguments in Cultural Theory* (Durham, N.C.: Duke University Press, 1999), 48–49. For Beverley's discussion of the "'cultured' vision of culture," see 13–14. See also Shelley Streeby, who makes a similar argument about the role of recording technology within what she calls the early-twentieth-century "Chicana/o countercultures of modernity" in Los Angeles ("Joaquín Murrieta and the American 1848," in *Post-Nationalist American Studies*, ed. John Carlos Rowe [Berkeley: University of California Press, 2000], 180–90).

16. Sánchez, *Becoming Mexican American*, 183–84.

17. This incident is briefly discussed by Escobar (*Race, Police, and the Making of a Political Identity*, 148) and Sánchez (*Becoming Mexican American*, 183). I further rely on the transcript of a 1983 interview with González for KPBS TV in San Diego, now housed at Stanford. I am grateful to Shelley Streeby for bringing this document to my attention. My discussion of González has been influenced by her essay "Joaquín Murrieta and the American 1848," 185–86; and Carl Gutiérrez-Jones, *Rethinking the Borderlands: Between Chicano Culture and Legal Discourse* (Berkeley: University of California Press, 1995).

18. KPBS interview with González, 102.

19. For a *Locura de Radio* ad, see *La Opinión*, 29 January 1934, 4. On the same page are ads for the films *One Man's Journey*, starring Lionel Barrymore, at Teatro Bonito and *La Llorona*, staring Ramón Pereda, at Teatro Electrico (advertised as "El Teatro de las Familias").

20. KPBS interview with González, 96–98. Novarro and González were schoolmates in northern Mexico (84). For a brief discussion of his experiences filming *Viva Villa*, see 188.

21. George Lipsitz, *The Possessive Investment in Whiteness: How White People Profit from Identity Politics* (Philadelphia: Temple University Press, 1998).

22. KPBS interview with González, 103–4.

23. Ibid., 108. The DA was quoted to similar effect in the local press (Escobar, *Race, Police, and the Making of a Political Identity*, 148).

24. Sánchez, *Becoming Mexican American*, 184.

25. KPBS interview with González, 123–25.

26. *La Opinión*, 30 March, 1, 6; and 31 March, 1, 8; and Carl J. Mora, *Mexican Cinema: Reflections of a Society, 1896–1988* (Berkeley: University of California Press, 1982); Gilbert M. Joseph and Daniel Nugent, eds., *Everyday Forms of State Formation: Revolution and the Negotiation of Rule in Modern Mexico* (Durham, N.C.: Duke University Press, 1994); and Chon A. Noriega

and Steven Ricci, eds., *The Mexican Cinema Project* (Los Angeles: UCLA Film and Television Archive, 1994).

27. *La Opinión*, 3 February 1934, 4, and 29 March 1934, 4.

28. Mike Davis, *City of Quartz* (New York: Vintage Books, 1992), 251.

29. "Police Prepare to Use Portable Radio Device," *Los Angeles Times*, 21 March 1934, sec. 2, 10. For the use of police car radios, see Escobar, *Race, Police, and the Making of a Political Identity*, 159.

30. See, for example, "KHJ to Help in Crime Appeal," *Los Angeles Times*, 7 November 1927, sec. 2, 8.

31. See Rick Altman, ed., *Sound Theory, Sound Practice* (New York: Routledge, 1992), 113–25; and Donald Crafton, *The Talkies: American Cinema's Transition to Sound, 1926–1931* (Berkeley: University of California Press, 1997), especially 38–47.

32. Tino Balio, *Grand Design: Hollywood as a Modern Business Enterprise, 1930–1939* (Berkeley: University of California Press, 1993), 11, 14.

33. Carey McWilliams, *Southern California Country: An Island on the Land* (1946; Salt Lake City: Peregrine Smith Books, 1995), 331–33.

34. According to McWilliams, in 1915 the film industry generated $20 million in payroll (ibid., 333).

35. See Bruce Long, ed., *Taylorology: A Continuing Exploration of the Life and Death of William Desmond Taylor*, on-line journal, www.uno.edu/~drcom/Taylorology; Richard Koszarski, *An Evening's Entertainment: The Age of the Silent Feature Picture, 1915–1928* (Berkeley: University of California Press, 1990), 206; and Kenneth Anger, *Hollywood Babylon* (New York: Dell Publishing, 1981), 47–60.

36. See *Long Beach Press*, 22 February 1922, included in "Drugs in Early Hollywood," *Taylorology*, issue 71 (November 1998).

37. *Milwaukee Journal*, 16 February 1922, included in "Drugs in Early Hollywood."

38. Richard Burritt, *Chicago Daily News*, 10 February 1922, included in *Taylorology*, issue 34 (October 1995); Thoreau Cronyn, "The Truth about Hollywood," Part II, *New York Herald*, 19 March–2 April 1922, included in *Taylorology*, issue 13 (January 1994).

39. Cronyn, "The Truth about Hollywood," Part II.

40. Koszarski, *An Evening's Entertainment*, 276.

41. As Anger indicates, high-profile drug scandals continued throughout the 1920s (*Hollywood Babylon*, 89–98).

42. Barrett C. Kiesling, *Talking Pictures: How They Are Made, How to Appreciate Them* (New York: Johnson Publishing Company, 1937), 165.

43. McWilliams, *Southern California Country*, 333–34.

44. Ibid., 336. Similarly, in his biography of Carl Laemmle, John Drinkwater notes that "Universal City" was "self-contained and self-sufficient" (*The Life and Adventures of Carl Laemmle* [New York: Putnam's Sons, 1931], 181–82).

45. See Donald Crafton, *The Talkies: American Cinema's Transition to*

Sound, 1926–1931 (Berkeley: University of California Press, 1997), 191, 195, 199, 201, 206–7.

46. Gerald Horne, *Class Struggle in Hollywood, 1930–1950: Moguls, Mobsters, Stars, Reds and Trade Unions* (Austin: University of Texas Press, 2001), 42.

47. Drinkwater, *Life and Adventures of Carl Laemmle,* 181.

48. Jack L. Warner, with Dean Jennings, *My First Hundred Years in Hollywood* (New York: Random House, 1964), 173.

49. Michael Rogin, *Blackface, White Noise: Jewish Immigration in the Hollywood Melting Pot* (Berkeley: University of California Press, 1996).

50. Quoted by Horne, *Class Struggle in Hollywood,* 265.

51. Ibid.

52. David Bordwell and Kristen Thompson, "Technological Change and Classical Film Style," in Balio, *Grand Design,* 123–25.

53. McWilliams, *Southern California Country,* 335.

54. Lary May, *Screening Out the Past: The Birth of Mass Culture and the Motion Picture Industry* (Chicago: University of Chicago Press, 1980), 190. See also McWilliams, *Southern California Country,* 337.

55. Thomas Doherty, *Pre-Code Hollywood: Sex, Immorality, and Insurrection in American Cinema, 1930–1934* (New York: Columbia University Press, 1999), 362. Although the code itself was drafted in 1930, it was not until 1934 that the PCA was founded in an effort to enforce it.

56. Ibid. 364. This part of the code was apparently modeled on similar prescriptions adopted in 1927 by the Motion Picture Producers and Distributors of America in response to controversy over Hollywood films in Mexico (Helen Delpar, "Goodbye to the 'Greaser': Mexico, the MPPDA, and Derogatory Films, 1922–1926," *Journal of Popular Film and Television,* 12:1 [spring 1984]: 39).

57. See the press file for the film at the Margaret Herrick Library, Academy of Motion Picture Arts and Sciences, Los Angeles.

58. "Villa Film to Be Seen in Mexico," *Los Angeles Times,* 22 February 1934, sec. I, 5.

59. Delpar, "Goodbye to the 'Greaser,'" 36.

60. Kerry Segrave, *American Films Abroad: Hollywood's Domination of the World's Movie Screens* (Jefferson, N.C.: McFarland and Company, 1997), 74.

61. Delpar, "Goodbye to the 'Greaser,'" 40; Segrave, *American Films Abroad,* 74.

62. Letter from Joseph Breen to Leslie Simmons, PCA file for *The Traitor,* Margaret Herrick Library.

63. Letter from Breen to M. J. Siegel, 7 February 1940, in the PCA file for *Rancho Grande* (Republic, 1940), Margaret Herrick Library.

64. *Border G-Man* research copy, Film and Television Library, UCLA.

65. *Lawless Border* (1935), for example, concerns a U.S. government agent who teams up with a Mexican agent in order to infiltrate a gang of smugglers who supply arms to revolutionary forces in Mexico. Films focusing on cattle

rustling include *The Cisco Kid* (Fox, 1931), *Land Beyond the Law* (1937), *Border Café* (1937), and *Borderland* (1937). Finally, *Pals of the Saddle* (1938), starring John Wayne, is about how three cowboys, a female federal agent, and a border division of the U.S. Cavalry work together to prevent foreign agents from smuggling a vital war-related material called "monium" out of the country via Mexico. All information is from the on-line *American Film Institute Catalog*.

66. Information for *Flirting with Fate* is from the on-line *American Film Institute Catalog*. See also Delpar, "Goodbye to the 'Greaser,'" 39.

67. See the PCA files for both films at the Margaret Herrick Library.

68. In addition to *Viva Villa* and *La Cucaracha*, both released in 1934, the song also appeared in the following films: *The Cisco Kid* (1931), *Viva Cisco Kid* (1940), *La Conga Nights* (1940), *Rancho Grande* (1940), *Prairie Pioneers* (1941), *Santa Fe Saddlemates* (1945), *Song of Mexico* (1945), *Sporting Chance* (1945), and *Trail to Mexico* (1946).

69. Armstrong recorded "La Cucaracha" in 1935 for Decca Records, re-released on the CD *Louis Armstrong: Rhythm Saved the World*, Decca Jazz, 1991.

70. See *Memories of Mexico Album: A Collection of Mexico's Most Popular Melodies, with English and Original Spanish Text* (New York: Edward B. Marks Music Corporation, 1934), 5–8; *Spanish Songs* (Chicago: Belmont Music Company, 1937), 4–5; *Treasure Chest of World-Wide Songs* (New York: Treasure Chest Publications, 1936), 2. "La Cucaracha" was also included in a boxed set of sheet music called *Symprovised Music* (New York: Symprovised Music, 1937), and somewhat earlier in Carl Sandburg's *The American Songbag* (New York: Harcourt, Brace and World, 1927), 289–91.

71. "Mexican La Cucaracha (The Cockroach Song)" (Chicago: Calumet Music Co., 1935); "La Cucaracha (La Cu-Ca-Ra-Cha), As Originally Introduced in the Metro-Goldwyn-Mayer Production 'Viva Villa'" (New York: Robbins Music Corporation, 1934); "La Cucaracha, the Mexican Cockroach Song, Sung in the Metro-Goldwyn-Mayer Film Production 'Viva Villa'" (New York: Edward B. Marks Music Corp., 1934); "La Cucaracha (La-Coo-Cah-Rah-Cha), the Authentic Song from RKO Picture!!" (New York: Irving Berlin Inc., Music Publishers, 1934). The song was also included in a collection of songs from contemporary films called the *Universal Dance Folio for Piano* (New York: Irving Berlin Inc., Music Publishers, 1936).

72. The film *La Conga Nights* references the dance in a song called "Carmenita McCoy," quoted in the film's PCA file, Margaret Herrick Library.

73. See, for example, Ramón Gutiérrez, "The Erotic Zone: Sexual Transgression on the U.S.–Mexican Border," in *Mapping Multiculturalism*, ed. Avery F. Gordon and Christopher Newfield (Minneapolis: University of Minnesota Press, 1996), 253–62.

74. KPBS interview with González, 43.

75. Ibid., 247.

76. Ibid., 222, 244–45.

77. Such an interpretation is consistent with greater Mexican music conventions that, according to Américo Paredes, tended to limit the performance of *rancheras* to cantinas and other male-dominated places because of the *grito's* sexual connotations. In the context of south Texas, Paredes notes that historically, singers in family gatherings "sang in soft or medium voices" and the loud shouts characteristic of performance "situations involving men without women, or men with 'women of the other kind,'" were strictly "taboo." See Américo Paredes, *A Texas-Mexican Cancionero: Folksongs of the Lower Border* (Austin: University of Texas Press, 1995), xviii–xxii; and José E. Limón, *American Encounters: Greater Mexico, the United States, and the Erotics of Culture* (Boston: Beacon Press, 1998), 180–81.

78. Nathaniel West, *The Day of the Locust, Novels and Other Writings,* ed. Sacvan Bercovitch (New York: Penguin Books, 1997), 298.

79. Ibid., 304.

80. Ibid., 306–7.

81. Ibid.

82. Rogin, *Blackface, White Noise,* 140.

83. *Motion Picture Daily,* 27 March 1934 (emphasis added), and Regina Crewe, *American,* no date or page numbers, *Viva Villa* press clipping file, Margaret Herrick Library.

84. William Tracy, "The Marquis de Villa," *Nation* 138, no. 359 (2 May 1934): 516.

85. Miriam Hansen, *Babel and Babylon: Spectatorship in American Silent Film* (Cambridge: Harvard University Press, 1991), 254.

86. Ibid., 245–48.

87. Hansen reproduces a still from *Blood in the Sand* depicting the sash (ibid., 265).

88. See ibid., 266–67.

89. Charles F. Altman, *The American Film Musical* (Bloomington: Indiana University Press, 1987), 19, 24.

90. For the "rumba fox-trot" arrangement of "La Cucaracha," see *Universal Dance Folio for Piano,* 42–43.

91. Publicity stills for the film can be found at the Margaret Herrick Library.

92. "La Cucaracha," *Symprovised Music,* no. 123, 1938.

93. In this regard, *La Cucaracha* bears comparison to mainstream musicals as analyzed in Rick Altman, *The American Film Musical* (Bloomington: Indiana University Press, 1987), 27.

94. "Mexican La Cucaracha." For similar "translations," see "La Cucaracha As Originally Introduced in the MGM Production 'Viva Villa,'" *Spanish Songs,* and *Treasure Chest of World-Wide Songs.*

95. According to Richard Dyer, because red tended to absorb rather than reflect light, color processes dominated by red did not make "white" char-

acters look "white" enough by dominant standards. In contrast, filmmakers viewed dark colors like red as a better match for the skin tones of nonwhite characters, even when, as in *La Cucaracha,* two of the three Mexican characters are seemingly played by Anglos. See Richard Dyer, *White* (New York: Routledge, 1997), 92–93.

96. Escobar, *Race, Police, and the Making of a Political Identity,* 122.

97. My reading has been influenced by Claudia Gorbman's in *Westerns: Film through History* (New York: Routledge, 2001). On the interpretation of film scores, see Kathryn Kalinak, *Settling the Score: Music and the Classical Hollywood Film* (Madison: University of Wisconsin Press, 1992).

98. See Philip Sonnichsen, liner notes, *Los Primeros Duetos Femininas/ The First Women Duets* (1930–1955), Folklyric Records, FL9035.

99. Lalo Guerrero, "Marijuana Boogie," *The Chicano Experience,* Arhoolie Records.

100. Hansen, *Babel and Babylon,* 97. This was done by partly dispensing with older, "distracting" spectacles and by attempting to construct larger and more coherent narratives.

101. Ibid., 16.

102. Although Hansen's discussion primarily concerns immigrants to the United States from eastern and southern Europe, my own conclusions regarding Mexican audiences are indebted to her formulations (ibid., 90–125).

103. This list of song subjects is based on the record of songs popular among Mexicans in the United States in the 1930s. See *The Chicano Experience,* as well as other Arhoolie selections such as *Corridos y Tragedias de la Frontera* (CD 7019/7020); *Lydia Mendoza: A Family Autobiography,* compiled and introduced by Chris Strachwitz with James Nicolopulos (Houston: Arte Público Press, 1993); Paredes, *A Texas-Mexican Cancionero;* and Nicolás Kanellos, *A History of Hispanic Theatre in the United States: Origins to 1940* (Houston: Arte Público Press, 1984).

104. Tomás Ybarra-Frausto, "I Can Still Hear the Applause," in Kanellos, *A History of Hispanic Theatre in the United States,* 56.

105. Ibid., 57.

106. Ibid., 46.

107. Hansen, *Babel and Babylon,* 94. The variety-show format may have further enabled Mexicans to take pleasure in and gain imaginary control over the jarring dislocations of immigrant life in southern California (108).

108. For relevant film listings, see *La Opinión,* 26 February 1933, 7; and 27 January 1934, 4. In addition to musicals, Mexican film exhibitors screened Hollywood dramas, westerns, and horror films like *Hell's Highway, The Mummy,* and *The Sagebrush Trail* (*La Opinión,* 11 February 1933, 4; 28 April 1934, 4; 27 January 1934, 4).

109. *La Opinión,* 19 February 1933, 7.

110. Ibid. *La Opinión,* 28 April 1933, 4.

111. *La Opinión,* 11 March 1933, 4.

112. Crafton, "Labor Troubles," in *The Talkies*, 217–24.

113. My use of the term "virtual *revista*" is indebted to Crafton's "Virtual Broadway, Virtual Orchestra: De Forest and Vitaphone," in *The Talkies*, 64–88, where he argues that many English-language sound films represented "virtual" versions of other forms of popular entertainment such as the Broadway musical, vaudeville, and radio variety shows.

114. Carl J. Mora, *Mexican Cinema: Reflections of a Society* (Berkeley: University of California Press, 1982), 32. As Douglas Gomery notes, Hollywood made a number of films in other languages as well, but Spanish production continued the longest and was the most rewarding (*Shared Pleasures: A History of Movie Presentation in the United States* [Madison: University of Wisconsin Press, 1992]). Thus, whereas some histories emphasize the poor returns and short lives of Hollywood's non-English productions, Spanish-language films were relatively remunerative and lasted for almost a decade (Crafton, *The Talkies*, 424–30, and Natasa Durovicova, "Translating America: The Hollywood Multilinguals, 1929–1933," in Rich Altman, *Sound Theory, Sound Practice* [New York: Routledge, 1992], 138–53).

115. *American Film Institute Catalog.*

116. For the popularity of the dance on the stages of Mexican L.A., see the testimony of "Isobel Sandoval" quoted in the previous chapter.

117. Hansen, *Babel and Babylon*, 99.

118. *El Caballero de la Noche* contains nine songs, with music by William Kernell, Troy Sanders, and Mojica, and Spanish lyrics by Mojica. See the entry for the film in the *American Film Institute Catalog*. Apparently, a copy of the film no longer exists and all information concerning it is drawn from a screen continuity and credit sheet, UCLA Special Collections.

119. See film listings, *La Opinión*, various issues, January 1934.

120. Non-Mexican theaters generally charged significantly more. In 1933, for example, Loews State Theater advertised the Eddie Cantor musical comedy called *The Kid From Spain* at the "SENSATIONAL LOEW PRICES" of 25 cents until 6 o'clock and 40 cents after that. At the same time, the even more expensive Grauman's Chinese Theater charged 50 cents, 75 cents, and $1.00 for matinees and 75 cents, $1.00, and $1.50 for night screenings (*Los Angeles Times*, 21 February 1933, sec. 2, 8).

6. COCAINE COLONIALISM

1. Although there are important chemical and cultural differences between coca and cocaine, I use the words interchangeably because, for my purposes, they share many of the same ideological meanings in U.S. and European contexts.

2. Joseph F. Spillane, "Making a Modern Drug: The Manufacture, Sale, and Control of Cocaine in the United States, 1880–1920," in *Cocaine: Global Histories*, ed. Paul Gootenberg (London: Routledge, 1999), 21–45.

3. Joseph Kennedy, *Coca Exotica* (London: Cornwall Books, 1985), 62–64, 83–87.

4. Paul Gootenberg, "Reluctance or Resistance?: Constructing Cocaine (Prohibitions) in Peru," in Gootenberg, *Cocaine,* 47–49.

5. Virginia Berridge and Griffith Edwards, *Opium and the People: Opiate Use in the Nineteenth Century* (New Haven: Yale University Press, 1987), 221.

6. Ernest Jones, *The Life and Work of Sigmund Freud,* vol. 1 (New York: Basic Books, 1953), 93.

7. Freud wrote that "the study of coca was an allotrion which I was eager to conclude" (quoted in ibid., 83–84). Jones explains that "the word 'allotrion,' with its punitive connotation, was one familiar to Freud from his schoolteachers' use of it to signify anything, such as a hobby, that detracted from the serious fulfillment of a duty" (84).

8. Robert Byck, ed., with notes by Anna Freud, *Cocaine Papers by Sigmund Freud* (New York: Meridian Books, 1975).

9. Johan Jacob Von Tschudi, *Travels in Peru,* trans. Thomasina Ross (London: David Bogue, 1847).

10. G. W. F. Hegel, *The Philosophy of History,* trans. J. Sibree (New York: Dover Press, 1956), 81–82.

11. Quoted in H. Guillaume's *The Amazon Provinces of Peru as a Field of European Emigration* (London: Wyman and Sons, 1888), 52.

12. See Michael Taussig, *Shamanism, Colonialism, and the Wild Man: A Study in Terror and Healing* (Chicago: University of Chicago Press, 1987), 60–66.

13. Quoted in Guillaume, *Amazon Provinces of Peru,* 137–38.

14. Joseph A. Gagliano, *Coca Prohibition in Peru: The Historical Debates* (Tucson: University of Arizona Press, 1994).

15. For Freud's citation of Tschudi, see "Über Coca," in Byck, *Cocaine Papers,* 51.

16. Tschudi, *Travels in Peru,* 452.

17. Ibid., 446.

18. Ibid., 457.

19. Ibid., 450.

20. Freud, "Über Coca," 50. Subsequent references are given in the text.

21. The question of Freud's relationship to anti-Semitism and his own Jewishness is a large and complex one to which I shall briefly return toward the end of this chapter. For more extensive treatments of the topic, see Sander L. Gilman, *The Case of Sigmund Freud: Medicine and Identity at the Fin de Siècle* (Baltimore: Johns Hopkins University Press, 1993); Carl E. Schorske, "Politics and Patricide in Freud's *Interpretation of Dreams,*" in *Fin-de-Siècle Vienna* (New York: Vintage Books, 1981), 181–203; and Marianna Torgovnick, "Entering Freud's Study," in *Gone Primitive: Savage Intellects, Modern Lives* (Chicago: University of Chicago Press, 1990), 194–209. The last author is my source for stereotypes of the "primitive" Jew. Subsequent references are given in the text.

22. Sigmund Freud, letter to Martha Bernays, 7 February 1884, in *The Letters of Sigmund Freud,* ed. Ernest L. Freud, ed. trans. Tania and James Stern (New York: Basic Books, 1960), 97.

23. Walter Boehlich, ed., trans. Arnold J. Pomerans, *The Letters of Sigmund Freud to Eduard Silberstein* (Cambridge: Harvard University Press, 1990), xv–xvi, xxix.

24. Freud to Eduard Silberstein, August 1874, in ibid., 55.

25. Boehlich, *Letters,* xvi.

26. Ernest L. Freud, *Letters,* 55.

27. Ibid., 126.

28. Freud, letter to Georg Groddeck, 18 February 1920, in Ernest L. Freud, *Letters,* 329.

29. Quoted by Frank J. Sulloway, *Freud: Biologist of the Mind* (New York: Basic Books, 1983), 477.

30. Curtis Marez, "The Rough Ride through Empire," in *Recovering the U.S. Hispanic Literary Heritage,* ed. José Aranda Jr. and Silvio Torres-Saillant (Houston: Arte Público Press, 2002).

31. Ernest L. Freud, *Letters,* 11.

32. Ibid., 12.

33. Frontispiece, W. Golden Mortimer, *History of Coca, the Divine Plant of the Incas* (San Francisco: And/Or Press, 1974).

34. Berridge and Edwards, *Opium and the People,* 218.

35. Tschudi, *Travels in Peru,* 478.

36. Ibid., 463–64.

37. Ibid., 467–68.

38. Herbert S. Klein, "Coca Production in the Bolivian Yungas," in *Drugs in the Western Hemisphere: An Odyssey of Cultures in Conflict,* ed. William O. Walker III (Wilmington, Del.: Scholarly Resources Books, 1996), 22–34.

39. Tschudi, *Travels in Peru,* 469.

40. Ibid.

41. Freud to Martha Bernays, quoted in Jones, *Life and Work,* 84.

42. Jones, *Life and Work,* 83.

43. Byck, *Cocaine Papers,* 197.

44. Freud, letter to Martha Bernays, quoted in ibid., 157–58.

45. Quoted in Jones, *Life and Work,* 90.

46. Sulloway, *Freud,* 26.

47. Quoted by Taussig, *Shamanism, Colonialism, and the Wild Man,* 76.

48. Ibid., 75.

49. For colonial representations of Indians as demonic, see ibid., 209–20.

50. Freud, "Craving for and Fear of Cocaine," in Byck, *Cocaine Papers,* 172.

51. Jones, for example, refers to Freud's early research as "The Cocaine Episode" and implies that it had little to do with his later, more significant, analytic work (*Life and Work,* 78–97). Following Jones, Sulloway labels his

two-page consideration of this topic "The Cocaine Episode" and subsumes it under the larger heading, "Freud's Early Neurological Career" (*Freud*, 25–28).

52. "It is possible, too, that [Freud's] use of cocaine ... may have mediated the change from physiological to mainly psychiatric interests" (Berridge and Edwards, *Opium and the People*, 219).

53. For extended discussions of these issues, see Sulloway, *Freud*; and Stephen Jay Gould, *Ontogeny and Phylogeny* (Cambridge, Mass.: Belknap Press, 1977), 155–64.

54. For a summary of psychic topography in Freud, see J. Laplanche and J.-B. Pontalis, *The Language of Psychoanalysis*, trans. Donald Nicholson-Smith (New York: Norton, 1973), 449–53; and Jacques Derrida, "Freud and the Scene of Writing," in *Writing and Difference*, trans. Alan Bass (Chicago: University of Chicago Press, 1978), 196–231.

55. See "Cocaine Habit among Negroes," *Philadelphia Medical Journal*, 15 November 1902, 73; and E. H. Williams, "Drug-Habit Menace in the South," *Medical Record*, 7 February 1914, 247–49, and "Negro Cocaine 'Fiends' Are New Southern Menace," *New York Times*, 8 February 1914, sec. 4, 12.

56. Quoted by Nancy Falbre, "Where Has All the Money Gone?" *Village Voice Literary Supplement*, April 1990, 12.

57. I have taken these figures for cocaine use and penalties from a groundbreaking essay article by *Los Angeles Times* reporter Ron Harris, "Experts Say the War on Drugs Has Turned into a War on Blacks," reprinted in the *San Francisco Chronicle*, 24 April 1990, A12.

58. For a discussion of such zones in Los Angeles, see Mike Davis, *City of Quartz* (New York: Vintage Books, 1992), 267–322.

7. Drug Wars Are Indian Wars

1. "An Interview with Leslie Marmon Silko," in *Conversations with Leslie Marmon Silko*, ed. Ellen L. Arnold (Jackson: University Press of Mississippi, 2000), 153–54.

2. See also Alexander Cockburn and Jeffrey St. Clair, *Whiteout: The CIA, Drugs and the Press* (New York: Verso, 1998); and Peter Dale Scott and Jonathan Marshall, *Cocaine Politics: Drugs, Armies and the C.I.A. in Central America* (Berkeley: University of California Press, 1991).

3. See Pola Reyburd, "Who Are the Bad Guys? Literary Images of Narcotraffickers," in *Drug Trafficking in the Americas*, ed. Bruce M. Bagley and William O. Walker III (Coral Gables, Fla.: North-South Center Publications, 1994), 535–46; and Pola Reydburd, "Issues in Narcotrafficking: A Fictional Outlook," in *Drug Trafficking Research in the Americas: An Annotated Bibliography*, ed. Bruce M. Bagley (Coral Gables, Fla.: North-South Center Publications, 1996), 63–74. To my knowledge, no comparable study of film exists.

4. Arnold, *Conversations*, 101.

5. For information on intelligence training and gathering at Fort Huachuca, see Timothy J. Dunn, *Militarization of the U.S.–Mexico Border, 1978–*

1992: Low-Intensity Conflict Doctrine Comes Home (Austin: University of Texas Press, 1996), 110, 132. For drone crash landings, see Christina O. Valdez, "Falling Drones Raise Concern," *Arizona Republic,* 29 October 1993, B1.

6. See Dunn, *Militarization of the U.S.–Mexico Border;* Peter Dale Scott and Jonathan Marshall, *Cocaine Politics: Drugs, Armies, and the CIA in Central America* (Berkeley: University of California Press, 1998); Bruce M. Bagley, "Myths of Militarization: Enlisting the Armed Forces in the War on Drugs," in *Drugs in the Americas,* ed. Peter H. Smith (Boulder, Colo.: Westview Press, 1992), 129–50; and Donald J. Mabry, "The U.S. Military and the War on Drugs," in Bagley, *Drug Trafficking in the Americas,* 43–60.

7. Cockburn and St. Clair, *Whiteout,* 235–53.

8. See Gerald Vizenor, *Manifest Manners: Postindian Warriors of Survivance* (Hanover, N.H.: Wesleyan University Press, 1994), 154–62. See also Ward Churchill's review of Vizenor's book, *American Indian Culture and Research Journal* 18:4 (1994): 313–18.

9. Mary Crow Dog, with Richard Erdoes, *Lakota Woman* (New York: HarperPerennial, 1990), 58. Subsequent references appear in the text.

10. Leslie Marmon Silko, *Almanac of the Dead* (New York: Penguin Books, 1991), 562. For similar remarks from Serlo, see 548–49. Subsequent references appear in the text.

11. See the quotation from Waters in the Introduction.

12. See Cockburn and St. Clair, *Whiteout,* 63–94.

13. Ibid., 66–67.

14. Martin A. Lee and Bruce Shlain, *Acid Dreams: The C.I.A., L.S.D., and the Sixties Rebellion* (New York: Grove Press, 1985).

15. Cockburn and St. Clair, *Whiteout,* 80.

16. Ibid., 81; emphasis added.

17. William E. Unrau, *White Man's Wicked Water: The Alcohol Trade and Prohibition in Indian Country, 1802–1892* (Lawrence: University Press of Kansas, 1996). I am grateful to Stephanie LeMenager for bringing this source to my attention.

18. Quoted by Luana Ross, *Inventing the Savage: The Social Construction of Native American Criminality* (Austin: University of Texas Press, 1998).

19. Ibid., 115–18.

20. Quoted by Cockburn and St. Clair, *Whiteout,* 81.

21. *American Indian Crime* "American Indians Are Violent Crime Victims at Double the Rate of the General Population," U.S. Department of Justice press release, 14 February 1999; and "American Indian Confinement Towers above National Average," *Corrections Professional* 4:14 (9 April 1999).

22. A study by the General Accounting Office concluded that during the 1990s the number of people in U.S. prisons doubled ("Female Prison Population Growing at Rapid Rate," Associated Press State and Local Wire Service, 7 August 2000, Lexis-Nexis news database). Further, according to the U.S. Justice Department, between 1997 and 1998, the prison population in Arizona

rose from 23,484, to 25,311—an increase of 7.8 percent. For the same period, the national rate was 4.8 percent. See "Arizona's Prison Population Grows Faster Than U.S. Average," Associated Press State and Local Wire Service, 16 August 1999, Lexis-Nexis news database.

23. Quoted in "Arizona's Prison Population Grows Faster Than U.S. Average," Associated Press State and Local Wire Service.

24. General Accounting Office, cited in "Female Prison Population Growing at Rapid Rate." For an account of drug laws in Arizona, see Judge Rudolph J. Gerber, "On Dispensing Injustice," *Arizona Law Review* (spring 2001), Lexis-Nexis law review database.

25. For rates of female imprisonment, see "Female Prison Population Growing at Rapid Rate." According to the last U.S. Census, whites make up 75 percent of the total population in Arizona but account for only 54 percent of prisoners. By contrast, American Indians represent 5 percent of the state's population but 6 percent of those in prison. In all likelihood, however, this last figure is actually higher, because historically, other categories such as "Mexican" or "Hispanic" tend to include and therefore obscure Indian populations (see Curtis Marez, "Signifying Spain, Making Mexicans, Becoming Comanche," *American Quarterly* 53:2 [June 2001]: 267–307). According to the census, "Hispanics" account for 25 percent of the state's population but make up 36 percent of its prisoners, and in all probability a number of such people could also be classified as Indians. See "Arizona Prison Demographics," Associated Press State and Local Wire Service, 17 July 2001, Lexis-Nexis news database.

26. Russell Means, with Marvin J. Wolf, *Where White Men Fear to Tread* (New York: St. Martin's Press, 1995), 125. Subsequent references are given in the text.

27. John (Fire) Lame Deer, with Richard Erdoes, *Lame Deer: Seeker of Visions* (1972; New York: Washington Square Press, 1994), 70–71.

28. Leonard Peltier, *Prison Writings: My Life Is My Sun Dance,* ed. Harvey Arden (New York: St. Martin's Press, 1999), 66–67.

29. See Ward Churchill and Jim Vander Wall, *Agents of Repression: The F.B.I.'s Secret Wars against the Black Panther Party and the American Indian Movement* (Boston: South End Press, 1990).

30. Peltier, *Prison Writings,* 54–55.

31. See Deborah Pacini and Christine Franquemont, eds., *Coca and Cocaine: Effects on People and Policy in Latin America* (Ithaca, N.Y.: Cornell University, Latin American Studies Program, 1986), 36, 77.

32. See John T. Cusack, former chief of staff for the House Select Committee on Narcotics Abuse and Control, in ibid., 65–71.

33. Macdonald, in Pacini and Franquemont, *Coca and Cocaine,* 145–60.

34. Mabry, "The U.S. Military and the War on Drugs," 54.

35. Marcos Avirama Avirama, personal conversation, 29 October 1991.

36. Ibid. See also Jorge Gomez Lizarazo, "Colombian Blood, U.S. Guns," *New York Times,* 28 January 1992, F3.

37. Bagley, "Myths of Militarization," 142.

38. Churchill and Vander Wall, *Agents of Repression,* 136–38; Peter Matthiessen, *In the Spirit of Crazy Horse* (New York: Penguin Books, 1992), 62–63.

39. Matthiessen, *In the Spirit of Crazy Horse,* 63.

40. Churchill and Vander Wall, *Agents of Repression,* 129–34.

41. Matthiessen, *In the Spirit of Crazy Horse,* 63.

42. Ibid., 126–49.

43. See also Leslie Marmon Silko, "Tribal Councils: Puppets of the U.S. Government," in *Yellow Woman and a Beauty of the Spirit* (New York: Simon and Schuster, 1997), 92–95.

44. Matthiessen, *In the Spirit of Crazy Horse,* 129.

45. Ibid., 128.

46. Ibid., 61.

47. Ibid., 68–69.

48. Ibid., 67.

49. Quoted in ibid.

50. Lame Deer, *Lame Deer,* 64–65.

51. For Durham's background, see Churchill and Vander Wall, *Agents of Repression,* 220.

52. Ibid., 272–81.

53. Ibid., 230–33.

54. Peltier, *Prison Writings,* 95–96.

55. Vine Deloria Jr. and David E. Wilkins, *Tribes, Treaties and Constitutional Tribulations* (Austin: University of Texas Press, 1999), 59–70.

56. Ibid., 75–76.

57. See Henry M. Teller, "Courts of Indian Offences," in *Documents of United States Indian Policy,* ed. Francis Paul Prucha (Lincoln: University of Nebraska Press, 1990), 161.

58. Thomas J. Morgan, "Rules for Indian Courts," in Prucha, *Documents of Unites States Indian Policy,* 187.

59. Ibid.

60. Teller, "Courts of Indian Offence," 161.

61. See Edward Spicer, *The Yaqui: A Cultural History* (Tucson: University of Arizona Press, 1980).

62. Ibid., 239.

63. See Ibid., 248.

64. See Ibid.

65. Ibid.

66. Ibid., 157.

67. Immanuel Wallerstein, "America and the World: Today, Yesterday, and Tomorrow," in *After Liberalism* (New York: New Press, 1995), 205.

68. Ibid.

69. José David Saldívar, *Border Matters: Remapping American Cultural Studies* (Berkeley: University of California Press, 1997), xii.

70. Leslie Marmon Silko, "The Border Patrol State," in *Yellow Woman,* 116–17.

71. Ibid., 123.

72. Ibid.

73. Wallerstein, "America and the World," 205.

Index

Curtis Marez is assistant professor of critical studies in the School of Cinema and Television at the University of Southern California.